Marguerite Patten's
All Colour Cookery

Hamlyn
London New York
Sydney Toronto

Some of the material in this book has been previously published in the Hamlyn All-Colour Cookbooks paperback series

Published by
The Hamlyn Publishing Group Limited
London · New York · Sydney · Toronto
Astronaut House, Feltham, Middlesex, England
© Copyright The Hamlyn Publishing Group Limited 1975
Tenth impression 1983

ISBN 0 600 31362 X
Printed in Czechoslovakia

Line drawings by John Scott Martin and others
52046/5

Acknowledgements

The author and publishers would like to thank the following for their help and co-operation in providing colour photographs for this book:

Angostura Aromatic Bitters: page 64.
Argentine Beef Bureau: page 63 bottom.
Armour: page 198 top.
Atora: pages 62 top, 91, 199 bottom.
Australian Recipe Service: page 92 top.
Ayds Reducing Plan: page 119 bottom.
Beechams Foods Limited: page 154 top.
British Egg Information Service: page 51 bottom.
Brown and Polson Limited: pages 57, 62 bottom.
Cadbury Typhoo Food Advisory Service: pages 156 top, 173 top, 187 bottom, 219 bottom.
Californian Prune Advisory Bureau: page 73 bottom.
Carnation Milk Bureau: pages 96 bottom, 212 top.
Cirio Company Limited: page 150 bottom.
Colmans Mustard: pages 61 bottom, 78 bottom.
Danish Food Centre: pages 80 bottom, 81, 82 bottom, 95 top, 149 top.
Dutch Dairy Bureau: pages 13 bottom, 148 top, 197 bottom.
Dutch Fruit and Vegetable Producers Association: pages 19 top, 20 bottom, 22 bottom, 74 bottom, 118 top, 126 bottom, 145 top.
Eden Vale Dairy Fresh Foods: pages 115 top, 200 top.
Electricity Council: page 131 bottom.
Flour Advisory Bureau: pages 171 top, 172 top.
Farrows Rice: pages 37 bottom, 45 bottom.
The Friends of Wine: page 201 top. .
Fruit Producers' Council: pages 28, 46 top, 74 top, 83 bottom, 86 top, 121 bottom, 135 top, 139 top, 144 bottom, 157 top, 160 bottom, 168 top, 180 top, 195 top, 198 bottom, 210 top, 212 bottom, 213.
Gale's Honey: pages 63 top, 99 top.
Green Giant: page 141 top.
Heinz Limited: pages 209 bottom, 211 bottom.
Herring Industry Bureau: pages 12 top, 35.
Isleworth Polytechnic: pages 11 top, 26 top, 105 top, 190 bottom.
Jif Lemon: page 44.
Jobling Housecraft Service (Pyrosil): page 21 top.
Kraft Foods Limited: page 116 bottom.
Lard Information Bureau: pages 85 bottom, 113 bottom, 172 bottom.
Lawry's Foods International Incorporated: page 189 bottom.
Lea and Perrins Worcestershire Sauce: page 103.
New Zealand Lamb Information Bureau: page 70 top.
George Newnes Limited: pages 70 bottom, 144 top.
Karl Ostmann Limited (Germany): pages 19 bottom, 23 bottom, 25 top, 26 bottom, 29 top, 30 bottom, 45 top, 87 bottom, 109, 125 top, 130 top, 147 top.
Potato Marketing Board: pages 23 top, 112, 205 top.
RHM Foods Limited: pages 58, 104 top, 141 bottom, 142 bottom, 143 bottom, 158 bottom, 159, 199 top.
Rice Information Service: pages 66, 121 top.
Stork Cookery Service: page 200 bottom.
Sunsweet Prunes: page 145 bottom.
Swiss Cheese Union: pages 15 top, 190 top.
Van den Berghs Limited: page 89 top.
John West Foods Limited: pages 36 bottom, 130 bottom.
White Fish Authority: pages 11 bottom, 34, 36 top, 39, 40 top, 41 bottom, 42 bottom, 150 top, 192 top, 215 bottom, 216 top.
Woman's Own: page 203 bottom.

Contents

Useful facts and figures

Oven temperatures

The following chart gives the conversions from degrees Fahrenheit to degrees Celsius (formerly known as Centigrade) recommended by the manufacturers of electric cookers.

Description	Electric setting	Gas mark
very cool	225°F – 110°C	$\frac{1}{4}$
	250°F – 130°C	$\frac{1}{2}$
cool	275°F – 140°C	1
	300°F – 150°C	2
very moderate	325°F – 170°C	3
moderate	350°F – 180°C	4
moderate **to**	375°F – 190°C	5
moderately hot	400°F – 200°C	6
hot	425°F – 220°C	7
	450°F – 230°C	8
very hot	475°F – 240°C	9

Note: This table is an approximate guide only. Different makes of cooker vary and if you are in any doubt about the setting, it is as well to refer to the manufacturer's temperature chart. Check also on the position of food in the oven.

Comparisons of weights and measures

It is useful to note that 3 teaspoons equal 1 tablespoon; the average English teacup is $\frac{1}{4}$ pint; the average English breakfast cup is $\frac{1}{2}$ pint; a B.S.I. measuring cup, used in recipes, holds $\frac{1}{2}$ pint or 10 fluid ounces.

It should be noted that the American pint is 16 fluid ounces, as opposed to the British Imperial and Canadian pints which are 20 fluid ounces. The American $\frac{1}{2}$-pint measuring cup is 8 fluid ounces and is, therefore, equivalent to $\frac{2}{5}$ British pint. In Australia, the metric system is now used, based on a 250-millilitre cup. In America, standard cup and spoon measurements are used.

Metrication

For quick and easy reference when buying food, it should be remembered that 1 kilogramme (1000 grammes) equals 2.2 pounds ($35\frac{3}{4}$ ounces) – i.e. as a rough guide, $\frac{1}{2}$ kilogramme is about 1 pound. In liquid measurements, 1 litre (10 decilitres or 1000 millilitres) equals almost exactly $1\frac{3}{4}$ pints (1.76), so $\frac{1}{2}$ litre is $\frac{7}{8}$ pint. As a rough guide, therefore, one can assume that the equivalent of 1 pint is a generous $\frac{1}{2}$ litre. In this book mainly millilitres and some decilitres have been used, i.e. sometimes you will find in a sauce 125 ml. used as an equivalent to $\frac{1}{4}$ pint, in this case it is because the slightly lower amount gives the desired result and sometimes 150 ml. has been used to balance a recipe correctly. In some cases you will find I have mentioned $1\frac{1}{2}$ dl. as an equivalent to $\frac{1}{4}$ pint, in this case it is because this rather more rounded amount is quite acceptable and we need to be familiar with both millilitres and decilitres.

A simple method of converting recipe quantities is to use rounded figures instead of an exact conversion, taking 25 grammes to 1 ounce, and a generous $\frac{1}{2}$ litre to 1 pint. Since 1 ounce is exactly 28.35 grammes and

1 pint is 568 millilitres, it can be seen that these equivalents will give a slightly smaller finished dish, but the proportion of liquids to solids will remain the same and a satisfactory result will be produced.

Note: All recipes have been individually converted so that each recipe preserves the correct proportions.

A guide for American users

Imperial	American
1 lb. butter or other fat	2 cups
1 lb. flour	4 cups
1 lb. granulated or castor sugar	2 cups
1 lb. icing or confectioners' sugar	$3\frac{1}{2}$ cups
1 lb. brown (moist) sugar	2 cups
12 oz. golden syrup or treacle	1 cup
14 oz. rice	2 cups
1 lb. dried fruit	3 cups
1 lb. chopped or minced meat	2 cups
2 oz. soft breadcrumbs	1 cup
1 oz. flour	$\frac{1}{4}$ cup
1 oz. sugar	2 tablespoons
$\frac{1}{2}$ oz. butter	1 tablespoon
1 oz. golden syrup or treacle	1 tablespoon
1 oz. jam or jelly	1 tablespoon
4 oz. grated cheese	1 cup
4 oz. button mushrooms	1 cup
4 oz. chopped nuts (most kinds)	1 cup
$\frac{1}{4}$ pint water, milk etc.	$\frac{2}{3}$ cup
$\frac{1}{2}$ pint water	$1\frac{1}{4}$ cups
1 pint water	$2\frac{1}{2}$ cups

Note: The British pint is 20 fluid ounces as opposed to the American pint which is 16 fluid ounces.

In this book you will find recipes for all occasions, ranging from simple family meals to new ideas for parties and celebrations of various kinds.

In order that you may find the right dish, for the right meal, in the shortest possible time, I have given Easy Guides to selections in each of the major sections.

Over the years so many enthusiastic cooks have told me how helpful they find colour photographs of the completed dishes; in this book, practically all the important recipes have been pictured, so you will have a clear idea of how the food should look.

Nowadays many of us make good use of a home freezer and so I have included information on the freezing techniques for all kinds of dishes; this means you can prepare the food at your leisure, freeze it, so it is ready to serve on a future day.

We have for so long been used to calculating weights, etc in Imperial measures, but very soon metrication will be standard practice. In each recipe, therefore, you will find both the old Imperial and the new metric measures side by side, to enable you to become familiar with the latter.

I hope you enjoy using this book, it has been a great pleasure to compile it and I would like to thank the Home Economists of the Hamlyn Group for their help in photographing the recipes.

Marguerite Patten

Introduction

Marguerite Patten in the Hamlyn Group test kitchen.

The art of good cooking

To cook well is not only a practical achievement, but it can give great pleasure to both the cook and the people for whom she, or he, cooks. In my opinion the essentials of good cooking are fairly simple, and I list them below:

Learn the basic principles of cooking, by this I mean know how to roast well, to fry food without it being overcooked or greasy, to make sauces that are smooth (almost like velvet), etc. In other words 'walk before you run'. When you have learned these basic 'do's and don'ts' – all of which are given in this book – you are then ready to move on to the more exciting dishes and these must be based upon the elementary cooking processes.

Be critical about the food you buy, in other words shop carefully and wisely. You will save money and have better results, for while you can disguise food that is less than perfect, you can never beat good cooking of food that is first class in quality.

Become very critical of all cooking, your own, as well as other peoples.
Taste as you cook – adjust seasonings, etc. slowly and surely.
Plan the way you will present the food – for appearance plays a big part in making food appetising.

Develop your own creative abilities; it is not wise to alter recipes, particularly those for cakes, etc., which have the correct balance of fat, sugar, eggs and other ingredients, before you have followed the recipe for the first time. After making the recipe, think how you can alter it slightly to make it *your own speciality*. It may be you can change the herbs in a savoury recipe, or have a new stuffing, etc. Perhaps you could flavour the cake mixture with another spice or a different fruit juice. In this way you will be gaining the satisfaction of being an original, as well as a practical cook.

Most wives and mothers have to cook for many days of the year. It is all too easy for this to become a somewhat boring job, but you can make it so much *less* boring, and so much *more* rewarding, both from the saving of money and time and the appreciation from the family, if you are willing to try *new* ideas and produce as varied meals as possible. Often people say their families enjoy only the familiar dishes, but this is where you can be clever – certainly base the recipe on familiar ingredients, but give it a new 'twist', a new presentation, and see if they do not enjoy this even more than usual. You will also benefit from the fact you are avoiding repetitive cooking.

Following a recipe

It is always wise to read through a recipe completely before you start the cooking, for nothing is more annoying than to start the dish and then find there is one essential ingredient you have not purchased, or that a certain stage of cooking will delay the dish more than you would wish. I hope you will find it helpful that recipes list separately:

The cooking time: Although this differs slightly due to the variations in cookers, etc., this should be a good guide.

The preparation time: Again this will vary according to the individual, but should be an indication as to whether you will have time to make that particular dish on that occasion.

Main cooking utensils: I would get these ready before you start making the dish, for it will save you last-minute rushing to the cupboard when the food is mixed and ready to cook.

The oven position: This is important, it makes a difference to cooking time and even baking.

The number of servings: Based upon an average appetite. Remember this will vary slightly, according to the rest of the menu.

Some cookery terms
Mixing food

The correct method of mixing ingredients is important and often makes a difference to the success of a dish. Here are some of the terms used:

Beat: To mix briskly, generally with a wooden spoon or with the mixer at a medium speed.

Blend: To incorporate ingredients together, could be food or liquids (e.g. a sauce). Equipment used varies with the kind of ingredients.

Fold: To mix very gently, used to incorporate sugar into egg whites (e.g. in meringues), flour into eggs, etc. (in light cakes); use a cutting or flicking movement with a metal spoon or flat-bladed knife.

Knead: To handle firmly with your hands (explained in greater detail on page 170), used for biscuit and bread doughs.

Whisk: To stir or beat very briskly; a hand or electric beater or whisk is used. Egg whites are whisked to make meringues; cream is whisked to thicken, *but do this very carefully so it does not become over-beaten.*

Some cookery beliefs

In cookery, as in many other spheres, there are certain beliefs about the correct technique to follow. Some of these are correct, others are not really true facts. Here are some of the points so often raised by people:

Q. When creaming fat and sugar, is it true that you must always cream in the same direction?
A. No, in fact it rests your arm if you cream in a clockwise manner for a time, then reverse the procedure and cream in an anti-clockwise direction. By the way, a folded cloth under the mixing bowl helps to stop the bowl slipping.

Q. Is it essential to whisk egg whites just before you need them?
A. No, you can whisk them some little time before being required, then cover the bowl tightly, or turn it upside-down on the table - the purpose is to exclude the air, which makes the egg whites 'watery' again.

Q. Does it help to leave a pancake or Yorkshire pudding batter standing before you use it?
A. Once upon a time this was the recognised procedure and many people today say it is not an advantage. Personally I do leave the batter standing in a refrigerator before I make a Yorkshire pudding, for I believe the change from the cold to the heat of the oven helps it to rise; I am less concerned to let the batter stand when using it to make pancakes. Always remember to whisk the batter just before cooking, as the flour tends to drop to the bottom of the bowl.

Q. Is it essential to mix short crust pastry, etc. with really cold water?
A. Yes, it does help to keep the pastry cool, and that is an advantage. I have found, however, that one can make very good short crust pastry by mixing it with milk, rather than water, and that this is a distinct advantage when you want to freeze the pastry.

Q. One is told that you should always roll pastry in the same direction; is this really necessary?
A. The purpose of this method of handling the pastry is to prevent it from stretching; you turn the pastry, not the rolling-pin.
   When you turn the pastry lift it carefully and do not stretch or pull this; pastry is a little like a fabric, you will spoil the shape of the pie or other pastry dish if you do not keep it a good shape.

Q. Must you bake a soufflé the moment it is mixed?
A. No, it will stand for about an hour if covered with a bowl and rise when baked, this means you can prepare the soufflé some little time before the meal; it is not necessary to make this a last-minute task. You cannot, of course, let a hot soufflé stand after baking if you use the usual recipes; the only way you can allow time for the soufflé to stand after cooking is if you omit the yolks from the recipe and simply mix it with the stiffly whisked egg whites.

Meal starters

There are many times when family meals consist of two courses only, without a 'starter'; but an interesting hors d'œuvre can turn a fairly simple meal into a more exciting one, and this extra course is generally considered one of the essentials of a special occasion dinner or luncheon.

This chapter has a varied selection of meal starters and this is followed by many ideas for soups, which could be served after, or instead of, an hòrs d'œuvre. Recipes for soups begin on page 19.

Choosing wisely

Do not be too conservative in your choice of hors d'œuvre. Why not depart from custom and serve a 'dip' or canapés with your pre-dinner drinks, then serve the main course when you go into the dining-room. This is a practical idea when entertaining a lot of people, with little help in cooking or serving. Recipes for these begin on pages 8 and 189.

Do not imagine your meal starter must be expensive, I hope this chapter will convince you to the contrary. Although some of the dishes are frankly luxurious, others are made from everyday ingredients. The Easy Selection guide on the next page will help you choose wisely, and sensible home freezing will enable you to buy when some foods are cheapest.

Take an interest in presenting familiar dishes in new ways; as page 15 shows, even a simple salad looks more interesting when served in a goblet.

Plan your meal starter with the rest of the meal in mind. Avoid a rich creamy hors d'œuvre if the other courses are fairly heavy or creamy; select a satisfying appetiser or soup if you plan a light main dish and dessert.

Never let the flavour of the hors d'œuvre or soup be too dominating; it could spoil your palate for the rest of the meal.

Freezing meal starters

Fruit juices and many fruits freeze well; grapefruit segments, melon, fresh tomato juice are particularly successful.

Salads should not be frozen, the ingredients lose their crispness, but many vegetables used in cooking freeze well. Page 107 gives more information.

Smoked fish and shellfish can be frozen, as well as many fish dishes, full information given on page 32.

Pâtés take time to make, so it is worthwhile preparing in advance. Cook, cover with melted butter, cool then wrap and freeze. Use within 6 weeks, thaw out at room temperature.

To serve hors d'oeuvre

The information below describes ways of serving fresh fruits; you can also add fruit to salads as part of an hors d'œuvre.

Grapefruit halves, sprinkled with sugar and topped with a glacé cherry, make an easy start to a meal. For something different, spread grapefruit halves with honey and sprinkle with brown sugar. Put into individual flameproof containers and grill the grapefruit for a few minutes until the surface begins to brown.

There is a variety of smoked fish available, and these are some of the most popular meal starters. They need no cooking or elaborate accompaniments. The most readily available smoked fish are eel, trout, mackerel and salmon, but smoked sprats are extremely good. Garnish the fish with a little lettuce, lemon and serve with cayenne pepper, brown bread and butter and horseradish sauce; although this is not usually served with smoked salmon.

Shellfish of all kinds make good fish cocktails or salads. Page 11 gives a prawn cocktail which is a little unusual. To make a change, serve the prawns in a tomato-flavoured mayonnaise on shredded lettuce.

Salami and other cooked meats can be served as part of a mixed hors d'œuvre or with pâté, as shown in the picture on page 16.

Easy guide to meal starters

The following gives you help in selecting the right hors d'œuvre or soup for the right occasion.

When you are short of time see pages 9, 10, 11, 14, 15.

When you are short of money see pages 9, 12, 13, 14, 15, 19, 21, 22, 23.

When you want a special dish see pages 11, 12, 15, 16, 17, 28, 29, 30, 31, 43, 53, 189, 192, 215.

For a snack or light meal see pages 10, 11, 12, 13, 14, 15, 17, 20, 21, 23, 24, 25, 29, 30, 31, 52.

When you are slimming see pages 9, 10, 15, 20, 21, 26, 27.

Fruit as an hors d'oeuvre

Many fruits or fruit juices make an interesting start to a meal.

Citrus fruits
1. Serve fresh or canned orange juice as cold as possible. To give a new flavour, pour the juice over mint leaves, bruised to bring out the maximum flavour. Strain into frosted glasses and top with glacé or Maraschino cherries. To frost glasses brush the citrus with a little egg white and roll in castor sugar.
2. Mix orange, lemon and pineapple juice together.
3. Serve fresh grapefruit mixed with segments of fresh orange and tangerine, and moistened with lemon juice to give a 'bite'.
4. Mix segments of grapefruit with shellfish, toss in oil, vinegar or lemon juice, season well or blend with yoghurt and lemon juice.
5. Roll thin slices of ham round chopped skinned segments of grapefruit, orange and grated raw apple; blend with mayonnaise.

Melon
Cut the melon into slices, remove the seeds, then cut the flesh into neat portions. Top with thin slices of orange and glacé or Maraschino cherries. Serve with powdered ginger and sugar.

Glazed melon
Cut the melon into slices, sprinkle very lightly with powdered ginger and brown sugar then put under the grill for 2 minutes until the sugar melts. Serve at once. Serve slices of melon with Parma ham.

Tomato
Flavour canned or bottled tomato juice with a little celery, salt, sherry and Worcestershire sauce.

Avocado pears as an hors d'oeuvre

Avocado pears vinaigrette
Halve the pears, remove the stone in each, then fill the centre of each halved pear with French dressing. If wished this dressing, also known as vinaigrette, can be given a sharper taste with extra vinegar or lemon juice.

Avocado pears with shellfish
Prepare the pears by halving them, then taking out the stones. Fill with shrimps, prawns, or flaked crab meat or lobster blended either with mayonnaise with a little extra lemon juice added, or with the dressing used for Prawn cocktail, (see page 11). If preferred use just the French dressing (see page 14) with the fish.

Avocado pears with grapefruit
Pull the skin away from the flesh of the pear, then cut this into neat slices, discarding the stone. Sprinkle with lemon juice or with French dressing. Arrange on a bed of crisp lettuce with segments of fresh or well drained canned grapefruit. Top with mayonnaise.

Avocado pears indienne
Blend a little curry powder with mayonnaise, toss the shellfish in this before putting into the centre of the pears. Serve with wedges of lemon.

Avocado pears and cheese
Crumble Danish blue cheese and blend with mayonnaise; fill the centres of the pears with this mixture.

Note: Avocado pears will discolour when cut unless sprinkled with lemon juice.

Jamaican prawn hors d'oeuvre

Imperial	Metric
16 prawns or 8–12 oz. small shrimps, chopped	16 prawns or 200–300 g. small shrimps, chopped
1 red chilli pepper, chopped	1 red chilli pepper, chopped
grated rind and juice of 1 lemon	grated rind and juice of 1 lemon
1 tablespoon olive oil	1 tablespoon olive oil
seasoning	seasoning
1 clove garlic, crushed	1 clove garlic, crushed
1 lettuce	1 lettuce
Garnish:	Garnish:
8 whole prawns	8 whole prawns

1. Shell the prawns, devein them and chop finely.
2. Mix with the chopped chilli pepper, lemon rind and juice, olive oil, seasoning and garlic.
3. Wash and dry the lettuce.
4. To serve, place a bed of lettuce on individual serving dishes and spoon the prawn mixture over. Serve with bread and butter or biscuits.

Avocado dressing for shellfish
Put the flesh of an avocado into a bowl and mash until smooth with the juice of a medium-sized lemon, 1 teaspoon olive oil, 1 teaspoon made mustard and 2–3 tablespoons mayonnaise. Season with chilli powder, cayenne pepper, a few drops Tabasco sauce and salt. Serve with prepared fish or shellfish.

Preparation time: 15 minutes
Serves: 4

Prawn cocktail

Imperial
4 oz. prawns (weight when
   skinned, see stage 1)
lettuce
Dressing:
4 tablespoons mayonnaise (see
   page 47)
½–1 tablespoon tomato purée or
   ketchup
1 teaspoon Worcestershire
   sauce (see note)
2 tablespoons thick cream
seasoning

Metric
100 g. prawns (weight when
   skinned, see stage 1)
lettuce
Dressing:
4 tablespoons mayonnaise (see
   page 47)
½–1 tablespoon tomato purée or
   ketchup
1 teaspoon Worcestershire
   sauce (see note)
2 tablespoons thick cream
seasoning

1. If using frozen prawns, defrost at room temperature. To hasten the process the packet could be put into cold water for a while; do not put in hot water otherwise the fish will be tough.
   If using fresh prawns, put them for 1 minute in hot water and the skins (or shells as they are often called) come away quickly and easily. Leave a few whole for garnish.
2. Blend all the ingredients together for the dressing.
3. Toss the prawns in the dressing.
4. Shred the lettuce very finely, for it has to be eaten with a spoon.
5. Put the lettuce into the glasses, top with the prawns and garnish with the reserved whole prawns as in the photograph. Serve with brown bread and butter and lemon.

Note: This can be increased up to 1 tablespoon if you want a more piquant flavour; or use a few drops of chilli sauce or soy sauce.

Preparation time: 15 minutes plus time to make mayonnaise
Main utensils: sharp knife, basin
Serves: 4

Creamed scampi

Imperial
2 oz. butter
8 oz. scampi, large size
seasoning
1 oz. flour
½ pint single cream or
   evaporated milk or top of
   the milk
lemon juice
Garnish:
chopped parsley or chives

Metric
50 g. butter
200 g. scampi, large size
seasoning
25 g. flour
250 ml. single cream or
   evaporated milk or top of
   the milk
lemon juice
Garnish:
chopped parsley or chives

1. Melt the butter in a frying pan or heat-resisting skillet.
2. Toss the scampi in seasoned flour and fry carefully for 4–5 minutes. Add more butter if necessary and keep shaking the pan. Take care not to overcook the scampi.
3. Pour in the cream, evaporated milk or top of the milk to make a smooth sauce. Cook, stirring all the time.
4. Season with salt and pepper and lemon juice.
5. Garnish with chopped parsley or chives.
6. Either serve in the dish in which it was cooked or turn out on to a hot dish. Hand rye bread or hot toast and lemon wedges.

Variation
Cut plaice or sole into small pieces and fry as the scampi.

Cooking time: 10–12 minutes
Preparation time: 10 minutes
Main cooking utensil: frying pan
Serves: 4

Marinated kipper salad

Imperial	Metric
8–10 oz. cooked, cold potatoes, old or new	200–250 g. cooked, cold potatoes, old or new
4 tablespoons mayonnaise	4 tablespoons mayonnaise
1 dessert apple	1 dessert apple
2 sticks celery	2 sticks celery
paprika pepper	paprika pepper
2 large kippers or 4 kipper fillets	2 large kippers or 4 kipper fillets
can sweetcorn	can sweetcorn
French dressing (see page 14)	French dressing (see page 14)
Garnish:	*Garnish:*
lemon	lemon

1. Dice the cooked potatoes and mix with the mayonnaise, then add the chopped peeled apple and celery and pile in the centre of the dish. Sprinkle with paprika.
2. Remove the bones from whole kippers.
3. Cut the raw kippers into very narrow strips.
4. Put into a basin and mix with the well drained sweetcorn and French dressing, made as directed on page 14.
5. Arrange the kipper mixture round the potato salad.
6. Garnish with lemon slices or wedges.
7. Serve as cold as possible with brown bread and butter.

Variation
Mock smoked salmon — raw kipper marinated in French dressing for several hours — may be served instead of smoked salmon as an hors d'oeuvre.

Cooking time: 20–30 minutes
Preparation time: 20 minutes
Main cooking utensil: saucepan
Serves: 4–6

Pickled herrings

Imperial	Metric
4 large salt or fresh herrings	4 large salt or fresh herrings
½ pint brown or white vinegar	275 ml. brown or white vinegar
½ pint water	275 ml. water
2–4 oz. sugar	50–100 g. sugar
2 teaspoons pickling spice	2 teaspoons pickling spice
2 bay leaves	2 bay leaves
bunch fresh dill or pinch dried dill	bunch fresh dill or pinch dried dill
2 carrots	2 carrots
1 turnip	1 turnip
2 onions	2 onions
2 leeks	2 leeks
stick celery	stick celery
seasoning	seasoning
Garnish:	*Garnish:*
red and green chilli peppers	red and green chilli peppers
1 medium-sized onion	1 medium-sized onion
2 lemons	2 lemons
2 firm tomatoes	2 firm tomatoes

1. If using salt herrings, cover with cold water and stand overnight. If using fresh herrings (as in picture) clean, divide into 2 fillets and do not soak; use at once.
2. Divide the salt fish into small pieces.
3. Put the vinegar, water, sugar and pickling spices into a pan, simmer steadily for 8 minutes, making sure the sugar is dissolved.
4. Put the herrings, bay leaves, dill and diced vegetables into a dish, cover with the hot pickling mixture.
5. Add seasoning to taste, fresh fish should be well salted.
6. Wait until liquid is no longer steaming, then put into a cool place, preferably a refrigerator. Fresh herrings should be stored for 1–2 days only if no refrigerator is available. Serve with the vegetables and garnish.

Cooking time: 8 minutes
Preparation time: 20 minutes, plus time to stand (see note and stages 1 and 6)
Main cooking utensil: saucepan
Serves: 4

Margareta sill

Imperial
4 large herrings
1 oz. butter
seasoning
2–3 teaspoons made mustard
3 teaspoons tomato purée
4 tablespoons single cream or
  top of milk
Garnish:
chopped parsley

Metric
4 large herrings
25 g. butter
seasoning
2–3 teaspoons made mustard
3 teaspoons tomato purée
4 tablespoons single cream or
  top of milk
Garnish:
chopped parsley

1. Clean, wash and fillet the herrings (see below).
2. Cut the fillets into two.
3. Divide the butter equally into eight pieces.
4. Place a piece of butter on each fillet and roll up with the skin side outside.
5. Pack upright into a casserole and season well.
6. Mix the mustard, tomato purée and cream to a smooth sauce and pour over the fish.
7. Bake until tender. Serve as a hot or cold hors d'oeuvre garnished with parsley.

To fillet herrings. Slit the under-side of the herrings, turn and place cut side downwards on to a board. Run your finger or thumb down the backbone very firmly, turn over, lift away the backbone, then cut the fish into two fillets.
To remove the smell of fish after handling: Rub the hands with a little dry mustard then wash in the usual way, the smell goes completely.

Variation
Use soured cream or yoghurt.

Cooking time: 30 minutes
Preparation time: 15 minutes
Main cooking utensil: covered casserole
Oven temperature: moderate to moderately hot (350–375°F., 180–190°C., Gas Mark 4–5)
Oven position: centre
Serves: 4

Mussels with cheese

Imperial
2 pints mussels
1 onion
6 sticks celery
salt
8 oz. tomatoes
4 oz. Gouda cheese

Metric
a generous litre mussels
1 onion
6 sticks celery
salt
200 g. tomatoes
100 g. Gouda cheese

1. Clean the mussels in cold water and remove the black weed. Discard any that will not close when tapped sharply.
2. Place the mussels in a pan with the chopped onion, celery and salt.
3. Cover, bring to the boil and simmer until all the shells are open.
4. Remove from the heat and drain. When cool remove the mussels from the shells and discard half the shells.
5. Skin the tomatoes, remove the pips and chop the fleshy part finely.
6. Place each mussel in one half of a shell and arrange on a dish.
7. Blend the chopped tomatoes, seasoning and finely grated cheese.
8. Spread the tomato mixture over the mussels.
9. Brown under the grill and garnish with parsley. Serve hot as an hors d'oeuvre or light supper dish with a green salad.

Variations
Canned mussels could be used; heat, then drain and put in a dish, top with the tomato mixture and brown under the grill. Another way of serving the ingredients above is to omit the onions and celery when cooking the mussels. Then fry the celery and onions with an extra onion. Put this cooked vegetable purée with tomatoes on to the mussels, then add the cheese and brown under the grill.

Cooking time: 20 minutes
Preparation time: 20 minutes
Main cooking utensils: large saucepan, ovenproof dish
Serves: 4–6

Herring and mushroom salad

Imperial	Metric
4 oz. button mushrooms	100 g. button mushrooms
4 bismarck or pickled herrings (see page 12)	4 bismarck or pickled herrings (see page 12)
French dressing:	*French dressing:*
2 teaspoons made mustard	2 teaspoons made mustard
pinch salt	pinch salt
shake pepper	shake pepper
pinch sugar	pinch sugar
4 tablespoons oil	4 tablespoons oil
2–3 tablespoons vinegar or lemon juice	2–3 tablespoons vinegar or lemon juice
Garnish:	*Garnish:*
chopped parsley	chopped parsley
wafer thin onion rings	wafer thin onion rings

1. Wash, dry, but do not peel the mushrooms, slice thinly.
2. Shake the French dressing ingredients together.
3. Toss the mushrooms in the dressing, arrange the herrings on a dish with the dressed mushrooms between them.
4. Garnish with chopped parsley and wafer thin onion rings.
5. Serve either as an hors d'oeuvre or as a light meal with brown bread and butter, and/or potato salad.

Note: Raw mushrooms are delicious in salads – choose firm button mushrooms where possible. Slice and add to other ingredients in green or mixed salads.

Variation
Add chopped cucumber to the mushrooms.

Preparation time: 15 minutes
Main utensil: sharp knife
Serves: 4 as an hors d'oeuvre or 2–3 as a main dish

Egg salad

Imperial	Metric
4 eggs	4 eggs
lettuce	lettuce
watercress	watercress
mayonnaise (see page 47)	mayonnaise (see page 47)
Garnish:	*Garnish:*
paprika pepper	paprika pepper

1. Put the eggs into boiling water and cook for just on 10 minutes.
2. Remove from the boiling water, plunge into the cold water to cool quickly, crack the shells, this ensures that there will be no dark line, due to over-cooking round the egg yolk.
3. Arrange a bed of salad and watercress on a dish, top with the halved eggs and coat with mayonnaise.
4. Garnish with paprika pepper. Serve with tomatoes, cucumber, or other salad vegetables, as a main meal or hors d'oeuvre.

Note: Do not shell eggs until ready to serve, then keep in a cool place for a limited time. Once eggs are sliced or cut they dry.

Variation
Remove the yolks and blend with a little curry powder or with grated Cheddar cheese.

Cooking time: 10 minutes
Preparation time: few minutes
Main cooking utensil: saucepan
Serves: 2 as a main meal or 4 as an hors d'oeuvre

Goblet salads

This way of serving a salad is particularly suitable for a buffet, as it can be eaten with a spoon or small fork. It can either form an hors d'oeuvre or part of a main course.

Salade de fromage et salami

Pull the leaves of a small lettuce heart apart, wash and dry, then shred coarsely and put into the bottom of the serving glasses or dishes. Drain a small can of asparagus tips and chop if wished, slice 2—3 small, raw button mushrooms neatly and cut 8 oz. (200 g.) Gruyère cheese into thick matchsticks. Mix together with 1—2 teaspoons capers and 1 oz. (25 g.) grated Parmesan cheese and put into the dishes. Moisten with dressing made by blending 3 tablespoons olive oil, salt, pepper, dry mustard and 1½ tablespoons lemon juice or vinegar together. Top with cones of salami, black olives and sprigs of parsley.

Salade parisienne

This French salad is another mixture of ingredients that could be served in a similar way to the cheese and salami salad. Cut 12 oz. (300 g.) mixed cooked meat (veal, tongue, ham or beef) into matchstick pieces, chop 2 hard-boiled eggs and dice 8 oz. (200 g.) potatoes. Mix together with a finely chopped or grated onion and put on a bed of shredded lettuce. Top with dressing, as above, and garnish with chopped chervil or parsley.

Preparation time: 20 minutes
Serves: 4

Salmon mousse

Imperial	Metric
1-pint packet aspic jelly	½-litre packet aspic jelly
approximately 1 pint hot water or well strained fish stock made with skin and bones of fish	approximately ½ litre hot water or well strained fish stock made with skin and bones of fish
little oil	little oil
few tarragon leaves	few tarragon leaves
2—3 gherkins	2—3 gherkins
1—2 cooked carrots	1—2 cooked carrots
2 level teaspoons powdered gelatine	2 level teaspoons powdered gelatine
2 tablespoons dry sherry	2 tablespoons dry sherry
1 lb. cooked or canned salmon	½ kg. cooked or canned salmon
3 tablespoons mayonnaise	3 tablespoons mayonnaise
grated rind and juice of ½ lemon	grated rind and juice of ½ lemon
seasoning	seasoning
2 egg whites	2 egg whites

1. Dissolve the aspic jelly in the hot water or stock (see packet instructions).
2. Allow to cool then spoon a little into each oiled mould (use approximately a third of the jelly).
3. As the jelly thickens turn it in the mould so that it coats the bottom and sides.
4. Arrange individual tarragon leaves, pieces of gherkin and carrot on the jelly.
5. Carefully spoon a very thin layer of cool but liquid jelly over the garnish. Allow to set.
6. Re-heat the remaining aspic, add the gelatine, softened in sherry, stir until dissolved. Cool and allow to stiffen slightly.
7. Add the flaked salmon, mayonnaise, grated lemon rind and juice, seasoning, and finally the stiffly beaten egg whites.
8. Spoon into the moulds, allow to set. Turn out and garnish with lettuce, tomato and lemon quarters.

Cooking time: few minutes
Preparation time: 15 minutes plus setting time
Main cooking utensils: 4 ½-pint (¼-litre) individual moulds or 6 smaller moulds, saucepan
Serves: 4—6

Liver loaf

Imperial	Metric
1–1¼ lb. calves' or pigs' liver	500–600 g. calves' or pigs' liver
4 oz. salt pork or fat bacon	100 g. salt pork or fat bacon
4 anchovy fillets (optional)	4 anchovy fillets (optional)
1 small onion	1 small onion
1 clove garlic	1 clove garlic
2 oz. soft breadcrumbs	50 g. soft breadcrumbs
seasoning	seasoning
2 small eggs, or 1 whole egg and 1 egg yolk	2 small eggs, or 1 whole egg and 1 egg yolk
12 rashers thin, long streaky bacon	12 rashers thin, long streaky bacon
Garnish:	*Garnish:*
gherkin	gherkin
canned or home-made potato salad	canned or home-made potato salad
chives	chives

1. Slice the liver and put it through the mincer with the pork and anchovies.
2. Add the chopped onion and crushed clove garlic to the liver etc. and put it through the mincer again (for a fine pâté put it through twice).
3. Blend with the breadcrumbs, seasoning and eggs, and mix very thoroughly.
4. Line the tin with most of the rashers and put in the mixture, pressing down firmly.
5. Cover with the rest of the bacon rashers cut into halves.
6. Stand in a tin of cold water, and bake until firm.
7. When cooked put a piece of foil or greaseproof paper and a weight on top and leave until cold.
8. Serve garnished with gherkin. Slice, and serve with potato salad, chives and a mixed salad.

Cooking time: 1½ hours
Preparation time: 25 minutes
Main cooking utensils: 2-lb. (1-kg.) loaf tin, roasting tin
Oven temperature: very moderate (350°F., 180°C., Gas Mark 3–4)
Oven position: centre
Serves: 6–8

Chicken liver pâté

Imperial	Metric
1 onion	1 onion
2 oz. fat	50 g. fat
1 lb. chicken livers	400 g. chicken livers
11–12 oz. fat pork	275–300 g. fat pork
3 oz. bread	75 g. bread
¼ pint milk	125 ml. milk
2 eggs	2 eggs
seasoning	seasoning
1 teaspoon paprika	1 teaspoon paprika
4 oz. bacon	100 g. bacon
½ red pepper	½ red pepper
1 oz. softened butter	25 g. softened butter
1 clove garlic, crushed	1 clove garlic, crushed
pinch cayenne pepper	pinch cayenne pepper

1. Chop the onion finely and soften it in the fat.
2. Mince the chicken livers and dice 1–2 oz. (25–50 g.) of the fat pork. Mix these with the onion.
3. Soak the bread in the milk, beat until smooth and add to the mixture with the eggs, seasoning and paprika.
4. Cut the rest of the fat pork into slices and form these into a neat oblong, spread the pâté on these.
5. Mince the bacon, dice the red pepper and mix both these with the softened butter, crushed garlic and cayenne pepper. Put this on top of the pâté.
6. Roll up firmly and either tie with several pieces of string or wrap in foil. The former gives a crisper coating to the fat.
7. Bake for the time and temperature given (if wrapping in foil allow an extra 15 minutes). Cool. Serve sliced thinly as an hors d'oeuvre or as a light main dish with salad.

Cooking time: 1 hour (see stages 6 and 7)
Preparation time: 30 minutes
Main cooking utensils: saucepan, baking tray
Oven temperature: moderate (325–350°F., 170–180°C., Gas Mark 3–4)
Oven position: centre
Serves: 4–5 as a main dish or 8–10 as an hors d'oeuvre

Fish and egg flan

Imperial	Metric
7–8 oz. shortcrust pastry, using 7–8 oz. flour, etc.	175–200 g. shortcrust pastry, using 175–200 g. flour, etc.
Filling:	*Filling:*
2 oz. mushrooms	50 g. mushrooms
1 oz. butter	25 g. butter
3 eggs	3 eggs
seasoning	seasoning
¼ pint thin cream	125 ml. thin cream
¼ pint milk	125 ml. milk
2 tomatoes	2 tomatoes
2–3 teaspoons chopped herbs (chervil, parsley, marjoram, tarragon)	2–3 teaspoons chopped herbs (chervil, parsley, marjoram, tarragon)
3–4 oz. canned or frozen mussels	75–100 g. canned or frozen mussels
4–6 oz. frozen prawns, defrosted	100–150 g. frozen prawns, defrosted
Garnish:	*Garnish:*
parsley	parsley

1. Roll out the pastry and line the flan ring.
2. Bake 'blind' for approximately 15 minutes, until just beginning to set, but not brown.
3. While the pastry is cooking, fry the finely chopped mushrooms until tender in the butter.
4. Beat the eggs, seasoning and cream, add the hot milk, the skinned, chopped tomatoes, chopped herbs, mussels and prawns.
5. Spoon into the flan case carefully.
6. Return to the oven, lower the heat to very moderate and cook until set.
7. Top with chopped parsley. Serve hot or cold as an hors d'oeuvre or main dish.

Cooking time: 50–60 minutes
Preparation time: 30 minutes
Main cooking utensils: 8- to 9-inch (20- to 23-cm.) flan ring, baking sheet, frying pan, saucepan
Oven temperature: (425°F., 220°C., Gas Mark 7) then (325°F., 170°C., Gas Mark 3) *Oven position:* centre
Serves: 5–6

Soufflé with poached eggs

Imperial	Metric
4 eggs	4 eggs
seasoning	seasoning
Soufflé mixture:	*Soufflé mixture:*
1 oz. butter	25 g. butter
1 oz. flour	25 g. flour
12 tablespoons milk	12 tablespoons milk
3 egg yolks	3 egg yolks
4 oz. finely grated Gruyère cheese	100 g. finely grated Gruyère cheese
5 egg whites	5 egg whites

1. Poach the eggs in boiling, salted water until set enough to handle; do not overcook.
2. Melt the butter in a pan, stir in the flour and cook for several minutes.
3. Gradually blend in the milk, bring to the boil and cook until thickened.
4. Season well, add the egg yolks and finely grated cheese.
5. Gradually fold in the stiffly beaten egg whites.
6. Put half the mixture into the greased soufflé dishes, top with the well-drained, poached eggs, then the rest of the soufflé mixture.
7. Bake for approximately 20 minutes until just set.

Note: This dish is equally suitable for an hors d'oeuvre or a savoury. Serve as soon as possible after cooking. This is eaten with a dessertspoon and fork.

Variation
Use a mixture of Parmesan and Cheddar cheese.

Cooking time: 30 minutes
Preparation time: 20 minutes
Main cooking utensils: 2 saucepans, soufflé dishes
Oven temperature: moderate (375°F., 190°C., Gas Mark 5)
Serves: 4

Soups

A soup can be an excellent start to a meal, but many soups make a satisfying light meal, particularly if followed by cheese and fruit.

Making stock

Many soups need stock to give additional flavour. When the recipe specifies a brown stock this is made by simmering bones or shin of beef, lamb or game in water to cover for several hours. Vegetables and herbs can be added. A white stock is made in the same way, but using bones of veal, chicken or turkey. If home-made stock is not available, substitute stock cubes. Stock is a highly perishable liquid, especially if vegetables have been used, so store carefully; reboil every other day, even when kept in a refrigerator. Stock freezes well, see the information right.

Types of soup

Soups can be made from most vegetables, so you can plan a variety of dishes throughout the year, based upon the recipes on pages 19 to 24. You can choose a clear soup with diced vegetables; a purée soup, where the vegetables are sieved or emulsified; or a creamed soup, where the vegetables are blended with cream or a creamy sauce.

Broths and chowders are both thick soups and could be served for a supper dish. Meat, fish and vegetables are all used to make this type of soup. The Lobster chowder on page 31 could be made with inexpensive white or smoked fish; the Vegetable chowder on page 24 could have pieces of cooked chicken, ham or other meat added.

Clear soups are ideal when you are not particularly hungry or when trying to lose weight. Serve jellied or frosted soups in hot weather or Continental fruit soups (see pages 26, 27 and 28).

To freeze soups

Stock freezes well. Pour the liquid into waxed or polythene containers allowing $\frac{1}{2}$ inch (1 cm.) 'head-room'. If you prefer to use polythene bags stand these in a firm container (such as a sugar carton), pour in the soup, seal, freeze, then remove the bag from the carton; this gives you a neat pack for easy storage. A more 'space-saving' method of freezing concentrated stock is to pour this into ice-cube trays, freeze, then store the cubes in suitable containers. Use within 3 months. Purée or meat soups should be used within the same length of time. For information on creamed soups or thickening see under sauces page 221.

Carrot soup

Imperial
1 large onion
1½ oz. butter or margarine
2 pints white stock or
   water
1 lb. carrots, peeled and
   chopped
1 clove garlic, crushed
seasoning
1½ oz. flour
½ pint milk
parsley

Metric
1 large onion
40 g. butter or margarine
generous litre white stock or
   water
½ kg. carrots, peeled and
   chopped
1 clove garlic, crushed
seasoning
40 g. flour
250 ml. milk
parsley

1. Chop the onion and toss in the butter or margarine.
2. Add the white stock or water and the carrots with the garlic.
3. Season well, being particularly generous with pepper, and simmer for 30–40 minutes until the carrots are tender.
4. Blend the flour and milk and work until smooth. Bring to the boil, stirring constantly, and cook until thickened.
5. Sieve the carrot mixture, blend with the thickened milk. Reheat and top with chopped parsley.
6. Serve with fried bread croûtons.

Variation
To give more colour and flavour, add two skinned tomatoes and 2 teaspoons paprika. Fry the tomatoes with the onion at stage 1 and blend the paprika with the flour at stage 4.

Cooking time: 1 hour
Preparation time: 15 minutes
Main cooking utensils: frying pan, saucepan
Serves: 4–5

Celery cream soup

Imperial
2 onions
2 oz. butter
2 pints white stock or water
   and 2–3 chicken stock
   cubes
1 lb. celery, chopped
2–3 teaspoons soup seasoning
2 teaspoons paprika
½–1 tablespoon tomato purée
1 oz. flour
¼ pint thin cream or evaporated
   milk
Garnish:
parsley

Metric
2 onions
50 g. butter
generous litre white stock or
   water and 2–3 chicken stock
   cubes
½ kg. celery, chopped
2–3 teaspoons soup seasoning
2 teaspoons paprika
½–1 tablespoon tomato purée
25 g. flour
125 ml. thin cream or evaporated
   milk
Garnish:
parsley

1. Chop the onions and fry in the butter until soft.
2. Add the white stock or water and stock cubes, the celery, soup seasoning, paprika and tomato purée.
3. Simmer for approximately 45 minutes then sieve the soup and reheat.
4. Blend the flour with the cream or evaporated milk. Stir into the hot soup and cook steadily until thickened. Do not cook too quickly.
5. Garnish with freshly chopped or dried parsley. If using the dried parsley, simmer in the soup for 5 minutes.

Cooking time: about 1 hour
Preparation time: 20 minutes
Main cooking utensil: saucepan
Serves: 5–6

Clear celery soup

Imperial	Metric
carcass of a roasted chicken	carcass of a roasted chicken
3–4 pints water, use the smaller amount in a pressure cooker	1¾–2¼ litres water, use the smaller amount in a pressure cooker
1 head celery	1 head celery
2 onions	2 onions
2 carrots	2 carrots
bouquet garni	bouquet garni
2 bay leaves	2 bay leaves
seasoning	seasoning
little jelly from the tin when roasting the chicken	little jelly from the tin when roasting the chicken

1. Break the carcass into convenient-sized pieces, put them into a large saucepan, add the water, simmer for 1½ hours or longer if wished; or put into a pressure cooker, cook at 15-lb. (7-kg.) pressure for 30 minutes, allow pressure to drop at room temperature (gradually).
2. Strain the stock carefully into a pan, add most of the celery stalks, saving the best part for garnish, the whole onions, carrots, bouquet garni, bay leaves and seasoning.
3. Simmer for 30 minutes or allow 10 minutes in a pressure cooker.
4. Strain again, re-heat with the jelly, the remaining chopped celery and extra seasoning. Serve topped with celery leaves.

Variation
Chicken broth: Make stock as above and add 2–3 stalks celery, 2 onions, 2 carrots, 1 leek, a small piece of turnip, all diced. Add the herbs and seasoning and the rice or barley and simmer for 45 minutes.

Cooking time: 2 hours
Preparation time: 20 minutes
Main cooking utensil: saucepan
Serves: 4–6

Dutch onion soup

Imperial	Metric
1¼ lb. onions	generous ½ kg. onions
2 oz. butter	50 g. butter
1½ oz. flour	40 g. flour
2½ pints brown stock	1¼ litres brown stock
seasoning	seasoning
2–3 slices bread	2–3 slices bread
grated Gruyère, Dutch Gouda or Edam cheese	grated Gruyère, Dutch Gouda or Edam cheese

1. Peel and slice the onions and toss in the butter until soft but not browned.
2. Stir in the flour and cook for a few minutes then gradually blend in the brown stock.
3. Bring to the boil and cook until slightly thickened, season well. Reduce the heat and let the soup simmer for about 45 minutes, stirring from time to time.
4. Cut bread into shapes to fit the top of the soup tureen or bowl. Pour in the soup and top with the bread. Cover this with a good layer of grated Gruyère, Dutch Gouda or Edam cheese and brown under the grill.

Cooking time: 1 hour
Preparation time: 10 minutes
Main cooking utensil: saucepan, grill
Serves: 5–6

Browned onion soup

Imperial
4 medium-sized onions
2 oz. butter
2 pints good brown stock (see note)
seasoning
4 rounds French bread
2–3 oz. Gruyère cheese, grated

Metric
4 medium-sized onions
50 g. butter
generous litre good brown stock (see note)
seasoning
4 rounds French bread
50–75 g. Gruyère cheese, grated

1. Cut the onions into thin rounds.
2. Fry in the hot butter until pale gold; do not allow to become too dark.
3. Add the stock and seasoning and simmer for approximately 20 minutes.
4. If using a 'cook and serve' dish as shown, add the rounds of bread (which can be toasted) to the soup in the pan, sprinkle on the grated cheese and brown under the grill. If preferred, put the bread into 4 soup bowls, add the soup and cheese and brown.

Note: Stock should be made with beef bones and can be flavoured with yeast or beef extract for additional flavour. Do not exceed the given amount of cheese and do not overcook.

Variations
Omit the bread or toast and the cheese and serve the soup topped with chopped parsley or chervil. Use a white stock and 1 pint (generous ½ litre) stock and 1 pint (generous ½ litre) milk. Cook as above, top with the cheese, but do not brown.

Cooking time: 35 minutes
Preparation time: 10 minutes
Main cooking utensil: saucepan
Serves: 4

Tomato vegetable broth

Imperial
2 lb. tomatoes including 8 oz. very small ones
4 medium-sized onions
2 cloves garlic (optional)
4 tablespoons oil
3-inch piece cucumber
water and 2 chicken stock cubes
seasoning
1 green pepper
about ¼ small cabbage

Metric
1 kg. tomatoes including 200 g. very small ones
4 medium-sized onions
2 cloves garlic (optional)
4 tablespoons oil
7-cm. piece cucumber
water and 2 chicken stock cubes
seasoning
1 green pepper
about ¼ small cabbage

1. Chop 1½ lb. (¾ kg.) large tomatoes, do not skin them for the soup is generally sieved.
2. Peel and chop 3 of the onions and crush the garlic cloves.
3. Heat 3 tablespoons oil and toss the tomatoes and onions in this, then add the stock, or water and stock cubes, season well and simmer for 15–20 minutes. Sieve and put on one side.
4. Slice the remaining onion, the cucumber and the pepper, discarding core and seeds, and shred the cabbage.
5. Toss in remaining oil for a few minutes, add the remaining skinned tomatoes, heat for a few minutes only.
6. Add the sieved tomatoes and heat together gently until the soup is very hot. Serve with crusty bread.

Note: Tomato soup is a favourite in Portugal, and tomatoes are used in soups with a variety of ingredients.

Variation
Add sliced hard-boiled eggs.

Cooking time: 30 minutes
Preparation time: 20 minutes
Main cooking utensil: saucepan
Serves: 6

Polish tomato soup

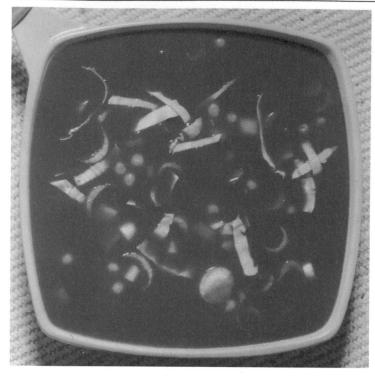

Imperial
1¼ lb. tomatoes
2 oz. fat or dripping
1½ oz. potato or ordinary flour
2½ pints stock
2–3 teaspoons sugar
seasoning

Metric
generous ½ kg. tomatoes
50 g. fat or dripping
40 g. potato or ordinary flour
scant 1½ litres stock
2–3 teaspoons sugar
seasoning

1. Skin the tomatoes and, if wished, deseed them. This makes a very smooth soup.
2. Fry the tomatoes in the fat or dripping until soft.
3. Blend in the flour, stock, sugar and seasoning; then bring to the boil and simmer for 30 minutes.

Variation
Add dried vegetables and cook these until soft (see picture) or add noodles.

Austrian tomato soup: Chop 1 carrot, 1 onion, 1 stick celery and toss in 2 oz. (50 g.) butter. Add 1¼ lb. (generous ½ kg.) tomatoes and cook for several minutes. Blend 1 oz. (25 g.) flour with 2 pints (generous litre) stock or water. Add to the vegetables with seasoning, a pinch paprika, 1 bay leaf, pinch marjoram and the juice and rind of 1 lemon. Simmer until tender, sieve and reheat. Stir in 2 oz. (50 g.) cooked rice before serving.

Cooking time: 45 minutes
Preparation time: 10 minutes
Main cooking utensil: saucepan
Serves: 4–6

Turnip top soup

Imperial
8–12 oz. turnip tops
1 large onion
2 medium-sized potatoes
1½ oz. butter
½ oz. flour
1 teaspoon curry powder
2½ pints white stock or water
   and 2–3 chicken stock cubes
1½ oz. rice
seasoning
Garnish (*optional*):
2 slices bread
1–2 oz. butter or fat

Metric
200–300 g. turnip tops
1 large onion
2 medium-sized potatoes
40 g. butter
15 g. flour
1 teaspoon curry powder
1¼ litres white stock or water
   and 2–3 chicken stock cubes
40 g. rice
seasoning
Garnish (*optional*):
2 slices bread
25–50 g. butter or fat

1. Shred the turnip tops very finely, discarding any tough old leaves.
2. Chop the onion and dice the potatoes.
3. Heat the butter and fry the onion until tender but not brown.
4. Blend in the flour and the curry powder.
5. Add the stock or water and stock cubes and bring to the boil.
6. Add the potatoes and rice and season well. Cook steadily for 10 minutes. Add the turnip tops and continue cooking for a further 10–15 minutes.
7. If wished, dice 2 slices of bread and fry in 1–2 oz. (25–50 g.) butter or fat until crisp and golden. Put on the soup just before serving.

Variation
Chinese vegetable soup: Bring 1½ pints (generous ¾ litre) white stock to the boil. Add 8 oz. (200 g.) very finely chopped turnip top leaves and 3–4 oz. (75–100 g.) finely diced, lean pork. Simmer steadily until tender then add seasoning, pinch monosodium glutamate and 2 tablespoons sherry.

Cooking time: 35 minutes
Preparation time: 15 minutes
Main cooking utensils: saucepan, frying pan
Serves: 4–5

Cream of potato soup

Imperial
1 lb. potatoes, peeled
1 pint chicken stock or water
and 2 stock cubes
2 large onions
bay leaf
seasoning
2 oz. butter
2 oz. flour
1 pint milk
½ pint thin cream
little cayenne pepper
little celery salt
Garnish:
chopped parsley

Metric
½ kg. potatoes, peeled
generous ½ litre chicken stock or
water and 2 stock cubes
2 large onions
bay leaf
seasoning
50 g. butter
50 g. flour
500 ml. milk
275 ml. thin cream
little cayenne pepper
little celery salt
Garnish:
chopped parsley

1. Put the potatoes — cut into small pieces — into the stock with the chopped onion, bay leaf and seasoning.
2. Cook until tender, do not boil too quickly.
3. Rub through a sieve.
4. Heat the butter in saucepan, stir in the flour, and cook for several minutes. Gradually stir in the milk, bring to the boil, cook until thick and smooth.
5. Add the potato purée and heat, then stir in the cream and seasoning, including the cayenne pepper and celery salt. Serve in individual soup cups or tureen, garnished with the parsley.

Variation
Make a potato leek soup with 10 oz. (300 g.) potatoes, 1 large onion, 12 oz. (300 g.) leeks, etc. Garnish with tiny croûtons of fried bread and paprika pepper and chopped watercress.

Note: The picture also shows potato salad.

Cooking time: 30 minutes
Preparation time: 25 minutes
Main cooking utensil: saucepan
Serves: 8–10

German potato soup

Imperial
6–8 oz. bacon (cut in one piece)
1 lb. old potatoes (weight when
peeled)
2 medium-sized leeks
1 onion
2½ pints water or stock
1–2 teaspoons soup seasoning
(see note)
3 white and 3 black peppercorns
4–5 pimento corns (see note)
2 bay leaves
pinch garlic salt

Metric
150 g. bacon (cut in one piece)
½ kg. old potatoes (weight when
peeled)
2 medium-sized leeks
1 onion
scant 1½ litres water or stock
1–2 teaspoons soup seasoning
(see note)
3 white and 3 black peppercorns
4–5 pimento corns (see note)
2 bay leaves
pinch garlic salt

1. Put the bacon, diced potatoes, finely chopped leeks and onion into a pan.
2. Add all the other ingredients and simmer gently until the vegetables are soft.
3. Remove the bacon, chop most of it finely, but save a few slices as a garnish. Return the bacon to the soup and heat.
4. Serve hot with rye bread, garnished with bacon.

Note: Available from German delicatessens.

Variation
Put 1 lb. (½ kg.) old potatoes, 2 leeks, 1 onion and 2 stalks celery (all prepared and chopped) into a pan with 2½ pints (1½ litres) stock, 2 sage leaves, a sprig of parsley and seasoning. Simmer until tender. Sieve the soup, add 2 oz. (50 g.) butter and reheat. Grill 2 oz. (50 g.) bacon and crumble. Sprinkle over the soup and serve with croûtons.

Cooking time: approximately 1 hour
Preparation time: 15 minutes
Main cooking utensil: large saucepan
Serves: 4

Vegetable chowder

Imperial	Metric
2–3 large leeks	2–3 large leeks
2 onions	2 onions
4 carrots	4 carrots
3–4 stalks celery	3–4 stalks celery
1 small turnip (optional)	1 small turnip (optional)
1 oz. butter	25 g. butter
2–3 oz. lean bacon, diced	50–75 g. lean bacon, diced
1 oz. flour	25 g. flour
1½ pints stock or water	¾ litre stock or water
seasoning	seasoning
3 oz. rice	75 g. rice
Topping:	*Topping:*
grated cheese	grated cheese

1. Dice the leeks, onions, carrots, celery and turnip.
2. Heat the butter in a saucepan and fry the diced bacon until crisp. Stir in the flour and cook for a few minutes.
3. Add the stock gradually and bring to the boil, stirring.
4. Add the vegetables and simmer until tender, seasoning well. Meanwhile boil the rice in salted water until tender. Drain and add to the chowder. Top with grated cheese and serve with hot rolls.

Note: The word chowder means a soup which is almost as thick and as filling as pot-au-feu. By adding cheese to vegetable chowder you can turn this into a complete and very satisfying meal.

Cooking time: 30 minutes
Preparation time: 15 minutes
Main cooking utensil: large saucepan
Serves: 4–5

Minestrone soup

Imperial	Metric
3 oz. haricot beans	75 g. haricot beans
1½ pints white stock	¾ litre white stock
1 large onion	1 large onion
2 tablespoons oil	2 tablespoons oil
1 clove garlic	1 clove garlic
2 oz. bacon	50 g. bacon
stick celery	stick celery
1 carrot	1 carrot
8 oz. tomatoes	200 g. tomatoes
seasoning	seasoning
8 oz. cabbage	200 g. cabbage
2 oz. macaroni or vermicelli	50 g. macaroni or vermicelli
Garnish:	*Garnish:*
chopped parsley	chopped parsley
grated Parmesan cheese	grated Parmesan cheese

1. Soak the beans overnight in the water or stock.
2. Chop the onion very finely and toss in the hot oil, for 2 minutes.
3. Add the crushed clove of garlic and the diced bacon and cook for a few minutes.
4. Put in the soaked haricot beans and the liquid in which they were soaked.
5. If using water, one or two chicken stock cubes could be put into the pan at this time.
6. Cover the pan and simmer gently for 1½ hours.
7. Add the finely chopped celery, diced carrot, skinned tomatoes and the seasoning; cook for 15 minutes.
8. Shred the cabbage very finely, put into the soup with the pasta — broken into short lengths — and continue cooking for 15–20 minutes until tender.
9. Taste the soup and re-season if necessary. Top with a generous amount of chopped parsley and grated cheese.

Cooking time: 2¼ hours
Preparation time: 30 minutes, plus overnight soaking of the haricot beans
Main cooking utensil: large saucepan
Serves: 4–6

Kidney soup

Imperial
8 oz. kidney (ox or lamb)
1 small onion
2 oz. butter
1 oz. flour
2 pints stock or water
   with 1–2 stock cubes
   (see note)
seasoning
sprig of parsley
little port or Burgundy

Metric
200 g. kidney (ox or lamb)
1 small onion
50 g. butter
25 g. flour
generous litre stock or water
   with 1–2 stock cubes
   (see note)
seasoning
sprig of parsley
little port or Burgundy

1. Chop the kidney very finely.
2. Fry with the finely chopped onion in hot butter for a minute or two. Be sure not to harden the outside of the meat.
3. Blend in the flour and gradually add the stock.
4. Bring to the boil, stir until smooth.
5. Simmer gently, adding seasoning and a sprig of parsley, for about 1½ hours.
6. To serve remove the parsley and add the port.

Note: With lamb's kidneys which need shorter cooking, use 1¼–1½ pints (¾ litre) only.

Variation

Oxtail soup: Soak one small chopped oxtail for 1–2 hours, discard the water. Fry 2 onions, 2 carrots and a little turnip at stage 2. Then continue as kidney soup.

Cooking time: lamb's kidneys 30 minutes, ox kidneys 1½ hours
Preparation time: 15 minutes
Main cooking utensil: large saucepan
Serves: 4–6

Liver dumpling soup

Imperial
Dumplings:
4 oz. calf's or lamb's or good
   quality ox liver
1 small onion
seasoning
pinch soup seasoning (see note)
2 oz. breadcrumbs
pinch marjoram
1 egg
little milk
Soup:
2 pints brown or white stock
   or water and stock cubes
Garnish:
chopped parsley and/or chives

Metric
Dumplings:
100 g. calf's or lamb's or good
   quality ox liver
1 small onion
seasoning
pinch soup seasoning (see note)
50 g. breadcrumbs
pinch marjoram
1 egg
little milk
Soup:
generous litre brown or white
   stock or water and stock cubes
Garnish:
chopped parsley and/or chives

1. To make the dumplings, chop the liver finely or put it through a coarse mincer.
2. Chop or grate the onion, then blend with the liver, seasoning, breadcrumbs and herbs.
3. Press together very firmly, add the egg and enough milk to bind.
4. Leave this mixture to stand for 30 minutes, so that the breadcrumbs absorb the liquid.
5. Heat the stock, or water and stock cubes, then press the liver mixture through a coarse sieve into the boiling soup, or spoon into the liquid with a teaspoon.
6. Cook for a few minutes only.
7. Garnish with chopped parsley and/or chives.

Note: Soup seasoning is available from German delicatessens.

Cooking time: 5 minutes
Preparation time: 15 minutes plus 30 minutes standing
Main cooking utensil: saucepan
Serves: 4

Consommé and garnishes

Imperial	Metric
12 oz. shin beef	300 g. shin beef
2 pints good brown stock (made from marrow bones)	generous litre good brown stock (made from marrow bones)
seasoning	seasoning
1 onion	1 onion
1 carrot	1 carrot
small piece celery	small piece celery
sprig parsley	sprig parsley
bay leaf	bay leaf

1. Cut the meat into neat pieces and put into the saucepan with the other ingredients.
2. Cover the pan tightly and simmer for 1 hour.
3. Strain through several thicknesses of muslin to give a clear liquid.
4. If the liquid is not clear, put in a whisked egg white and the clean shell.
5. Simmer for 20 minutes — any small particles of food collect on the shell and white.
6. Restrain carefully.
7. Heat the soup and add a little sherry or the garnishes given below.

Variations

Consommé julienne: Cut some carrot, turnip and cabbage into matchstick pieces, toss in butter and simmer in a little hot consommé until tender.
Consommé jardinière: As above but dice the vegetables.
With egg white: Hard-boil an egg and cut the white into fancy shapes — the yolk can also be used.
Jellied consommé: Dissolve 1–2 teaspoons powder gelatine in the hot consommé. Allow to set lightly, then whisk or chop and pile into soup cups.

Cooking time: 1 hour
Preparation time: 20 minutes (including straining)
Main cooking utensil: large saucepan
Serves: 4

Clear soup with pancakes

Imperial	Metric
chicken carcass or beef bones	chicken carcass or beef bones
2 pints water	generous litre water
2 onions	2 onions
2 carrots	2 carrots
2–3 teaspoons soup seasoning (see note)	2–3 teaspoons soup seasoning (see note)
Savoury pancake:	*Savoury pancake:*
2 oz. plain or self-raising flour	50 g. plain or self-raising flour
pinch salt	pinch salt
2 eggs	2 eggs
¼ pint milk	125 ml. milk
pinch powdered nutmeg	pinch powdered nutmeg
½–1 teaspoon dried parsley	½–1 teaspoon dried parsley
butter	butter

1. Simmer the chicken carcass or the beef bones in the water with the onions and carrots for about 2 hours.
2. Strain the liquid into a saucepan, add the soup seasoning and simmer for about 10 minutes.
3. Meanwhile, make a savoury pancake by beating together the flour, salt, eggs, milk, nutmeg and dried parsley.
4. Heat some butter in a small frying pan and cook thin layers of the batter. Cut into strips and put on to the hot soup with a little chopped parsley.

Note: Soup seasoning is available from German delicatessens.

Cooking time: 2¼ hours
Preparation time: 20 minutes
Main cooking utensils: saucepan, mixing bowl, small frying pan
Serves: 4–5

Clear tomato soup

Imperial	Metric
chicken carcass	chicken carcass
about 4 oz. bacon pieces	about 100 g. bacon pieces
1 or 2 onions	1 or 2 onions
bouquet garni	bouquet garni
seasoning	seasoning
4 large tomatoes	4 large tomatoes
sprig fresh thyme or ½ teaspoon powdered thyme	sprig fresh thyme or ½ teaspoon powdered thyme
1 bay leaf	1 bay leaf
pinch sugar (optional)	pinch sugar (optional)

1. Put the chicken carcass into the pan, add the bacon pieces, onions, herbs and seasoning.
2. Cook with water to cover for approximately 1½ hours in an ordinary saucepan or for 30 minutes in a pressure cooker at 15-lb. (7-kg.) pressure. Allow the pressure to drop at room temperature.
3. Strain the liquid carefully; for a clear soup without fat it is a good idea to let the strained liquid stand for some hours until cold, then remove any fat from the top.
4. For a tomato soup completely free from pips it is advisable to sieve the tomatoes, or they can be skinned and deseeded.
5. Put the chopped tomatoes or the tomato purée into the pan with the clear stock, add the sprig of thyme, a bay leaf and a little extra seasoning if desired.
6. Many people like a slightly sweet taste to a tomato soup so a good pinch of sugar, preferably brown, can be added.
7. Cook until smooth then sieve if wished, to remove the thyme.
8. Serve with fresh rolls or bread.

Variation

For a thicker soup the tomatoes should be skinned and chopped and added to the stock with 2 diced potatoes, and 1 diced leek, then cooked until tender.

Cooking time: 2 hours or see stage 2
Preparation time: 15 minutes
Main cooking utensil: saucepan
Serves: 5–6

Frosted soups

The clear soups on pages 26, 30 and above are very suitable for frosting. As you will see from the picture of the Jellied fish consommé on page 30, the soup looks delicious when served in glasses, or it can be put into chilled soup cups. If you want to frost the fish soup on page 30, instead of serving it as a jellied soup, follow the directions below.

Frosted consommé: Make the consommé as the recipe on page 26. If you intend to serve this within 1–2 days, cool, pour into freezing trays, freeze in the refrigerator or home freezer. Take out 10–15 minutes before serving, so the mixture is not too hard. Break up with a fork, spoon into chilled soup cups. Top with finely diced pepper (discard core and seeds), diced skinned tomato, etc., or with yoghurt. If, on the other hand, you are making the soup for storage, follow the directions for the Jellied consommé on page 26, cool and freeze. The gelatine prevents the formation of ice splinters in the consommé. Bottled or canned tomato juice can be used instead of meat stock. If preferred, use the following recipe:

Frosted tomato soup: Follow the directions for the Clear tomato soup above, cool, then frost lightly. Top with diced cucumber or gherkins.

Frosted celery soup: This is a particularly interesting clear soup. Follow the directions for Clear celery soup on page 20 to the stage where the chicken jelly is added. Frost the soup *very lightly*, then fold in a little soured cream or yoghurt and very finely chopped celery heart. Spoon into chilled soup cups. This soup is better served when freshly prepared.

Gazpacho

This Spanish soup can be frosted *very lightly* or served very well chilled.

Skin 4–5 large ripe tomatoes, chop coarsely; chop about 8 small spring onions or 1 onion, 1–2 cloves garlic and ½ medium-sized skinned cucumber. Either sieve the vegetables, or emulsify in a liquidiser (blender) goblet or pound them until a fairly smooth pulp. Add enough iced water to give a thinner consistency, together with 1–2 tablespoons olive oil (you may even like more oil) and seasoning to taste. Chill or frost *very lightly*. Serve the soup in chilled soup cups and hand dishes of diced green and/or red pepper (discard core and seeds), diced cucumber, finely chopped onion and finely diced fresh bread. You can freeze the basic pulp of this soup, but not the diced vegetables. **Serves 4–6.**

Some unusual soups

Every country has their own traditional soups and while we may find the recipes unusual, they are often considered quite commonplace in other parts of the world. Scandinavia and France both have traditional fish soups and you will find these on pages 30 and 31. The Lobster chowder is one of the famous American soups and is a very good way of making expensive lobster serve the maximum number of people.

I am always surprised at the relatively few people who have tried a fruit soup. A typical recipe is given below, this can be varied according to the fruits available. One golden rule is that the soup should not be too sweet, for it should sharpen one's appetite for the rest of the meal. If the soup is well sweetened, as one would a fruit purée to be served for a dessert, it will spoil your palate for the rest of the meal.

If you want to make a soup into a light meal nothing could be better than a cheese soup, see recipe page 29. It is also possible to serve this as a well-chilled soup, providing it is emulsified or sieved just before serving, so it is very smooth with no trace of a skin. Children often enjoy this soup and it is an excellent way of giving them protein. Lemon-flavoured soups are often served in Greece, although the recipe on page 29 is not from that country, it is equally delicious.

Chicken and game soups

It is a pity to waste the carcase of poultry or game, for you have the basis for an excellent stock and/or soup. The simplest way of preparing poultry or game soup is to put the carcase into a pan, cover with water, add vegetables and herbs to taste, season. Simmer for several hours or cook for 1 hour in a pressure cooker at 15 lb. (7 kg.); allow pressure to drop at room temperature. Let the liquid cool. Remove any particles of meat and discard the bones. Sieve the tiny pieces of flesh, vegetables, etc. or emulsify in a warmed liquidiser (blender). Tip back into the liquid and reheat.

For a clear soup rather like the consommé on page 26, prepare the soup as above, strain carefully. Reheat the liquid, add a little sherry (or port wine with game). If you find the stock lacking in flavour add a chicken stock cube, then be sparing with seasoning as these are generally well seasoned.

For a creamed chicken soup follow directions in the first paragraph. Blend the smooth mixture with a thin white sauce. To about 1 pint (scant ½ litre) of chicken and vegetable purée, allow ½ oz. (15 g.) butter, margarine or chicken fat, ½ oz. (15 g.) flour and ½ pint (3 dl.) milk. This should give the right consistency, but naturally you can alter the proportions as desired.

Summer fruit soup

Imperial	Metric
1 lb. cooking apples or soft pears	½ kg. cooking apples or soft pears
2–3 fresh peaches or small can peaches (see note)	2–3 fresh peaches or small can peaches (see note)
1¼ pints water	¾ litre water
rind and juice of 2 lemons	rind and juice of 2 lemons
2 teaspoons cornflour	2 teaspoons cornflour
3–4 oz. sugar	75–100 g. sugar
1–2 teaspoons powdered cinnamon	1–2 teaspoons powdered cinnamon
Garnish:	*Garnish:*
lemon slice	lemon slice
watercress	watercress
To serve:	*To serve:*
¼ pint soured or thick cream	125 ml. soured or thick cream

1. Peel, core and slice the apples or pears, remove the skin from the peaches but retain the stones, as these give a good flavour to the soup.
2. Put the fruit into a saucepan with the water and lemon rinds; be careful to use the top 'zest' of the lemon rinds only, so that the soup is not bitter.
3. Cook until the fruit is quite soft, then sieve and put into the saucepan.
4. Blend the cornflour with the lemon juice, stir into the soup, cook until thickened.
5. Add the sugar and cinnamon gradually, tasting as you do so, to make sure the mixture is refreshing with a certain 'bite'.
6. Chill thoroughly.
7. Serve garnished with lemon and watercress. The cream may be put on top of soup or served separately.

Note: If using canned peaches, use the syrup instead of some of the water and use a little less sugar.

Cooking time: 25–30 minutes
Preparation time: 15 minutes
Main cooking utensil: saucepan
Serves: 4–5

Lemon soup

Imperial
2 pints water or half water
  and half apple juice or half
  water and half wine
3 oz. sago
3 lemons
2 egg yolks
½–1 oz. vanilla sugar
pinch powdered ginger
sugar to taste
Topping:
2 egg whites
½–1 oz. sugar
little powdered cinnamon
a few ratafia biscuits (tiny
  macaroons)

Metric
generous litre water or half water
  and half apple juice or half
  water and half wine
75 g. sago
3 lemons
2 egg yolks
15–25 g. vanilla sugar
pinch powdered ginger
sugar to taste
Topping:
2 egg whites
15–25 g. sugar
little powdered cinnamon
a few ratafia biscuits (tiny
  macaroons)

1. Bring the water, or apple juice and water or wine and water to the boil.
2. Put in the sago and stir for a few minutes to prevent it dropping to the bottom of the pan.
3. Lower the heat, add the rind of 1–2 lemons and simmer the sago until quite clear. The soup can be sieved, then re-heated if wished.
4. Blend the lemon juice with the egg yolks, add to the soup together with the vanilla sugar and powdered ginger.
5. Simmer gently until slightly thickened by the egg yolks, but do not allow to boil.
6. Taste the soup and add sugar as required, do not make this too sweet for it should be refreshing on a hot day. Chill thoroughly.
7. Pour into the serving dish or dishes.
8. Whisk the egg whites until very stiff, drop in spoonfuls on soup, top with sugar and 'bands' of powdered cinnamon. Serve at once, with ratafias.

Cooking time: 1 hour
Preparation time: 15 minutes
Main cooking utensil: saucepan
Serves: 4–5

Cheese soup

Imperial
2 small onions
2 oz. butter
2 oz. flour
1 pint milk
1 pint white stock or water
1 level teaspoon salt
pinch pepper
6 oz. Cheddar cheese
Garnish:
grated cheese
croûtons

Metric
2 small onions
50 g. butter
50 g. flour
500 ml. milk
500 ml. white stock or water
1 level teaspoon salt
pinch pepper
150 g. Cheddar cheese.
Garnish:
grated cheese
croûtons

1. Slice the onions very thinly and cook in the butter for a few minutes, add the flour and cook for another minute.
2. Stir in the milk and stock or water, bring to the boil.
3. Season and simmer gently for about 5 minutes.
4. Grate or dice the cheese, toss in the soup and simmer until melted. Do not allow to boil.
5. Serve at once, sprinkled with grated cheese, and croûtons. To make croûtons, cut slices of bread into small cubes and fry until golden brown.

Variation

Cream of corn soup: Prepare the soup as above to stage 3, then add a large packet of frozen corn and cook for a further 10–15 minutes. Sieve if wished. Serve topped with grated cheese if desired or with cheese added to the soup as in the recipe above.

Cooking time: 15 minutes
Preparation time: 10 minutes
Main cooking utensil: large saucepan
Serves: 4–6

Copenhagen consommé

Imperial	Metric
1 lb. firm white fish (hake, halibut or cod)	½ kg. firm white fish (hake, halibut or cod)
1 lb. fish bones	½ kg. fish bones
bouquet garni of parsley, celery and fennel	bouquet garni of parsley, celery and fennel
2 teaspoons salt	2 teaspoons salt
pepper	pepper
2 tablespoons lemon juice	2 tablespoons lemon juice
¼ pint white wine	125 ml. white wine
1½ pints water	generous ¾ litre water
1 egg white (see note)	1 egg white (see note)
¾ oz. gelatine	20 g. gelatine
1 leek	1 leek
2 sticks celery and 3 carrots cut into fine julienne shreds	2 sticks celery and 3 carrots cut into fine julienne shreds
lemon slices	lemon slices

1. Place the fish, fish bones, bouquet garni of herbs tied in muslin, salt, pinch pepper, lemon juice, wine and water in a large saucepan.
2. Bring to the boil and simmer covered for 15 minutes.
3. Strain through a fine sieve.
4. Whisk in the egg white and strain again.
5. Add the gelatine dissolved in a little water.
6. Taste and season again if necessary.
7. Leave to set lightly.
8. Cook julienne shreds for 3–4 minutes in fast boiling salted water. Drain and cool and add to the fish jelly. Leave to set.
9. When set, chop and pile in soup dishes, serve with lemon slices.

Note: An egg white is used to clear soups – any tiny particles that might spoil the clarity cling to this.

Cooking time: 20 minutes
Preparation time: 15 minutes
Main cooking utensils: large saucepan, sieve
Serves: 6–8

Finnish fish soup

Imperial	Metric
dried herbs	dried herbs
2½ pints water	scant 1½ litres water
2–3 oz. rice	50–75 g. rice
4 oz. green peas	100 g. green peas
seasoning	seasoning
8 oz. skinned, filleted fish	200 g. skinned, filleted fish
2 tablespoons concentrated tomato purée	2 tablespoons concentrated tomato purée
1 oz. cornflour	25 g. cornflour
¼ pint water	125 ml. water
good pinch salt	good pinch salt
paprika	paprika
garlic salt	garlic salt

1. Put dried herbs to taste into the water and add the rice, peas and seasoning.
2. Simmer for 15 minutes, then add the fish, cut into neat pieces, the tomato purée blended with the cornflour and the ¼ pint (125 ml.) water, salt, paprika and garlic salt.
3. Simmer for a further 10–15 minutes and garnish with parsley if wished.

Variation
Greek fish soup: Heat 2 tablespoons olive oil and toss 2 medium-sized chopped onions, 2 medium-sized chopped carrots and a crushed clove of garlic in it. Add 2½ pints (scant 1½ litres) water, rind of ½–1 lemon and seasoning and simmer for 30 minutes. Add 12 oz. (300 g.) skinned, dried fish, the juice of a lemon and a little chopped celery. Cook for a further 10 minutes. Lift out pieces of fish and strain the stock; put this back in the saucepan after blending it with 2 egg yolks and a little extra lemon juice if required. Thicken gently over a low heat without boiling, stirring constantly. Replace the fish and heat for a few minutes.

Cooking time: 30 minutes
Preparation time: 10 minutes
Main cooking utensil: saucepan
Serves: 4–6

Bouillabaisse

Imperial	Metric
fish bones	fish bones
2½ pints water	scant 1½ litres water
seasoning	seasoning
1 strip orange peel	1 strip orange peel
bouquet garni	bouquet garni
3–4 tablespoons olive oil	3–4 tablespoons olive oil
5 medium-sized onions	5 medium-sized onions
4 cloves garlic	4 cloves garlic
1 tablespoon pimento	1 tablespoon pimento
6 peeled tomatoes	6 peeled tomatoes
¼ teaspoon nutmeg	¼ teaspoon nutmeg
2 lb. mixed filleted fish	1 kg. mixed filleted fish
2 pinches saffron	2 pinches saffron
1 tablespoon tomato purée	1 tablespoon tomato purée
¼ pint white wine	125 ml. white wine
few peeled prawns	few peeled prawns
chopped parsley	chopped parsley
To serve:	*To serve:*
croûtons or French bread	croûtons or French bread

1. Clean the fish bones and put into a pan with the water, seasoning, chopped orange peel and bouquet garni.
2. Boil rapidly until reduced to just less than 2 pints (1¼ litres).
3. Put the oil in another pan, add the finely sliced onions and chopped garlic.
4. Allow to brown. Add the chopped pimento, tomatoes and nutmeg, cook for a few minutes.
5. Increase the heat, add strained fish stock, chopped fish, saffron, tomato purée and wine.
6. Season to taste and simmer until the fish is well cooked but do not allow this to break.
7. Add the prawns and parsley immediately before serving. This could be served as a main dish.

Cooking time: 40 minutes
Preparation time: 30 minutes
Main cooking utensils: 2 saucepans
Serves: 8

Lobster chowder

Imperial	Metric
1 medium-sized cooked lobster	1 medium-sized cooked lobster
1 pint water	550 ml. water
1–2 rashers bacon	1–2 rashers bacon
tiny onion	tiny onion
1½ oz. flour	40 g. flour
1 medium-sized potato	1 medium-sized potato
generous ¼ pint top of milk or single cream	150 ml. top of milk or single cream
seasoning	seasoning
pinch sugar	pinch sugar
chopped parsley	chopped parsley

1. Remove all the flesh from the lobster.
2. Simmer the shell in the water for 15 minutes, then strain and add to the resulting liquid enough water to make up to 1 pint (550 ml.) again.
3. Fry the chopped bacon and chopped onion for a few minutes then sprinkle over the flour. Stir in the lobster stock and bring to the boil, stirring until thickened.
4. Add the diced potato, lobster meat, seasoning and sugar and heat gently for 10 minutes.
5. Serve hot, sprinkled with chopped parsley, with croûtons or French bread.

Variation
Hamburger chowder: Heat a can of oxtail soup and add 4 oz. (100 g.) cooked minced beef, some cooked diced vegetables, and a little cooked rice. Heat for a few minutes and serve sprinkled with parsley.

Cooking time: 30 minutes
Preparation time: 15 minutes
Main cooking utensils: large saucepan, frying pan
Serves: 4–6

Fish dishes

Fish is one of the important protein foods that can be cooked in a great variety of ways. It is a highly perishable food, so buy wisely to make certain it is fresh (see below) and store in the refrigerator or a cool place as soon as you bring it home. Most fish freezes well, the column on the right gives advice on home freezing of fish.

To tell if fish is fresh
Check that the shop or store from where the fish is purchased is careful about cleanliness and keeps fish on ice or a cold slab.

Fresh fish has a pleasant smell, if it gives off a strong odour of ammonia it is stale.

Fresh fish looks firm, if it is limp it could be stale; the eyes should look bright and clear and the scales bright and shiny.

Shellfish can be judged in the same way as other fish, i.e. the colour should be bright and the fish firm. Another way to tell when lobster is fresh is to pull the tail out firmly, if it springs back then the lobster is fresh. Mussels, and similar shellfish, should be bought alive. It is essential to check this. Tap the shells sharply, if they do not close then discard those, for the fish inside the shell could have been dead for some time. Shellfish is particularly perishable.

Types of fish
Fish is generally described under four groups: The first is white fish, which covers many well-known types, ideal for most forms of cooking, see page 38. On page 48 are listed most shellfish. Oily fish (page 44) which provide natural oils in the diet, range from inexpensive herring to luxurious fresh salmon. Freshwater fish, caught in rivers and lakes, are given on page 47 and smoked fish on page 34. Many fish are frozen and canned, see page 35.

To freeze fish
Never try to freeze fish that is not 100 per cent fresh. Prepare ready for cooking, wrap firmly in foil or freezer polythene. Divide large quantities of fish into convenient-sized portions. You can coat suitable fish with seasoned flour and beaten egg and crumbs, ready for frying. Freeze the coated fish on flat trays, then wrap; this stops the coating sticking to the wrapping. Fish is spoiled by over-cooking; if you want to freeze dishes either prepare then freeze and cook later, or, if cooked and frozen, do not overcook when reheating. Use *raw* frozen fish within 4 months (shellfish and smoked fish 2 months), *cooked* fish within 2 months (shellfish 1 month). Wrap fish for freezing very thoroughly.

Ways to prepare fish

Fish can be cooked whole or cut into slices, generally called 'steaks' or 'cutlets', or many fish can be filleted. The fishmonger will generally bone whole fish (such as herrings), or fillet white fish, i.e. plaice and sole for you, but it may be that you have to do this yourself. The instructions are given below. None of these processes is really difficult.

To fillet fish: Choose a sharp and pliable knife. Flat fish (such as sole and plaice) can be cut into 4 fillets; other fish into 2 fillets. To fillet flat fish remove the head first, then make a sharp cut down the centre of the fish. Insert the knife under the flesh, ease the flesh slowly and carefully away from the backbone. This gives the first fillet. Repeat the process with the other 3 fillets. A little salt on both the knife and your fingertips helps to do this easily.

To skin fish: Hold the tail of the fish, or the tail end of a fillet of fish firmly. Make a small cut across the fillet at the tail end. Insert the tip of the knife under the cut and ease the flesh away slowly and carefully from the skin.

To bone whole fish: Many fish are difficult to eat because of the large number of bones. Herrings are a typical fish, where it is better to bone them before cooking.

Slit the whole fish under the stomach, remove the roes (these can be used in cooking), then discard the rest of the intestines. Insert the knife into the flesh and cut this until you can 'open out' the fish. Turn the fish, with the skin side uppermost on to a board. Run your finger very firmly down the centre of the fish, this loosens the backbone. Now turn the fish over again and you will find you can not only lift away the backbone, but most of the tiny bones as well.

The boned fish may now be cut into 2 fillets if wished.

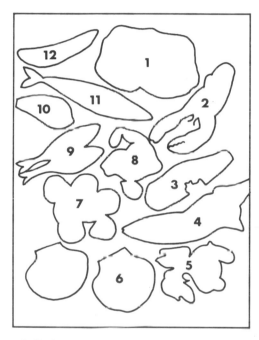

1 Crab
2 Lobster
3 Whiting
4 Trout
5 Shrimps
6 Scallops
7 Oysters
8 Mussels
9 Red mullet
10 Salmon
11 Mackerel
12 Halibut

Methods of cooking fish

There are various ways in which fish is cooked and the recipes in this chapter are all based upon the basic methods below:

To bake fish: This means cooking the fish in the oven; it could be baked in just a little seasoned butter, or it could have a variety of other ingredients added, as the recipes on pages 39 and 40. If you want the fish to keep moist cover the dish, but if you want the fish to brown slightly on top leave the dish uncovered. Bake whole fish for approximately 12 minutes per lb. ($\frac{1}{2}$ kg.), fillets for 12–20 minutes, depending upon the thickness and most fish cutlets take about 20 minutes. The oven should be set to a moderate to moderately hot temperature, unless stated to the contrary.

To fry fish: There are two basic ways of frying fish, the first in shallow fat or oil, the second in deep fat or oil.

When frying fish you can coat the fish with seasoned flour, or to give a better coating, with the flour then with beaten egg and fine crisp breadcrumbs. This coating is suitable for both shallow or deep frying.

You can, however, coat the fish with a batter, directions for making this are given under the Fried scampi recipe on page 51.

If frying in shallow fat allow enough fat or oil to give a good coating in a large frying pan. Put in the fish and fry rapidly on one side, then turn and fry on the second side. Thin fillets of fish take only about 4 minutes, but thicker fish will take up to 10 minutes. Lower the heat after browning the fish on either side.

If frying in deep fat or oil make sure this is really hot, you will find advice on testing the temperature in the recipe on page 51 (stage 5). The cooking time when deep frying is a little shorter than when frying in shallow fat or oil.

To grill fish: Make sure the grill is really hot before putting the fish under this. Either cover the grill pan with buttered or oiled foil, or brush the grid of the grill pan with butter. or oil. Cook for the same time as shallow frying, and baste the fish with butter or oil to prevent it drying.

To poach fish: Often one is told to 'boil' fish, this is a mistake, for fish should not be boiled quickly; it spoils the texture and breaks the fish. Put the fish into seasoned cold water, or white wine or fish stock (made by simmering bones and skin). Bring to simmering point, then allow 7–10 minutes per lb. ($\frac{1}{2}$ kg.); in some recipes the fish is put into the heated liquid and simmered.

Smoked fish and ways to serve

Name	Buy	Ways of cooking
Smoked cod	Filleted.	As haddock.
Smoked eel	Portions with bone or fillets.	Serve raw as smoked salmon.
Smoked haddock Known as 'Finnan' haddock.	Whole or filleted.	Poach in water or milk. Can top with poached egg.
Smoked herrings The most versatile of smoked fish.	Whole or filleted.	See kippers, bloaters, buckling.
Kippers Split, salted smoked herrings.	Whole or filleted.	Grill, fry, poach in water, bake in oven.
Bloaters Smoked whole herrings.	Whole.	As kippers.
Buckling A form of smoked herring.	Whole.	Serve as smoked trout.
Smoked salmon	Cut in wafer-thin slices.	Never cooked. Serve raw.
Smoked sprats	Whole.	Grill, fry or serve as smoked trout.
Smoked trout	Whole.	Serve raw as smoked salmon.
Smoked whiting	Filleted, often called 'golden fillets'.	As smoked haddock.

Allow 1–2 kippers or bloaters per person, 8–12 oz. (200–300 g.) smoked haddock, etc. (greater weight on bone), 2–3 oz. (50–75 g.) smoked salmon or filleted eel, 1 smoked trout or buckling, 6 oz. (150 g.) smoked sprats.

Jugged kippers

Kippers may be grilled or fried; they need little fat, since they have such an amount of natural oil. One of the best ways to cook the kippers, for it keeps them moist and does not over-crisp them, is to put the fish into a strong tall jug (hence the name) or into a large shallow dish. Pour boiling water over the fish and cook as recipe on page 35, or lift out of the liquid and top with butter.

Kippers in salads

Raw kippers can be used in salads, etc. Buy filleted kippers, skin and divide into strips, cover with French dressing (page 14). Soak overnight or for several hours. Drain, serve with lemon as an hors d'œuvre or put on a bed of lettuce and garnish with olives, tomatoes, etc. If preferred use lightly cooked kippers instead; the method of cooking, above, would be ideal, lift from the liquid, then skin, etc.

Grilled cod cutlets garnished with grilled tomatoes, lemon wedges and parsley sprigs.

Canned and frozen fish

Many fish are either canned or commercially frozen, it is useful to have these in either your store cupboard or freezing compartment of the refrigerator or the freezer.

The official recommendations about storing canned fish is to keep fish in tomato sauce for only up to 1 year and fish in oil for up to 5 years. The most useful canned fish is sardines, for savoury toast or sandwiches or used in quick recipes as page 130 or instead of kippers on page 36. Canned salmon is invaluable for many dishes, see page 45. Choose the cheaper pink salmon for cooking. Also keep some shellfish and/or tuna, together with herrings or pilchards. Canned cod's roe could be used in place of the fresh roe on page 53.

There is a wide variety of frozen fish available, much of this can be cooked from the frozen state. Read, and follow, the manufacturers' instructions on the packet. Shellfish, however, is generally better thawed out at room temperature. If you are in a hurry, stand the container in cold, not hot, water to hasten defrosting.

REMEMBER when canned fish is removed from the can or the can is opened and when frozen fish is defrosted, these are as perishable as fresh fish.

Easy guide to fish dishes

The following gives you help in selecting the right fish dishes for the right occasion.

When you are short of time see pages 35, 42, 44, 46, 47, 52, 208, 215, 216.

When you are short of money see pages 12, 13, 14, 35, 36, 37, 39, 40, 147, 150, 203.

When you want a special dish see pages 15, 39, 40, 41, 42, 43, 44, 45, 49, 50, 51, 52, 53, 191, 193.

For a snack or light meal see pages 17, 31, 36, 37, 52.

When you are slimming see pages 36, 50, 115, 119, 191.

Kipper and lemon

Imperial	Metric
2 kippers	2 kippers
boiling water	boiling water
Garnish:	*Garnish:*
slices of orange or lemon	slices of orange or lemon
parsley	parsley

1. Put the fish in a dish, then pour over the boiling water.
2. Leave for a few minutes until tender, lift out of the water.
3. Put under the grill if wished to crisp slightly, brushing first with a little melted butter.
4. Garnish with slices of orange and parsley or use lemon instead, and serve.

Note: Kippers make a good breakfast or supper dish.

Variation

Grill the kippers with a knob of butter.

Cooking time: few minutes
Preparation time: few minutes
Main utensil: dish or jug
Serves: 2

Haddock omelette

Imperial	Metric
4 oz. smoked haddock	100 g. smoked haddock
Filling:	*Filling:*
few cooked peas	few cooked peas
little butter	little butter
Omelette:	*Omelette:*
3–4 eggs	3–4 eggs
seasoning	seasoning
1 tablespoon water	1 tablespoon water
1 oz. butter	25 g. butter
Garnish:	*Garnish:*
sprig of parsley	sprig of parsley

1. Poach the haddock in a little water or milk until tender.
2. Strain, flake and heat with the peas and the butter while making the omelette.
3. Beat the eggs lightly. For this type of plain omelette the eggs should not be over-beaten. Season, add the water.
4. Heat the butter in the omelette pan.
5. Pour in the eggs and leave for a few seconds until the bottom of the egg sets lightly. Tip the pan and loosen the edges of the omelette so the liquid egg flows under all the time. Continue like this, 'working' the omelette, until set.
6. Put in the filling. Fold the omelette away from the handle, tip on to a hot plate or dish, and add the garnish.

Variations

Many fillings may be used instead, for instance, other fish, grated cheese, cooked vegetables.

Cooking time: few minutes plus time for cooking haddock
Preparation time: few minutes
Main cooking utensils: saucepan, omelette pan
Serves: 2

Kipper pizza

Imperial	Metric
Dough:	*Dough:*
½ oz. yeast	15 g. yeast
½ pint water	250 ml. water
1 lb. plain flour	400 g. plain flour
seasoning	seasoning
2 teaspoons sugar	2 teaspoons sugar
2 tablespoons oil	2 tablespoons oil
Topping:	*Topping:*
1 16-oz. can tomatoes	1 453-g. can tomatoes
1 7-oz. can kipper fillets	1 198-g. can kipper fillets
½–1 teaspoon chopped parsley	½–1 teaspoon chopped parsley
½ teaspoon mixed chopped fresh herbs or pinch dried herbs	½ teaspoon mixed chopped fresh herbs or pinch dried herbs
2 oz. Gruyère cheese	50 g. Gruyère cheese
1–2 oz. Parmesan cheese	25–50 g. Parmesan cheese
few black and stuffed olives	few black and stuffed olives

1. Dissolve the yeast in tepid water.
2. Sieve the flour and seasoning, add the sugar and oil then the yeast liquid; knead well to form a smooth dough.
3. Cover the dough with a cloth or polythene bag and allow to prove (rise) in a warm place for about 1½–2 hours until double in bulk.
4. Open the can of tomatoes and the kipper fillets and drain.
5. Knead the risen dough and shape, or roll, if preferred, into a round or oblong on a greased, warmed tin.
6. Chop the tomatoes and mix with most of the kipper fillets, parsley and herbs, put on the dough.
7. Cook for about 30 minutes; meanwhile grate the cheese.
8. Top the pizza with the cheese, the rest of the kipper fillets and the olives.
9. Return to the oven for a further 10 minutes. Serve hot or cold as an appetiser or light meal.

Cooking time: 40 minutes
Preparation time: 40 minutes plus time for dough to prove
Main cooking utensil: baking tin or sheet
Oven temperature: hot (425–450°F., 220–230°C., Gas Mark 7–8)
Serves: 6 as a main course or 12 as an appetiser

Smoked cod with duchesse potatoes

Imperial	Metric
large packet frozen peas	large packet frozen peas
2 fillets (1 lb.) smoked cod	2 fillets ($\frac{1}{2}$ kg.) smoked cod
$\frac{1}{4}$ pint milk	125 ml. milk
1 oz. butter	25 g. butter
Duchesse potatoes:	*Duchesse potatoes:*
12 oz. potato	300 g. potato
1 oz. butter	25 g. butter
1 egg	1 egg
2 tablespoons cream (optional)	2 tablespoons cream (optional)
seasoning	seasoning
little grated nutmeg (optional)	little grated nutmeg (optional)
Sauce:	*Sauce:*
1 oz. butter or margarine	25 g. butter or margarine
1 oz. flour	25 g. flour
$\frac{1}{2}$ pint milk	125 ml. milk
good pinch dried fennel	good pinch dried fennel

1. First make the Duchesse potatoes. Cook the potatoes in boiling salted water; strain and sieve.
2. Mix to a smooth purée with the butter, egg, cream, season well and add the nutmeg.
3. Pipe the mixture into rosettes round the edge of an oven-proof serving dish, brown under the grill or in the oven.
4. Cook the peas as directed and place in bottom of dish.
5. Meanwhile poach the fish gently in the milk and butter for 10 minutes, flake into large pieces, pile into the centre of the potato-lined dish and keep hot.
6. To make the sauce, heat the butter in a saucepan, stir in the flour.
7. Cook for 2–3 minutes, remove from the heat, gradually stir in the milk.
8. Return to the heat, cook until thickened and smooth, stirring all the time, add the seasoning and the fennel.
9. Pour over the fish. Serve hot with mixed vegetables

Cooking time: 30 minutes
Preparation time: 20 minutes
Main cooking utensils: 3 saucepans
Serves: 4

Smoked haddock kedgeree

Imperial	Metric
1 medium-sized smoked haddock	1 medium-sized smoked haddock
water	water
3 oz. long-grain rice	75 g. long-grain rice
seasoning	seasoning
bay leaf	bay leaf
slice lemon	slice lemon
2 oz. butter	50 g. butter
1 small onion	1 small onion
Garnish:	*Garnish:*
1–2 hard-boiled eggs	1–2 hard-boiled eggs
parsley	parsley
paprika pepper	paprika pepper

1. Cut the haddock into neat pieces and put into a pan with cold water, bring just to the boil, then remove the pan from the heat — this method of poaching the fish prevents over-cooking.
2. Put the rice into the second pan with $\frac{1}{4}$ pint (125 ml.) water only; add seasoning, the bay leaf and lemon.
3. Bring the water to the boil, stir briskly, cover the pan tightly, then lower the heat and cook slowly for approximately 15 minutes — by this time the water will have been absorbed and the rice will be tender.
4. Heat the butter and fry the finely chopped onion until tender, then add the fish and the rice and heat together.
5. Pile on to a hot dish and top with halved eggs, sprigs of parsley and paprika pepper. Serve with crisp toast.

Variations
Omit the onion, and add a little cream. Omit the onion and fry a little chopped bacon with the butter.

Cooking time: 30 minutes
Preparation time: 15 minutes
Main cooking utensils: 2 saucepans
Serves: 4–6

White fish and ways to cook

Name – Season	Buy	Ways to cook
Bass May–Sept.	Whole, steaks or fillets.	Poach, steam, fry, grill or bake.
Bream July–Dec.	Sea or fresh water. Small fish whole – larger filleted.	Grill, fry or bake.
Brill May–August.	Usually filleted.	As plaice.
Cod Throughout year best Oct.–March.	Codling – whole large fish – fillets or steaks.	All methods.
Flounder Nov.–March.	Whole or filleted.	As plaice.
Haddock Throughout year best Oct.–Feb.	As cod.	As cod.
Hake June–Jan.	As cod.	As cod.
Halibut July–April.	Whole, steaks or cutlets.	Poach, grill or fry.
Huss or Dogfish Sept.–May.	Filleted.	Bake or fry.

Name – Season	Buy	Ways to cook
John Dory or Dory Sept.–Jan.	Filleted.	As plaice.
Plaice Throughout year best May–Dec.	Whole or filleted.	Steam, poach, grill, fry or bake.
Rock salmon (coal-fish, coley or saithe) Throughout year best Sept.–May.	Filleted.	As cod.
Skate Nov.–May.	Triangular portions.	Poach, bake or fry.
Sole Throughout year.	As plaice, but more expensive.	As plaice.
Turbot April–Sept.	As halibut.	As halibut.
Whiting Oct.–April.	Whole or fillets.	As plaice.

Allow 1 whole fish, 2 medium fillets or 6–8 oz. (150–200 g.) per person.

Cutlets espagnole

Imperial	Metric
3 large cod cutlets	3 large cod cutlets
juice of 1 lemon	juice of 1 lemon
seasoning	seasoning
½ oz. melted butter	15 g. melted butter
6 oz. grated cheese	150 g. grated cheese
1 tablespoon mixed herbs	1 tablespoon mixed herbs
1 small finely chopped onion	1 small finely chopped onion
1 oz. butter	25 g. butter
1 large tomato	1 large tomato
Garnish:	*Garnish:*
parsley	parsley
lemon slices	lemon slices

1. Wash the cutlets and dry thoroughly.
2. Squeeze lemon juice on each cutlet and season well; brush with melted butter.
3. Grill on underside for 3–5 minutes.
4. Mix grated cheese, herbs and chopped onion together. Add a little lemon juice.
5. Divide mixture into three portions and form each portion into a firm ball.
6. Place a portion of cheese mixture on each of the cutlets, add a knob of butter on each cutlet.
7. Place under a hot grill and cook for about 4–5 minutes, or until cutlets are cooked through, adding sliced tomato topped with butter towards the end of cooking time. Dish up immediately after cooking as cheese mixture may toughen. Garnish with parsley and tomato, and slices of lemon.

Note: The cheese must be formed into a ball otherwise it will have melted long before the fish is cooked.

Cooking time: 10 minutes
Preparation time: 10–15 minutes
Main cooking utensil: grill pan
Serves: 3

38

Baked cod Danish style

Imperial	Metric
1 thick cutlet of cod weighing approximately 2 lb.	1 thick cutlet of cod weighing approximately 1 kg.
salt	salt
pepper	pepper
2 oz. streaky bacon	50 g. streaky bacon
4 oz. button mushrooms	100 g. button mushrooms
2 oz. butter	50 g. butter
Garnish:	*Garnish:*
lemon	lemon
parsley	parsley
tomatoes	tomatoes
cooked peas	cooked peas

1. Rub the fish with salt and pepper.
2. Cut the rashers of bacon in small pieces, peel the button mushrooms. Place at the bottom of a casserole.
3. Place the fish on top, dab with butter. Do not cover.
4. Bake as directed for 40–50 minutes according to the thickness of the fish.
Baste frequently with the butter. Serve with butterflies of lemon on top of the fish with a little parsley. Top the tomatoes with a few cooked peas; serve with extra peas.

Variation
Used sliced tomatoes instead of mushrooms; use a mixture of wafer thin slices of onion and tomatoes in place of mushrooms; brush the fish with melted butter and sprinkle very lightly with curry powder before baking.

Cooking time: 40–50 minutes
Preparation time: 5 minutes
Main cooking utensil: large shallow casserole
Oven temperature: moderately hot (375°F., 190°C., Gas Mark 5)
Oven position: centre
Serves: 4–6

Sicilian baked fish

Imperial	Metric
3 portions brill, skinned	3 portions brill, skinned
2 tablespoons olive oil	2 tablespoons olive oil
1 medium onion	1 medium onion
8-oz. can peeled tomatoes	226-g. can peeled tomatoes
salt, freshly ground black pepper	salt, freshly ground black pepper
1 level tablespoon capers	1 level tablespoon capers
1 level tablespoon chopped parsley	1 level tablespoon chopped parsley
2 tablespoons chopped celery	2 tablespoons chopped celery

1. Arrange portions of brill in a buttered shallow dish.
2. Heat the oil and fry the chopped onion gently until soft and golden.
3. Add the tomatoes and seasoning.
4. Bring to the boil and cook over a moderate heat for about 5 minutes, or until the liquid is reduced to a thin purée.
5. Stir in the capers, parsley and celery and spoon the sauce evenly over the fish.
6. Cover and cook for about 25 minutes. Serve hot, with lemon.

Note: Brill is an excellent fish for casseroling or baking, since it keeps its firm texture. To skin fish dip knife in salt to make it easier to cut away the skin; do this slowly and gently so that the fish is not broken.

Variation
Chicken turbot (young turbot) can be used instead of brill; a little chopped garlic can be added to the onion.

Cooking time: 25 minutes
Preparation time: 15 minutes
Main cooking utensils: saucepan, shallow ovenproof dish
Oven temperature: moderately hot (375–400°F., 190–200°C., Gas Mark 5–6)
Oven position: above centre
Serves: 3

Welsh cod bake

Imperial
2–3 leeks
1½ oz. butter
1–1½ lb. cod (on the bone)
seasoning
juice of 1 lemon
2 oz. walnuts, chopped
1 tablespoon chopped parsley
Garnish:
sliced lemon

Metric
2–3 leeks
40 g. butter
½–¾ kg. cod (on the bone)
seasoning
juice of 1 lemon
50 g. walnuts, chopped
1 tablespoon chopped parsley
Garnish:
sliced lemon

1. Cut the white and pale green parts of the well washed leeks into thin slices and cook very gently in the butter in a covered casserole for 15 minutes.
2. Lay the cod on top, season well, sprinkle with the lemon juice, walnuts and chopped parsley.
3. Cover with buttered paper or foil and continue cooking until the fish is just tender and the walnuts brown.
4. Garnish with sliced lemon and serve hot, with brown bread and butter, green salad and cooked peas, or cold with salad.

Variation
Use hake or fresh haddock. Add 2–3 sliced tomatoes to the leeks.

Cooking time: 35–45 minutes
Preparation time: 10 minutes
Main cooking utensils: greaseproof paper or foil, covered casserole
Oven temperature: moderately hot (375°F., 190°C., Gas Mark 5)
Oven position: centre
Serves: 4

Sole in cream sauce

Imperial
seasoning
4 large or 8 smaller fillets sole
1½ oz. butter
2 shallots or small onions
good sprig parsley
1 small bay leaf
12 tablespoons white wine
Sauce:
1½ oz. butter
1½ oz. flour
½ pint thin cream
2 egg yolks
3 tablespoons thick cream
1 tablespoon lemon juice
Garnish:
about 4 oz. cooked prunes

Metric
seasoning
4 large or 8 smaller fillets sole
40 g. butter
2 shallots or small onions
good sprig parsley
1 small bay leaf
12 tablespoons white wine
Sauce:
40 g. butter
40 g. flour
250 ml. thin cream
2 egg yolks
3 tablespoons thick cream
1 tablespoon lemon juice
Garnish:
about 100 g. cooked prunes

1. Season the fillets of fish lightly and put into a buttered dish.
2. The fillets may either be folded or rolled, if the latter they take a little extra time to cook.
3. Add the chopped shallots or onions together with the herbs, do not chop the parsley.
4. Pour over the wine, cover the dish with well-buttered paper and cook until the fish is tender.
5. Melt the butter in the pan, stir in the flour, then add the cream to the roux. Stir in the strained liquid from the fish, bring the sauce to the boil, cook until thickened.
6. Whisk the egg yolks with the thick cream, add to the sauce with the lemon juice, and cook until thickened without boiling; season well.
7. Add the cooked prunes to the sauce, pour over the fish.

Cooking time: 25–30 minutes
Preparation time: 15 minutes (classic version would take longer due to the garnishes)
Main cooking utensils: ovenproof dish, saucepan
Oven temperature: moderate (375°F., 190°C., Gas Mark 5)
Oven position: just above centre
Serves: 4

Grilled cod steaks with almonds and mushrooms

Imperial	Metric
3–4 oz. butter	75–100 g. butter
4 cod steaks (preferably from tail)	4 cod steaks (preferably from tail)
seasoning	seasoning
1 oz. grated Parmesan cheese	25 g. grated Parmesan cheese
4 oz. blanched almonds	100 g. blanched almonds
4 oz. small button mushrooms	100 g. small button mushrooms
Garnish:	*Garnish:*
2–3 small tomatoes	2–3 small tomatoes
sprigs parsley	sprigs parsley

1. Melt the butter in a frying pan.
2. Brush the cod steaks on one side with a little butter and season lightly.
3. Put on the grid of the grill pan and cook until golden brown, then turn.
4. Season the second side, brush with butter and sprinkle with the cheese.
5. Continue cooking until golden brown and tender.
6. Meanwhile fry the almonds and mushrooms in the remaining butter.
7. Place the fish in the hot serving dish, then add the nuts and mushrooms.
8. Garnish with wedges of tomato and sprigs of parsley. Serve with a green vegetable and new or creamed potatoes.

Variation
Use turbot or other white fish, or whole trout. Instead of grilling the fish fry it in the pan before adding the nuts and mushrooms.

Cooking time: 15 minutes
Preparation time: 15 minutes
Main cooking utensils: frying pan, grill pan
Serves: 4

Creamed fish with onions

Imperial	Metric
1¼ lb. cod fillet	good ½ kg. cod fillet
seasoning	seasoning
2 oz. butter	50 g. butter
6–8 anchovy fillets	6–8 anchovy fillets
3 small onions	3 small onions
3 tomatoes	3 tomatoes
1½ tablespoons chopped parsley	1½ tablespoons chopped parsley
4–8 tablespoons thin cream	4–8 tablespoons thin cream

1. Cut the fish into three or four portions, season well.
2. Melt half the butter and fry the chopped anchovies and chopped onions until a pale golden brown.
3. Skin and divide the tomatoes into portions and cook for 3 minutes.
4. Add the parsley and put the mixture into a wide ovenproof dish.
5. Top with the fish portions, the rest of the butter and seasoning and put under a hot grill and cook for about 5 minutes.
6. Add the cream and continue cooking with the heat lowered for a further 5 minutes. Serve in the cooking dish with either a green salad or green beans.

Variation
Use folded fillets of plaice or sole instead of cod, or portions of fresh haddock.

Cooking time: 25 minutes
Preparation time: 15 minutes
Main cooking utensils: frying pan, ovenproof dish
Serves: 3–4

Goujons à la valencienne

Imperial	Metric
1 medium-sized onion	1 medium-sized onion
1 clove garlic	1 clove garlic
2 medium-sized tomatoes	2 medium-sized tomatoes
½ oz. butter	15 g. butter
1 tablespoon olive oil	1 tablespoon olive oil
pinch chilli powder	pinch chilli powder
pinch saffron powder	pinch saffron powder
4 tablespoons water or white wine	4 tablespoons water or white wine
1 teaspoon lemon juice	1 teaspoon lemon juice
1 tablespoon chopped parsley	1 tablespoon chopped parsley
2–3 large fillets plaice or other flat white fish (skinned)	2–3 large fillets plaice or other flat white fish (skinned)
seasoning	seasoning

1. Chop the onion very finely.
2. Crush the clove of garlic.
3. Skin, halve and de-seed the tomatoes then chop finely.
4. Heat the butter and oil in the pan.
5. Fry the vegetables very slowly until tender then add the chilli and saffron powder, water or wine and the lemon juice.
6. Stir until a smooth sauce is formed, add half the parsley.
7. Cut the fillets of fish into narrow ribbons and season well.
8. Poach in the sauce for a few minutes only.
9. Add the rest of the parsley. Serve in a border of creamed potatoes or boiled rice.

Note: This recipe may also be served as an hors d'oeuvre and in this case would serve 4 people.

Variation
Omit the chilli and saffron powders.

Cooking time: 25 minutes
Preparation time: 20 minutes
Main cooking utensil: frying pan
Serves: 2–4

Fried fish in chive butter

Imperial	Metric
1½ lb. white fish, either whole fillets of sole, plaice or whiting or portions of cod, fresh haddock, turbot or halibut	¾ kg. white fish, either whole fillets of sole, plaice or whiting or portions of cod, fresh haddock, turbot or halibut
1 level tablespoon flour	1 level tablespoon flour
seasoning	seasoning
2–3 oz. butter	50–75 g. butter
2 tablespoons chopped chives	2 tablespoons chopped chives
Garnish:	*Garnish:*
parsley	parsley
lemon	lemon

1. Wash and fry the fish, coat lightly in the seasoned flour.
2. Melt the butter and fry the fish until tender.
3. Lift on to a hot dish.
4. Add the chives to the remaining butter and heat thoroughly.
5. Pour over the fish.
6. Garnish with parsley and lemon. Serve with plain boiled potatoes tossed in chopped parsley.

Variation
Fish meunière: Allow the butter to brown and add chopped parsley in place of chopped chives — use a little more butter than in the recipe above.

Cooking time: 5–10 minutes according to type of fish used
Preparation time: 5–8 minutes
Main cooking utensil: frying pan
Serves: 4

Fish and vegetable platter

Imperial	Metric
1–1½ lb. mixed vegetables or the equivalent in frozen vegetables	½–¾ kg. mixed vegetables or the equivalent in frozen vegetables
seasoning	seasoning
1 oz. butter	25 g. butter
4–5 portions white fish (cod, turbot or halibut)	4–5 portions white fish (cod, turbot or halibut)
1 level tablespoon flour	1 level tablespoon flour
3 tablespoons oil	3 tablespoons oil
grated rind and juice of 1 lemon	grated rind and juice of 1 lemon
1 good tablespoon capers	1 good tablespoon capers
3–4 gherkins	3–4 gherkins
3–4 anchovy fillets	3–4 anchovy fillets
1 tablespoon chopped parsley	1 tablespoon chopped parsley
Garnish:	*Garnish:*
2 lemons	2 lemons

1. Prepare the vegetables and cook in boiling, salted water until just tender, drain and toss in butter.
2. Wash and dry the fish, coat in the flour, which should be seasoned well; do not exceed the small amount of flour since the fish should not have a thick coating.
3. Heat the oil and fry the fish in this until nearly tender on both sides.
4. Add the grated lemon rind, lemon juice, capers, diced gherkins and chopped anchovy fillets, heat thoroughly with the fish.
5. Lift the fish with the other ingredients from the pan, drain away any surplus oil.
6. Arrange the vegetables and fish with the capers, gherkins and anchovies on a hot dish, top with the chopped parsley and garnish with the lemons.

Cooking time: 30 minutes
Preparation time: 25 minutes
Main cooking utensils: saucepan, frying pan
Serves: 4–5

Fish Mediterranean style

Imperial	Metric
6 oz. white fish (weight without skin and bones)	150 g. white fish (weight without skin and bones)
1½-inch piece cucumber	4-cm. piece cucumber
¼ pint water	125 ml. water
seasoning	seasoning
1 small onion	1 small onion
1 oz. butter or margarine	25 g. butter or margarine
½ oz. flour	15 g. flour
4 tablespoons milk	4 tablespoons milk
1 oz. mushrooms	25 g. mushrooms
1 oz. prawns, shelled	25 g. prawns, shelled
2 large tomatoes	2 large tomatoes
1 oz. cheese, grated (Cheddar or Gruyère)	25 g. cheese, grated (Cheddar or Gruyère)
Garnish:	*Garnish:*
chopped parsley	chopped parsley

1. Put the fish and the peeled diced cucumber into a saucepan with the water and plenty of seasoning, bring to the boil.
2. Simmer for 10 minutes only until the fish is just cooked.
3. Drain the fish and flake just a little; reserve and strain the stock.
4. Dice the onion and toss in half the butter or margarine.
5. Add the flour, stir over a gentle heat, gradually add the milk and bring to the boil.
6. Measure the fish stock and add ¼ pint (125 ml.) of this to the sauce, with the fish, cucumber, diced raw mushrooms and prawns.
7. Heat for a few minutes only, season well, spoon into scallop shells; keep hot.
8. Meanwhile skin, slice the tomatoes and fry to a thick purée, season.
9. Pile over the fish mixture, top with cheese.
10. Brown under the grill or in the oven for a very short time.

Cooking time: 25 minutes
Preparation time: 20 minutes
Main cooking utensils: saucepan, frying pan, 2 scallop shells
Serves: 2–4

Oily fish and ways to cook

Name – Season	Buy	Ways to cook
Herrings Throughout year best June–Feb.	Whole – easier to eat if boned and filleted.	Grill, fry, bake, pickle or souse.
Mackerel March–July.	Must be fresh. Buy as herrings.	As herrings.
Mullet April–August.	Grey or red. Buy whole.	Bake or grill. Liver of mullet can be cooked.
Salmon March–August.	Cutlets or steaks.	Poach – use hot or cold. Grill or bake or fry.
Salmon trout April–August.	Whole.	As salmon.
Sprats Oct.–March.	Similar to herrings.	Grill, fry or bake.
Whitebait May–August.	Whole – as tiny fish.	Fry – do not remove heads.

Allow 1–2 white fish, 6 oz. (150 g.) sprats, whitebait or salmon, per person.

Red mullet provençale

Cooking time: 20–25 minutes
Preparation time: 10 minutes
Main cooking utensil: shallow ovenproof dish
Oven temperature: moderate to moderately hot (350–375°F., 180–190°C., Gas Mark 4–5)
Oven position: above centre
Serves: 2

Imperial
2 red mullet
little oil
1 small onion
1 clove garlic (optional)
2 tablespoons lemon juice
1 tablespoon chopped parsley
seasoning
Mustard butter:
1 oz. butter
2 teaspoons French mustard
squeeze lemon juice
good pinch chopped fresh
   or dried herbs
Garnish:
olives
parsley

Metric
2 red mullet
little oil
1 small onion
1 clove garlic (optional)
2 tablespoons lemon juice
1 tablespoon chopped parsley
seasoning
Mustard butter:
25 g. butter
2 teaspoons French mustard
squeeze lemon juice
good pinch chopped fresh
   or dried herbs
Garnish:
olives
parsley

1. Split the mullet along the stomachs and insert the knife into the flesh, so the fish may be laid flat.
2. Remove the backbones and as many small bones as possible.
3. Put the fish into the oiled dish with the flesh side uppermost.
4. Sprinkle with the very finely chopped onion and garlic, the lemon juice, parsley and seasoning.
5. Bake for 20–25 minutes (depending upon the size of the fish) until just tender.
6. Make the mustard butter while the fish are cooking; to make this blend all the ingredients together, form into neat pats.
7. Lift the fish on to the serving dish, garnish with the olives and sprigs of parsley and top with the mustard butter.

Variation

Use mackerel instead of red mullet.

Peppers stuffed with fish

Imperial
3 oz. long-grain rice
approximately 1½ pints water
seasoning
1 red pepper
4 medium-sized green peppers
8 small Bismarck herrings
1½ tablespoons olive oil
2 teaspoons white or brown
   malt vinegar or tarragon
   vinegar
1 dessert apple
2 hard-boiled eggs
1 teaspoon fish seasoning or
   ½–1 teaspoon chopped mixed
   fresh or dried herbs

Metric
75 g. long-grain rice
approximately ¾ litre water
seasoning
1 red pepper
4 medium-sized green peppers
8 small Bismarck herrings
1½ tablespoons olive oil
2 teaspoons white or brown
   malt vinegar or tarragon
   vinegar
1 dessert apple
2 hard-boiled eggs
1 teaspoon fish seasoning or
   ½–1 teaspoon chopped mixed
   fresh or dried herbs

1. Cook the rice in the boiling water with seasoning until just soft; do not overcook.
2. While the rice is cooking prepare the peppers; cut the red pepper in half. Chop one half finely and cut the second half into neat strips, discarding the seeds and core.
3. Cut a slice from the top of each green pepper, this slice may also be finely chopped.
4. Remove the core and seeds from the green peppers and simmer the shells for 5 minutes in boiling, salted water, then drain. They need not be blanched if preferred firmer.
5. Chop half the Bismarck herrings.
6. Strain the rice, and while still hot blend it with the oil, vinegar, peeled, diced apple, chopped fish and 1 chopped egg. Add the fish seasoning or herbs, then the diced red and green pepper, saving a little for garnish. Pile the mixture into the green peppers.
7. Top with sliced egg and piece of pepper, arrange on a dish with remaining herrings and strips of red pepper.

Cooking time: 20 minutes
Preparation time: 20 minutes
Main cooking utensils: 3 saucepans
Serves: 4

Salmon pie

Imperial
12 oz. puff pastry
3 oz. quick-cooking rice
1 small onion
½ oz. butter
3 tablespoons cream or white
   sauce
1 tablespoon chopped parsley
12-oz. can salmon
2 hard-boiled eggs
seasoning
little butter (about ½ oz.)
Garnish:
parsley
lemon

Metric
300 g. puff pastry
75 g. quick-cooking rice
1 small onion
15 g. butter
3 tablespoons cream or white
   sauce
1 tablespoon chopped parsley
300-g. can salmon
2 hard-boiled eggs
seasoning
little butter (about 15 g.)
Garnish:
parsley
lemon

1. If using frozen puff pastry allow it to defrost enough to roll out.
2. Cook the rice as directed, then drain and dry.
3. Chop the onion and cook in the hot butter, then add the cream, parsley, flaked salmon, and rice.
4. Roll out the pastry to an oblong about 15 inches by 12 inches (35 by 30 cm.). Put the salmon mixture on this, then cover with the sliced hard-boiled eggs, seasoning and tiny pieces of butter.
5. Damp the edges of the pastry and fold to cover the filling.
6. Secure the ends of the pastry; snip the top pastry to allow steam to escape.
7. Bake for time and at temperature given, reducing the heat after about 20 minutes. Garnish with parsley and lemon slices.

Note: This pie is excellent for taking on a picnic as it can be wrapped in foil and carried safely.

Cooking time: 40 minutes
Preparation time: 30 minutes
Main cooking utensils: saucepans, flat baking tray or sheet
Oven temperature: hot (425–450°F., 220–230°C., Gas Mark 7–8)
   then moderately hot (400°F., 200°C., Gas Mark 6)
Oven position: centre
Serves: 4–6

Mackerel and cider apple sauce

Imperial	Metric
2 mackerel	2 mackerel
¼ pint cider	125 ml. cider
1 tablespoon vinegar	1 tablespoon vinegar
1 bay leaf	1 bay leaf
squeeze lemon juice	squeeze lemon juice
bouquet garni	bouquet garni
seasoning	seasoning
Sauce:	*Sauce:*
½ oz. butter	15 g. butter
1 oz. sugar	25 g. sugar
8 oz. cooking apples	¼ kg. cooking apples
4 tablespoons cider	4 tablespoons cider
Garnish:	*Garnish:*
lemon or orange slices	lemon or orange slices
sprigs fresh tarragon	sprigs fresh tarragon
watercress	watercress
paprika pepper	paprika pepper

1. Cut the heads off the fish, clean out the intestines, and remove the backbones.
2. Put the fish into the dish with the ingredients for cooking, cover with foil or a lid and bake until tender but unbroken — the time varies as mackerel is sometimes very solid.
3. Allow to cool in the dish.
4. Make the sauce. Melt the butter, add the sugar and peeled and sliced apples and cider, then simmer to a thick purée.
5. Either sieve or beat until smooth.
6. Lift the mackerel on to a fresh serving dish and top with 'butterflies' of lemon or orange. Garnish with watercress and paprika pepper. Serve with sauce and green and potato salad.

Variation
Fresh herrings or trout could be used — this dish makes a pleasant change and is much more economical than cold shellfish or salmon.

Cooking time: 20–35 minutes
Preparation time: 20 minutes
Main cooking utensils: baking dish, lid or foil
Oven temperature: moderately hot (375°F., 190°C., Gas Mark 5)
Oven position: centre
Serves: 2

Swiss herrings

Imperial	Metric
4 herrings	4 herrings
seasoning	seasoning
about 3 teaspoons French mustard	about 3 teaspoons French mustard
4 portions processed Swiss Gruyère cheese	4 portions processed Swiss Gruyère cheese
Garnish:	*Garnish:*
parsley	parsley
lemon	lemon

1. Split open the herrings and remove backbone. Season.
2. Brush the flesh side with French mustard and place under the grill for 3 minutes, folding the herring again.
3. When nearly cooked arrange a portion of processed Gruyère cheese horizontally on each fillet and continue gently grilling until the cheese has melted and the fillets are cooked.
4. Garnish with parsley and lemon and serve at once.

Variation
A pinch of curry powder could be added to the French mustard and a few drops of Worcestershire sauce.

Cooking time: 7–10 minutes
Preparation time: few minutes
Main cooking utensil: grill pan
Serves: 4

Freshwater fish and ways to cook

Name – Season	Buy	Ways to cook
Carp Oct.–Feb.	Generally whole.	Bake slowly.
Eel Sept.–May.	Fresh.	Generally stewed or in jelly.
Trout April–Sept.	Whole.	Grill, fry or bake. As this is a dry fish, use plenty of fat.
Perch May–Feb.	Generally whole. Cut away fins before cooking. Plunge into boiling water for 1 minute, remove scales then cook.	Fry or grill.
Bream July–Dec.	Also under 'White fish'.	Grill, fry or bake.
Smelt Sept.–March.	Becoming very rare. Buy whole.	Grill or fry. Keep head on fish.

Trout and mustard sauce

Imperial	Metric
4 trout	4 trout
$\frac{1}{2}$ oz. flour	15 g. flour
seasoning	seasoning
2–3 oz. butter	50–75 g. butter
2–3 oz. blanched almonds	50–75 g. blanched almonds
Sauce rémoulade:	*Sauce rémoulade:*
$\frac{1}{4}$ pint mayonnaise	150 ml. mayonnaise
$\frac{1}{2}$ teaspoon made mustard	$\frac{1}{2}$ teaspoon made mustard
2 teaspoons chopped herbs (parsley, chervil, tarragon, chives)	2 teaspoons chopped herbs (parsley, chervil, tarragon, chives)
few capers	few capers

1. Remove the heads from the fish and clean out the intestines.
2. Wipe the fish and dry well. Coat lightly in seasoned flour.
3. Fry steadily for about 8 minutes in hot butter, then lift on to a hot dish.
4. Add the almonds to the butter remaining in the pan and fry for a few minutes. Spoon over the top of the fish.
5. To make the sauce, blend the mayonnaise with the mustard and chopped herbs and capers.
6. Serve the fish with the sauce in a sauceboat.

Variation
Omit the sauce and serve the trout and almonds with a little extra butter, allowed to darken to golden brown, with a little chopped parsley and capers added.

Mayonnaise
Blend 1 egg yolk with a pinch of salt, pepper, mustard and sugar. Add 1 tablespoon vinegar or lemon juice, then gradually blend in the oil, drop by drop, beating well with a wooden spoon to make a smooth sauce. 1 egg yolk takes $\frac{1}{4}$–$\frac{1}{2}$ pint (150–200 ml.) oil, but a less oily dressing can be made.

Cooking time: 12 minutes
Preparation time: 15 minutes
Main cooking utensil: frying pan
Serves: 4

47

Shellfish (Crustaceans) and ways to serve

Name – Season	Buy	Ways of cooking and serving
Clams Sept.–April.	Usually shelled or canned.	Generally put into soup or sauce.
Cockles Sept.–April.	Generally ready cooked and shelled.	Serve cold with bread and butter. Add to sauce.
Crab May–April.	Generally cooked, but if alive cook as page 221.	'Dress' crab as page 52. Serve cold, or in hot dishes.
Crawfish May–August.	Like lobster but no claws.	As lobster.
Crayfish (Ecrevisse) Oct.–March.	Small freshwater fish – like lobster.	As lobster.
Lobster Feb.–Oct.	Generally cooked. Good lobster feels heavy for size. If not, it is full of water. If alive cook as page 221.	Serve cold with salad, or as hot dish, see page 49.
Mussels Sept.–April.	Sold in shells or in jars ready prepared.	Scrub shells. Discard any which do not close tightly when tapped. See pages 13 and 50.

Name – Season	Buy	Ways of cooking and serving
Oysters Sept.–April. (also imported).	In shells. Sold by the dozen. Expensive.	Eat raw – swallow whole. Sometimes added to sauces.
Prawns Feb.–Dec.	Generally cooked, sometimes ready shelled, or cook as page 221.	Serve cold in salads or add to sauces, etc. See pages 43 and 52.
Scallops Oct.–March.	Occasionally called 'scollops' or 'escalopes'. Sold on shells by fishmonger.	Remove from shells, wash thoroughly. Poach in milk or see page 49.
Scampi Imported.	Name given to large prawns. Buy fresh or frozen.	Generally coated and fried. See page 51.
Shrimps Feb.–Oct.	As prawns.	As prawns.
Whelks Sept.–April.	Generally sold cooked.	Remove from shells with a pin, eat raw.
Winkles Sept.–April.	Like small whelks.	As whelks.

Cozze gratinate

Imperial
2 pints mussels
4 tablespoons water
4 tablespoons white wine
1 clove garlic
small bunch parsley
1–2 sprigs fennel
seasoning
Topping:
1 tablespoon olive oil
1 tablespoon chopped parsley
1 clove garlic
2 oz. soft breadcrumbs
Sauce:
1 egg yolk
4 tablespoons thick cream

Metric
1 litre mussels
4 tablespoons water
4 tablespoons white wine
1 clove garlic
small bunch parsley
1–2 sprigs fennel
seasoning
Topping:
1 tablespoon olive oil
1 tablespoon chopped parsley
1 clove garlic
50 g. soft breadcrumbs
Sauce:
1 egg yolk
4 tablespoons thick cream

1. Scrub the mussels in plenty of cold water; discard any that do not close when tapped sharply.
2. Put the mussels into a large pan with the water, wine, crushed garlic, parsley, fennel and seasoning.
3. Heat steadily until the mussels open, this takes only a few minutes.
4. Allow the fish to cool until easy to handle then remove one shell from each and any small weeds; discard any mussels that do not open.
5. Put the mussels, still on the halved shells, on to a flameproof dish.
6. Mix the oil, parsley, crushed garlic and breadcrumbs together, season well.
7. Spread over the top of the mussels and heat under the grill.
8. Meanwhile strain liquid from the pan then return to the pan.
9. Beat the egg yolk and cream, add to the liquid and cook gently, without boiling, for a few minutes. Spoon a little sauce on to large plates, add the mussels. Garnish with lemon and eat with fresh bread.

Cooking time: 20 minutes
Preparation time: 25 minutes
Main cooking utensils: large saucepan, flameproof dish, grill
Serves: 3–4

Scallops in saffron and cheese sauce

Imperial	Metric
few saffron strands or	few saffron strands or
¼ teaspoon saffron powder	¼ teaspoon saffron powder
8 tablespoons white wine	8 tablespoons white wine
8 small scallops	8 small scallops
1 small shallot or onion	1 small shallot or onion
½ tablespoon lemon juice	½ tablespoon lemon juice
1 oz. butter	25 g. butter
1 oz. flour	25 g. flour
¼ pint milk	125 ml. milk
seasoning	seasoning
3 oz. Gruyère cheese, grated	75 g. Gruyère cheese, grated

1. Put the saffron to soak in the wine for 30 minutes, strain the wine.
2. Remove the scallops from the shells and put them into the pan with the finely chopped shallot or onion.
3. Add the saffron-flavoured wine and lemon juice and simmer gently for 10 minutes or until the scallops are tender. Do not overcook as this will toughen the fish.
4. Lift the scallops from the pan on to the shells, strain the liquid.
5. Heat the butter, stir in the flour and cook for several minutes.
6. Gradually blend in the milk then bring to the boil and cook until the sauce is very thick. Gradually blend in the liquid from stage 4. Season well.
7. Stir in 2 oz. (50 g.) grated cheese, coat the scallops with the sauce and top with the remaining cheese.
8. Heat under the grill or in the oven for a few minutes. Serve as an hors-d'oeuvre or light supper dish.

Variation

Instead of scallops, cook white fish cut into neat portions in the wine, or heat portions of lobster in the wine.

Cooking time: 20 minutes
Preparation time: 15 minutes plus 30 minutes for saffron to soak
Main cooking utensils: saucepan, 4 scallop shells
Oven temperature: hot (425–450°F 220–230°C., Gas Mark 7–8)
Oven position: above centre
Serves: 4

Devilled lobster

Imperial	Metric
2 medium-sized lobsters	2 medium-sized lobsters
2 oz. butter	50 g. butter
1 clove garlic (optional)	1 clove garlic (optional)
2 teaspoons curry powder	2 teaspoons curry powder
shake cayenne pepper	shake cayenne pepper
Sauce:	*Sauce:*
2 egg yolks	2 egg yolks
1–2 teaspoons French mustard	1–2 teaspoons French mustard
1 teaspoon curry powder	1 teaspoon curry powder
shake cayenne pepper	shake cayenne pepper
pinch salt	pinch salt
pinch sugar	pinch sugar
up to ½ pint olive oil	up to 275 ml. olive oil
1 tablespoon lemon juice	1 tablespoon lemon juice
2 teaspoons finely chopped	2 teaspoons finely chopped
tarragon	tarragon

1. If the lobsters are alive, tie the claws firmly. Put them into a pan of cold water and bring the water slowly to the boil, or plunge them into boiling water.
2. Boil steadily until the shells turn scarlet (about 15–20 minutes), allow to cool. Alternatively, buy cooked lobsters.
3. Split the lobsters down the centre and remove the intestinal veins (the long thread-like vein in the body); also discard the 'lady fingers' (the grey fingers that are found where the claws join the body).
4. If wished, the large claws may be used in a separate dish or crack these, remove the flesh and put this into the body of the lobsters.
5. Cream the butter with the crushed garlic, curry powder and cayenne and spread over the lobsters. Heat under the grill.
6. To make the curry sauce, blend the egg yolks with the seasoning and sugar, very gradually blend in the oil, lemon juice and herbs. Garnish with lettuce.

Cooking time: few minutes plus time to cook the lobsters
Preparation time: 10 minutes
Main cooking utensils: large saucepan, grill pan
Serves: 4

49

Mussels in white wine

Imperial	Metric
at least 4 pints mussels	at least 2¼ litres mussels
1 onion	1 onion
bouquet garni	bouquet garni
½ pint white wine	300 ml. white wine
seasoning	seasoning
Sauce:	*Sauce:*
1½ oz. butter or margarine	40 g. butter or margarine
1½ oz. flour	40 g. flour
1–2 teaspoons curry powder	1–2 teaspoons curry powder
¾ pint milk or half milk and half white wine	375 ml. milk or half milk and half white wine
2 tablespoons thick cream (optional)	2 tablespoons thick cream (optional)
seasoning	seasoning
Garnish:	*Garnish:*
parsley	parsley

1. Scrub the mussels well and wash in plenty of cold water, discard any whose shells are open and will not close when tapped sharply.
2. Put the mussels into the pan with the onion; leave this whole if not required in the sauce or chop finely if you wish to add it to the final dish.
3. Put in the bouquet garni, wine and seasoning and simmer steadily until the shells open.
4. Lift the fish out of the pan when cool enough to handle, pull off one shell, and cut away any weed-like growths.
5. Heat the butter or margarine, stir in the flour and curry powder, cook for several minutes, then blend in the milk and bring to the boil.
6. Add the strained liquid from the mussel pan and the cream and season well. Replace the mussels and heat. Serve on large plates, garnished with parsley.

Cooking time: 25 minutes
Preparation time: 25 minutes
Main cooking utensils: 2 good-sized saucepans
Serves: 6 as an hors d'oeuvre or 4 as a main dish

Moules à la marinière

Imperial	Metric
4 oz. onions, finely chopped	100 g. onions, finely chopped
1 tablespoon butter	1 tablespoon butter
4 oz. tomatoes	100 g. tomatoes
small bunch mixed herbs	small bunch mixed herbs
¼ pint water or white wine and water	125 ml. water or white wine and water
1 pint mussels	550 ml. mussels
pepper	pepper
breadcrumbs (optional)	breadcrumbs (optional)
Garnish:	*Garnish:*
chopped parsley	chopped parsley

1. Fry the onions gently for 10 minutes in the butter, with a lid on the pan.
2. Remove the cover to brown, add the tomatoes cut in pieces and the bunch of mixed herbs.
3. Cover again and cook for 15 minutes.
4. In another large wide pan put the water and mussels.
5. Place a tea towel wrung out in boiling water on top of them, and leave for 2–3 minutes over a fierce heat until their shells open.
6. Remove the top halves of the shells, leave the mussels on the bottom shell. Remove the tiny fungus growth, i.e., the beard.
7. Strain the liquor and mix it together with the mussels into the onion and tomato purée.
8. Add plenty of pepper and heat gently through. If the mixture looks too thin for your taste, thicken by adding some soft white breadcrumbs, but do not use flour. Serve sprinkled with parsley.

Cooking time: 25 minutes
Preparation time: 20 minutes
Main cooking utensils: 2 saucepans
Serves: 2

Fried scampi

Imperial	Metric
about 12 scampi or equivalent in smaller prawns or frozen prawns	about 12 scampi or equivalent in smaller prawns or frozen prawns
½ oz. flour	15 g. flour
seasoning	seasoning
Batter:	*Batter:*
4 oz. flour	100 g. flour
pinch salt	pinch salt
2 eggs	2 eggs
¼ pint milk	125 ml. milk
3 tablespoons water	3 tablespoons water
Tartare sauce:	*Tartare sauce:*
mayonnaise (see page 47)	mayonnaise (see page 47)
1–2 teaspoons each chopped parsley, gherkins and capers	1–2 teaspoons each chopped parsley, gherkins and capers

1. Remove the shells from the fish, or if using frozen scampi these are ready shelled, but may not be pre-cooked.
2. Coat the fish lightly with seasoned flour – there is no need to allow frozen scampi to defrost completely.
3. Coat in batter, made by sieving the flour and salt, then beating in the eggs and liquid.
4. In the case of frozen scampi, it is a good idea to allow them to stand in the batter for a short time, or they may be a little watery.
5. Heat oil or fat. To test if it is the correct heat, put in a cube of day-old bread; it should brown in oil in about 30 seconds, or 1 minute in fat.
6. Put in the scampi and fry for several minutes. Pre-cooked scampi will take about 3–4 minutes, frozen uncooked scampi, 6–7 minutes.
7. Drain on absorbent paper and garnish with lemon and parsley. Serve with tartare sauce made by blending the mayonnaise with chopped parsley, gherkins and capers.

Cooking time: few minutes
Preparation time: 10 minutes
Main cooking utensils: frying basket and deep pan, absorbent paper
Serves: 4

Crab and cheese soufflé

Imperial	Metric
1 oz. butter	25 g. butter
½ oz. flour	15 g. flour
¼ pint milk	125 ml. milk
3 egg yolks	3 egg yolks
seasoning	seasoning
little cayenne pepper	little cayenne pepper
4 oz. crab meat	100 g. crab meat
2 oz. Parmesan cheese	50 g. Parmesan cheese
4 egg whites	4 egg whites

1. Make a sauce by melting the butter in a large pan, stirring in the flour and cooking slowly for a minute.
2. Gradually add the milk, return to the heat, stir vigorously over a moderate heat until the sauce thickens.
3. Cool a little, stir in the beaten egg yolks, seasoning and cayenne pepper. Add the flaked crab meat and finely grated cheese.
4. Whip the egg whites until stiff, fold carefully into the egg and crab mixture.
5. Turn into a buttered soufflé dish, bake for about 25–30 minutes, or until risen and brown. Serve at once either as an hors d'oeuvre or light main dish.

Variation
Use flaked smoked haddock in place of crab.
Cheese soufflé: Use 4 oz. (100 g.) cheese – all Parmesan or half Parmesan and half Gruyère.

Cooking time: 25–30 minutes
Preparation time: 20 minutes
Main cooking utensils: large pan, soufflé dish
Oven temperature: moderate (350–375°F., 180–190°C., Gas Mark 4–5)
Oven position: centre
Serves: 4–5

Hasty prawn curry

Imperial	Metric
1 large onion	1 large onion
1 oz. butter	25 g. butter
½ oz. flour	15 g. flour
1 level dessertspoon curry powder	1 level dessertspoon curry powder
1 tablespoon mango chutney	1 tablespoon mango chutney
¾ pint water	375 ml. water
1 dessert apple	1 dessert apple
4-oz. packet frozen prawns	113-g. packet frozen prawns
2 16-oz. cans curried beans with sultanas	2 454-g. cans curried beans with sultanas
4–6 oz. Patna rice	100–150 g. Patna rice
1 level teaspoon turmeric	1 level teaspoon turmeric
Garnish:	*Garnish:*
a few unshelled prawns (optional)	a few unshelled prawns (optional)

1. Chop the onion and fry in the butter until lightly browned.
2. Blend the flour, curry powder and chutney together with a little of the water, add to the onion and cook for 3 minutes, stirring all the time.
3. Add the rest of the water and peeled chopped apple and bring to the boil.
4. Leave to simmer gently for 10–15 minutes, adding the prawns and beans after 10 minutes.
5. Meanwhile cook the rice with the turmeric in boiling salted water for 15 minutes.
6. Drain the rice and arrange on a serving dish with the curry in the middle. Garnish with prawns.

Variation
Use hard-boiled eggs instead of prawns or a mixture of eggs and prawns or shrimps.

Cooking time: 20 minutes
Preparation time: 15 minutes
Main cooking utensils: 2 saucepans
Serves: 4–6

King crab mayonnaise

Imperial	Metric
1 medium-sized onion	1 medium-sized onion
1 tablespoon oil	1 tablespoon oil
1 dessertspoon curry powder	1 dessertspoon curry powder
1 dessertspoon tomato purée	1 dessertspoon tomato purée
1 tablespoon clear honey	1 tablespoon clear honey
1 wineglass red wine	1 wineglass red wine
¾ wineglass water	¾ wineglass water
seasoning	seasoning
juice of ½ lemon	juice of ½ lemon
½ pint mayonnaise (see page 47)	250 ml. mayonnaise (see page 47)
1 lb. frozen crab meat or 1 large crab	½ kg. frozen crab meat or 1 large crab
Garnish:	*Garnish:*
3–4 tomatoes	3–4 tomatoes
few black olives	few black olives

1. Fry the chopped onion in oil for 3–4 minutes.
2. Add the curry powder and cook for a further 2 minutes.
3. Add the tomato purée, honey, wine and water. Bring to the boil, season and add lemon juice.
4. Simmer until it has become thick and syrupy. Strain and leave to cool. Stir into the mayonnaise and crab meat.
5. Arrange in a long shallow dish and garnish with tomato and black olives. Serve with a green salad.

Note: If using a fresh crab, pull the body away from the shell, remove the meat from the body, discard the stomach bag and the grey parts (dead men's fingers), remove the meat from the crushed claws also. Serve dark and light meat separately, or mix together as in this salad.

Cooking time: 10–15 minutes
Preparation time: 10–20 minutes (depending on whether fresh or frozen crab is used)
Main cooking utensil: saucepan
Serves: 6

Fish roes and ways to serve

Name	Buy	Ways of cooking
Cod's roe	Fresh, uncooked.	Steam for 10 minutes, skin. Add to sauce or slice and fry.
	Fresh, ready cooked.	Add to sauces or slice and fry.
	Smoked.	Use as sandwich filling or blend with butter to make paste, or see below.
Herring roe	Hard roe, fresh uncooked.	Nicer fried in a little fat.
	Soft roe, fresh uncooked.	Either poach in milk or fry in butter.

To use smoked roe

Smoked cod's roe can be used to make one of the most famous fish pâtés, i.e. *Taramasalata*. While there are many recipes for this, basically it is a mixture of mashed smoked cod's roe, flavouring, butter and/or cream to soften.

Buy the smoked roe wisely; if the red skin looks dry and hard it probably means the roe is not fresh and will also be dry. Remove the roe from the skin, mash this, add pepper, but no salt, a little crushed garlic and lemon juice to flavour. Blend in enough butter and single cream to give the consistency of a soft pâté. Serve with hot toast, butter and lemon wedges. I find you have a softer, more delicate pâté if you put the cod's roe (in the skin) into warm water for at least 1 hour, then skin and proceed as above.

Smoked cod's roe is quite expensive so if you want to make an economical hors d'œuvre for a party, hard boil eggs, halve and remove the yolks, sieve or mash these, mix with the Taramasalata (above). Pile the mixture back into the hard-boiled egg whites and serve on a bed of salad.

Smoked cod's roe or the pâté, made from this, freeze well. Cover the pâté with melted butter, wrap and freeze. Use within 4–6 weeks.

Fish pâté

Imperial
1–1¼ lb. white fish (hake, halibut, etc.) without skin or bone
seasoning
1–2 cloves garlic
2 oz. butter
¼ pint thick cream
2 teaspoons very finely chopped parsley
½ teaspoon very finely grated lemon rind
2 teaspoons lemon juice
Topping:
6 tablespoons thick mayonnaise (see page 47)
1 tablespoon tomato purée
Garnish:
capers
lettuce
lemon

Metric
generous ½ kg. white fish (hake, halibut, etc.) without skin or bone
seasoning
1–2 cloves garlic
50 g. butter
125 ml. thick cream
2 teaspoons very finely chopped parsley
½ teaspoon very finely grated lemon rind
2 teaspoons lemon juice
Topping:
6 tablespoons thick mayonnaise (see page 47)
1 tablespoon tomato purée
Garnish:
capers
lettuce
lemon

1. Put the fish into a pan with a very little water (just enough to prevent the fish from burning) and seasoning.
2. Cook over a low heat for about 10 minutes until just tender.
3. Drain very well, then mince the fish or flake and pound it until very smooth; if preferred emulsify in a liquidiser.
4. Add the crushed garlic, the softened butter and cream.
5. Beat well until very smooth.
6. Add the parsley, lemon rind and juice and season well.
7. Put into a dish to give a depth of about 1½ inches (4 cm.).
8. Chill well then top with the mayonnaise, blended with the tomato purée. Serve cut into neat slices, topped with a few capers with lettuce and slices of lemon. Serve with hot toast.

Cooking time: 10 minutes
Preparation time: 20 minutes
Main cooking utensil: saucepan
Serves: 6–8

Meat dishes

Meat is probably the most important protein food in most households; it also is one of the more costly, that is why it is important to know the various ways of cooking meat, so you can take advantage of cheaper cuts and make appetising meals from these. Learn to recognise good-quality meat and meat that is fresh. Many people save money by bulk buying meat for their freezers and the column on the left of page 56 gives advice on home freezing of meat.

To tell if meat is fresh

Check you buy from a butcher or supermarket where absolute cleanliness is practised.

Beef: The lean should be a clear bright red; the fat firm and pale cream in colour. A good joint of beef must have a certain amount of fat.

Mutton and lamb: The lean should be a dull pink-red and firm; the fat white in colour. Mutton has more fat than lamb and always takes longer slower cooking.

Pork: The lean must look a pale pink; very young pork has white-pink lean. The fat should be white and dry.

Veal: The lean should be pale pink and dry; the fat, of which there is very little, firm and white.

Bacon and ham: Both must look pleasantly moist with a reasonable, but not excessive, amount of fat. Note: When the word 'dry' is applied to meat it does not mean hard and dry, but not damp.

Types of meat

The meats mentioned on the left, with the exception of bacon and ham, are all described as fresh meats, i.e. they have not been subjected to any form of curing. Beef, lamb and mutton are also listed under red meats and bones from these meats are used to give a brown stock, see to make stock below. Pork is really a red meat, but does not produce a good stock. Veal is a white meat and the bones produce a white stock.

Bacon and ham are examples of cured meat, and it is possible to buy cured beef (salted beef – either brisket or silverside) or tongue. There is a recipe using salted meat on page 65. If cooking a joint of salted meat, it is advisable to soak it before cooking. Allow about 12 hours in cold water to cover. Green bacon or 'sweet cure' bacon joints do not need soaking before cooking, they are milder. Since offal (often called 'variety' meats) are very varied, you will find information about these starting on page 56. Many of these are highly nutritious and they lend themselves to many different ways of cooking.

To make stock: Cover the washed bones with water, add seasoning and herbs or vegetables to taste. Simmer for several hours or 1 hour at 15 lb. (7 kg.) in a pressure cooker. Strain and use.

Methods of cooking meat

The recipes that follow give you new ideas for serving meat, but they all are based upon the following classic ways of cooking:

To bake meat: As this means cooking the meat in the oven, it is really correct to consider roasting a form of baking. You will find timing for roasting meat in the tables on pages 57, 66, 71, 75 and recommended temperatures in the recipes on pages 58, 66, 71, 76, etc.

Roast best end neck of lamb garnished with halved pineapple rings and served with pasta shapes.

To boil meat: This term is a little misleading in that it implies meat is cooked in boiling liquid whereas the liquid should simmer gently. Too quick cooking toughens the meat and it also causes the outside to overcook before the centre of the meat is really tender.

To braise meat: This method of cooking is a combination of frying and stewing. The meat is first browned in hot fat, then cooked above a layer of vegetables, etc., known as a 'mirepoix' (see page 91).

To casserole meat: This is similar to stewing, except that the meat, etc. is cooked in a casserole in a slow to very moderate oven. If you are adapting a stew for cooking in a casserole you can use a little less liquid, since there is less evaporation in the oven.

To fry meat: This method of cooking is only suitable for tender pieces of meat (these are detailed in the various tables). Make sure any fat used is hot before the meat is placed into the pan. Cook the meat quickly on either side to seal in the flavour, then lower the temperature to ensure it is cooked right through to the middle. Chops, etc. do not need draining on absorbent paper, but rissoles or similar fried meat dishes should be well drained. It is a good idea to coat rissoles with flour, then egg and crumbs before frying; this gives them a good crisp coating and more attractive appearance.

To grill meat: This, like frying, is meant for the prime cuts of meat. Always preheat the grill, so you seal the outside of the meat quickly. The one exception to this rule is when cooking thick bacon, such as gammon steaks, etc., if the grill is too hot it causes the fat to curl and burn before the meat is cooked. Keep lean meats 'basted' with melted fat during cooking, so they do not become dry.

To stew meat: This means cooking meat in a liquid; often this is thickened and vegetables, etc. added to give additional flavour to the meat. Stewing is a long slow method of cooking, therefore it is ideal for the less tender pieces of meat.

Canned and frozen meat

Canned meats are a useful ingredient to have in the store cupboard; they should be used within 5 years. Some of the most versatile are:

Stewing steak: To use in place of fresh meat, add cooked vegetables or flavour with herbs, curry, etc.

Corned beef: This can be served cold, or sliced and coated with seasoned flour or with a batter and fried. You can coat the whole piece of corned beef with melted fat and heat it thoroughly in the oven. You will find a more interesting recipe using this meat on page 83.

Canned tongue can be served cold, or sliced and heated in a sauce, a suitable sauce is the one given in the recipe on page 89.

Canned ham could be substituted for freshly cooked ham, it tends to crumble slightly when sliced, otherwise is very good; so are various kinds of luncheon meat.

Frozen meats should be treated like the meat you freeze yourself, see page 56. Frozen hamburgers are a general favourite with most children and they can be cooked from the frozen state. Always note the directions for correct storage of frozen meat which you will find on the packets.

Easy guide to meat dishes

The following gives you help in selecting the right meat dishes for the right occasion.

When you are short of time see pages 59, 60, 69, 72, 74, 77, 81, 82, 83, 86, 87, 88, 208.

When you are short of money see pages 62, 63, 64, 65, 66, 70, 78, 83, 84, 85, 86, 87, 88, 141, 143, 204, 205.

When you want a special dish see pages 58, 59, 60, 61, 67, 68, 69, 71, 72, 73, 76, 80, 81, 82, 89, 192, 193, 194, 208, 216.

For a snack or light meal see pages 64, 65.

When you are slimming see pages 58, 59, 71, 77, 81, 121.

To freeze meat

Divide large joints into convenient-sized pieces. Wrap in foil, then in polythene wrap or bags. Press all wrappings firmly round the joint, so excluding the maximum of air; this ensures the meat freezes in the shortest time and improves both texture and taste. Use raw beef within 9 months, pork in 6 months, mutton and lamb within 9 months, veal in 4 months. If the meat is very fat remove excess fat before freezing or use in a shorter time.

Raw salted meats should be used within 3 months. Raw offal should be used within about 3 months. Cooked meat dishes (casseroles, etc.) should be used within 2–3 months and cooked salt meat or dishes based upon these meats within 1 month.

Although a steak and kidney pudding or pie contains offal, I find I can freeze it for up to 3 months, but most cooked offal dishes are better used within 2 months.

When freezing steaks or chops, separate each portion with a square of waxed paper before wrapping, so making it easier to remove as many pieces as desired for that particular meal. Cook steaks, etc. from the frozen state, but either allow joints to thaw out completely, this takes at least 24 hours in the refrigerator, or cook from the frozen state, using a meat thermometer or the slower roasting as page 91.

Either defrost cooked casserole dishes completely before heating or heat very slowly to begin with, for if you try to heat too quickly you burn the outside of the meat, etc. before it is thawed. To save keeping casseroles in the freezer either:
a. Line dish with double foil before putting in meat, etc. for cooking; cook, cool, freeze then lift out and wrap (see sketch below), or
b. Cook in an unlined dish, cool and freeze in the casserole, then tip out and wrap.

Return the meat, etc. to the original dish to heat again. Meat puddings are better cooked for 3 hours (to give light suet pastry), cooled then frozen and cooked for a further 2–3 hours after taking from the freezer. Line basins as suggested above (point a). *NEVER PUT AN OVENPROOF DISH OR BASIN STRAIGHT FROM THE FREEZER INTO AN OVEN OR STEAMER*, allow to return to room temperature first.

Choosing and cooking offal

Offal is a nourishing meat that is often neglected. There are many of these variety meats that are not easily obtained, so I can concentrate on those that are readily available.

Head: Calf's, pig's and lamb's heads can be used to make a brawn. As a lamb's head is smaller it will only take 2 hours to cook instead of the 2½–3 hours needed for a pig's head. It will make a smaller brawn, that serves 4–6 people. A head is also delicious served hot. Soak the split head in cold water for several hours or overnight. Remove from the water and rinse well. Simmer with vegetables and herbs to flavour then serve hot with a parsley or brain sauce. To make the brain sauce, remove the white brains from the head, soak separately for only 1 hour in cold water with a few drops of vinegar or lemon juice added, then simmer in fresh salted water for 15 minutes. Add to a well-seasoned white sauce (page 123).

Heart: The comparatively tender lamb's hearts can be stuffed and roasted. Wash well, cut away the tough arteries, then put in your favourite stuffing. Wrap in well-greased foil and cook for 1¼–1½ hours in a moderate to moderately hot oven.

The less tender calf's or ox heart are better stewed or cooked in a casserole; while calf's heart can be cooked whole, as the recipe on page 87, ox heart should be sliced before cooking. Ox heart makes a good alternative to stewing steak in many recipes. Heart, like liver and kidney, is an excellent source of iron.

Kidney: Lambs' kidneys make a delicious savoury with bacon or on toast. Skin, remove hard gristle and fry steadily; ox kidney should be cooked slowly. See page 88 for kidney recipes.

Liver: Calf's liver is the tenderest and most easily digested, and ideal for children or invalids. Lamb's liver or pig's liver (if good quality) can be cooked quickly, there are several recipes on pages 86 and 87. Ox liver is better cooked more slowly. Remember overcooking toughens liver, so time your cooking carefully.

Oxtail: This makes one of the most delicious stews or casserole dishes. Fry the oxtail in a little fat, together with various sliced vegetables. Lift out of the pan, then make a thickened sauce, seasoning this well. Replace the oxtail and vegetables in the sauce and simmer gently for about 3 hours. Leave overnight, remove the surplus fat and reheat.

Tongue: A recipe for pressed ox tongue is given on page 89 together with a delicious way of serving smaller tongues. Pressed tongue makes an excellent dish when you are having a buffet meal.

To cook sweetbreads and tripe

These are appetising and easily digested offal and are particularly good for invalids. Both meats need 'blanching' before cooking, i.e. put the meat into a pan of cold water, bring the water to the boil, then throw the water away. This ensures the meat is white.

After blanching sweetbreads, simmer until tender for

20–30 minutes in seasoned water or chicken stock. Cool enough to handle, remove from the stock and take away any pieces of gristle and skin. You can then press the meat and slice it neatly. The sweetbreads can be put into a brown sauce made with the stock, or a white sauce made partially with stock and partially with milk (see page 123). They also can be coated with seasoned flour, then egg and crumbs and fried until crisp and brown. Serve fried sweetbreads with tartare sauce, see page 51.

After blanching tripe, put it into a mixture of milk and water or milk and stock, with sliced onions. Season and simmer until tender. Modern 'dressed tripe' will need about 1 hour. The liquid can then be thickened with flour or cornflour.

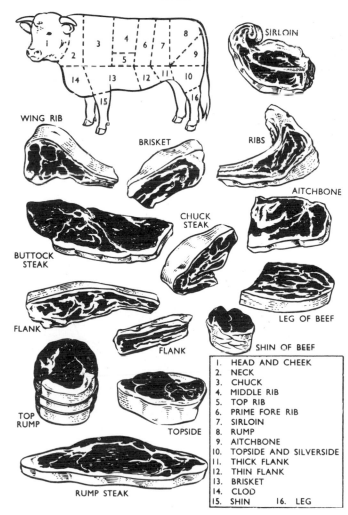

Grilled steak served with a baked potato and coleslaw — a mixture of shredded cabbage, diced apple and raisins tossed in mayonnaise.

Beef

Method of cooking	Cut	Cooking time	To serve
Roasting	Sirloin on or off bone Ribs Fillet Aitch-bone (good quality) Topside Rump Leg of mutton cut.	15 minutes per lb. (½ kg.) plus 15 minutes over. Well done, 20 minutes per lb. (½ kg.) plus 20 minutes over, or 40 minutes per lb (½ kg.) in very slow oven (see page 58).	Mustard Horseradish sauce Yorkshire pudding Roast potatoes Thin gravy (see page 58).
Grilling or frying	Rump steak Fillet Sirloin Entrecôte.	5–15 minutes depending on thickness and personal preference (see page 59).	Chipped or mashed potatoes Salad Tomatoes Mushrooms (see page 59).
Stewing or braising	Skirt or chuck Bladebone Leg of mutton cut Brisket Flank.	1½–3 hours, see also under Pressure cooking (page 64).	Mixed vegetables Dumplings Thickened gravy.
Boiling some joints also **pickled**	Brisket (fresh or salted) Silverside (fresh or salted) Aitch-bone Shin or leg Flank.	30 minutes per lb. (½ kg.) plus 30 minutes over (see pages 55 and 65).	Vegetables Dumplings (recipe page 62) Salad when served cold.
Stock for soup, etc.	Neck Shin or leg Clod Marrowbone Oxtail (see also page 56) Flank.	1½–3 hours (see pages 18 and 65) or ½–1 hour in pressure cooker (see page 64).	Add vegetables, herbs, etc.

BEEF

1. HEAD AND CHEEK
2. NECK
3. CHUCK
4. MIDDLE RIB
5. TOP RIB
6. PRIME FORE RIB
7. SIRLOIN
8. RUMP
9. AITCHBONE
10. TOPSIDE AND SILVERSIDE
11. THICK FLANK
12. THIN FLANK
13. BRISKET
14. CLOD
15. SHIN   16. LEG

Roast beef

Cooking time: see stages 1, 2, 3, 4
Preparation time: few minutes
Main cooking utensil: roasting tin
Oven temperature: hot (425–450°F., 220–230°C., Gas Mark 7–8); for slow roasting very moderate (325–350°F., 170–180°C., Gas Mark 3–4)
Oven position: above centre

Joints to choose for roasting:
sirloin
ribs
fillet
aitch-bone (good quality)
topside (better with slow roasting)
brisket (only suitable for slow roasting) and rump

1. Weigh the meat – cooking time depends on this. For under-done ('rare'), allow 15 minutes cooking time per lb. (450 g.) and 15 minutes over. If slow roasting allow 30 minutes per lb. and 30 minutes over.
For medium-done – i.e., well-done on outside, less well done in centre – allow nearly 20 minutes per lb. and 20 minutes over. If slow roasting allow 35 minutes per lb. and 35 minutes over.
For well-done allow a good 20 or even 25 minutes per lb. and 20 minutes over; if slow roasting, nearly 40 minutes per lb. and 40 minutes over.
If using a covered roasting tin or foil allow an extra 20 minutes cooking time or 25°F. (14°C.) higher temperature or one mark higher on a gas cooker. After about 45 minutes the heat can be reduced to moderately hot (400°F., 200°C., Gas Mark 6). This does not apply when slow roasting. Meat that has been frozen is often better if roasted more slowly.
2. To prepare for roasting, season the joint lightly and add a very little fat over the lean part of the meat.
3. Roast the meat as described in stage 1.
4. To make the gravy, drain all but 1 tablespoon fat from the tin. Stir in 1 tablespoon flour or flour and gravy flavouring, cook for several minutes making sure all the sediment is scraped up, then gradually add ½ pint (250 ml.) brown stock, bring to the boil, cook for a few minutes, and strain. Serve with Yorkshire pudding and roast potatoes.

Yorkshire pudding

Cooking time: 15 minutes or 35 minutes
Preparation time: 10 minutes
Main cooking utensil: small patty tins or Yorkshire pudding tin
Oven temperature: hot to very hot (425–475°F., 220–240°C., Gas Mark 7–9)
Oven position: towards top of oven
Serves: 4

Imperial	Metric
4 oz. plain flour	100 g. plain flour
pinch salt	pinch salt
1 egg	1 egg
½ pint milk or milk and water	250 ml. milk or milk and water
½–1 oz. fat	15–25 g. fat

1. Sieve flour and salt into a basin.
2. Add the egg and beat well, then beat in enough liquid to give a stiff batter. Allow to stand for a few minutes, then gradually beat in the remainder of the liquid.
3. Either rub patty tins with the fat or put a knob into a larger tin and heat for a few minutes in the oven.
4. It is a good idea to raise the temperature of the oven by 25°F., (14°C.) or one mark with a gas cooker, so the pudding is cooked very quickly.
5. Give batter a final whisk, put into a tin or tins. Bake small puddings for a shorter time; the larger one until firm and brown.
6. Alternatively, lift the meat on to a trivet and pour off all fat but 1 tablespoon, add batter, return meat and batter to oven.

Roast potatoes
Use a little extra fat with the beef. Dry the potatoes, put in hot fat, roast for approximately 45 minutes.

Grilled steak

Cuts of beef to choose for grilling:
minute — very thin slice
rump — excellent flavour
fillet — very tender
sirloin — very tender
entrecôte — from ribs of sirloin
point — from pointed end of
   rump
porterhouse — large sirloin
   steak for 4
tournedos — fillet tied into rounds
To cook:
little butter or oil

1. Light or switch on the grill for several minutes before cooking the steak.
2. Put the steak on the grid of grill pan and brush with melted butter or oil.
3. Cook on one side, then turn with tongs — do not put the prongs of a fork into meat. Brush the second side with butter and cook to taste.
Minute steak: 1 minute cooking each side
Under-done steak ('rare'): About ¾ inch (2 cm.) thick, 3—4 minutes each side.
Medium done: Cook as under-done, then lower heat for a further 3 minutes.
Well-done steak: Cook as under-done, then lower heat for further 5—6 minutes.
4. Serve with grilled tomatoes, chips, watercress and maître d'hôtel butter.

Parsley butter
Work chopped parsley and lemon juice into butter, chill before shaping. (Parsley butter is the English name for maître d'hôtel butter.)

Cooking time: see method
Preparation time: few minutes
Main cooking utensil: grill pan
Allow: 6—8 oz. (150—200g.) per person

Pot roast

Imperial	Metric
6 large onions	6 large onions
6 large carrots	6 large carrots
3 small turnips	3 small turnips
2 oz. good dripping	50 g. good dripping
2- to 3-lb. piece boned top rib, rolled (see note)	1- to 1½-kg. piece boned top rib, rolled (see note)
seasoning	seasoning

1. Peel the vegetables and leave whole.
2. Melt the dripping in pan or casserole and fry the vegetables until a good brown colour, lift out of the pan.
3. Fry the meat on all sides over a fierce heat to seal in juices.
4. Return the vegetables to the pan, with just enough water to give approximately 1½ inch (3 cm.) in depth.
5. Season well.
6. Put the meat on top of vegetables and cover pan. If you are unsure whether the lid fits tightly, put piece of foil or a cloth under this.
7. Either cook very gently on top of the stove or in the oven allowing 30 minutes per lb. (½ kg.). The vegetables should not be too small otherwise they break badly during cooking.
8. Carve the meat as you would a roast joint. The liquid at the bottom of the pan makes delicious gravy.

Note: Other pieces of meat which are excellent for pot roasting are fresh brisket, i.e., unsalted, half leg lamb, etc.

Variation
Large potatoes may be added.

Cooking time: 3 hours
Preparation time: 15—20 minutes
Main cooking utensil: strong saucepan or cast-iron casserole with
   well-fitting lid
Oven temperature: moderate (350°F., 180°C., Gas Mark 4)
Oven position: centre
Serves: 6—8

Tournedos of fillet steak with herbs

Imperial
1 lb. potatoes (weight when peeled)
fat or oil for frying
4 medium-sized fillet steaks
4 strips bacon fat
seasoning
½–1 teaspoon mixed dried tarragon or rosemary
3 oz. butter
Garnish:
parsley
tomatoes

Metric
½ kg. potatoes (weight when peeled)
fat or oil for frying
4 medium-sized fillet steaks
4 strips bacon fat
seasoning
½–1 teaspoon mixed dried tarragon or rosemary
75 g. butter
Garnish:
parsley
tomatoes

1. Peel the potatoes, cut them into matchstick shapes, dry well.
2. Fry them steadily in hot fat or oil until tender and pale golden, but not brown. Lift out of the pan.
3. Form each steak into a round shape with your hands, arrange the bacon fat round the sides and tie with fine string.
4. Season lightly, press the herbs into both sides of the meat very firmly with the back of a knife.
5. Heat the butter and fry the steaks; allow 2 minutes over a fairly high heat on each side for very rare steaks, then lower the heat and cook for a further 4–6 minutes according to personal taste.
6. Meanwhile, re-heat the fat or oil, put in the matchstick potatoes, fry until crisp and drain on absorbent paper.
7. Arrange the potatoes on individual plates, top with a tournedos, garnish with parsley and segments of tomato, serve with salad.

Note: To save time, heat commercial potato crisps instead of making matchstick potatoes.

Cooking time: 15 minutes
Preparation time: 15 minutes
Main cooking utensils: saucepan for fat or oil and frying basket, frying pan
Serves: 4

Tournedos à la Rossini

Imperial
4 fillet steaks
4 slices of bread
3 oz. butter or 2 oz. butter and 1 tablespoon oil
Sauce:
4 tablespoons brown stock
4 tablespoons Madeira
Garnish:
4 slices pâté
4 truffles (see note)

Metric
4 fillet steaks
4 slices of bread
75 g. butter or 50 g. butter and 1 tablespoon oil
Sauce:
4 tablespoons brown stock
4 tablespoons Madeira
Garnish:
4 slices pâté
4 truffles (see note)

1. Tie the meat into rounds, unless this has been done by the butcher.
2. Fry rounds or squares of bread in hot butter or butter and oil until crisp and golden brown.
3. Put onto a hot dish and keep warm.
4. Fry the meat on both sides. For underdone steak this should be served almost at once without further cooking; for medium-done steak, cook for 2–3 minutes each side, lower the heat and cook for a further 2–3 minutes; for well done steak, cook on each side for 2–3 minutes, then allow a further 4–5 minutes. Lift on to the bread.
5. Blend the stock and Madeira together in the pan, and pour round the steaks.
6. Top with pâté and truffles. Serve at once with sauté potatoes and watercress.

Note: If you cannot get truffles use cooked mushrooms instead. You can grill the steaks instead of frying them if you prefer.

Sauté potatoes
Fry diced or sliced cooked potatoes in hot fat until brown.

Cooking time: see stage 4
Preparation time: few minutes
Main cooking utensils: large frying pan, pan for potatoes
Serves: 4

Meatballs with cheese

Imperial

Meatballs:
12 oz. beef (rump steak, sirloin
  or topside)
4 oz. bacon
1 onion
pinch oregano (wild marjoram)
little grated nutmeg
seasoning
2 oz. breadcrumbs
little stock or milk (optional)
To coat:
1 oz. seasoned flour or
  1 egg and 2 oz. crisp
  breadcrumbs
To fry:
2 oz. butter
1 tablespoon oil
Cheese topping:
8 oz. Bel Paese, Mozzarella
  or Gruyère cheese

Metric

Meatballs:
300 g. beef (rump steak, sirloin
  or topside)
100 g. bacon
1 onion
pinch oregano (wild marjoram)
little grated nutmeg
seasoning
50 g. breadcrumbs
little stock or milk (optional)
To coat:
25 g. seasoned flour or
  1 egg and 50 g. crisp
  breadcrumbs
To fry:
50 g. butter
1 tablespoon oil
Cheese topping:
200 g. Bel Paese, Mozzarella
  or Gruyère cheese

1. Put the meat, bacon and onion through the mincer at least once.
2. Blend with the rest of the ingredients for the meatballs.
3. If dry, blend with a little stock or milk.
4. Form into balls, roll either in seasoned flour or egg and crumbs.
5. Fry steadily in hot butter and oil until crisp and golden brown.
6. Put on to skewers, top with a little cheese and put a slice of cheese between each ball.
7. Heat under the grill until the cheese has melted. Serve at once — in the picture the balls are served on cooked cabbage leaves to set off their colour.

Cooking time: 10–15 minutes
Preparation time: 20 minutes
Main cooking utensils: frying pan, skewers and grill pan
Serves: 4

Oven pot roast with mustard sauce

Imperial

3–3½ lb. fresh brisket
  or topside of beef
seasoning
1 clove garlic
2 oz. dripping or fat
about 8 good-sized onions
8 large carrots
8 large potatoes
½ pint brown stock or red wine
Mustard sauce:
½ oz. flour
1 level tablespoon dry mustard

Metric

1½–1¾ kg. fresh brisket
  or topside of beef
seasoning
1 clove garlic
50 g. dripping or fat
about 8 good-sized onions
8 large carrots
8 large potatoes
300 ml. brown stock or red wine
Mustard sauce:
15 g. flour
1 level tablespoon dry mustard

1. Dry the meat, season well.
2. Skin the garlic, and cut into narrow strips, press these into the meat.
3. Heat the dripping or fat in the bottom of the roasting tin or the casserole and turn the meat in this.
4. Cook for 40 minutes, turning once or twice until the meat is golden brown.
5. Lift the meat on to a plate or dish, add the vegetables to the tin or casserole (if there is too much fat pour away a little before adding the vegetables, but leave at least 1 tablespoon fat).
6. Season the vegetables, add stock or wine.
7. Place the meat on top of the vegetables.
8. Cover the tin or casserole and cook in the centre of a moderate oven for 1½ hours.
9. Put the meat on to the serving dish with the vegetables. Strain off the liquid.
10. Blend with the flour and mustard and cook until thickened slightly. Serve the meat with the sauce.

Cooking time: 2¼ hours
Preparation time: 20 minutes
Main cooking utensils: covered roasting tin or casserole, saucepan
Oven temperature: moderate (325–350°F., 170–180°C.,
  Gas Mark 3–4)
Oven position: towards the top of the oven, then centre
Serves: 6–8

Stewed steak and dumplings

Imperial	Metric
1–1½ lb. beef steak	½–¾ kg. beef steak
seasoning	seasoning
1½ oz. fat	40 g. fat
2 onions	2 onions
2 or 3 large carrots	2 or 3 large carrots
¾ pint water	425 ml. water
½ bay leaf	½ bay leaf
little nutmeg or mixed herbs	little nutmeg or mixed herbs
Dumplings:	*Dumplings:*
4 oz. flour (with plain flour use ¾ teaspoon baking powder)	100 g. flour (with plain flour use ¾ teaspoon baking powder)
seasoning	seasoning
2 oz. shredded suet	50 g. shredded suet
water to mix	water to mix

1. Cut the meat into neat squares.
2. Season, then brown in the fat.
3. Add the sliced onions and carrots, water and flavourings.
4. Transfer the contents to a casserole and cook for 2 hours in the oven.
5. Make the dumplings: Sieve the dry ingredients together, add the suet and mix to a soft dough with the water.
6. Roll into balls with lightly floured hands.
7. Check there is sufficient liquid in the stew, then drop in the dumplings and cook for 15–20 minutes.
8. Serve the stew with the dumplings and a green vegetable.

Variation
Extra vegetables may be added to the stew. A good flavour is given by adding 2 cloves and 2 teaspoons vinegar, or for a stew with a thicker consistency, coat the meat in 1 oz. (25 g.) seasoned flour.

Dumplings may be varied by adding chopped herbs, etc.

Cooking time: 2½ hours
Preparation time: 15 minutes
Main cooking utensils: large saucepan, casserole
Oven temperature: moderate (350°F., 180°C., Gas Mark 4)
Oven position: centre
Serves: 4

Beef and mushroom casserole

Imperial	Metric
1 lb. stewing steak	½ kg. stewing steak
1 oz. cornflour	25 g. cornflour
seasoning	seasoning
2 tablespoons corn oil	2 tablespoons corn oil
2 onions	2 onions
1 clove garlic	1 clove garlic
2 beef stock cubes	2 beef stock cubes
1 pint hot water	½ litre hot water
5 tablespoons red wine (optional)	5 tablespoons red wine (optional)
2 carrots	2 carrots
1 small green pepper	1 small green pepper
1 small red pepper and/or a few tomatoes	1 small red pepper and/or a few tomatoes
2 oz. mushrooms	50 g. mushrooms
Garnish:	*Garnish:*
black olives	black olives

1. Cut the meat into neat pieces.
2. Coat with the cornflour blended with seasoning.
3. Heat the oil in the pan and toss the sliced onion and finely chopped garlic in this for 2–3 minutes.
4. Put the coated meat into the pan and cook gently for 5 minutes stirring all the time.
5. Blend the stock cubes with the hot water, pour into the pan.
6. Bring to the boil, add the wine and stir as the mixture thickens.
7. Add the sliced carrots, then spoon the mixture into the casserole.
8. Cover and cook for 1½ hours in a cool to moderate oven.
9. Remove from the oven, add the diced green pepper and the diced red pepper (discard cores and seeds) and/or the skinned tomatoes and the sliced mushrooms.
10. Return to the oven for a further 30 minutes. Serve topped with olives and with mashed potatoes or boiled rice.

Cooking time: 2¼–2½ hours
Preparation time: 25 minutes
Main cooking utensils: saucepan, covered casserole
Oven temperature: cool to moderate (300–325°F., 150–170°C., Gas Mark 2–3)
Oven position: centre
Serves: 4

African beef stew

Imperial	Metric
1¼–1½ lb. stewing steak	½–¾ kg. stewing steak
2 large onions	2 large onions
2 large carrots	2 large carrots
1–2 cloves garlic	1–2 cloves garlic
1½ oz. butter or peanut butter	40 g. butter or peanut butter
2 level tablespoons tomato purée or ketchup	2 level tablespoons tomato purée or ketchup
1 bay leaf	1 bay leaf
pinch powdered cloves	pinch powdered cloves
pinch powdered ginger	pinch powdered ginger
shake cayenne pepper	shake cayenne pepper
seasoning	seasoning
tablespoon lemon juice or vinegar	tablespoon lemon juice or vinegar
¾ pint stock or water and 2 stock cubes	375 ml. stock or water and 2 stock cubes
1 oz. peanut butter	25 g. peanut butter
1 oz. flour	25 g. flour
2–3 tablespoons water	2–3 tablespoons water

1. Cut the meat into neat pieces, then peel and slice the onions and carrots and crush the cloves of garlic.
2. Melt the butter or peanut butter and toss the meat and vegetables in this for a few minutes.
3. Stir in the tomato purée, bay leaf, spices and seasoning, together with the lemon juice and stock.
4. Transfer to a casserole and cook for 2–2½ hours in the oven.
5. Add the peanut butter and the flour blended with the water.
6. Cook, stirring well, for a few minutes until well thickened. Taste, and re-season if wished. Serve with mashed sweet or ordinary potatoes.

Variation

Use diced boiling chicken instead of beef. A very little honey added gives a faintly sweet taste to this type of stew.

Cooking time: 2¾ hours
Preparation time: 35 minutes
Main cooking utensil: saucepan, casserole
Oven temperature: moderate (350°F., 180°C., Gas Mark 4)
Oven position: centre
Serves: 4–5

Beef olives

Imperial	Metric
1½ lb. beef topside or silverside, cut into 6 thin slices	¾ kg. beef topside or silverside, cut into 6 thin slices
seasoning	seasoning
Stuffing:	*Stuffing:*
1 medium-sized onion	1 medium-sized onion
2 oz. butter or margarine	50 g. butter or margarine
3 oz. soft white breadcrumbs	75 g. soft white breadcrumbs
1 oz. Parmesan cheese, grated	25 g. Parmesan cheese, grated
1 tablespoon chopped parsley	1 tablespoon chopped parsley
2 tablespoons finely chopped celery (optional)	2 tablespoons finely chopped celery (optional)
1 egg	1 egg
seasoning	seasoning
Sauce:	*Sauce:*
2 onions	2 onions
4 tablespoons oil	4 tablespoons oil
4 large tomatoes	4 large tomatoes
½ pint beef stock	300 ml. beef stock
¼ pint red wine	150 ml. red wine
2 bay leaves	2 bay leaves

1. Chop the onion for the stuffing and fry for a few minutes in the hot butter or margarine.
2. Remove pan from heat and add other stuffing ingredients.
3. Lay the slices of beef on a board and season lightly, then roll with a rolling pin until paper thin.
4. Spread with the stuffing and roll firmly, secure with cotton.
5. Chop onions for sauce and fry in oil for a few minutes.
6. Add the beef rolls and brown these in the onion mixture.
7. Add the skinned chopped tomatoes, stock or water and stock cube, wine, bay leaves and seasoning.
8. Cover the pan and simmer for 1 hour until the meat is tender.
9. Lift the meat rolls on to a hot dish, boil the sauce until reduced in quantity. Pour the sauce over the rolls and serve with carrots, peas and creamed potatoes.

Cooking time: 1½ hours
Preparation time: 30 minutes
Main cooking utensils: 1 or 2 saucepans (1 with lid)
Serves: 6

Buying and cooking minced beef

When beef is minced it becomes a very versatile and economical purchase, for there is no wastage and the meat can be mixed with other ingredients. In most recipes, minced stewing steak could be chosen, although you could use a better-quality meat if you make your own hamburgers or other similar dishes. Buy minced beef carefully, it must look pleasantly moist and bright in colour; the many cut surfaces means it deteriorates very quickly, so use as soon as possible after purchase. If you freeze minced meat, or cooked dishes with minced meat, use within 2 months.

Mince collops: This is one of the traditional ways of cooking minced beef. Fry 1–2 finely chopped onions in 1 oz. (25 g.) fat, then stir in 1 oz. (25 g.) flour and blend in a **generous** ½ pint (3 dl.) stock, or water with ½–1 beef stock cube. Bring the sauce to the boil, stir as it thickens, then add 1 lb. (½ kg.) raw minced beef. Stir well until the meat blends with the sauce, add seasoning, chopped herbs or any other flavourings desired. Cover the pan, lower the heat and simmer gently for 45 minutes to 1 hour. Serve with toast, creamed potatoes, cooked rice or noodles. **Serves 4.**

Using a pressure cooker

A pressure cooker is an ideal way of producing stock, or cooking stews, etc., in a very short time. To make stock put the bones in the cooker with water to cover; do not use as much liquid as you would require in an ordinary pan, for there is little loss due to evaporation in a pressure cooker. It is important that the cooker is not more than two-thirds filled with food, etc. Place the lid into position, together with the weight. Follow the instructions given by the manufacturer and bring pressure to 15 lb. (7 kg.). Lower the heat and maintain the pressure for ½–1 hour, then allow the pressure to **drop** at room temperature and use the stock (see also pages 18 and 65).

If making a stew in a pressure cooker, follow the recipe as given for an ordinary pan, but reduce the amount of liquid to about two-thirds of the recommended amount. Fry the vegetables and/or meat in the pressure cooker, without the lid in position, then add the rest of the ingredients as given in the recipe. Place the lid in position, bring to 15 lb. (7 kg.) pressure, lower the heat and time accordingly. A beef stew takes 15 minutes at this pressure; allow pressure to drop at room temperature, then serve the stew.

Spicy cottage pie

Cooking time: 1 hour 20 minutes
Preparation time: 20 minutes
Main cooking utensils: frying pan, covered casserole, saucepan
Oven temperature: moderate to moderately hot (350–375°F.,
   180–190°C., Gas Mark 4–5)
Oven position: centre
Serves: 4–6

Imperial	Metric
1–2 onions	1–2 onions
3 oz. margarine or butter	75 g. margarine or butter
1 lb. minced beef	½ kg. minced beef
1 tablespoon flour	1 tablespoon flour
¼ pint water or chicken stock	150 ml. water or chicken stock
1–2 tablespoons Angostura bitters	1–2 tablespoons Angostura bitters
seasoning	seasoning
1–1½ lb. potatoes	½–¾ kg. potatoes
1 tablespoon milk	1 tablespoon milk
little grated nutmeg	little grated nutmeg
1 egg, separated	1 egg, separated

1. Peel and chop the onions very finely.
2. Heat 2 oz. (50 g.) margarine or butter in the frying pan.
3. Cook the onions and the beef until a pleasant golden colour.
4. Sprinkle with the flour, then stir in the water or stock and the Angostura.
5. Heat steadily, stirring all the time, then add seasoning to taste.
6. Transfer to a casserole, cover and cook for 30 minutes in a moderate oven.
7. Meanwhile cook the potatoes in salted water until soft.
8. Strain, mash, then beat in the rest of the margarine or butter, milk, nutmeg and seasoning, together with the egg yolk.
9. Remove the casserole from the oven. Spread or pipe the potatoes over the top and brush with the egg white.
10. Return to the oven, without a lid and continue cooking for a further 30 minutes. Serve with mixed vegetables.

Note: Angostura bitters are not only excellent in drinks but add interest to many dishes.

Cold boiled beef and coleslaw

Imperial
1 lb. cold sliced beef
Coleslaw:
½ small white cabbage (see note)
1 diced apple
few sticks celery
few raisins
French dressing (see page 14)
2–3 tablespoons mayonnaise (see page 47)

Metric
½ kg. cold sliced beef
Coleslaw:
½ small white cabbage (see note)
1 diced apple
few sticks celery
few raisins
French dressing (see page 14)
2–3 tablespoons mayonnaise (see page 47)

1. Slice the beef neatly and arrange on a dish.
2. Shred the cabbage very finely.
3. Mix with the peeled, diced apple, chopped celery and the raisins. Mix the French dressing with the mayonnaise. Spoon this over the salad and toss well.

Note: If white cabbage is unobtainable then use the inside of any cabbage. Do not use coarse outer leaves. Sprouts can also be shredded and used.

Variations
Use cold roasted beef, boiled brisket or silverside of beef, salted if wished.
Add a little grated horseradish to dressing.

Preparation time: 15 minutes
Main utensils: sharp knife
Serves: 4

To boil meat

As explained on page 55, the term 'boiling' is not a correct one to describe the cooking of meat in liquids; the water, or other liquid used, should simmer gently, so that the meat cooks slowly and evenly. Times for boiling meat are given in the various tables, but remember this is the minimum cooking time; if you buy a rather thick piece of meat you could increase the time slightly, without harming the meat in any way.

Often when meat is cooked in liquid, you find you have a slight grey 'scum' at the top of the liquid, and this should be removed during the early stages of cooking.

Meat may be cooked in water; if the meat is ready salted, as tongue, brisket or silverside, bacon or ham, you do not add salt, but just pepper, herbs and vegetables. You could use stock, but check this is not too salt. A little wine may be added to the stock or water, or try cooking the meat in a cheap cider. Bacon is very good cooked in cider or in a mixture of ginger ale or ginger beer and water. Dumplings, as the recipe on page 62, may be added towards the end of the cooking time. If you intend serving the boiled meat as a cold dish, allow it to cool in the stock.

Making dripping

Page 18 gives details of making stock and this can always be produced from the bones of a joint or after boiling meat (see above).

After cooking meat you may find you have a quite appreciable amount of fat in the roasting tin or top of the stock. Do not waste this, use in cooking as it gives flavour and saves spending money on other fats for frying, etc. Dripping should be cleaned, the correct term is 'clarified'. If you want to store it allow the dripping to set, put into a pan with water to cover. Heat slowly until the dripping melts again. Cool once more; you will find most of the tiny pieces of meat, etc. have dropped into the water. Lift the solid dripping from the water, turn upside-down, scrape away the remaining tiny particles of meat. Beef dripping is best, as this is a particularly rich fat.

Meat jelly: When you have let the dripping set, (before clarifying), you will probably find you have a layer of meat jelly under the dripping. This is delicious added to soups, stews, etc. and since it is remarkably rich in flavour a little of the jelly adds a great deal of additional taste to the food.

Lamb or mutton

Method of cooking	Cut	Cooking time	To serve
Roasting	Leg Loin and saddle Best end of neck (lamb) Shoulder Breast stuffed and rolled.	20 minutes per lb. ($\frac{1}{2}$ kg.) plus 20 minutes over (see page 67).	Mutton: Redcurrant jelly Lamb: mint jelly or mint sauce Fresh peas.
Grilling or frying	Loin chops Gigot chops Cutlets (use as part of mixed grill).	10–15 minutes (see page 69).	Chipped potatoes Tomatoes Mushrooms Peas Salad.
Stewing, braising or boiling	Neck Breast Leg Shoulder.	$1\frac{1}{2}$–$2\frac{1}{2}$ hours (see page 70).	Mixed vegetables Creamed potatoes.
Soups or stock	Scrag end of neck Head Trotters.	$1\frac{1}{2}$–$2\frac{1}{2}$ hours (see page 18).	

LAMB OR MUTTON

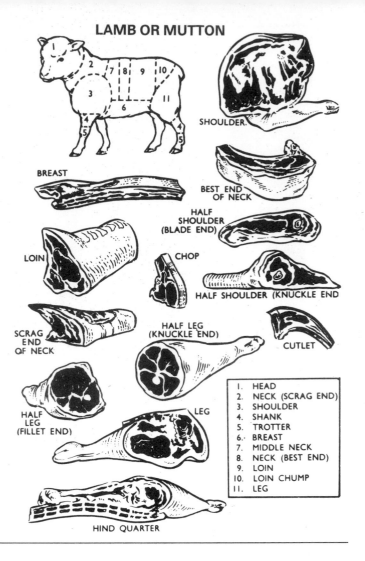

SHOULDER
BREAST
BEST END OF NECK
HALF SHOULDER (BLADE END)
LOIN
CHOP
HALF SHOULDER (KNUCKLE END)
SCRAG END OF NECK
HALF LEG (KNUCKLE END)
CUTLET
HALF LEG (FILLET END)
LEG
HIND QUARTER

1. HEAD
2. NECK (SCRAG END)
3. SHOULDER
4. SHANK
5. TROTTER
6. BREAST
7. MIDDLE NECK
8. NECK (BEST END)
9. LOIN
10. LOIN CHUMP
11. LEG

Rolled breast of lamb

Imperial
1 large or 2 smaller breasts of lamb
seasoning
Stuffing:
3 oz. cooked long-grain rice
1$\frac{1}{2}$ oz. melted margarine or shredded suet
3 oz. seedless raisins
1–2 tablespoons chopped parsley
seasoning
1 egg

Metric
1 large or 2 smaller breasts of lamb
seasoning
Stuffing:
75 g. cooked long-grain rice
40 g. melted margarine or shredded suet
75 g. seedless raisins
1–2 tablespoons chopped parsley
seasoning
1 egg

1. Remove the bones from the lamb and put these bones into a pan with seasoned water to cover.
2. Put a lid on the pan and simmer for 45 minutes.
3. Mix all the ingredients for the stuffing together and spread over the meat.
4. Roll firmly and tie or skewer.
5. Put into the casserole, do not cover, cook for 25 minutes in a moderately hot oven to extract surplus fat.
6. Pour this fat away then pour the strained stock from stage 1 round the meat (this ensures a very moist flavour) to a depth of 1 inch (2 cm.).
7. Cover the casserole, lower the heat to moderate and cook for 45 minutes. Serve hot or cold, cut into neat slices, with a mixed salad.

Variation
Chopped soaked (but not cooked) prunes can be used in place of the raisins.

Cooking time: nearly 2 hours (including making the stock)
Preparation time: 20 minutes
Main cooking utensils: covered saucepan, covered deep casserole
Oven temperature: moderately hot (400°F., 200°C., Gas Mark 6) then moderate (325–350°F., 170–180°C., Gas Mark 3–4)
Oven position: centre
Serves: 4

Lamb with mushroom sauce

Imperial	Metric
2½ lb. loin of lamb	1¼ kg. loin of lamb
3 oz. butter	75 g. butter
seasoning	seasoning
8 oz. small mushrooms	200 g. small mushrooms
1 oz. flour	25 g. flour
½ pint white stock	250 ml. white stock
2 tablespoons brandy (optional)	2 tablespoons brandy (optional)
2 tablespoons thin cream	2 tablespoons thin cream
1 tablespoon chopped marjoram or oregano (wild marjoram)	1 tablespoon chopped marjoram or oregano (wild marjoram)
4 large or 8 smaller tomatoes	4 large or 8 smaller tomatoes

1. Brush the lean part of the lamb with some of the butter.
2. Roast until tender, allowing 20 minutes per lb. (½ kg.) and 20 minutes over, and reducing the heat from hot to moderately hot after about 30 minutes.
3. Towards the end of the cooking time, spoon a little lamb dripping into a saucepan, add the remaining butter and toss the well-seasoned mushrooms in this. Lift out, keep hot, blend in the flour, cook for several minutes, then gradually blend in the stock.
4. Bring to the boil, cook until thickened, add the brandy, if used, and cream, replace the mushrooms and add half the marjoram or oregano.
5. Bake the tomatoes until just soft, seasoning them well.
6. Put the mushrooms and sauce round the meat, add the tomatoes and top with the remaining marjoram or oregano.

Cooking time: 1 hour 10 minutes
Preparation time: 15 minutes
Main cooking utensils: roasting tin, saucepan
Oven temperature: hot (425–450°F., 220–230°C., Gas Mark 7–8) then moderately hot (375–400°F., 190–200°C., Gas Mark 5–6)
Oven position: above centre
Serves: 4

Garlic-flavoured lamb

Imperial	Metric
1–2 cloves garlic	1–2 cloves garlic
1 small leg or shoulder of young lamb	1 small leg or shoulder of young lamb
4 oz. butter	100 g. butter
French mustard	French mustard
pepper	pepper
little flour	little flour

1. Peel the garlic cloves and slice them thinly lengthwise into slivers. Make slits in the meat and push the garlic slivers into the cuts.
2. Spread the meat with the butter and a thin layer of mustard.
3. Sprinkle lightly with pepper and a little flour to give a crisp finish to the meat.
4. Roast in a hot oven, reducing the heat to moderately hot after the first 20 minutes. Serve the lamb with matchstick potatoes, made by frying tiny strips of potato until golden brown and crisp.

Note: This method of cooking lamb with garlic is suitable for very young lamb, which is not too fat. Older meat is more fatty and with the generous amount of butter in the recipe would give a greasy result.

Variation
Very young lamb is usually served underdone in France, where this recipe comes from. Roast the meat for 15 minutes per lb. (½ kg.) and 15 minutes over if you prefer lamb less well cooked.

Cooking time: 20 minutes per lb. (½ kg.) and 20 minutes over
Preparation time: 15 minutes
Main cooking utensil: roasting tin
Oven temperature: hot (425°F., 220°C., Gas Mark 7) then moderately hot (400°F., 200°C., Gas Mark 6)
Serves: 6

Roast lamb with rosemary

Imperial	Metric
2 oz. butter	50 g. butter
small leg of lamb	small leg of lamb
seasoning	seasoning
rosemary	rosemary
clove garlic (optional)	clove garlic (optional)
2 lb. potatoes	1 kg. potatoes
Garnish:	*Garnish:*
sprigs rosemary	sprigs rosemary

1. Spread butter over lamb and season well.
2. Stick rosemary leaves into the fat of the meat.
3. Insert a clove of garlic near the bone if you like.
4. Place the joint on a rack in a meat tin.
5. Roast for 20 minutes to the lb. (450 g.) and 20 minutes over.
6. Peel potatoes and cut into ½-inch (1-cm.) thick slices.
7. Place them under the meat after it has been cooking for 30 minutes.
8. Baste joint from time to time.
9. When cooked, garnish with sprigs of rosemary. Serve with roast onions or leeks in a white sauce or tossed in butter.

Variation

Roast meat more slowly, i.e., 30 minutes per lb. and 30 minutes over, in a moderately hot oven (375–400°F., 190–200°C., Gas Mark 5–6).

Cooking time: see stage 5
Main cooking utensils: rack, roasting tin
Oven temperature: hot (425–450°F., 220°–230°C., Gas Mark 7–8)
Oven position: above centre
Serves: 6

Crown roast of lamb

Imperial	Metric
1 or 2 joints of loin, approximately 12–14 chops	1 or 2 joints of loin, approximately 12–14 chops
1 oz. butter or fat	25 g. butter or fat
seasoning	seasoning
Prune and apricot stuffing:	*Prune and apricot stuffing:*
1 oz. butter	25 g. butter
1 medium onion, chopped	1 medium onion, chopped
2 oz. boiled rice	50 g. boiled rice
4 oz. prunes, chopped and stoned	100 g. prunes, chopped and stoned
1 oz. ground almonds	25 g. ground almonds
3–4 whole apricots, fresh or canned	3–4 whole apricots, fresh or canned
1 tablespoon chopped parsley	1 tablespoon chopped parsley
grated rind of 1 lemon	grated rind of 1 lemon
juice of 1 lemon	juice of 1 lemon
1 egg	1 egg
seasoning	seasoning

1. Ask the butcher to cut and tie the meat into a round (crown roast), brush with melted butter or fat and season.
2. Melt the butter and cook the chopped onion until transparent.
3. Add the rice and prunes and cook together for a few minutes.
4. Mix in ground almonds, sliced apricots, parsley, lemon rind and juice.
5. Bind with egg and season.
6. Place the stuffing in the centre of the crown roast.
7. Wrap a piece of kitchen foil around each bone to protect it while cooking.
8. Roast for 25 minutes to the lb. (½ kg.) and 25 minutes over, weighing the roast after stuffing.
9. Remove the foil and place a cutlet frill on the end of each bone.

Cooking time: see stage 8
Preparation time: 20 minutes
Main cooking utensils: saucepan, roasting tin
Oven temperature: moderately hot (375–400°F., 190–200°C., Gas Mark 5–6)
Oven position: centre
Serves: 6–14 (depending on the size of the chops)

Lamb cutlets in pastry cases

Imperial	Metric
6 large lamb cutlets	6 large lamb cutlets
seasoning	seasoning
½ tablespoon chopped chives	½ tablespoon chopped chives
1 teaspoon chopped mint	1 teaspoon chopped mint
Pastry:	*Pastry:*
10–12 oz. plain flour	250–300 g. plain flour
pinch salt	pinch salt
6 oz. butter	150 g. butter
water to bind	water to bind
Glaze:	*Glaze:*
1 egg	1 egg

1. Grill or fry the lamb cutlets for about 5–10 minutes depending upon thickness, season, sprinkle with chopped chives and mint. Allow to cool.
2. Meanwhile, make the pastry. Sieve the flour and salt, rub in the butter, bind with water to form a rolling consistency.
3. Roll out thinly and cut into triangles large enough to cover meat.
4. Lay a cutlet on each triangle of pastry. Brush the edges with water, wrap round the meat. Garnish with leaves of pastry and brush with beaten egg.
5. Bake for approximately 25 minutes in a moderately hot to hot oven, then lower the heat to very moderate and leave for a further 15 minutes.
6. Serve hot with flageolets or young broad beans tossed in butter and chopped parsley.

Variation

Spread the cutlets with a stuffing made of pork sausage meat and chopped herbs, then wrap in pastry.

Cooking time: 45–50 minutes
Preparation time: 15 minutes
Main cooking utensils: frying or grill pan, baking tray
Oven temperature: moderately hot to hot (400–425°F., 200–220°C., Gas Mark 6–7) then very moderate (325°F., 170°C., Gas Mark 3)
Oven position: just above centre
Serves: 6

Lamb with peppercorns

Imperial	Metric
6 large lamb chops	6 large lamb chops
6 oz. butter	150 g. butter
about 24–30 peppercorns	about 24–30 peppercorns
(depending on taste)	(depending on taste)
Duchesse potatoes:	*Duchesse potatoes:*
2¼ lb. potatoes (weight when peeled)	generous 1 kg. potatoes (weight when peeled)
3 oz. butter	75 g. butter
3 egg yolks	3 egg yolks
seasoning	seasoning
Garnish:	*Garnish:*
3 large tomatoes	3 large tomatoes
1½ lb. French beans	¾ kg. French beans
parsley	parsley

1. Cut away the bone from each chop so that the meat may be rolled into a round called a noisette.
2. Brush the lean part of the meat with a little melted butter, press the crushed peppercorns into one side of the meat, turn the noisettes over and repeat on the second side.
3. Boil the potatoes in salted water until just soft, strain and mash, add the butter, egg yolks and seasoning. Divide into 12 portions and form into 12 cakes with a palette knife.
4. Heat half the butter in a pan, fry rounds of Duchesse potatoes until golden coloured on both sides.
5. Put on a hot dish, top half the rounds with halved, seasoned tomatoes; heat these in the oven while frying the noisettes.
6. Fry the noisettes in the remaining butter until tender.
7. Lift the noisettes on to the rounds of Duchesse potatoes, put on to a serving dish with the drained cooked beans and parsley.

Cooking time: 45 minutes
Preparation time: 20 minutes
Main cooking utensils: 2 saucepans, grill pan, ovenproof serving dish
Oven temperature: very moderate (350°F., 180°C., Gas Mark 4)
Oven position: centre
Serves: 6

New Zealand style lamb

Imperial
1½ lb. neck of lamb (see note)
seasoning
1 oz. flour
1 large onion
8 small onions
3–4 tomatoes
1 green pepper
2 oz. fat or 2 tablespoons oil
1 pint brown stock or ¾ pint
   brown stock and ¼ pint
   red wine
pinch marjoram

Metric
¾ kg. neck of lamb (see note)
seasoning
25 g. flour
1 large onion
8 small onions
3–4 tomatoes
1 green pepper
50 g. fat or 2 tablespoons oil
575 ml. brown stock or 425 ml.
   brown stock and 150 ml.
   red wine
pinch marjoram

1. Divide the meat into neat pieces and coat in seasoned flour.
2. Peel and slice the large onion, but leave the smaller ones whole.
3. Slice the tomatoes thickly; cut the green pepper into rings, discarding seeds and core.
4. Heat the fat.
5. Toss the meat in the hot fat for a few minutes, then add the vegetables and cook for a further 2–3 minutes.
6. Gradually blend in the stock, or stock and wine. Bring to the boil and cook until thickened.
7. Add the marjoram and transfer to the casserole.
8. Cook for approximately 1¾ hours.
9. Serve with rather thick slices of fresh bread or rolls. Spread with butter and flavour with crushed garlic or garlic salt.

Note: Choose middle or scrag end of neck. For a more luxurious dish, use best end of neck or even loin chops.

Variation
Garlic may be added to the other vegetables.

Cooking time: 1¾ hours
Preparation time: 20 minutes
Main cooking utensils: frying pan, casserole
Oven temperature: moderate (325–350°F., 170–180°C., Gas Mark 3–4)
Oven position: centre
Serves: 4

Savoury lamb and dumpling stew

Imperial
1–1½ lb. middle neck lamb
¾ oz. dripping
½–¾ lb. onions
1 lb. carrots
1¼ pint stock or water and
   stock cube
2 tablespoons tomato purée
seasoning
pinch sage or mixed herbs
1–2 teaspoons gravy browning
Dumplings:
8 oz. self-raising flour
1 teaspoon salt
½ teaspoon pepper
3–4 oz. suet
water to mix
Garnish:
parsley

Metric
½–¾ kg. middle neck lamb
20 g. dripping
225–350 g. onions
½ kg. carrots
scant ¾ litre stock or water and
   stock cube
2 tablespoons tomato purée
seasoning
pinch sage or mixed herbs
1–2 teaspoons gravy browning
Dumplings:
200 g. self-raising flour
1 teaspoon salt
½ teaspoon pepper
75–100 g. suet
water to mix
Garnish:
parsley

1. Divide the lamb into pieces and remove any excess fat.
2. Heat the dripping.
3. Fry the peeled and sliced onions and carrots.
4. Add the meat and fry for a further 1–2 minutes.
5. Gradually stir in the stock and tomato purée.
6. Bring to the boil, add remaining ingredients, cover pan tightly.
7. Simmer gently for 1½–2 hours.
8. Meanwhile make the dumplings. Sift the flour, salt and pepper together. Stir in the suet and add enough cold water to give a soft but not sticky dough. Divide the mixture into eight and shape each into a ball.
9. Thirty minutes before the end of the cooking time, add the dumplings to the stew. Place in a serving dish and garnish with parsley.

Cooking time: about 2½ hours
Preparation time: 25 minutes
Main cooking utensils: large saucepan
Serves: 4

Pork

Method of cooking	Cut	Cooking time	To serve
Roasting	Loin Leg Bladebone Spare rib.	25 minutes per lb. (½ kg.) plus 25 minutes over (see below).	Sage and onion stuffing Mustard Apple sauce Orange salad.
Frying or grilling	Chops from loin Chump chops Spare rib chops.	15–20 minutes (see page 74).	Apple sauce Apple rings Sage and onion stuffing Tomatoes Mushrooms.
Boiling or stewing	Head Hand and spring Belly Cuts given for roasting.	2½ hours.	Salads Mixed vegetables.

To produce crisp crackling

Most people like the fat skin of pork to become very crisp and have a good 'crackling'. First score with a knife, i.e. cut at regular intervals. Rub with oil or melted lard. You may like to sprinkle the fat with salt, as in the recipe below. This is not essential, but it gives a good flavour to the crackling

PORK

LEG
CHOP
LOIN
SPARE RIB
BLADE BONE
BELLY
HAND AND SPRING

1. HEAD
2. SPARE RIB
3. HAND
4. BELLY
5. LOIN
6. LEG.

Jellied loin of pork

Imperial	Metric
1 pint clear white stock	550 ml. clear white stock
3–4 lb. loin of pork	1½–2 kg. loin of pork
salt and little oil	salt and little oil
1–2 tablespoons sherry	1–2 tablespoons sherry
1–2 tablespoons lemon juice	1–2 tablespoons lemon juice
seasoning	seasoning
½ oz. gelatine (1 envelope)	15 g. gelatine (1 envelope)

1. Make the stock by simmering veal, pork or poultry bones with water for several hours. If liked a pig's trotter may be cooked with the bones, this adds to the setting quality and flavour of the stock, and therefore one should use slightly less gelatine at stage 4.
2. Whilst the stock is simmering roast the meat. Rub the meat with salt, brush it with a little oil and set it in a roasting tin. Cook the joint, allowing 25 minutes per lb. (½ kg.) and 25 minutes over, and reducing the heat to moderate after 20 minutes. When cooked, leave to cool.
3. Strain the stock very carefully indeed as it must be extremely clear and measure 1 pint (550 ml.). Blend the sherry with the lemon juice (the proportion of these is a matter of personal taste but the total amount must not exceed 3 tablespoons) and add to the stock. Taste and season well.
4. Dissolve the gelatine carefully in the warm stock. If the weather is warm reduce the amount of stock to give a total of 1 pint (550 ml.) after the addition of the sherry and lemon juice, this will give a stiffer jelly. If a pig's trotter was used in the stock at stage 1, use slightly less gelatine.
5. Cool the stock and allow it to stiffen slightly.
6. Remove any crisp skin from the meat and reserve.
7. Brush or spread the jelly over the meat and leave to set. Garnish with strips of crackling and parsley or chervil leaves. Brush this with liquid jelly and allow to set, then add the final coating. Serve garnished with watercress and tomatoes.

Cooking time: see stage 2 plus 2–3 hours for the stock
Preparation time: 30 minutes
Main cooking utensils: saucepan, roasting tin
Oven temperature: hot (425°F., 220°C., Gas Mark 7) then moderate (375°F., 190°C., Gas Mark 5)
Serves: 8

Loin of pork with piquant sauce

Imperial	Metric
1 loin of pork, approximately 5 lb. in weight	1 loin of pork, approximately 2½ kg. in weight
Glaze:	*Glaze:*
8-oz. can pineapple pieces	226-g. can pineapple pieces
½ pint water	300 ml. water
2 oz. black treacle	50 g. black treacle
1 level teaspoon dry mustard	1 level teaspoon dry mustard
1 level teaspoon salt	1 level teaspoon salt
¼ level teaspoon pepper	¼ level teaspoon pepper
½ oz. cornflour	15 g. cornflour
1 stock cube	1 stock cube
1 tablespoon redcurrant jelly	1 tablespoon redcurrant jelly
1 tablespoon vinegar	1 tablespoon vinegar

1. Place the meat in a tin or casserole.
2. Drain the pineapple and mix the juice with the water.
3. Blend the treacle, mustard, salt and pepper with the fruit juice and water.
4. Pour this over the meat, cover with foil or a lid and cook, basting every 30 minutes.
5. Remove the cover 30 minutes before the end.
6. When cooked, transfer the meat to a heated dish.
7. Blend the cornflour, crushed stock cube, redcurrant jelly, vinegar and the liquid from the baking tin, bring to the boil on top of the cooker, stirring all the time.
8. Chop the pineapple and add this to the sauce, re-season. Serve with sprigged cauliflower or carrots tossed in melted butter.

Note: This is delicious served cold with salad.

Variation
Use golden syrup instead of treacle.

Cooking time: approximately 3 hours
Preparation time: 10 minutes
Main cooking utensils: deep covered casserole, saucepan
Oven temperature: moderate (350–375°F., 180–190°C., Gas Mark 4–5)
Oven position: centre
Serves: 8–10

Apricot pork chops

Imperial	Metric
4 pork loin chops	4 pork loin chops
1 oz. butter	25 g. butter
1 small onion	1 small onion
½ oz. flour	15 g. flour
1 small can halved apricots	1 small can halved apricots
1 tablespoon tomato purée	1 tablespoon tomato purée
grated rind of 1 small orange	grated rind of 1 small orange
1 bay leaf	1 bay leaf
2 tablespoons vinegar	2 tablespoons vinegar
seasoning	seasoning
Garnish:	*Garnish:*
orange slices	orange slices
parsley	parsley

1. Trim the chops if necessary and remove the rind.
2. Fry in the hot butter until just brown.
3. Place in a shallow casserole or heatproof dish.
4. Chop the onion and fry in the fat left in the pan.
5. Stir in the flour, cook for several minutes. Remove from the heat.
6. Reserve 2 apricots for garnish and sieve the rest to form a purée.
7. Stir the purée into the pan with the tomato purée, orange rind, bay leaf, vinegar and seasoning to taste.
8. Bring to the boil, stirring, and cook for 1–2 minutes.
9. Pour over the chops, cover and cook in the oven.
10. Remove the pith from the orange and slice the flesh.
11. Lift the chops from the casserole on to a hot dish.
12. Garnish with orange slices, apricots and parsley sprigs. Serve with the juice from the casserole in a sauceboat, and with green salad.

Variation
Use apple purée instead of apricot purée.

Cooking time: 35–40 minutes
Preparation time: 15 minutes
Main cooking utensils: frying pan, casserole
Oven temperature: moderately hot (400°F., 200°C., Gas Mark 6)
Oven position: centre
Serves: 2–4

Spare ribs of pork with barbecue sauce

Imperial	Metric
8 spare ribs of pork	8 spare ribs of pork
1 oz. butter	25 g. butter
seasoning	seasoning
Barbecue sauce:	*Barbecue sauce:*
1 oz. butter	25 g. butter
2 sliced onions	2 sliced onions
1 clove garlic	1 clove garlic
4 oz. mushrooms	100 g. mushrooms
medium-sized can tomatoes	medium-sized can tomatoes
1 teaspoon Worcestershire sauce	1 teaspoon Worcestershire sauce
1 teaspoon made mustard	1 teaspoon made mustard
½ teaspoon mixed herbs	½ teaspoon mixed herbs
½ teaspoon castor sugar	½ teaspoon castor sugar
seasoning	seasoning
Garnish:	*Garnish:*
watercress	watercress

1. Brush the spare ribs with melted butter and season well.
2. Grill for 15–20 minutes, turning once or twice and lowering heat after 10 minutes.
3. Melt butter in a pan.
4. Gently fry the onions and crushed clove of garlic, add chopped mushrooms and fry for a few minutes.
5. Add tomatoes, Worcestershire sauce, mustard, herbs, sugar and seasoning.
6. Simmer for about 10 minutes.
7. Pour over chops and garnish with fresh watercress. Serve with boiled carrots and creamed or jacket potatoes.

Variation
Use 6 large skinned fresh tomatoes and ¼ pint (125 ml.) stock instead of canned tomatoes.

Cooking time: 20 minutes
Preparation time: 15 minutes
Main cooking utensils: grill pan, saucepan
Serves: 4

Loin of pork with prunes

Imperial	Metric
4–6 oz. prunes	100–150 g. prunes
little sugar	little sugar
1–1½ lb. loin or fillet of pork	½–¾ kg. loin or fillet of pork
seasoning	seasoning
3–4 oz. butter	75–100 g. butter
glass schnapps or brandy	glass schnapps or brandy

1. Soak the prunes for several hours, or overnight, in water to cover, then simmer until tender with sugar to taste.
2. Cut the pork into neat pieces.
3. Season lightly, then fry in butter until tender, adding the prunes towards the end of the cooking time.
4. Add the schnapps or brandy, heat gently, then ignite and serve. Serve with boiled potatoes, topped with chopped dill, and cooked peas or beans.

To ignite brandy and other spirits: Make sure that you have a sufficient quantity, this is important when adding brandy to a very liquid mixture, and that it is warm before trying to light it.

Variation
Flavour pork with a little powdered ginger; fry a finely chopped onion in a pan with the pork; use sliced apples instead of prunes; add a little thin cream to the butter at stage 3.

Cooking time: 15 minutes plus time for cooking and soaking prunes
Preparation time: few minutes
Main cooking utensils: saucepan, frying pan
Serves: 4

Pork chops and frankfurters

Imperial
4 small pork chops (see note)
seasoning
2–3 oz. melted butter
4–8 frankfurters
1 green pepper (optional)
2 small eating apples
1 can sauerkraut (about 12 oz.)
Garnish:
parsley

Metric
4 small pork chops (see note)
seasoning
50–75 g. melted butter
4–8 frankfurters
1 green pepper (optional)
2 small eating apples
1 can sauerkraut (about 340 g.)
Garnish:
parsley

1. Season the pork chops. If they are very lean brush with a little melted butter. Grill until tender, turning over and lowering the heat when browned on either side.
2. Simmer the frankfurters in boiling water for 5 minutes, then drain.
3. Fry the cored sliced pepper and apples in the rest of the butter, add the sauerkraut and heat thoroughly.
4. Put the apple mixture on to a hot dish, top with the chops and frankfurters and garnish with parsley. Sliced raw tomatoes are a good accompaniment, or grilled mushrooms.

Note: Choose loin or spare rib chops.

Variation
Use canned corn instead of sauerkraut.

Cooking time: 20 minutes
Preparation time: 20 minutes
Main cooking utensils: grill pan, saucepan, frying pan
Serves: 4

Pork and vegetable ragoût

Imperial
8 oz. Brussels sprouts
8 oz. carrots
4 oz. turnips
2 onions
2 leeks
1 lb. lean pork, cut from leg or
 shoulder
3 oz. butter or margarine
1¼ pints chicken stock
seasoning
4 oz. long- or medium-grain
 rice
6 large tomatoes
2 teaspoons concentrated
 tomato purée
½–1 teaspoon yeast or meat
 extract

Metric
200 g. Brussels sprouts
200 g. carrots
100 g. turnips
2 onions
2 leeks
½ kg. lean pork, cut from leg or
 shoulder
75 g. butter or margarine
625 ml. chicken stock
seasoning
100 g. long- or medium-grain
 rice
6 large tomatoes
2 teaspoons concentrated
 tomato purée
½–1 teaspoon yeast or meat
 extract

1. Prepare the vegetables. Remove the outer leaves from sprouts, cut the peeled carrots and turnips into strips and the onions and leeks into thin slices.
2. Cut the pork into small pieces, season lightly.
3. Heat 2 oz. (50 g.) butter or margarine, toss the pork in it, add the vegetables and blend with the pork.
4. Stir in ¾ pint (375 ml.) of the stock, season and simmer steadily until the vegetables and meat are tender and the liquid absorbed.
5. Meanwhile, simmer the rice in the remainder of the stock until tender, and the liquid absorbed, about 15 minutes.
6. Simmer the skinned, deseeded tomatoes and the tomato purée with the remaining butter and add the yeast extract.
7. Put the tomato mixture into the mould, cover with the rice and leave in a warm place for a short time. Turn out and serve with the ragoût.

Cooking time: 45 minutes
Preparation time: 25 minutes
Main cooking utensils: 3 saucepans, 1-pint (½-litre) mould
Serves: 4–5

Veal

Method of cooking	Cut	Cooking time	To serve
Roasting	Shoulder Breast Best end of neck Loin Fillet Chump end of loin.	25 minutes per 1 lb. (½ kg.) plus 25 minutes over (see page 76).	Sausages Veal stuffing or other well-flavoured stuffing. Keep well basted.
Grilling or frying	Chops from loin Fillet Best end of neck chops Thin slices from leg — called 'fillets' and when cooked 'escalopes'.	15—20 minutes (see page 77).	Chipped potatoes Tomatoes Mushrooms.
Stewing or braising	Breast Fillet Knuckle Middle or scrag end of neck.	1½—2½ hours (see page 78).	Mixed vegetables Various sauces.
Boiling	Head Feet Breast.	1½—2½ hours (see page 56).	Mixed vegetables Salads.
Stock for soup, etc.	Feet Knuckle.	1½—2½ hours (see page 18).	

VEAL

FILLET (KNUCKLE END)
FILLET
FILLET STEAK
LEG
BREAST
MIDDLE NECK
SCRAG END
BEST END OF NECK
LOIN
KNUCKLE
SHOULDER
HALF SHOULDER

1. HEAD
2. NECK (SCRAG END)
3. SHOULDER
4. BREAST
5. NECK (BEST END)
6. LOIN
7. FILLET
8. KNUCKLE

Larding veal

Mention is made in the recipe for Veal with spring vegetables (page 76) of 'larding' veal. This is the classic way of incorporating fat into this exceptionally lean meat. You need strips of very fat bacon or belly of pork and a special larding needle. This is very like a carpet needle so the latter could be sterilised in boiling water and used instead. If you cannot 'lard' the meat, cover with plenty of fat and baste with the hot fat during cooking, or wrap the meat in well-greased foil.

Making interesting gravy

A good gravy makes a great deal of difference to the taste of roasted joints. The method of making gravy is given under Roast beef on page 58; it is traditional to serve a thicker gravy with joints such as veal, pork, etc. so use nearly twice the amount of flour given in the recipe. Add extra flavour to gravy by using the tiny particles of meat, stuffing, etc. that are in the roasting tin, then strain the gravy before serving. You may add a little wine.

A veal escalope coated with breadcrumbs and fried in butter (for other veal recipes see pages 76—78).

75

Veal or beef with spring vegetables

Imperial	Metric
12 oz. fat from bacon or fat pork	300 g. fat from bacon or fat pork
about 3½—4 lb. meat (see note)	about 1½—1¾ kg. meat (see note)
1 pint red wine	550 ml. red wine
1½ lb. small onions	¾ kg. small onions
8 oz. mushrooms	200 g. mushrooms
1½—2 lb. carrots	¾—1 kg. carrots
2 lb. peas	1 kg. peas

1. Cut the fat into long thin strips, put it into a larding needle (or use a carpet needle) and thread through the meat.
2. Cover the outside with more fat bacon.
3. For veal allow 25 minutes per lb. (½ kg.) and 25 minutes over, for beef allow 15—20 minutes to the lb. (½ kg.) and 15—20 minutes over. Roast in a hot oven, reducing the heat to moderately hot after 1½ hours if wished.
4. At the end of 1 hour pour the wine into the roasting tin, baste the meat and continue basting at 30 minute intervals.
5. Add the onions 45 minutes before the end of the cooking time, and add the mushrooms 15 minutes before the end of the cooking time.
6. Meanwhile cook the carrots in boiling, salted water for about 15 minutes.
7. Add the peas and continue cooking until both vegetables are tender.
8. Serve the veal hot with the vegetables. If wished the liquid may be thickened.

Note: Choose a joint of veal fillet or boned and rolled loin, beef topside or fresh brisket, châteaubriand steak or sirloin.

Variation

Other vegetables can be used, for example, young turnips, celeriac or young parsnips; cook these with the carrots.

Cooking time: see stage 3
Preparation time: 30 minutes
Main cooking utensils: roasting tin, saucepan
Oven temperature: hot (425—450°F., 220—230°C., Gas Mark 7—8) then moderately hot (400°F., 200°C., Gas Mark 6)
Oven position: above centre
Serves: 8

Rolled stuffed veal

Imperial	Metric
1 3-lb. boned joint veal (loin, shoulder or leg)	1 1½-kg. boned joint veal (loin, shoulder or leg)
2—3 oz. fat for basting	50—75 g. fat for basting
Stuffing:	*Stuffing:*
2 oz. butter	50 g. butter
4—5 large tomatoes	4—5 large tomatoes
1 green pepper	1 green pepper
1 red pepper	1 red pepper
2 onions	2 onions
6 oz. fat pork or bacon	150 g. fat pork or bacon
seasoning	seasoning
1 teaspoon mixed chopped fresh herbs or good pinch dried herbs	1 teaspoon mixed chopped fresh herbs or good pinch dried herbs

1. Cut the boned veal to make 2 'pockets', leave the very bottom of the meat uncut.
2. To make the stuffing, heat the butter, and fry the skinned, sliced tomatoes, strips of green and red pepper (discard the seeds and core) and finely chopped onions.
3. Blend with the strips of fat pork or bacon, seasoning and chopped herbs.
4. Insert a quarter of the mixture into the first pocket, another quarter into the second and spread half the rest over the top of the veal.
5. Roll, tie or skewer. If possible put it under a board with a weight on top (for easy slicing).
6. Brown the veal in hot fat in a tin, then roast for 1 hour, basting several times with the hot fat.
7. Spread the remaining stuffing mixture on the top of the meat and continue cooking for another hour.
8. When the veal is cooked, remove the string or skewers and slice.

Cooking time: 2 hours 20 minutes
Preparation time: 20 minutes
Main cooking utensils: frying pan, roasting tin
Oven temperature: moderately hot to hot (400—425°F., 200—220°C., Gas Mark 6—7)
Oven position: hottest part
Serves: 6—7

Veal escalopes and mushrooms

Imperial	Metric
4 oz. butter	100 g. butter
4 slices fillet of veal (see note)	4 slices fillet of veal (see note)
seasoning	seasoning
sprig tarragon	sprig tarragon
8 oz. mushrooms (see note)	200 g. mushrooms (see note)
½ pint thin cream	275 ml. thin cream
Garnish:	*Garnish:*
small sprigs tarragon	small sprigs tarragon

1. Heat the butter, then fry the slices of well-seasoned veal steadily until golden brown.
2. Lift on to a dish and keep hot.
3. Chop the tarragon finely and mix with the sliced mushrooms, season well, then fry these steadily until soft.
4. Arrange the mushrooms on the dish with the meat.
5. Stir the cream into the pan and blend with the meat and vegetable juices.
6. Either pour the cream sauce over the meat or serve separately.
7. Garnish the escalopes with sprigs of tarragon.
8. Serve hot with vegetables or salad, or this is ideal to cook in a large pan over a barbecue. Use a large pan, fry the veal, push to one side of the pan while cooking the mushrooms, then add the cream.

Note: Veal fillet is cut from the top of the leg. If the slices are too thick, beat them out thinly with a mallet or rolling pin. Girolles are a type of edible fungi, not unlike mushrooms in flavour but of a firmer texture, ordinary mushrooms could be used instead.

Cooking time: 15–20 minutes
Preparation time: 10 minutes
Main cooking utensil: large frying pan
Serves: 4

Veal with Tyrol sauce

Imperial	Metric
4 fillets veal	4 fillets veal
To coat:	*To coat:*
½ oz. flour	15 g. flour
seasoning	seasoning
1 egg	1 egg
crisp breadcrumbs	crisp breadcrumbs
lard or butter for frying	lard or butter for frying
Sauce:	*Sauce:*
¼ pint soured cream or fresh cream	125 ml. soured cream or fresh cream
1 tablespoon lemon juice	1 tablespoon lemon juice
1 egg yolk	1 egg yolk
seasoning	seasoning
½ teaspoon made mustard	½ teaspoon made mustard
2 tablespoons sliced olives	2 tablespoons sliced olives
Garnish:	*Garnish:*
rolled anchovy fillets	rolled anchovy fillets

1. Trim off any fat from the meat.
2. If the slices are too thick, flatten with a rolling pin.
3. Mix the flour and seasoning.
4. Coat the meat in this, then in beaten egg and crisp breadcrumbs.
5. Heat the fat.
6. Fry the meat until golden brown on the underside, turn and brown on the second side.
7. Then lower the heat and cook for several minutes to make certain the veal is tender.
8. Put all the ingredients for the sauce into the top of the double saucepan, or basin over hot water, and heat gently.
9. Pour sauce over fillets just before serving, and top with anchovy fillets.

Cooking time: 10 minutes
Preparation time: 10 minutes
Main cooking utensils: frying pan, basin and saucepan or double saucepan
Serves: 4

Veal goulash

Imperial	Metric
3 medium-sized onions	3 medium-sized onions
3 oz. butter	75 g. butter
1 oz. flour	25 g. flour
1 tablespoon paprika	1 tablespoon paprika
seasoning	seasoning
$1\frac{1}{2}$–2 lb. stewing veal	$\frac{3}{4}$–1 kg. stewing veal
1 pint white stock or water (a chicken stock cube can be added)	550 ml. white stock or water (a chicken stock cube can be added)
$\frac{1}{2}$ pint dry white wine	275 ml. dry white wine
juice of $\frac{1}{2}$ lemon	juice of $\frac{1}{2}$ lemon
$\frac{1}{4}$–$\frac{1}{2}$ pint soured cream or fresh thin cream and little lemon juice	150–275 ml. soured cream or fresh thin cream and little lemon juice

1. Chop the onions finely, then toss them in the hot butter.
2. Blend the flour with the paprika and plenty of seasoning.
3. Cut the meat into neat pieces and roll in the seasoned flour.
4. Add to the butter, cook for several minutes, taking care the outside does not harden.
5. Gradually blend in the stock and wine, bring to the boil, add lemon juice and continue cooking until the meat is very tender.
6. Stir the soured or fresh cream in just before serving, the amount according to personal taste; heat gently without boiling for a few minutes.
7. Serve with noodles or rice.

To cook noodles or other pasta (spaghetti, etc.): Allow 2 pints (generous litre) water to every 4 oz. (100 g.) pasta, together with 1 teaspoon salt. Bring the water to the boil, add the pasta and allow it to cook quickly until tender, but not too soft; drain well.

Cooking time: $1\frac{1}{2}$–2 hours
Preparation time: 15 minutes
Main cooking utensil: saucepan
Serves: 4–5

Ossobuco

Imperial	Metric
$1\frac{1}{2}$–2 lb. stewing veal or knuckle of veal	$\frac{3}{4}$–1 kg. stewing veal or knuckle of veal
1 oz. flour	25 g. flour
seasoning	seasoning
$\frac{1}{2}$ teaspoon dry mustard	$\frac{1}{2}$ teaspoon dry mustard
3 onions	3 onions
1 oz. butter	25 g. butter
1 tablespoon oil	1 tablespoon oil
3 carrots	3 carrots
piece celery	piece celery
3 tomatoes, skinned	3 tomatoes, skinned
bunch mixed herbs	bunch mixed herbs
grated rind and juice of 1 lemon	grated rind and juice of 1 lemon
$\frac{1}{2}$ pint white wine	300 ml. white wine
1 level tablespoon concentrated tomato purée	1 level tablespoon concentrated tomato purée
Garnish:	*Garnish:*
chopped parsley	chopped parsley

1. Cut the meat into neat pieces.
2. Roll in flour sifted with seasoning and mustard.
3. Fry the sliced onions in hot butter and oil until pale golden.
4. Add the meat, diced carrots, celery, chopped tomatoes, herbs (tied in muslin) and seasoning.
5. Toss with the onions for 2–3 minutes.
6. Stir in the lemon juice and rind, the white wine, and tomato purée diluted with $\frac{1}{2}$ pint (300 ml.) water.
7. Season well and simmer for 2 hours.
8. Lift meat on to a hot dish, remove the bag of herbs.
9. Rub the sauce through a sieve.
10. Pour over the meat and top with chopped parsley, if liked. Serve with rice, topped with melted butter and grated cheese.

Cooking time: $2\frac{1}{4}$ hours
Preparation time: 25 minutes
Main cooking utensil: large saucepan
Serves: 4–6

Bacon and ham

Method of cooking	Cut	Cooking time	To serve
Roasting or baking	Gammon slipper Middle gammon Back and ribs Joint top streaky.	20 minutes per lb. ($\frac{1}{2}$ kg.) and 20 minutes over. If liked well done, cook as pork for 25 minutes per lb. ($\frac{1}{2}$ kg.) (see page 80).	Mustard Salads Unusual garnishes such as baked apples, oranges, pineapple, apple, etc.
Grilling or frying	Top streaky Prime streaky Thin streaky Gammon slipper Middle gammon Corner gammon Long back Short back Back and ribs Top Prime collar.	Few minutes only for thin rashers, with thick slices of gammon cook outside fairly quickly then reduce heat to cook through to the middle. Keep gammon well brushed with fat when grilling (see page 81).	Eggs, tomatoes mushrooms, etc. for breakfast Vegetables or salads for main meals.
Boiling or braising	Forehock Prime streaky Flank back Gammon slipper	Soak well if you want very mild flavour, then simmer gently for	Vegetables – beans and peas are particularly good with boiled bacon

Method of cooking	Cut	Cooking time	To serve
Boiling or braising	Gammon hock Middle Corner gammon Long back Back and ribs Top back Prime collar End of collar Oyster cut	20–25 minutes per lb. ($\frac{1}{2}$ kg.) and 20–25 minutes over. The cheaper cuts need about 35 minutes per lb. ($\frac{1}{2}$ kg.) and 35 minutes over. Do not boil too quickly. A pressure cooker can be used (see page 64). Ham or bacon stock is excellent for soups.	Salads, etc.

Boiled gammon garnished with fruit (see opposite).

BACON

1. BUTT
2. SMALL HOCK | FOREHOCK
3. FORE SLIPPER |
4. TOP STREAKY
5. PRIME STREAKY
6. THIN STREAKY
7. FLANK
8. GAMMON SLIPPER
9. GAMMON HOCK
10. MIDDLE GAMMON
11. CORNER GAMMON
12. LONG BACK
13. OYSTER
14. SHORT BACK
15. BACK AND RIBS
16. TOP BACK
17. PRIME COLLAR
18. END COLLAR

Fruit with bacon and ham

Fruit blends extremely well with bacon and ham; try frying rings of cooking apple with the breakfast bacon. Serve cooked prunes with hot or cold boiled bacon or ham. Peaches, pineapple rings, apricots or apple rings or even slices of orange can be heated under the grill, when grilling bacon rashers or thicker steaks of gammon, etc. Brush the fruit with a little melted butter so it does not scorch under the heat of the grill. To give an interesting sweet taste sprinkle the fruit with brown sugar, then grill for 1–2 minutes only, as the sugar burns very easily.

Treacle-glazed gammon

Imperial	Metric
5 lb. middle gammon	2½ kg. middle gammon
4 tablespoons black treacle	4 tablespoons black treacle
12 peppercorns	12 peppercorns
1 bay leaf	1 bay leaf
cloves	cloves
¼ pint dry cider	125 ml. dry cider

1. Soak the gammon overnight, rinse in cold running water, place in a saucepan and cover with cold water.
2. Add 2 tablespoons black treacle, the peppercorns and the bay leaf; bring slowly to the boil and simmer gently for 1½ hours.
3. Drain the joint, strip off the skin and score the fat into diamonds with a sharp knife. Insert a clove in each diamond.
4. Warm the remaining 2 tablespoons of black treacle and pour over the fat surface. Place the joint in a roasting tin and pour the cider over the top.
5. Cook for approximately 1 hour basting frequently with the cider.
6. Serve hot with vegetables, or cold on a bed of lettuce.

Note: Store the gammon in the refrigerator. It is delicious cold.

Variation
Use half treacle and half golden syrup or honey.

Cooking time: 2½ hours
Preparation time: few minutes, plus overnight soaking
Main cooking utensils: large saucepan, roasting tin
Oven temperature: moderate to moderately hot (350–375°F., 180–190°C., Gas Mark 4–5)
Oven position: centre
Serves: 8–10

Boiled bacon

Imperial	Metric
Per person:	*Per person:*
6–9 oz. boiling bacon or ham	150–225 g. boiling bacon or ham
pepper	pepper
Parsley sauce:	*Parsley sauce:*
1 oz. butter	25 g. butter
1 oz. flour	25 g. flour
¼ pint bacon stock	125 ml. bacon stock
¼ pint milk	125 ml. milk
seasoning	seasoning
1–2 tablespoons chopped parsley	1–2 tablespoons chopped parsley

1. Wash salted bacon or ham and soak overnight or for several hours in cold water.
2. Put the bacon into a saucepan and cover with cold water.
3. Bring to the boil, skim and add pepper (no salt).
4. Cover and simmer for the time given.
5. If you wish to add vegetables put in prepared carrots, potatoes and onions ½ hour before the end of cooking time.
6. To make the parsley sauce, heat the butter in a saucepan, stir in the flour and cook for a few minutes. Remove the pan from the heat and stir in the stock and milk gradually. Return to the heat and bring to the boil, stirring constantly, then add the seasoning and parsley.
7. Serve the drained bacon hot, with vegetables and parsley sauce separately.

Note: If you buy sweet-cured or mild-cured bacon joints you do not need to soak them. Prepacked polythene wrapped joints can be cooked in their wrapping. The polythene helps to keep the meat moist.

Cooking time: 30 minutes per lb. (½ kg.) for thin joints, 35 minutes per lb. for thicker joints
Preparation time: depends on vegetable added
Main cooking utensil: large saucepan

Grilled gammon and pineapple

Imperial	Metric
3 gammon steaks (see note)	3 gammon steaks (see note)
1 oz. butter	25 g. butter
small can pineapple rings	small can pineapple rings
Garnish:	*Garnish:*
few glacé cherries	few glacé cherries
parsley	parsley

1. Remove the skin from the pieces of gammon.
2. Snip the fat at intervals — this prevents the rashers curling and helps the fat to crisp.
3. Put the gammon on the grid of the grill pan and brush the lean meat with melted butter.
4. It is important not to preheat the grill when cooking gammon or bacon, otherwise it curls before it is cooked, and the fat could burn. Grill quickly on each side, then lower the heat and cook through to the middle.
5. Just before serving add the rings of pineapple and heat thoroughly. Arrange on a hot dish, top the pineapple with glacé cherries and parsley.

Note: Gammon is a lean piece of bacon, so brush well with butter as it cooks.

Variation
Use peaches instead of pineapple.

Cooking time: 15 minutes
Preparation time: few minutes
Main cooking utensil: grill pan
Serves: 3

Casserole of bacon

Imperial	Metric
6–9 oz. bacon or ham per person (see note)	150–225 g. bacon or ham per person (see note)
pepper or peppercorns	pepper or peppercorns
mixed vegetables to taste	mixed vegetables to taste

1. Soak the bacon. Bacon with a mild cure needs only a limited soaking in cold water.
2. Put it into the casserole and cover with cold water.
3. Add pepper or peppercorns, and cover with a lid.
4. Allow approximately 40 minutes per lb. ($\frac{1}{2}$ kg.) for a wide thin joint, a little longer for a thicker joint.
5. Add the vegetables during cooking.
6. Serve hot with the liquid in which the bacon was cooked as a sauce and the vegetables.

Note: You must allow the larger amount when you buy bacon with a thick skin and large amount of fat. Choose a piece of foreback, prime streaky, flank, gammon slipper, gammon hock, middle gammon, corner gammon, long back, back and ribs, top back, prime collar, end of collar or oyster cut.

If some of the stock is left after cooking the bacon, do not waste this as it gives an excellent flavour in stews or soups — particularly pea or lentil soup.

The rind of the bacon can always be added to the soup and taken out before serving.

Variation
Use cider or ginger ale in place of water.

Cooking time: see stage 4
Preparation time: depends on the vegetables added
Main cooking utensil: ovenproof casserole
Oven temperature: moderate (325–350°F., 170–180°C., Gas Mark 3–4)
Oven position: centre

Quiche Danoise

Imperial
Shortcrust pastry:
8 oz. plain flour
pinch salt
4 oz. fat
approximately 2 tablespoons
    water
Filling:
5 slices bacon
1 oz. fat
2 eggs
¼ pint cream
good 6 tablespoons milk
seasoning
Garnish:
watercress

Metric
Shortcrust pastry:
200 g. plain flour
pinch salt
100 g. fat
approximately 2 tablespoons
    water
Filling:
5 slices bacon
25 g. fat
2 eggs
125 ml. cream
good 6 tablespoons milk
seasoning
Garnish:
watercress

1. Sieve the flour and salt, rub in the fat until the mixture resembles fine breadcrumbs.
2. Bind with the water, and roll out, then line the tin.
3. Bake blind for about 10 minutes, remove the paper or foil and bread or beans.
4. Fry the bacon slices for a few minutes in the fat, put into the pastry.
5. Beat the eggs, cream, milk and seasoning, then strain over the bacon.
6. Bake for a further 25 minutes until the filling is set at the lower heat. Serve cold, garnished with watercress, with a green salad and French bread.

Note: Carry this flan in the tin to prevent the filling breaking.

Variation
Use all milk instead of cream. Use canned luncheon meat or pork and ham instead of bacon.

Cooking time: 25 minutes
Preparation time: 25 minutes
Main cooking utensils: 8-inch (20-cm.) flan ring and baking sheet
Oven temperature: hot (425–450°F., 220–230°C., Gas Mark 7–8)
    then moderate (375°F., 190°C., Gas Mark 5) .
Oven position: centre
Serves: 4–6

Gammon and asparagus rolls

Imperial
8 oz. asparagus or 1 medium
    can asparagus
salt
4 thin rashers gammon, rinds
    removed
Sauce:
1 oz. butter
1 oz. flour
½ pint milk
4 tablespoons asparagus stock
4 oz. grated Cheddar cheese
seasoning
Garnish:
2 tomatoes
chopped parsley

Metric
200 g. asparagus or 1 medium
    can asparagus
salt
4 thin rashers gammon, rinds
    removed
Sauce:
25 g. butter
25 g. flour
250 ml. milk
4 tablespoons asparagus stock
100 g. grated Cheddar cheese
seasoning
Garnish:
2 tomatoes
chopped parsley

1. Cook the asparagus in boiling salted water until tender, or open the can of asparagus, drain carefully.
2. Wrap the thin gammon rashers round the asparagus, put into a dish and cook in the oven for 15 minutes.
3. Meanwhile make the cheese sauce. Melt the butter, stir in the flour and cook for several minutes.
4. Add the milk and asparagus stock, bring to the boil and cook until thickened.
5. Stir in the cheese and seasoning and pour the sauce over the asparagus.
6. Arrange halved tomatoes round the asparagus rolls, return to the oven to brown. Top with parsley. Serve hot with salad.

Variation
For a party: Prepare the rolls. Make the cheese sauce and pour over the rolls. Cover tightly and reheat in a moderately hot oven. Do not cook the sauce once cheese has been added as this will make it tough with the heating in the oven.

Cooking time: 45 minutes if using fresh asparagus
Preparation time: 15 minutes
Main cooking utensils: saucepan, strainer, ovenproof dish
Oven temperature: moderately hot (375°F., 190°C., Gas Mark 5)
Oven position: above centre
Serves: 4

Stew of bacon and vegetables

Imperial	Metric
about 12 oz. gammon or back bacon, cut in thick rashers	about 300 g. gammon or back bacon, cut in thick rashers
2 oz. butter	50 g. butter
8 oz. onions	200 g. onions
seasoning	seasoning
1½ lb. peas, weight before shelling, or equivalent in frozen peas (see stages 5 and 6)	¾ kg. peas, weight before shelling, or equivalent in frozen peas (see stages 5 and 6)
12 oz. new carrots, scraped	300 g. new carrots, scraped

1. Remove the bacon rinds and put them into the pan with the bacon. Cut the bacon into fingers.
2. Fry steadily until golden coloured, lift out, put on a plate, then add the butter to the pan.
3. Peel and slice the onions, toss in the butter until translucent, do not allow to brown.
4. If a great deal of fat remains, some could be spooned out, but a little fat is a good thing as it adds flavour to the vegetables; leave the bacon rinds in the pan.
5. Add approximately ½ pint (250 ml.) water and seasoning (be sparing with the salt); put in the fresh shelled peas and sliced carrots. Cook steadily for about 15–20 minutes, covering the pan tightly. If using frozen peas, cook the carrots for 15–20 minutes and add the peas with the bacon at stage 6.
6. Replace the bacon and continue cooking until the vegetables are quite soft. Remove the bacon rinds.
7. The liquid should have evaporated by the time the vegetables are cooked; if necessary remove the lid to increase evaporation.

Variation

Blend a little thin cream into the cooked vegetables and bacon. Soaked dried peas could be used, in which case increase the cooking time and the amount of liquid.

Cooking time: 35 minutes
Preparation time: 25 minutes
Main cooking utensil: large saucepan
Serves: 4

Potato and corned beef hash

Imperial	Metric
4 medium sized potatoes or 2 really large ones	4 medium-sized potatoes or 2 really large ones
½–1 oz. butter or margarine	15–25 g. butter or margarine
2 oz. shortening or fat	50 g. shortening or fat
2 onions or equivalent in spring onions	2 onions or equivalent in spring onions
3–4 oz. streaky bacon	75–100 g. streaky bacon
12 oz. corned beef	300 g. corned beef
2 dessert apples	2 dessert apples
seasoning	seasoning
Topping:	*Topping:*
knob butter	knob butter
parsley	parsley

1. Wash and dry the potatoes, prick them to prevent the skins breaking, brush the skins with butter or margarine.
2. Put on a baking sheet and bake until soft, approximately 1¼–1½ hours in a moderately hot oven.
3. Split the potatoes through the centre and scoop out the centre pulp, trying to keep this in reasonable-sized pieces rather than allowing it to become soft and mashed.
4. Heat the shortening or fat in a pan and fry the chopped onions until nearly soft. Remove from the heat and add the finely chopped bacon, flaked corned beef, pieces of potato and diced apple (leave the peel on for extra flavour and colour). Season lightly.
5. Season the potato cases, pile the mixture back into them and return to the oven for about 10 minutes to heat through.
6. Serve topped with a knob of butter and a little chopped parsley; this is excellent for supper or as a main dish with a green vegetable.

Cooking time: 1¼–1½ hours
Preparation time: 15 minutes
Main cooking utensils: baking tray, frying pan
Oven temperature: moderately hot (375°F., 190°C., Gas Mark 5)
Oven position: centre
Serves: 4

Savoury bacon pudding

Imperial	Metric
Suet crust pastry:	*Suet crust pastry:*
8 oz. self-raising flour	200 g. self-raising flour
pinch salt	pinch salt
4 oz. shredded suet	100 g. shredded suet
cold water to mix	cold water to mix
Filling:	*Filling:*
8–12 oz. streaky bacon	200–300 g. streaky bacon
1–2 chopped onions	1–2 chopped onions
1–2 chopped tomatoes	1–2 chopped tomatoes
1–2 diced carrots	1–2 diced carrots
small piece sliced cucumber (optional) or diced marrow (optional)	small piece sliced cucumber (optional) or diced marrow (optional)
little chopped parsley	little chopped parsley
water	water
pepper	pepper

1. Sieve the flour and salt, add the suet and enough water to make a rolling consistency.
2. Roll out on a floured board, use two-thirds to line a 1½- to 2-pint (¾- to 1-litre) basin.
3. Fill with the diced bacon, vegetables, parsley and a very little water. Add pepper, no salt should be needed unless using green bacon.
4. Roll out remaining suet crust to form a lid, press over the top of the mixture, cover with greased greaseproof paper or foil.
5. Steam over boiling water for the time given. When cooked, either turn out or serve from the basin. Garnish with watercress if you like.

Cooking time: 3 hours
Preparation time: 25 minutes
Main cooking utensils: 1½- to 2-pint (¾- to 1-litre) basin, greaseproof paper or foil, steamer, saucepan.
Serves: 4–5

Savoury minced steak with soufflé topping

Imperial	Metric
1 small green pepper	1 small green pepper
1 small onion	1 small onion
2 oz. mushrooms	50 g. mushrooms
2 tomatoes	2 tomatoes
1 tablespoon oil	1 tablespoon oil
16-oz. can minced steak	450-g. can minced steak
pinch of oregano or mixed herbs	pinch of oregano or mixed herbs
seasoning	seasoning
Soufflé topping:	*Soufflé topping:*
2 oz. finely grated Cheddar cheese	50 g. finely grated Cheddar cheese
3 tablespoons evaporated milk	3 tablespoons evaporated milk
2 eggs	2 eggs
salt	salt
pinch cayenne pepper	pinch cayenne pepper
Garnish:	*Garnish:*
sprig of parsley	sprig of parsley

1. Chop the pepper, removing seeds and core, skin and chop the onion, skin and slice the mushrooms and tomatoes.
2. Heat the oil and lightly fry all the vegetables until onion is golden brown.
3. Place the minced steak in the ovenproof dish, top with the vegetables.
4. Sprinkle seasonings on top.
5. Make the soufflé by melting the cheese in the evaporated milk in a basin over hot water. Allow to cool slightly.
6. Stir in the egg yolks.
7. Whisk egg whites stiffly, then fold in the cheese mixture. Season.
8. Place on top of the meat and vegetables.
9. Bake until the soufflé is well risen and lightly browned, 20–25 minutes. Serve at once, garnished with parsley.

Cooking time: 40 minutes
Preparation time: 20 minutes
Main cooking utensils: frying pan, ovenproof dish, basin over hot water
Oven temperature: moderate (375°F., 190°C., Gas Mark 5)
Oven position: centre
Serves: 4

Sausage and savoury cabbage

Imperial	Metric
1 oz. margarine	25 g. margarine
10 oz. skinless sausages	250 g. skinless sausages
1 large onion	1 large onion
1 large leek or another onion	1 large leek or another onion
1 lb. firm cabbage (use heart of cabbage or white Dutch cabbage)	½ kg. firm cabbage (use heart of cabbage or white Dutch cabbage)
8 oz. tomatoes	200 g. tomatoes
seasoning	seasoning

1. Melt the margarine in the flameproof casserole. If you do not have this type of casserole then use a frying pan plus an ovenproof casserole.
2. Fry the sausages until golden brown, lift out of the pan on to a plate.
3. Peel the onion and slice thinly; wash and slice the leek.
4. Toss the onion and leek in the fat remaining in the pan for 5 minutes.
5. Add the finely shredded cabbage and the skinned, deseeded and chopped tomatoes; continue cooking for a few minutes.
6. Season the mixture well, if using a flameproof casserole put on the lid and transfer it to the oven; if using an ordinary frying pan tip the mixture into the ovenproof casserole and cover.
7. Bake for 20 minutes. Remove the lid, add the sausages and heat for a further 10 minutes. Serve hot with jacket potatoes.

Note: There is no need to defrost frozen sausages before cooking.

Variation
This dish, like many other casserole dishes, may be cooked in a covered pan over a very low heat.

Cooking time: 40 minutes
Preparation time: 15 minutes
Main cooking utensil: shallow flameproof casserole with lid (stage 1)
Oven temperature: moderate to moderately hot (350–375°F., 180–190°C., Gas Mark 4–5)
Oven position: above centre
Serves: 4

Bean and meat casserole

Imperial	Metric
2 lb. haricot beans	1 kg. haricot beans
6-oz. piece salt pork	150-g. piece salt pork
8 oz. lamb or mutton	200 g. lamb or mutton
1 small garlic sausage	1 small garlic sausage
3 oz. lard	75 g. lard
1 onion	1 onion
3–4 cloves	3–4 cloves
1 clove garlic or 1 teaspoon garlic salt	1 clove garlic or 1 teaspoon garlic salt
2 sprigs parsley	2 sprigs parsley
2 tablespoons concentrated tomato purée	2 tablespoons concentrated tomato purée
seasoning	seasoning
8 oz. tomatoes	200 g. tomatoes
3 oz. breadcrumbs	75 g. breadcrumbs
2 oz. butter	50 g. butter

1. Soak the haricot beans overnight. Drain.
2. Dice the meats and sausage and fry in the lard until evenly browned.
3. Place the beans, meats, onion stuck with cloves, crushed garlic or garlic salt, parsley, tomato purée and seasoning in a deep casserole.
4. Just cover with water and cook steadily for approximately 2 hours in a moderate oven.
5. Add the quartered tomatoes. Fry the breadcrumbs in butter and sprinkle on top.
6. Bake for a further few minutes. Serve with a green vegetable.

Cooking time: 2¼ hours
Preparation time: 30 minutes plus overnight soaking for beans
Main cooking utensils: strong saucepan, deep casserole
Oven temperature: moderate (325–350°F., 170–180°C., Gas Mark 3–4)
Oven position: centre
Serves: 8

Lamb and apple curry

Imperial	Metric
1 lb. lamb from leg or shoulder	½ kg. lamb from leg or shoulder
1 level tablespoon flour	1 level tablespoon flour
seasoning	seasoning
½–1 tablespoon curry powder	½–1 tablespoon curry powder
1 oz. fat	25 g. fat
1 onion	1 onion
1–2 peeled apples	1–2 peeled apples
¾ pint stock	400 ml. stock
1 green pepper	1 green pepper
2–3 tomatoes	2–3 tomatoes
juice of ½ lemon	juice of ½ lemon
1–2 oz. sultanas	25–50 g. sultanas
1 teaspoon sugar	1 teaspoon sugar
6 oz. long-grain rice	150 g. long-grain rice
½ pint plus 2 tablespoons water	275 ml. water
½ teaspoon salt	½ teaspoon salt
Garnish:	*Garnish:*
paprika pepper	paprika pepper

1. Dice the lamb neatly and roll in the flour, mixed with seasoning and curry powder.
2. Fry in hot fat for 5 minutes, add the chopped onion and sliced apple, turn in the fat for 2 minutes.
3. Gradually blend in the stock, bring to the boil and cook until thickened.
4. Simmer for 30 minutes, add chopped green pepper, skinned quartered tomatoes, lemon juice, sultanas and sugar; continue cooking in a covered pan for 45 minutes.
5. While the curry is cooking prepare the rice. Put the rice, water and salt into a pan.
6. Bring to the boil, stir, cover tightly and lower heat so the liquid simmers gently. Cook for 15 minutes. At the end of this time the rice should be tender and the liquid absorbed. Garnish with paprika pepper. Serve with chutney and lemon.

Cooking time: 1½ hours
Preparation time: 25 minutes
Main cooking utensils: 2 saucepans
Serves: 4

Liver tournedos

Imperial	Metric
approximately 1½ lb. calves' liver, cut into 2–3 slices	approximately ¾ kg. calves' liver, cut into 2–3 slices
seasoning	seasoning
pinch dried sage	pinch dried sage
grated rind of 1 lemon	grated rind of 1 lemon
½ oz. flour	15 g. flour
1 large onion	1 large onion
3 oz. butter	75 g. butter
2 large tomatoes	2 large tomatoes
Garnish:	*Garnish:*
6 sage leaves	6 sage leaves

1. Cut the liver into 12 rounds or neat portions, tie these into a round shape with cotton or fine string.
2. Mix together the seasoning, dried sage, finely grated lemon rind and flour.
3. Coat the liver with this mixture.
4. Peel the onion and cut into 6 slices.
5. Fry in the hot butter over the barbecue until just tender.
6. Take 6 large slices from the tomatoes, fry for 1–2 minutes only, so they are still very firm.
7. Put the onion and tomato slices on foil over the fire to keep hot while cooking the liver. Fry this until just tender, do not overcook.
8. Put a slice of tomato on each plate, top with a liver tournedos, a slice of onion, a second round of liver and a sage leaf.

Cooking time: 15 minutes
Preparation time: 10 minutes
Main cooking utensils: large frying pan, barbecue
Serves: 6

Creamed liver loaf

Imperial	Metric
2 medium-sized onions	2 medium-sized onions
1 clove garlic (optional)	1 clove garlic (optional)
3 oz. butter	75 g. butter
1 oz. flour	25 g. flour
$\frac{1}{4}$ pint milk	125 ml. milk
$\frac{1}{4}$ pint thick cream	125 ml. thick cream
2 eggs	2 eggs
grated rind and juice of 1 lemon	grated rind and juice of 1 lemon
2 tablespoons brandy	2 tablespoons brandy
1$\frac{1}{4}$ lb. lamb's liver	generous $\frac{1}{2}$ kg. lamb's liver
8 oz. pig's liver	200 g. pig's liver
seasoning	seasoning
8–10 oz. streaky bacon rashers	200–250 g. streaky bacon rashers
Garnish:	*Garnish:*
watercress	watercress
1–2 pickled cucumbers	1–2 pickled cucumbers

1. Chop or grate the onions finely, crush the garlic; heat the butter in a pan and toss the onions and garlic in it, then stir in the flour and cook gently for 2–3 minutes.
2. Gradually add the milk, bring to the boil and cook until thickened (the mixture will look very buttery but that is correct).
3. Gradually add the cream, whisked with the eggs, the rind and juice of the lemon and the brandy.
4. Put the two kinds of liver through a fine mincer twice, to give a very smooth texture. Blend with the sauce and season well.
5. Remove the rinds from the bacon; line the tin with the rashers, letting them overlap slightly.
6. Press in the liver mixture and cover with greased foil.
7. Stand in the tin of water and cook for 1$\frac{1}{4}$ hours at the temperature given.
8. Put a weight on the loaf as it cools; garnish with sliced pickled cucumber and watercress, serve with potato salad.

Cooking time: 1$\frac{1}{2}$ hours
Preparation time: 25 minutes
Main cooking utensils: saucepan, 2-lb. (1-kg.) loaf tin, tin for water
Oven temperature: cool to moderate (300–325°F., 150 170°C., Gas Mark 2–3)
Oven position: centre
Serves: 6 as a main course or 12 as an hors-d'oeuvre

Savoury heart

Imperial	Metric
1 calf's heart	1 calf's heart
2–3 onions	2–3 onions
2–3 oz. inexpensive bacon	50–75 g. inexpensive bacon
3 sticks celery	3 sticks celery
2 oz. fat	50 g. fat
good pinch salt and sugar	good pinch salt and sugar
shake black pepper	shake black pepper
1 teaspoon soup seasoning	1 teaspoon soup seasoning
$\frac{1}{2}$ teaspoon dried thyme	$\frac{1}{2}$ teaspoon dried thyme
2 teaspoons cornflour	2 teaspoons cornflour
$\frac{1}{4}$ pint cheap red wine	125 ml. cheap red wine
approximately 1 pint stock	approximately 550 ml. stock
about 10 juniper berries	about 10 juniper berries
$\frac{1}{4}$ pint soured cream	125 ml. soured cream
6 oz. spaghetti	150 g. spaghetti
seasoning	seasoning

1. Wash the heart in cold water and cut away any tough arteries; if this spoils the shape of the heart sew it together.
2. Chop onions, bacon and celery finely, toss in hot fat.
3. Add the heart, coated in the seasonings, thyme and cornflour.
4. Turn the heart several times in the bacon and vegetable mixture and fat until golden brown.
5. Add the wine and water or stock.
6. If a strong flavour is required crush the juniper berries before adding them, but for a milder taste tie these in a piece of muslin so they may be removed.
7. Put a lid on the pan and simmer steadily until the heart is tender, this will take about 1$\frac{3}{4}$ hours.
8. Lift the heart on to a hot dish and slice fairly thickly.
9. Stir the soured cream into the liquid; if wished this may be made thicker by blending with a little more cornflour. Serve with well-seasoned boiled pasta, tomato and parsley.

Cooking time: 2 hours
Preparation time: 30 minutes
Main cooking utensils: 2 large saucepans
Serves: 5–6

Kidney and bacon milanese

Imperial	Metric
3–4 pints water	1¾–2 litres water
seasoning	seasoning
6–8 oz. spaghetti	150–200 g. spaghetti
2 onions	2 onions
2–3 oz. margarine	50–75 g. margarine
4 rashers streaky bacon	4 rashers streaky bacon
1 medium-sized can tomatoes or 12 oz. tomatoes and ¼ pint water	1 medium-sized can tomatoes or 300 g. tomatoes and 125 ml. water
4 lambs' kidneys	4 lambs' kidneys
2–3 oz. grated cheese	50–75 g. grated cheese
little chopped parsley	little chopped parsley

1. Bring the water to the boil, season well and put in the spaghetti to cook until just tender.
2. Peel and slice the onions.
3. Heat the margarine in the second pan (use the smaller quantity if the bacon is fat).
4. Fry the onions for a few minutes, then add the chopped bacon and continue cooking for 2–3 minutes.
5. Add the canned tomatoes, with the liquid from the can, or the skinned chopped tomatoes and water; simmer for a few minutes.
6. Skin the kidneys, cut into slices, add to the tomato mixture with seasoning.
7. Cover the pan and simmer for 10 minutes.
8. Drain the spaghetti, mix with the cheese and parsley. Pile the spaghetti on to a hot dish and top with the kidney mixture. Serve with a green salad.

Variation
Add 1–2 crushed cloves garlic to the onions at stage 4, add a little red wine at stage 7.

Cooking time: 25 minutes
Preparation time: 25 minutes
Main cooking utensils: 2 saucepans
Serves: 4

Kidney and bacon pilaff

Imperial	Metric
4–6 lambs' or pigs' kidneys	4–6 lambs' or pigs' kidneys
4 oz. streaky bacon	100 g. streaky bacon
1 large onion	1 large onion
1–2 oz. fat or butter	25–50 g. fat or butter
½ pint stock	250 ml. stock
seasoning	seasoning
1 level dessertspoon cornflour	1 level dessertspoon cornflour
2–3 tablespoons water	2–3 tablespoons water

1. Skin and core the kidneys, cut into small pieces; cut the bacon into small pieces, slice the onion.
2. Heat the fat in the pan and fry the kidneys, bacon and onion together until the onion is soft and golden brown.
3. Pour in the stock, simmer for approximately 15 minutes, seasoning well.
4. Blend the cornflour with the water, add to the kidney mixture and cook for several minutes, stirring all the time. Arrange in a border of cooked rice or on toast.

Variations
Use ¼ pint (125 ml.) stock and ¼ pint (125 ml.) tomato juice; add 2–4 oz. (50–100 g.) sliced mushrooms to the onion; blend the cornflour with port wine instead of water.

Cooking time: 25–30 minutes
Preparation time: 15 minutes
Main cooking utensil: saucepan
Serves: 4

Pressed ox tongue

Imperial	Metric
1 salted tongue (see note)	1 salted tongue (see note)
water	water
1 large onion	1 large onion
1 large carrot	1 large carrot
bay leaf	bay leaf
1 teaspoon powdered gelatine	1 teaspoon powdered gelatine

1. Soak the tongue overnight in cold water.
2. Put it into a pan with enough fresh cold water to cover. Bring to the boil and add the onion, carrot and bay leaf.
3. Cover the pan and simmer very gently allowing 40 minutes per lb. ($\frac{1}{2}$ kg.).
4. Lift the tongue out of the stock and cool.
5. Boil the stock in an open pan until there is just under $\frac{1}{2}$ pint (250 ml.) left.
6. Remove the skin of the tongue and any tiny bones at the root of the tongue.
7. Place the tongue in a tin or pan, curling it round to give a good shape. It needs to be a fairly tight fit.
8. Dissolve the gelatine in the stock, strain it over the tongue and put a plate and weight on top to press the tongue into shape. Leave until cold.
9. Remove the weight, etc., dip the base of the tin into hot water for $\frac{1}{2}$ minute to loosen the jelly round the meat, and turn out. Serve sliced thinly, with salad.

Note: The size varies quite considerably. Salted meat shrinks, so allow a good 8 oz. (200 g.) per person.

Variation

Cook unsalted ox tongue (the colour will not be as good) with salt to taste.

Cooking time: see stage 3
Preparation time: few minutes
Main cooking utensils: large covered saucepan, round cake tin or saucepan, plate, weight
Serves: 10–18

Tongue with almond sauce

Imperial	Metric
6–8 small calves' or lambs' tongues	6–8 small calves' or lambs' tongues
water	water
seasoning	seasoning
bay leaf	bay leaf
2 onions	2 onions
4–6 carrots	4–6 carrots
Sauce:	*Sauce:*
4 oz. fat pork or bacon	100 g. fat pork or bacon
1 oz. butter	25 g. butter
1 oz. flour	25 g. flour
just over $\frac{1}{2}$ pint stock	275 ml. stock
2 oz. ground almonds or finely chopped almonds	50 g. ground almonds or finely chopped almonds
grated rind and juice of 1 lemon	grated rind and juice of 1 lemon
2 oz. raisins (optional)	50 g. raisins (optional)
$\frac{1}{4}$ pint red wine	125 ml. red wine
Garnish:	*Garnish:*
chopped parsley	chopped parsley
cooked peas	cooked peas

1. Put the whole tongues with water to cover, seasoning and the bay leaf into a pan, add the finely chopped onions.
2. Simmer for 45 minutes, then add the sliced carrots, cook for a further 30 minutes.
3. Allow to cool sufficiently to handle. Skin and halve the tongues.
4. Dice the pork and fry it in a pan with the butter, stir in the flour, gradually blend in the generous $\frac{1}{2}$ pint (275 ml.) strained stock.
5. Bring to the boil and cook until thickened, add the almonds, lemon rind and juice, raisins and wine. Blend well, add the sliced carrots and tongues. Do not add the onions.
6. Put half the tongues into a hot dish, top with the sauce. Arrange remaining tongues on top with parsley and peas.

Cooking time: $1\frac{1}{2}$ hours
Preparation time: 30 minutes
Main cooking utensil: saucepan
Serves: 6

Poultry dishes

Due to modern methods of breeding and rearing, poultry today is available at comparatively reasonable prices and of uniform quality throughout the year.

When buying poultry look for the following:

Chicken: This should have a plump white breast, with plump and pliable legs. A very good test of a young fowl is to check that the breast bone is pliable. If buying an older boiling fowl, check that there is not an undue amount of fat, although there will be a layer of fat under the skin.

It is also possible to buy fresh or frozen chicken or chicken portions.

Turkey: This should have the same characteristics as chicken, above. If you have several birds from which to choose buy those with broad plump breasts rather than a thinner breast and longer legs, for you will be able to have a number more portions from the same weight of bird.

Some stores sell halved turkeys or turkey portions today, and these are ideal for small families.

Duck and goose: Both have a layer of fat under the skin, but check this is not too thick; a breast of duck or goose should have a reasonable layer of meat, and the under-bill should be soft and pliable.

To freeze poultry
Commercially frozen poultry has become very popular; these are an excellent purchase.

Allow sufficient time for the bird to thaw out (about 24 hours for a small chicken or duck; up to 72 hours for a large turkey) in a refrigerator. *Small* pieces of poultry can be cooked from the frozen state.

To freeze your own poultry: First remove the giblets and wrap separately in a polythene bag. These can be then placed inside the bird or frozen separately, but label carefully, so you know where to find them when required.

Wrap the bird very well; I use foil, then polythene. Make sure the wrapping is pressed firmly against the bird, so it follows the shape, and protect the wrapping from the sharp ends of the bones; these should have extra foil or cotton wool round the ends. If freezing jointed birds, wrap each joint separately or separate with pieces of waxed paper or polythene, so you can remove the number required. Use raw frozen poultry within 5–6 months. Cooked poultry can be frozen, it becomes a little soft in texture; use within 2–3 months. Cooked poultry dishes freeze well (time for storage depends upon ingredients used; generally they should be kept for 1–2 months).

Roast turkey garnished with the traditional accompaniments — chipolata sausages, bacon rolls and forcemeat balls (for cooking times see below).

Roasting poultry

Chicken and turkey are poultry that can be cooked in a variety of ways, see recipes given in this section. Duck and goose are less versatile and better roasted or cooked in a casserole, use recipe for guinea fowl (see page 100).

All these birds can be roasted, provided they are young and tender, see the left-hand column, page 90. Weigh the bird *including the stuffing*.

Fast roasting: Allow 15 minutes per lb. ($\frac{1}{2}$ kg.) and 15 minutes over at the temperature given on page 92. This can be reduced slightly, see the recipe for roasting turkey on page 98. Stage 4 details the timing for very large birds.

Slower roasting: Allow 25 minutes per lb. ($\frac{1}{2}$ kg.) and 25 minutes over in a very moderate to moderate oven (325–350°F., 170–180°C., Gas Mark 3–4). Allow 22 minutes per lb. ($\frac{1}{2}$ kg.) for additional weight over 12 lb. ($5\frac{1}{2}$ kg.)

Very slow roasting: This is helpful if you want to cook a very large bird during the night; allow $1\frac{1}{4}$ hours for the first lb. ($\frac{1}{2}$ kg.), then 25 minutes per lb. ($\frac{1}{2}$ kg.). Set the oven to cool, i.e. 275–300°F., 140–150°C., Gas Mark 1–2. Allow only 20 minutes per lb. ($\frac{1}{2}$ kg.) for additional weight over 12 lb. ($5\frac{1}{2}$ kg.).

The recipes in this chapter give stuffings for poultry, including apricot stuffing (see page 92). Other traditional stuffings are given on page 122 and sauces are opposite.

To braise meat, poultry and game

The basic method of braising is the same for meat, poultry or game; it produces a rich flavour. First divide the meat, poultry or game into large pieces, or leave joints, etc. whole. Heat a little fat in a large strong saucepan, brown the meat thoroughly in this; it can be coated in seasoned flour first, but this is not essential.

Lift the meat or poultry from the pan, then toss a little chopped bacon and mixed vegetables in any fat remaining in the pan. Add seasoning to the mixture and a little chopped parsley or other herbs. Pour just enough water, stock or wine over the savoury mixture to cover, then replace the meat or poultry in the pan. Place a tightly fitting lid on the pan and turn the heat low.

Timing for braised meats: If using prime cuts (these are listed in the various tables), allow about 20–25 minutes per lb. ($\frac{1}{2}$ kg.) and 20–25 minutes over; less tender cuts of meat should have the same time as for stewing.

Timing for braised chicken or game: If young and tender, allow the same time as for prime meat. If older, increase the timing as for boiled chicken (see page 94). The vegetable mixture, known as the 'mirepoix', can be sieved and served as a sauce with the meat.

Sauces for poultry

For turkey and chicken choose bread or cranberry sauce; for duck or goose serve apple or orange sauce.

Bread sauce: Warm $\frac{1}{2}$ pint (3 dl.) milk, add a peeled onion (this can be stuck with 2–3 cloves) and infuse in a warm place for a time. Add 2 oz. (50 g.) soft breadcrumbs, a good-sized knob of butter and seasoning. Remove the onion before serving, beat a little cream into the sauce at the last minute.

Cranberry sauce: Make a syrup of a little water with sugar to taste, add the cranberries and simmer until softened. Add a little port wine to flavour or use orange juice in place of water.

Apple sauce: Simmer peeled, thinly sliced cooking apples in water with sugar to taste. Sieve or emulsify until a smooth sauce. A knob of butter improves the texture and the sauce can be flavoured with grated orange rind, sultanas or mixed spice.

Orange sauce: Cut the rind from 2 oranges, then cut away all the white bitter pith and make thin match-stick shapes of the orange part. Simmer in a little giblet stock or water until tender. Blend 1 oz. (25 g.) flour with $\frac{1}{2}$ pint (3 dl.) strained giblet stock and $\frac{1}{4}$ pint ($1\frac{1}{2}$ dl.) orange juice. Cook until thickened and clear, add 2 tablespoons redcurrant jelly and the orange peel, seasoning to taste and heat.

Easy guide to poultry and game dishes

The following gives you help in selecting the right poultry or game dish for the right occasion.

When you are short of time see pages 93, 94.

When you are short of money see pages 97, 103.

When you want a special dish see pages 92, 93, 94, 95, 96, 97, 98, 99, 100, 101, 105, 218.

For a snack or light meal see pages 92, 93, 94.

When you are slimming see pages 93, 115, 120.

Apricot-stuffed chicken

Imperial	Metric
1 3-lb. chicken	1 1½-kg. chicken
1–2 oz. butter	25–50 g. butter
Apricot stuffing:	*Apricot stuffing:*
2 large onions, peeled	2 large onions, peeled
½ pint water	250 ml. water
salt	salt
1 large can apricots	1 large can apricots
1 oz. suet or butter	25 g. suet or butter
2 oz. breadcrumbs	50 g. breadcrumbs
1 egg (optional)	1 egg (optional)
1 teaspoon powdered sage	1 teaspoon powdered sage
Garnish:	*Garnish:*
6–8 apricots from can	6–8 apricots from can
parsley	parsley

1. Boil the onions in salted water for 20 minutes. Drain onions and chop finely.
2. Meanwhile drain the juice from the can of apricots. Put half the juice into a saucepan and heat.
3. Chop the apricots, reserving 6 or 8 for garnish. Add the chopped onions and apricots to the remaining stuffing ingredients and bind with the hot juice.
4. Stuff the bird, spread butter over the breast, and wrap in foil.
5. Bake for 1 hour.
6. Open the foil for the bird to brown. Add the reserved apricots and the remaining juice to the roasting tin and cook for a further 15–20 minutes.
7. Serve garnished with the apricots and a sprig of parsley, and the pan juices.

Variation

Use pineapple instead of apricots.

Cooking time: 1 hour 20 minutes plus time to make stuffing
Preparation time: 20 minutes
Main cooking utensils: saucepan, roasting tin, foil
Oven temperature: hot (425–450°F., 220–230°C., Gas Mark 7–8)
Oven position: towards top
Serves: 4–6

Fried chicken

Imperial	Metric
4 joints of young chicken	4 joints of young chicken
To coat:	*To coat:*
1 oz. flour	25 g. flour
seasoning	seasoning
OR	OR
1 egg	1 egg
little water	little water
3 tablespoons crisp breadcrumbs (raspings)	3 tablespoons crisp breadcrumbs (raspings)
For frying:	*For frying:*
3 oz. butter, fat or oil for shallow frying	75 g. butter, fat or oil for shallow frying
OR	OR
at least 1 lb. fat or 1 pint oil for deep frying	at least 450 g. fat or 550 ml. oil for deep frying

1. Put the flour and seasoning on to a plate, on greaseproof paper or in a bag.
2. Either turn the chicken (very well dried) in it or drop it into the bag and shake well until coated.
3. To coat in egg and breadcrumbs, beat egg on a plate – a little water can be added to make it go further.
4. Brush chicken with this, roll in breadcrumbs until evenly coated. Shake off surplus before cooking.
5. To shallow fry, heat fat in pan.
6. Add chicken cook for 4 minutes, then turn and cook for a further 4 minutes. Lower heat, cook for a further 10–12 minutes, turning once or twice.
7. To deep fry, heat oil or fat until a cube of day-old bread turns golden brown in ½–1 minute. Put in chicken and cook for approximately 12–15 minutes; lower heat when it goes in.
8. Whether shallow or deep fried, drain on crumpled tissue or kitchen paper. Serve with vegetables or salad.

Cooking time: 15–20 minutes
Preparation time: 5–8 minutes
Main cooking utensil: either large frying pan or deep fat pan with basket
Serves: 4

Chicken in a basket

Imperial	Metric
2 small broilers (young chickens)	2 small broilers (young chickens)
seasoning	seasoning
1 oz. flour	25 g. flour
1 egg	1 egg
3 oz. fine soft breadcrumbs	75 g. fine soft breadcrumbs
To fry:	*To fry:*
minimum 1½ pints oil or 1½ lb. fat	minimum 1 litre oil or ¾ kg. fat
Barbecue sauce:	*Barbecue sauce:*
3 oz. butter	75 g. butter
½ pint water	300 ml. water
juice of 1 lemon	juice of 1 lemon
seasoning	seasoning
good pinch each cayenne, paprika, chilli powder and sugar	good pinch each cayenne, paprika, chilli powder and sugar
1 onion, chopped	1 onion, chopped
1 clove garlic, crushed	1 clove garlic, crushed
½ tablespoon mustard	½ tablespoon mustard
few drops Tabasco and Worcestershire sauces	few drops Tabasco and Worcestershire sauces

1. Cut the chickens into joints. Coat in seasoned flour.
2. Brush with beaten egg and press soft crumbs against joints. It is possible to use crisp breadcrumbs, but they can become over-cooked before the chicken joints are tender, so particular care must be taken to watch them when frying.
3. Test the temperature of the oil or fat — put in a cube of day-old bread, this should turn golden in just over ½ minute with oil, just over 1 minute with fat. If this time is any shorter, the solid chicken meat will over-brown before being cooked.
4. Fry the chicken until tender, drain on absorbent paper.
5. Serve with the barbecue sauce, made by blending all ingredients together in a pan until hot. To give a thick sauce, blend in 1 oz. (25 g.) flour.

Cooking time: 15 minutes
Preparation time: 10 minutes
Main cooking utensils: pan and frying basket, saucepan
Serves: 4

Fried chicken and orange

Imperial	Metric
1 small roasting chicken	1 small roasting chicken
2–3 onions	2–3 onions
seasoning	seasoning
4 oranges (bitter Seville or sweet type)	4 oranges (bitter Seville or sweet type)
4 oz. butter or 4 tablespoons oil	100 g. butter or 4 tablespoons oil
1 clove garlic, crushed	1 clove garlic, crushed
¼ pint white wine	125 ml. white wine
Garnish:	*Garnish:*
slices fresh orange	slices fresh orange
1–2 tablespoons finely chopped parsley	1–2 tablespoons finely chopped parsley

1. Simmer the chicken in a pan of water with onions and seasoning for 45 minutes, until almost cooked.
2. Lift the chicken out of the stock, drain well. When cool enough to handle cut into half, flatten as much as possible.
3. While the chicken is simmering, remove the peel from 2–3 oranges, cut this into neat strips, removing some of the pith. Simmer the peel in water to cover for 1 hour.
4. Remove the pulp from all the oranges, discarding the skin, pips and any pith.
5. Heat the butter or oil in a pan, fry the garlic. Add the chicken halves and turn these in the garlic-flavoured butter or oil until quite tender, taking care not to over-brown. Add the wine towards the end of the cooking time with the well-drained orange peel and pulp.
6. Put the chicken halves on a dish, top with the orange peel and pulp, parsley and the orange slices.

Variation

Use 1 Seville and 3 sweet oranges for an interesting flavour.

Cooking time: 1 hour
Preparation time: 20 minutes
Main cooking utensils: large saucepan, frying pan, small saucepan
Serves: 4

Chicken with walnuts

Imperial	Metric
2 small or 1 large young chicken, suitable for frying	2 small or 1 large young chicken, suitable for frying
3 oz. butter	75 g. butter
2 tablespoons oil	2 tablespoons oil
1 clove garlic (optional)	1 clove garlic (optional)
1 onion	1 onion
4–6 oz. walnuts	100–150 g. walnuts
seasoning	seasoning
4 tablespoons white wine	4 tablespoons white wine
1 lb. fresh shelled or frozen peas	½ kg. fresh shelled or frozen peas
grated rind of 1 orange	grated rind of 1 orange
Potato balls:	*Potato balls:*
1 lb. potatoes	½ kg. potatoes
pan of oil or butter and oil	pan of oil or butter and oil

1. Cut the chicken into four serving pieces. Wash and dry very well, but do not flour.
2. Heat 2 oz. (50 g.) butter and the oil in a pan, fry the crushed garlic and finely chopped onion for a few minutes.
3. Add the chicken and continue cooking in pan, turning well, until nearly tender.
4. Add the coarsely chopped nuts and continue frying for a few minutes. Season the chicken, add the wine.
5. Meanwhile toss the shelled peas in the remaining 1 oz. (25 g.) butter, add the orange rind and a very little water.
6. Season well. Cook steadily until tender and all the liquid is absorbed.
7. Meanwhile, make the potato balls. Scoop out balls of raw potato with a vegetable scoop, turning it so that you have a complete round. Either fry steadily in hot oil or butter and oil until tender, or cook in a hot oven in 4–6 tablespoons oil.
8. Lift the chicken on to a hot dish, top with the nuts. Arrange the peas round the chicken together with the potato balls.

Cooking time: 20–25 minutes
Preparation time: 15 minutes
Main cooking utensils: large frying pan, deep-frying pan, saucepan
Serves: 4

Spanish boiled chicken

Imperial	Metric
1 boiling fowl, about 4 lb.	1 boiling fowl, about 2 kg.
6 good-sized onions	6 good-sized onions
6 large carrots	6 large carrots
1 lemon	1 lemon
seasoning	seasoning
about 12 oz. Spanish sausage (chorizo)	about 300 g. Spanish sausage (chorizo)
Sauce:	*Sauce:*
3 oz. butter	75 g. butter
2 oz. flour	50 g. flour
2–4 oz. mushrooms	50–100 g. mushrooms
½ pint milk	250 ml. milk
½ pint chicken stock	250 ml. chicken stock
nutmeg	nutmeg

1. Wash the fowl well and put it into a pan. The giblets may be added but the liver tends to give a bitter taste to the stock which people may not like.
2. Add the whole, peeled onions, the halved, peeled carrots, the sliced lemon and seasoning and pour in water to cover.
3. Bring to the boil, lower the heat and cook gently for 1¾ hours. Add the sausage, cut into pieces, and heat for a further 15 minutes.
4. Meanwhile prepare the sauce. Heat 2 oz. (50 g.) butter in the pan, stir in the flour, cook for several minutes.
5. Heat the remainder of the butter in a small pan and fry the mushrooms.
6. Blend the milk and chicken stock (spooned out from chicken pan) into the butter and flour roux. Bring to the boil and cook until thickened. Add the mushrooms and grated nutmeg.
7. Put the chicken, vegetables and sausage on to a hot dish with some of the clear stock, serve the sauce separately. Garnish with parsley.

Cooking time: 2 hours
Preparation time: 20 minutes
Main cooking utensils: 3 saucepans
Serves: 6

Chicken and bacon casserole

Imperial	Metric
1 small chicken, about 2 lb. when trussed, with giblets	1 small chicken, about 1 kg. when trussed, with giblets
¼ pint water	125 ml. water
seasoning	seasoning
1 bay leaf	1 bay leaf
bouquet garni	bouquet garni
1–2 onions	1–2 onions
2 oz. butter	50 g. butter
12-oz. piece streaky bacon	300-g. piece streaky bacon
1 oz. flour	25 g. flour
small packet frozen peas or about 8 oz. fresh peas	small packet frozen peas or about 200 g. fresh peas

1. Cut the chicken into neat pieces. If using frozen chicken make sure it is completely thawed, and pat dry on paper.
2. Simmer the giblets with the water, seasoning, bay leaf and bouquet garni for about 15 minutes; strain the liquid and use as stock.
3. While the giblets are cooking, peel and slice the onions, fry gently in the hot butter, put into the casserole.
4. Cut the bacon into neat pieces, fry in the pan until golden brown on the outside, add to the onions.
5. Coat the chicken pieces in flour mixed with seasoning but do not overseason as the bacon gives flavour.
6. Fry the chicken until golden, put it into the casserole.
7. Strain the stock over the chicken in the casserole.
8. Cover the casserole and cook for 45 minutes or until tender.
9. If using frozen peas add them to the casserole 8 minutes before the end of the cooking time; if using fresh peas shell and add about 20 minutes before the end of the cooking period. Serve hot with young beans and creamed or boiled potatoes.

Cooking time: 1 hour
Preparation time: 15 minutes plus time for chicken to defrost
Main cooking utensils: frying pan, casserole
Oven temperature: moderate to moderately hot (350–375°F., 180–190°C., Gas Mark 4–5)
Oven position: centre
Serves: 5–6

Coq au vin

Imperial	Metric
1 young roasting chicken (preferably a cock bird)	1 young roasting chicken (preferably a cock bird)
4–6 oz. button mushrooms	100–150 g. button mushrooms
about 12–15 small shallots or onions	about 12–15 small shallots or onions
1–2 cloves garlic (optional)	1–2 cloves garlic (optional)
4–6 oz. fat bacon or pork	100–150 g. fat bacon or pork
2 oz. butter	50 g. butter
1 oz. flour or ½ oz. cornflour	25 g. flour or 15 g. cornflour
seasoning	seasoning
2 tablespoons brandy	2 tablespoons brandy
1 pint red wine or ½ pint red wine and ½ pint chicken stock made by simmering the chicken giblets	500 ml. red wine or 250 ml. red wine and 250 ml. chicken stock made by simmering the chicken giblets

1. Joint the chicken. Simmer the giblets to make stock if this is to be used.
2. Peel the mushrooms, or just wash them and remove the base of the stalks.
3. Peel the shallots or onions. Slice the mushrooms or leave whole. The garlic should be chopped very finely.
4. Either dice the bacon or pork or halve the rashers, chop some and roll the remainder to make bacon rolls as in the picture.
5. Fry the chopped bacon or pork until crisp, lift out, toss the vegetables in the fat in the pan, remove.
6. Add the butter to the bacon fat. Coat the chicken joints in the flour or cornflour and seasoning, fry until golden.
7. Pour over the brandy and ignite; when the flame has gone out gradually add the wine or wine and stock.
8. Return the vegetables and bacon or pork to the pan, cover tightly, simmer for about 1 hour. Put the bacon rolls on top and cook for a further 15 minutes.

Cooking time: 1¼ hours
Preparation time: 25 minutes
Main cooking utensils: saucepan
Serves: 4–6

Indian chicken curry

Imperial	Metric
1¼ lb. boned chicken	generous ½ kg. boned chicken
¼–½ teaspoon powdered ginger	¼–½ teaspoon powdered ginger
½ teaspoon turmeric	½ teaspoon turmeric
¼ teaspoon powdered chillis	¼ teaspoon powdered chillis
¼ teaspoon cumin	¼ teaspoon cumin
seasoning	seasoning
pinch sugar	pinch sugar
1 oz. flour	25 g. flour
3 medium-sized onions	3 medium-sized onions
3 oz. butter	75 g. butter
1 pint white stock	500 ml. white stock
juice of 1 lemon	juice of 1 lemon
¼ pint yoghurt	125 ml. yoghurt
Rice:	*Rice:*
3 medium-sized carrots	3 medium-sized carrots
½ large swede	½ large swede
4 oz. peas	100 g. peas
8 oz. long-grain rice	200 g. long-grain rice
generous ¾ pint water	400 ml. water

1. Dice the chicken neatly
2. Turn the meat in the spices, seasoning and sugar which should be blended with the flour.
3. Chop the onions finely, fry in butter until soft, not brown.
4. Fry the meat with the onions for a few minutes.
5. Gradually blend in the stock and lemon juice, cook until thickened.
6. Lower the heat, cover tightly and cook for 1 hour, stir in the yoghurt.
7. Meanwhile cook chopped vegetables in well seasoned water.
8. Put the rice, seasoning and water into a pan, bring to the boil, cover tightly, lower the heat, simmer gently for 15 minutes, blend with the drained vegetables and form into a ring on a serving dish. Spoon the curry and sauce into the centre of the rice, garnish with endive, paprika and parsley.

Cooking time: 1 hour 20 minutes
Preparation time: 15 minutes
Main cooking utensils: 3 saucepans
Serves: 4

Creamed chicken and mushrooms

Imperial	Metric
1 (3 lb.) young chicken	1 (1½ kg.) young chicken
1½ oz. flour	40 g. flour
seasoning	seasoning
3 oz. butter or margarine	75 g. butter or margarine
1 tablespoon oil	1 tablespoon oil
4 oz. small mushrooms	100 g. small mushrooms
8-oz. can unsweetened evaporated milk	226-g. can unsweetened evaporated milk
1–2 tablespoons sherry	1–2 tablespoons sherry
7-oz. can sweetcorn	198-g. can sweetcorn
chopped parsley	chopped parsley
Garnish:	*Garnish:*
parsley sprigs	parsley sprigs

1. Joint the chicken into six pieces.
2. Coat the chicken in about ½ oz. (15 g.) of the flour mixed with seasoning.
3. Heat 2 oz. (50 g.) butter or margarine and the oil in the frying pan.
4. Fry the joints of chicken steadily until nearly tender, turning frequently so they become golden brown, but do not burn; this takes about 25 minutes.
5. Meanwhile heat the rest of the butter or margarine in the saucepan, toss the mushrooms in it for a good 5 minutes.
6. Add sufficient water to the evaporated milk to make up to 1 pint (550 ml.).
7. Blend this with the remaining flour, then stir into the mushrooms and continue stirring until the sauce thickens.
8. Remove from the heat, add the sherry, seasoning and well-drained sweetcorn.
9. Put the chicken joints in the casserole. Add the sauce and cook for 15 minutes in a moderate oven.
10. Stir chopped parsley into the sauce in the casserole and top with sprigs of parsley.

Cooking time: 40–45 minutes
Preparation time: 14 minutes
Main cooking utensils: large frying pan, saucepan, covered casserole
Oven temperature: moderate to moderately hot (350–375°F., 180–190°C., Gas Mark 4–5)
Oven position: centre
Serves: 6

Poulet chasseur

Imperial	Metric
1 young boiling fowl	1 young boiling fowl
seasoning	seasoning
2 oz. flour	50 g. flour
3 oz. fat or butter	75 g. fat or butter
4 oz. mushrooms	100 g. mushrooms
1–2 onions	1–2 onions
8 oz. tomatoes	200 g. tomatoes
4–6 oz. fat bacon (optional)	100–150 g. fat bacon (optional)
6–8 oz. sausages (optional)	150–200 g. sausages (optional)
1 pint chicken stock	500 ml. chicken stock
3 tablespoons red or white wine	3 tablespoons red or white wine
2 oz. raisins or sultanas (optional)	50 g. raisins or sultanas (optional)
bay leaf	bay leaf
bouquet garni	bouquet garni
Garnish:	*Garnish:*
chopped parsley	chopped parsley

1. Cut the fowl into neat joints. Simmer the giblets in seasoned water for 1 hour to make the stock.
2. Coat the chicken pieces in 1 oz. (25 g.) seasoned flour
3. Fry in 2 oz. (50 g.) fat or butter until golden brown. Put into the casserole.
4. Add the remaining 1 oz. (25 g.) fat to the pan and fry the mushrooms, chopped onions and skinned chopped tomatoes.
5. Add these to the casserole. Fry the diced bacon and sausages, put them into the casserole.
6. Stir the remaining 1 oz. (25 g.) flour into the pan, then blend in the stock (from simmering the giblets) and wine, cook until thickened slightly, pour over the chicken, adding the raisins or sultanas, bay leaf and bouquet garni.
7. Cover the casserole and cook for about 1½ hours in a very moderate oven or longer for an older bird. Serve topped with chopped parsley.

Cooking time: 2½ hours
Preparation time: 30 minutes
Main cooking utensils: saucepan, casserole
Oven temperature: very moderate (325–350°F., 170–180°C., Gas Mark 3–4)
Oven position: centre
Serves: 4–6

Kentish chicken pudding

Imperial	Metric
Suet crust:	*Suet crust:*
8 oz. self-raising flour (with plain flour use 2 level teaspoons baking powder)	200 g. self-raising flour (with plain flour use 2 level teaspoons baking powder)
½ level teaspoon salt	½ level teaspoon salt
3 oz. shredded suet	75 g. shredded suet
¼ pint less 1 tablespoon water	110 ml. water
Filling:	*Filling:*
8 oz. salt pork belly	200 g. salt pork belly
4 small chicken joints or 12 oz. uncooked chicken meat	4 small chicken joints or 300 g. uncooked chicken meat
1 large onion, chopped	1 large onion, chopped
seasoning	seasoning
1 heaped tablespoon chopped parsley	1 heaped tablespoon chopped parsley

1. Sieve together the flour and salt, mix in suet and add water.
2. Mix to a soft dough, knead until smooth.
3. Cut off a third of the pastry for a lid and roll out the rest.
4. Carefully line a basin with pastry.
5. Cut the pork into 1-inch (2½-cm.) cubes.
6. Put into the pastry-lined basin with the chicken joints, onion, seasoning and parsley.
7. Fill the basin three-quarters full with water and put on pastry lid.
8. Cover with a double layer of greased greaseproof paper or foil.
9. Cook for the time given. Serve with a green vegetable.

Variation

Add mixed vegetables instead of pork.

Cooking time: 2½–3 hours
Preparation time: 20 minutes
Main cooking utensils: 2-pint (1-litre pudding basin, steamer, saucepan, foil
Serves: 4

Chicken and mushroom pie

Imperial	Metric
Rough puff pastry:	*Rough puff pastry:*
3 oz. cooking fat mixed with 3 oz. margarine	75 g. cooking fat mixed with 75 g. margarine
8 oz. plain flour	200 g. plain flour
pinch salt	pinch salt
1 teaspoon lemon juice	1 teaspoon lemon juice
cold water	cold water
Filling:	*Filling:*
2 oz. butter	50 g. butter
2 oz. flour	50 g. flour
1 pint milk	550 ml. milk
seasoning	seasoning
8–12 oz. cooked chicken	200–300 g. cooked chicken
4 oz. mushrooms	100 g. mushrooms
Glaze:	*Glaze:*
1 egg	1 egg
1 tablespoon milk	1 tablespoon milk

1. Make the pastry. Cut the fat into the sieved flour and salt, mix to a soft dough with the lemon juice and water, put on a floured board.
2. Roll to an oblong, fold in three, seal ends and turn, repeat for further three times. Cool well before using.
3. Make the filling. Heat the butter, stir in the flour and cook for several minutes, then gradually blend in the milk. Bring to the boil and cook until thickened and smooth; stir well.
4. Add seasoning, chopped chicken, sliced uncooked mushrooms.
5. Put into the pie dish, cover with pastry.
6. Seal edges and decorate with leaves of pastry. Glaze with egg and milk.
7. Bake for 15 minutes in a hot oven, then lower the heat to moderate for a further 20 minutes until the pastry is brown and filling hot. Serve hot or cold with vegetables or a green salad.

Cooking time: 35 minutes
Preparation time: 30 minutes plus time for pastry to stand
Main cooking utensil: 2-pint (1-litre) pie dish
Oven temperature: hot (425–450°F., 220–230°C., Gas Mark 7–8), then moderate (375°F., 190°C., Gas Mark 5)
Oven position: just above centre
Serves: 6

Stuffed turkey

Imperial	Metric
1 10- to 12-lb. turkey	1 5- to 5½-kg. turkey
4 oz. fat pork, thinly sliced or 2–3 oz. butter	100 g. fat pork, thinly sliced or 50–75 g. butter
Stuffing:	*Stuffing:*
6 oz. veal	150 g. veal
6 oz. cooked ham	150 g. cooked ham
4 oz. butter	100 g. butter
4 oz. soft breadcrumbs	100 g. soft breadcrumbs
1 lemon	1 lemon
6 oz. seedless raisins	150 g. seedless raisins
2 small shallots or onions	2 small shallots or onions
seasoning	seasoning
1 egg	1 egg
white wine	white wine

1. Mince the veal, dice the ham and toss in the hot butter for several minutes. Add to the breadcrumbs with the grated lemon rind, raisins and chopped shallots. Season.
2. Add the egg and enough wine to bind the mixture.
3. Stuff the turkey with this, weigh and cover it with fat pork or butter, or wrap in buttered foil.
4. Allow 15 minutes cooking time per lb. (½ kg.) and 15 minutes over up to 12 lb. (5½ kg.). After this weight add an extra 12 minutes cooking time for each additional lb. (½ kg.). (Broad-breasted turkeys need about 20 minutes per lb. (½ kg.) and 20 minutes over.)
5. If using a covered roasting tin or foil, allow an extra 20 minutes cooking time or 25°F. (15°C.) higher temperature or one mark higher on a gas cooker.
6. After 45 minutes reduce the heat to moderately hot.
7. To brown the turkey, remove the lid of a covered roaster or open the foil approximately 30 minutes before the end of the cooking time.

Cooking time: see stages 4, 5, 6
Preparation time: 30 minutes
Main cooking utensils: frying pan, roasting tin
Oven temperature: hot (425–450°F., 220–230°C., Gas Mark 7–8) then moderately hot (400°F., 200°C., Gas Mark 6)
Oven position: above centre
Serves: 10–12

Honeyed turkey

Imperial
1 turkey (about 6 lb. when trussed)
Stuffing:
12 prunes (soaked overnight in water to cover)
15 whole fresh walnuts or about 4–6 oz. dried walnuts
3 tablespoons honey (thin or thick)
1 lb. pork sausage meat
1 medium-sized onion
1 egg
To coat:
2 oz. butter
4 tablespoons honey

Metric
1 turkey (about 3 kg. when trussed)
Stuffing:
12 prunes (soaked overnight in water to cover)
15 whole fresh walnuts or about 100–150 g. dried walnuts
3 tablespoons honey (thin or thick)
½ kg. pork sausage meat
1 medium-sized onion
1 egg
To coat:
50 g. butter
4 tablespoons honey

1. Dry the turkey and simmer the giblets for the gravy.
2. Drain and stone the prunes.
3. Chop the walnuts coarsely and press these into the prunes, then dip the prunes into the honey; be sure to use all the honey.
4. Put the sausage meat into a bowl, add the prunes and the finely chopped onion.
5. Lastly add the egg and mix well.
6. Put the stuffing into the turkey and wrap in well-buttered foil.
7. Roast for 3 hours in the centre of a moderate oven, but unwrap after 1½ hours' roasting and baste with the juices in the foil, then spread with the honey.
8. Wrap the turkey again and continue cooking.
9. If you want a crisp skin, then unwrap the turkey for the last 40 minutes of the cooking time. Serve with a thickened gravy; add some of the honey-flavoured juices to the gravy.

Cooking time: 3 hours
Preparation time: 15 minutes plus overnight soaking of prunes
Main cooking utensils: roasting tin
Oven temperature: moderate (325°F., 170°C., Gas Mark 3)
Oven position: centre
Serves: 8–10

Goose and chestnuts

Imperial
1½ lb. chestnuts
4 rashers streaky bacon
3 large onions
3 oz. butter or margarine
2–3 cooking apples
2 teaspoons finely chopped fresh sage
seasoning
1 goose, about 10 lb. when trussed, with giblets
1½ pints water
3 tablespoons goose fat
2 oz. flour
¼ pint red wine
2 teaspoons chopped herbs

Metric
¾ kg. chestnuts
4 rashers streaky bacon
3 large onions
75 g. butter or margarine
2–3 cooking apples
2 teaspoons finely chopped fresh sage
seasoning
1 goose, about 5 kg. when trussed, with giblets
generous ¾ litre water
3 tablespoons goose fat
50 g. flour
125 ml. red wine
2 teaspoons chopped herbs

1. Slit the chestnuts and boil for 5–10 minutes in water.
2. Cool enough to handle, remove the skins.
3. Chop the bacon; peel and slice the onions.
4. Heat the butter or margarine, fry the onions until slightly softened then add the bacon and cook for a few minutes.
5. Blend with half the chestnuts, the peeled diced apples, sage, seasoning and the diced raw goose liver.
6. Put the stuffing into the goose and weigh the bird, then stand in the tin.
7. Cook for 15 minutes per lb. (½ kg.) (weight when stuffed) and 15 minutes over.
8. Prick from time to time to allow the fat to run out.
9. Simmer the giblets in the water to make stock, strain.
10. To make the sauce heat the goose fat, stir in the flour and cook for several minutes.
11. Gradually blend in 1¼ pints (625 ml.) of the stock, bring to the boil and cook until thickened.
12. Add the rest of the chestnuts, the wine and chopped herbs.
Carve the goose on to a hot dish, and serve with the sauce.

Cooking time: see method
Preparation time: 25 minutes
Main cooking utensils: saucepan, roasting tin
Oven temperature: moderately hot (400–425°F., 200–220°C., Gas Mark 6–7)
Oven position: above centre
Serves: 8–10

Guinea fowl and cabbage

Imperial
1 good-sized young guinea fowl
2–3 oz. butter
1 cabbage
2 large carrots
1–2 large onions
8 oz. fairly fat bacon
seasoning
6 Strasbourg sausages
 (see note)
Stuffing:
good knob of butter
3 oz. cream cheese or 2–3 oz.
 grapes, moistened with
 white wine

Metric
1 good-sized young guinea fowl
50–75 g. butter
1 cabbage
2 large carrots
1–2 large onions
200 g. fairly fat bacon
seasoning
6 Strasbourg sausages
 (see note)
Stuffing:
good knob of butter
75 g. cream cheese or 50–75 g.
 grapes, moistened with
 white wine

1. Weigh the guinea fowl, stuff if liked, put into the tin and cover with butter.
2. Roast until tender, allowing 15 minutes per lb. ($\frac{1}{2}$ kg.) and 15 minutes over and basting well with the butter.
3. Meanwhile, cut the cabbage into pieces, chop the carrots finely, and the peeled onions into rings.
4. Remove the rind from the bacon, cut into pieces, fry in the pan for a few minutes, add the vegetables, toss with the bacon, pour in some juice from the roasting tin, add just enough water to prevent the cabbage burning, season lightly.
5. Cook until the vegetables are tender, approximately 30 minutes, and the liquid is absorbed.
6. Add the sausages to the meat tin; cook or heat thoroughly.
7. Serve as shown in the picture with the vegetables and bacon on the dish and the guinea fowl and sausages on top.

Note: Strasbourg sausages are strongly flavoured; frankfurters could be used instead.

Cooking time: see stage 2
Preparation time: 20 minutes
Main cooking utensils: roasting tin, large saucepan
Oven temperature: hot (425–450°F., 220–230°C., Gas Mark 7–8)
Oven position: centre
Serves: 4–5

Casserole of guinea fowl and prunes

Imperial
4–6 oz. prunes
1 large or 2 small guinea fowl
seasoning
1 oz. flour
1 oz. fat or dripping
1 large sliced onion
4–6 oz. diced pickled pork
 or bacon
1 small cabbage
1 wineglass red wine
4 smoked sausages or
 rashers bacon

Metric
100–150 g. prunes
1 large or 2 small guinea fowl
seasoning
25 g. flour
25 g. fat or dripping
1 large sliced onion
100–150 g. diced pickled pork
 or bacon
1 small cabbage
1 wineglass red wine
4 smoked sausages or
 rashers bacon

1. Soak the prunes overnight in cold water, drain and remove the stones.
2. Roll the bird in well seasoned flour.
3. Fry in hot fat until golden brown.
4. Remove the fowl, fry the sliced onion and pork for 5 minutes.
5. Shred and wash the cabbage, mix with the onion and pork, season well and put half at the bottom of a casserole.
6. Put the bird and some prunes on this, cover with the cabbage mixture, prunes and red wine. Arrange the smoked sausages or extra bacon on top, cover with a lid.
7. Cook for 2 hours.
8. Lift bird from the casserole, carve or joint, arrange the prunes, etc., around. Serve with new or creamed potatoes and a green vegetable. No sauce needed.

Variation
Use more red wine for extra liquid.

Cooking time: 2¼ hours
Preparation time: 15 minutes and overnight soaking of prunes
Main cooking utensils: saucepan, large covered casserole
Oven temperature: moderate (325–350°F., 170–180°C.,
 Gas Mark 3–4)
Oven position: centre
Serves: 4

Duck and olives

Imperial
2 duckling with giblets
seasoning
3 oz. butter
2 onions
1 oz. flour
pinch saffron powder
pinch curry powder
1 lemon
1–2 teaspoons sugar
18–24 green olives
4 slices bread

Metric
2 duckling with giblets
seasoning
75 g. butter
2 onions
25 g. flour
pinch saffron powder
pinch curry powder
1 lemon
1–2 teaspoons sugar
18–24 green olives
4 slices bread

1. Roast the duckling for 30 minutes in a hot oven until golden brown; prick the skin gently so the excess fat runs out.
2. Lower the heat to moderate, continue cooking until tender (just over 1 hour).
3. Meanwhile simmer the giblets in 1 pint (500 ml.) well-seasoned water for 1 hour; strain the liquid, remove the liver and mash with 1 oz. (25 g.) of the butter and the seasoning.
4. Heat the rest of the butter in the pan, fry the finely chopped onions until tender.
5. Stir in the flour blended with the saffron and curry powder.
6. Gradually blend in ¾ pint (375 ml.) of the giblet stock.
7. Bring to the boil, stirring, and cook until thickened.
8. Add a little lemon juice, finely grated lemon rind, seasoning, sugar and the olives. Toast the bread, spread with the liver and cut into fingers.
9. Cut the duckling into portions. Arrange on the dish with the sauce around, not over, the poultry; garnish with the toast fingers.

Cooking time: 1¼ hours
Preparation time: 15 minutes
Main cooking utensils: roasting tin, saucepan
Oven temperature: hot (425–450°F., 220–230°C., Gas Mark 7–8) then moderate (350–375°F., 180–190°C. Gas Mark 4–5)
Oven position: just above centre
Serves: 4–6

Duck nantaise

Imperial
1 oven-ready duck, about 4½ lb.
4–6 oz. fairly lean bacon
3–4 medium-sized onions, cooked for 15–20 minutes in salted water

Metric
1 oven-ready duck, about 2¼ kg.
100–150 g. fairly lean bacon
3–4 medium-sized onions, cooked for 15–20 minutes in salted water

1. Weigh the duck and allow to cook for 15 minutes per lb. (½ kg) and 15 minutes over.
2. After the duck has been cooking for approximately 30 minutes, prick the skin gently with a fine skewer to allow surplus fat to run out, and add the chopped rashers of bacon and the quartered onions. Toss in the duck fat and continue cooking.
3. Place the duck on a dish and garnish with cooked peas, pieces of onion and bacon.
4. Serve with thickened gravy made as follows: make a stock by simmering the giblets. Pour away the fat from the roasting tin, leaving 1 tablespoon. Blend in 1 oz. (25 g.) flour, gravy flavouring, seasoning and ½ pint (250 ml.) stock. Bring to the boil, stirring, and simmer for 1–2 minutes.

Note: This is the name given in France to a duckling from the Nantaise area; in this particular recipe the duck has an interesting garnish, but has not been stuffed. To carve large ducks, divide into 4 portions — 2 breasts and wings, and 2 legs. Divide smaller ducks, down the centre, into 2 portions.

Variation
Use new young parboiled baby turnips in place of the onions.

Cooking time: see stage 1
Preparation time: 10 minutes
Main cooking utensil: roasting tin
Oven temperature: hot (425–450°F., 220–230°C., Gas Mark 7–8)
Oven position: above centre
Serves: 4

Game dishes

In many parts of the country, game is easily available and this makes a pleasant change from meat and poultry.

There are widely differing views on the time that game should be hung, so check that the poulterer is aware of your particular requirements. Game that is 'well hung' has a very strong flavour, which pleases many people, but would offend others.

Care must be taken in choosing the method of cooking as older birds are very tough and are only palatable if cooked slowly in a casserole.

You can tell if game birds are young in very much the same way as you would judge poultry. The legs should be pliable, not rigid and sinewy; the breast bone pliable too and the breast plump.

Methods and timing for roasting are given on the opposite page.

Casseroled game is delicious and the recipes in this section can be used for every type of game with the following adaptations.

The Tinker's casserole on page 103 would be very successful with whole grouse or pheasant. All the casseroles on pages 104 and 105 are suitable for jointed grouse or other older birds but the Pheasant with apples would only be suitable for a young bird.

To freeze game

Game is a highly seasonal food and it is, therefore, very sensible to freeze any surplus.

Make sure the game is hung to your personal taste *before* freezing, for it cannot be hung successfully after you bring it from the freezer.

Wrap the game carefully in foil and polythene or all polythene and label the birds, etc. as to whether they are young for roasting or older for using in a casserole or stew; it is surprising how one forgets exactly what has gone into the freezer. Uncooked game can be stored for 6–8 months and it is highly successful; there is little, if any, loss of flavour or change in texture.

Cooked game is less successful, it loses flavour and some of the firm texture, unless frozen in a completed dish. Use cooked game within 2–3 months or cooked game dishes within about 1 month.

It is worth freezing small bags of fried crumbs, the traditional accompaniment to roast game. Fry the coarse crumbs in hot butter, margarine or dripping, until crisp and golden. Drain on absorbent paper, freeze on flat trays, then pack in polythene. You can then remove the number of bags required.

Freeze game giblets separately (see under To freeze poultry, page 90).

Ways to cook game

The accompaniments to roast game are fried crumbs, see under To freeze, bread sauce (page 91) or redcurrant jelly, game chips (wafer-thin slices of potato, fried until crisp) — the commercial potato crisps can be heated and served.

The larger game birds — grouse, partridge, pheasant — should be roasted for the same time and at the same temperature as that given for poultry (see page 91). Small snipe and woodcock need a total of 30 minutes' cooking. It is not essential to stuff game, but a piece of butter or cream cheese placed inside the bird helps to keep it moist, and the bird should be covered with fat bacon, clarified dripping or butter so it does not dry during cooking.

Young hare, known as 'leveret', or young rabbit can be roasted. You can roast all the young hare or just the back joints, known as the 'saddle'. The traditional accompaniments here are sage and onion stuffing (see page 122), redcurrant jelly and the stuffing (often called 'forcemeat') balls, which you will find under Pigeon casserole (see page 104). It is quite a good idea to roast the saddle of a young hare then cook the legs in a casserole as page 105. Venison is another game that is covered in this section. If you prefer to roast venison treat it as veal (see pages 75 and 76) but see the column on right.

To marinate game, etc.

Venison is a game meat that is much improved by soaking in a marinade. Many meats can also be soaked in the same way. The purpose is to impart flavour to the meat and, by using acid, wine, vinegar, etc., to tenderise meat. Often oil is added, and this adds the necessary fat to lean meats.

I am not giving definite quantities of marinades, but you need enough to let the joint soak in this; not enough to cover a large joint, as when soaking salted meats. Turn the joint several times, and do leave for a day, or at least 12 hours for game, or several hours for meat.

Wine marinade: Blend red wine with chopped onion, garlic, seasoning and a little oil.

Wine and vinegar marinade: Blend red wine with seasoning, a little sugar and made mustard, crushed garlic and chopped onion. Add vinegar and olive oil. I use about $\frac{1}{4}$ pint ($1\frac{1}{2}$ dl.) vinegar and oil to each $\frac{1}{2}$ pint (3 dl.) wine.

Beer marinade: Season beer, add a little oil, sugar, garlic and chopped herbs.

Any marinade left can be added to the gravy.

Tinker's casserole

Imperial	Metric
1½ lb. stewing steak or venison or 1 rabbit	¾ kg. stewing steak or venison or 1 rabbit
1 pint stout or use ½ pint stock and ½ pint stout	600 ml. stout or use 300 ml. stock and 300 ml. stout
2 oz. fat or dripping	50 g. fat or dripping
1½ oz. flour	40 g. flour
seasoning	seasoning
½ teaspoon dried mixed herbs or 2 teaspoons freshly chopped mixed herbs	½ teaspoon dried mixed herbs or 2 teaspoons freshly chopped mixed herbs
8–12 oz. carrots	200–300 g. carrots
1 tablespoon Worcestershire sauce	1 tablespoon Worcestershire sauce
4 oz. mushrooms	100 g. mushrooms

1. Cut the steak or venison into neat pieces, joint the rabbit.
2. Put into a bowl, add ½ pint (300 ml.) stout (or beer or wine) and leave to marinate for 1–2 hours.
3. Heat the fat or dripping in the pan, stir in the flour and cook for 2–3 minutes, stirring well.
4. Blend in the other ½ pint (300 ml.) stout (or other liquid), bring to the boil and stir well as the mixture thickens.
5. Add the meat and liquid, seasoning, herbs, sliced carrots and sauce.
6. Mix thoroughly then tip into the casserole, cover and cook steak or venison for nearly 2 hours in a cool to moderate oven; young rabbit needs 1½ hours only.
7. Remove the lid, add the thickly sliced mushrooms, stir to make sure they are covered with the sauce.
8. Replace the lid and cook for another 25 minutes.

Variation

In place of the stout or stock and stout you can use ½ pint (300 ml.) strained tea and ½ pint beer, or ½ pint red wine and ½ pint stock.

Cooking time: 2½ or 2 hours (see stage 6)
Preparation time: 20 minutes plus time to stand
Main cooking utensils: saucepan, covered casserole
Oven temperature: cool to moderate (300–325°F., 150–170°C., Gas Mark 2–3)
Oven position: centre
Serves: 4–6

Pigeon casserole

Imperial	Metric
4 oz. diced fat bacon	100 g. diced fat bacon
1 oz. butter or dripping	25 g. butter or dripping
4 small pigeons	4 small pigeons
2 small onions	2 small onions
1½ oz. sieved flour	40 g. sieved flour
1 pint stock	550 ml. stock
shake of pepper	shake of pepper
1 level teaspoon salt	1 level teaspoon salt
4 oz. mushrooms	100 g. mushrooms
Forcemeat balls:	*Forcemeat balls:*
4 oz. fresh breadcrumbs	100 g. fresh breadcrumbs
2 oz. suet	50 g. suet
1 tablespoon chopped parsley	1 tablespoon chopped parsley
grated rind of ½ lemon	grated rind of ½ lemon
seasoning	seasoning
beaten egg to bind	beaten egg to bind
Garnish:	*Garnish:*
fried bread	fried bread
parsley	parsley

1. Fry the bacon in heated fat until brown, remove from pan.
2. Clean the pigeons and remove the feet. Fry until brown; fry the onion lightly; drain and remove.
3. Stir in the flour, heat gently until brown, stirring all the time.
4. Add the stock, season to taste, bring to the boil.
5. Replace the fried ingredients, transfer all to a casserole, and cook in a cool to moderate oven until tender, 1¼–1½ hours.
6. Meanwhile mix all the ingredients for the forcemeat together and roll into small balls.
7. Add sliced mushrooms and forcemeat balls to the casserole; cook a further 15 minutes.
8. Garnish with triangles of fried bread, if desired, and chopped parsley.

Cooking time: 1¾–2 hours
Preparation time: 15 minutes
Main cooking utensils: large saucepan, casserole
Oven temperature: cool to moderate (300–325°F., 150–170°C., Gas Mark 2–3)
Serves: 4

Casserole of rabbit and sausages

Imperial	Metric
1 good-sized young rabbit	1 good-sized young rabbit
seasoning	seasoning
rabbit stock (see stage 1)	rabbit stock (see stage 1)
2 oz. butter	50 g. butter
1–2 tablespoons oil	1–2 tablespoons oil
4 oz. fairly fat bacon	100 g. fairly fat bacon
2 large onions	2 large onions
4 good-sized sausages	4 good-sized sausages
1 small cabbage or piece of cabbage	1 small cabbage or piece of cabbage

1. Wash the rabbit well and soak in cold water with a little salt for about 1 hour to whiten the flesh. Meanwhile, simmer the liver with about ½ pint (300 ml.) water to make the stock.
2. Remove the rabbit from the water and dry it well. Brown it all over in the hot butter and oil.
3. Place in a casserole or saucepan.
4. Dice the bacon, fry this with the chopped onions and add them to the rabbit.
5. Season lightly, add about ¼ pint (150 ml.) rabbit stock.
6. Cover and cook for approximately 45 minutes, then add the halved sausages, shredded cabbage and remaining stock, re-season and cook for a further hour.
7. The stock becomes absorbed by the cabbage, etc., and there is no need to make a sauce as the whole dish is very succulent and moist.
8. Carve or joint the rabbit and serve on a hot dish with the cabbage and sausages.

Variation
Red wine could be used in place of some of the stock.

Cooking time: 2 hours
Preparation time: 25 minutes plus time to soak rabbit (see stage 1)
Main cooking utensils: large frying pan, flameproof casserole or saucepan
Oven temperature: moderate (325–350°F., 170–180°C., Gas Mark 3–4)
Oven position: centre
Serves: 4–5

Jugged hare

Imperial	Metric
1 hare, jointed, with liver and blood	1 hare, jointed, with liver and blood
seasoning	seasoning
1½ pints water	¾ litre water
vinegar	vinegar
1 large onion	1 large onion
1 large carrot	1 large carrot
2 oz. dripping or fat	50 g. dripping or fat
2 oz. flour	50 g. flour
¼ pint port	125 ml. port
1 tablespoon redcurrant jelly	1 tablespoon redcurrant jelly
Forcemeat balls (opposite)	Forcemeat balls (opposite)
Garnish:	*Garnish:*
slices of bread	slices of bread
fat or butter	fat or butter
redcurrant jelly	redcurrant jelly

1. Cook the liver in the water with the seasoning for 30 minutes; strain off the stock and add enough water to give 1½ pints (¾ litre) again. Mash or sieve the liver.
2. Soak the hare in cold water and 1 tablespoon vinegar for 1–2 hours, lift out and dry well.
3. Fry the sliced onion and carrot in the hot dripping or fat.
4. Stir in the flour, cook for a few minutes, then blend in the 1½ pints (¾ litre) stock, blood from hare, port, jelly and liver. Bring to boil, cook until thickened, season.
5. Put the hare in a casserole, cover with the sauce and cook.
6. Make the forcemeat. Mix the breadcrumbs, suet, parsley, lemon rind and seasoning. Bind with the egg. Roll the mixture into small balls and bake them on a tin in the oven.
7. Cut the slices of bread into the desired shape, fry until crisp.
8. Serve, topped with the fried bread and redcurrant jelly. Serve the forcemeat balls and extra redcurrant jelly separately

Cooking time: 3–4 hours (depending on size of hare) plus time to cook liver and sauce
Preparation time: 40 minutes
Main cooking utensils: pan, covered casserole, tin
Oven temperature: (300–325°F., 150–170°C., Gas Mark 2–3)
Oven position: centre
Serves: 6

Pheasant with apples

Imperial	Metric
2 oz. butter or lard	50 g. butter or lard
1 plump pheasant (see note)	1 plump pheasant (see note)
seasoning	seasoning
small portion cream cheese (optional)	small portion cream cheese (optional)
Apple mixture:	*Apple mixture:*
2 oz. butter	50 g. butter
2 oz. sugar	50 g. sugar
4 tablespoons cider or mixture of cider and Calvados	4 tablespoons cider or mixture of cider and Calvados
juice of ½ lemon	juice of ½ lemon
2–3 dessert apples	2–3 dessert apples
Garnish:	*Garnish:*
parsley sprig	parsley sprig

1. Heat the butter or lard, spread this over the bird or birds and season lightly.
2. A portion of cream cheese, about 1–1½ oz. (25–40 g.) gives a moist texture to the bird, or put a small piece of butter or lard inside the bird.
3. Roast in a hot oven, basting the bird from time to time.
4. Meanwhile prepare the apple mixture. Heat the butter in a saucepan, stir in the sugar and heat gently until golden brown. Add the cider, or cider and Calvados, and lemon juice.
5. Add the sliced apples. Turn in the syrup and cook gently until tender but unbroken.
6. Arrange the apple mixture round the bird. Garnish with parsley.

Note: Although they are small birds a good-sized pheasant has a plump breast; if small use 2 pheasants. Always make sure game is well hung so that it will be tender — if hung for a considerable period it becomes 'high', which many people like, but it is not so suitable for this dish.

Cooking time: about 1 hour
Preparation time: 20 minutes
Main cooking utensils: roasting tin, large shallow saucepan
Oven temperature: hot (425–450°F., 220–230°C., Gas Mark 7–8)
Oven position: above centre
Serves: 3–4

Vegetable dishes

Vegetables are one of the important natural foods, for green vegetables provide much of the Vitamin C (the protective ascorbic acid) we need; and most vegetables contain some minerals that help to keep us well.

Do not be too conservative about the vegetables you buy; we are fortunate that we can choose from a very varied selection and in this chapter I have given ideas for using some of the less usual.

Fresh vegetables lose much of their value if they are not used within a short time after purchase; the column on the right gives hints on buying these. Remember there are large stocks of frozen vegetables from which to choose. Read the instructions carefully and do not over-cook; for in 'blanching', explained on page 107, top right, you partially cook the vegetables, so that the final heating time should be shortened.

Canned vegetables have been cooked in the process of canning, these need heating only. Use canned vegetables within 2 years.

There are two forms of dried vegetables, the older type, which should be soaked overnight, then cooked for quite a long period, and the modern form of drying, i.e. A.F.D. (Accelerated Freeze Dried), means the vegetables need short cooking only, see the instructions on the packets.

To buy vegetables

Be very fussy when you buy vegetables, for you will save money by the fact you will have little, if any, wastage and your family will enjoy the better flavour of the cooked vegetable.

Green vegetables should be firm and bright in colour, cabbages should feel heavy for their size. If there are many yellow leaves, then the green vegetables are not fresh.

Cauliflowers should be white, with firm green leaves; stale cauliflower or the smaller green broccoli have an unpleasantly strong flavour if they are stale. Spinach spoils quickly, it must be green with firm, almost crisp leaves.

Root vegetables, such as carrots, should be firm, if wrinkled they are very stale. Many people prefer to buy the ready washed vegetables, but these should be used quickly, since they spoil more rapidly than those coated with earth.

Tomatoes should be firm, and give off a strong smell, they lose this when not fresh. If tomatoes feel very light for their size they are dry and rather 'hollow' in the centres. Often one can buy slightly misshapen tomatoes cheaper.

Mushrooms should be firm, not wrinkled.

To cook vegetables
To boil vegetables
The basic way of cooking vegetables is to boil them in salted water. Over the years we have learned that valuable vitamins and mineral salts are lost if:

a. The vegetables are soaked for too long before cooking, so prepare just before you are ready to cook them.
b. The vegetables are placed into cold water; they should be added to rapidly boiling water. Do not use too much water; green vegetables can be cooked in about 1 inch (2½ cm.) water, although cauliflower needs rather more and spinach needs only the water adhering to the leaves.

Root vegetables can also be put into boiling water, even potatoes (which contain an appreciable amount of Vitamin C; especially when new and cooked with their skins on).

Bring the water to the boil, add a little salt, put in the vegetables gradually, so the water does not go off the boil and cook as quickly as you can. Strain and serve as soon as possible after cooking.

The vegetable water contains valuable mineral salts, do not waste this, use it in gravy or sauces, or even flavour it and drink it.

Most left-over cooked vegetables can be used in salads; toss in French dressing or mayonnaise, garnish with chopped herbs.

To fry vegetables
Many vegetables can be fried, the most popular being potatoes. Peel the potatoes, cut into slices or chips. You can fry in shallow fat or cook in deep oil or fat. Dry the potatoes, fry steadily until tender, remove from the oil or fat; reheat this, replace potatoes, fry again for 2 minutes until crisp and brown. Page 112 gives Potato croquettes, stage 5 outlines the method of testing the temperature of the fat or oil.

Onion rings should be coated in seasoned flour, egg white or milk and flour and fried.

Sliced courgettes or aubergines should be coated with flour or a thin batter and fried. Drain the food on absorbent paper before serving.

To bake potatoes
Page 205 gives an interesting way to stuff baked potatoes as well as instructions for cooking.

To roast vegetables
Potatoes, parsnips, etc. are delicious roasted in fat. Turn in hot fat, cook quickly for 1 hour. Parsnips are better boiled for about 10 minutes before roasting, potatoes can be parboiled too.

To freeze vegetables
The method of freezing vegetables is simple, it must be done carefully to ensure a satisfactory result.

Choose vegetables that are perfect in quality and very fresh. Many vegetables can be frozen, those that are not satisfactory are the salads (lettuce, etc.) which lose their crispness; tomatoes, which make a pulp, but no longer retain their shape. 'Watery' vegetables, such as marrow, courgettes, etc., are better cooked before freezing. The following is a brief outline only of the way to freeze vegetables; full information will be given in a freezer manufacturer's book.

1. Prepare the vegetables, as though for cooking.
2. 'Blanch' these for the recommended time, this is approximately 2 minutes, but does vary a little. The purpose of 'blanching' is to destroy any harmful enzymes that may be present in the vegetables, and to help retain both colour and flavour.
3. Plunge the vegetables into iced water, this makes sure they do not become too soft after 'blanching'.
4. Cool, then pack into suitable polythene containers or waxed cartons, following instructions for expelling air and sealing. Frozen vegetables can be stored for up to 1 year.

Easy guide to vegetable dishes and salads
The following gives you help in selecting the right salad or vegetable dish for the right occasion.

When you are short of time see pages 15, 108, 116, 117, 118.

When you are short of money see pages 108, 109, 112, 113, 205.

When you want a special dish see pages 108, 109, 110, 111, 112, 116, 117, 118.

For a snack or light meal see pages 110, 111, 115, 116, 117, 119, 120.

When you are slimming see pages 108, 111, 115, 116, 117, 118.

Asparagus with hard-boiled eggs

Imperial	Metric
1 good-sized bundle of asparagus	1 good-sized bundle of asparagus
seasoning	seasoning
3 eggs	3 eggs
parsley	parsley
radishes	radishes
Dressing:	*Dressing:*
good pinch salt	good pinch salt
pepper	pepper
sugar	sugar
mustard	mustard
1 tablespoon lemon juice	1 tablespoon lemon juice
1 tablespoon tarragon vinegar	1 tablespoon tarragon vinegar
4 tablespoons olive oil	4 tablespoons olive oil

1. Cut the base from the asparagus, then scrape the remaining white part of the stalks to clean.
2. Wash well in cold water, taking care not to break the tips.
3. Drain well, then tie into 3–4 bundles. It is better to cook the asparagus in smaller bundles to make sure of even cooking; in one large bundle the outer stalks tend to be cooked before the inner ones.
4. Stand upright in a pan of well seasoned water and cook steadily. If the water boils too rapidly the asparagus tends to fall over.
5. Test to see if it is cooked by pressing the stalks; they should feel very tender. Drain carefully and season.
6. Meanwhile, boil the eggs for 10 minutes to hard-boil, shell, chop the yolks and whites separately, chop the parsley, slice the radishes.
7. Blend together the ingredients for the dressing, coat the asparagus with this. Garnish it with lines of egg yolk, egg white, parsley and radishes.

Cooking time: 20–25 minutes
Preparation time: 15 minutes
Main cooking utensils: 2 saucepans
Serves: 4

Bean and tomato hotpot

Imperial	Metric
8 oz. butter beans	200 g. butter beans
seasoning	seasoning
about 1–1½ lb. neck of mutton or lamb	about ½–¾ kg. neck of mutton or lamb
2 large onions	2 large onions
1 clove garlic (optional)	1 clove garlic (optional)
2 oz. butter or fat	50 g. butter or fat
1–2 rashers bacon	1–2 rashers bacon
1 oz. flour	25 g. flour
¾–1 lb. tomatoes	300–400 g. tomatoes
sprinkling chopped rosemary or thyme, or pinch dried herbs	sprinkling chopped rosemary or thyme, or pinch dried herbs
¼ pint white wine (optional)	125 ml. white wine (optional)

1. Put the beans into a large container, cover with cold water, leave overnight. If preferred, soak in white stock for a richer flavour.
2. Put the beans, liquid and seasoning into a pan, simmer for 2 hours. Drain, save the liquid.
3. Cut the meat into convenient sized pieces.
4. Peel the onions, slice thickly, crush the garlic.
5. Heat the butter or fat, fry the onions and garlic, taking care they do not brown. Fry the finely chopped bacon.
6. Lift out of the pan; fry the meat, coated in seasoned flour, until well browned.
7. Lift this out of the pan, then return the beans, skinned sliced tomatoes, herbs, the onions, etc., to the pan, together with ¼ pint (125 ml.) bean liquid and white wine, or use ½ pint (250 ml.) bean liquid.
8. Add the meat, cover the pan tightly, simmer for 1 hour, add a little extra liquid from time to time if necessary. Serve with green salad or vegetable.

Cooking time: 3¼ hours
Preparation time: 15 minutes plus time for beans to soak overnight
Main cooking utensil: large saucepan
Serves: 4–5

Celery in creamed egg sauce

Imperial
1 lb. celery or celeriac
  (celery root)
seasoning
½ oz. butter
3 eggs
good pinch black pepper
1 teaspoon paprika pepper
good pinch grated or powdered
  nutmeg
½ pint evaporated milk or thin
  cream
Garnish:
chopped parsley

Metric
½ kg. celery or celeriac
  (celery root)
seasoning
15 g. butter
3 eggs
good pinch black pepper
1 teaspoon paprika pepper
good pinch grated or powdered
  nutmeg
250 ml. evaporated milk or thin
  cream
Garnish:
chopped parsley

1. Scrape and wash celery, cut into portions, peel and slice celeriac.
2. Cook the vegetable in well-seasoned water.
3. When tender, drain and put into a buttered dish.
4. Beat the eggs with the remaining ingredients.
5. Pour over the vegetable, bake for approximately 30 minutes, garnish with parsley.

Note: If using celeriac, add 1 tablespoon vinegar or lemon juice to the cooking water at stage 2; this helps keep it white.

Variation
Use broccoli or asparagus.

Cooking time: 55 minutes
Preparation time: 15 minutes plus time to stand (see stage 1)
Main cooking utensils: saucepan, ovenproof dish
Oven temperature: moderate to moderately hot (350–375°F., 180–190°C., Gas Mark 4–5)
Oven position: centre
Serves: 4 as a main dish or 8 as an hors d'oeuvre

Fried courgettes

Imperial
8–12 courgettes
seasoning
½ oz. flour
12 tablespoons olive oil
2 oz. butter
6 oz. cooked ham
Garnish:
1–2 oz. Parmesan cheese,
  grated
2–3 teaspoons freshly chopped
  parsley and sweet basil

Metric
8–12 courgettes
seasoning
15 g. flour
12 tablespoons olive oil
50 g. butter
150 g. cooked ham
Garnish:
25–50 g. Parmesan cheese,
  grated
2–3 teaspoons freshly chopped
  parsley and sweet basil

1. Wash and dice the courgettes, sprinkle with a little salt and leave to stand for 30 minutes, this removes some of the bitter taste.
2. Drain off any liquid and coat the courgettes in the seasoned flour.
3. Heat the oil and butter in a pan and toss the courgette cubes in this, add the chopped ham when the courgettes are nearly tender.
4. Sprinkle with the cheese and chopped herbs just before serving.

Variation
Coat the sliced courgettes thickly in 1½ oz. (40 g.) flour and fry them in deep hot oil until crisp and golden brown on the outside. Drain on absorbent paper, pour a little white wine, vinegar or lemon juice over them and top with chopped parsley and a little chopped oregano.

Cooking time: few minutes
Preparation time: 10 minutes plus time to stand
Main cooking utensil: frying pan
Serves: 4

Fennel with paprika pepper sauce

Imperial	Metric
6 roots of sweet fennel (see note)	6 roots of sweet fennel (see note)
seasoning	seasoning
Sauce:	*Sauce:*
2 oz. butter	50 g. butter
1 clove garlic (optional)	1 clove garlic (optional)
1½ oz. flour	40 g. flour
½ pint milk	250 ml. milk
¼ pint thin cream	125 ml. thin cream
2–3 teaspoons paprika pepper	2–3 teaspoons paprika pepper
½–1 tablespoon tomato purée	½–1 tablespoon tomato purée
Garnish:	*Garnish:*
cooked bacon or chopped ham	cooked bacon or chopped ham
chopped parsley	chopped parsley

1. Pull off any damaged layers on the outside of the fennel roots, put to soak in cold water for an hour if possible, this makes the roots very firm and crisp.
2. Put into boiling, salted water, cook until just tender.
3. Meanwhile make the sauce. Heat butter, stir in the crushed garlic and flour, add the milk, cook until thick and smooth.
4. Stir in the cream, blended with paprika, cook for several minutes.
5. Remove the pan from the heat, add the tomato purée, do not re-boil the sauce.
6. Dice the grilled or fried bacon or ham.
7. Pour the sauce over the well-drained fennel, garnish with bacon or ham and parsley.

Note: These are 2 kinds of fennel, one is a herb with feathery leaves, the other, as in the picture, is a thick root. Add the chopped herb or leaves to sauces served with fish. If the fennel is purchased with leaves, remove these and use in salads and sauces.

Cooking time: 25 minutes
Preparation time: 15 minutes plus time for fennel to soak
Main cooking utensils: 2 saucepans, grill pan or frying pan
Serves: 6

Caesar hotpot

Imperial	Metric
1 lb. young carrots	400 g. young carrots
8 oz. fresh peas	200 g. fresh peas
8 oz. diced new potatoes or very small potatoes	200 g. diced new potatoes or very small potatoes
seasoning	seasoning
Dressing:	*Dressing:*
seasoning	seasoning
1 teaspoon made mustard	1 teaspoon made mustard
2 tablespoons vinegar	2 tablespoons vinegar
4 tablespoons oil	4 tablespoons oil
Croûtons:	*Croûtons:*
2 slices bread	2 slices bread
2 oz. butter or fat	50 g. butter or fat
6 oz. white Cheddar or Gruyère cheese	150 g. white Cheddar or Gruyère cheese
Garnish:	*Garnish:*
olives	olives

1. Scrape the carrots and dice neatly.
2. Cook these with the peas and new potatoes in boiling, salted water until just tender.
3. Drain very well.
4. For the dressing, blend the seasoning with the vinegar and oil and toss the hot vegetables in this, they absorb the flavour better when warm.
5. Dice the bread and fry in the hot butter or fat until crisp and golden brown.
6. Dice the cheese neatly.
7. Arrange the vegetables in a deep dish or a shallow dish on a bed of lettuce if preferred, and top with the croûtons of bread (these should be hot for they make a pleasing contrast to the cold vegetables and cheese).
8. Put the cheese and olives on the salad, turn and serve.

Cooking time: 15 minutes
Preparation time: 15 minutes
Main cooking utensils: saucepan, frying pan
Serves: 4

Mushrooms in wine

Imperial
1½ lb. mushrooms
2 oz. butter
2 tablespoons oil
juice and finely grated rind of
   1 large lemon
½ pint white wine
seasoning
Garnish:
coarsely chopped parsley

Metric
¾ kg. mushrooms
50 g. butter
2 tablespoons oil
juice and finely grated rind of
   1 large lemon
275 ml. white wine
seasoning
Garnish:
coarsely chopped parsley

1. If the mushrooms are in good condition do not skin them as the skin contains much of the flavour. Wash the mushrooms well and trim the base of the stalks.
2. Heat the butter and oil in a large pan and toss the mushrooms in this taking care they do not brown or dry.
3. Add the lemon juice and rind, white wine and seasoning. Cook for about 20 minutes turning frequently to keep them moist. Leave the lid off the pan so that the liquid reduces and gives the mushrooms a good flavour.
4. Turn into a serving dish and top with coarsely chopped parsley. Serve with omelettes or other egg dishes.

Variation

Chopped onion and/or garlic can be fried in the butter and oil before adding the mushrooms. Small sausages can also be added. Fry these with the mushrooms, remove and add to the saucepan 10 minutes before serving.

Cooking time: 20 minutes
Preparation time: 10 minutes
Main cooking utensil: saucepan
Serves: 5—6

Mushroom mould

Imperial
2 lb. old potatoes, weight before
   peeling
seasoning
5 oz. butter
2–3 oz. cheese, Gruyère,
   Cheddar or Parmesan
3 tablespoons thick cream
1 tablespoon chopped parsley
1 clove garlic (optional)
2 medium-sized onions
8 oz. mushrooms
4 tablespoons concentrated
   tomato purée
good pinch sugar (optional)
Garnish:
celery leaves or parsley

Metric
1 kg. old potatoes, weight before
   peeling
seasoning
125 g. butter
50–75 g. cheese, Gruyère,
   Cheddar or Parmesan
3 tablespoons thick cream
1 tablespoon chopped parsley
1 clove garlic (optional)
2 medium-sized onions
200 g. mushrooms
4 tablespoons concentrated
   tomato purée
good pinch sugar (optional)
Garnish:
celery leaves or parsley

1. Peel and cook the potatoes steadily in boiling, salted water, do not allow them to cook too quickly or they become watery, drain, sieve or mash well until very smooth.
2. Add 2 oz. (50 g.) butter, the grated cheese and cream to the potatoes together with the parsley; season the mixture well.
3. Heat the remaining butter, fry the finely chopped garlic and onions, remove from the pan and fry the mushrooms in the butter remaining in the pan.
4. Blend the onion and garlic with the tomato purée, add a pinch sugar to give a slightly sweet flavour.
5. Put half the tomato purée into the greased mould, then one third of the potato, the remaining tomato mixture, more potato, then half the fried mushrooms.
6. Cover with the remaining potato mixture (keep the remaining mushrooms hot).
7. Bake for approximately 20 minutes and turn out. Top and garnish with mushrooms and celery leaves or parsley.

Cooking time: 45 minutes
Preparation time: 35 minutes
Main cooking utensils: saucepan, frying pan, 2- to 3-pint
   (1- to 1½-litre) mould
Oven temperature: moderately hot (400°F., 200°C., Gas Mark 6)
Oven position: centre
Serves: 6

Potato croquettes

Imperial	Metric
1–1½ lb. old potatoes	½–¾ kg. old potatoes
1–2 oz. margarine or butter	25–50 g. margarine or butter
seasoning	seasoning
little milk	little milk
Coating:	*Coating:*
1 tablespoon flour	1 tablespoon flour
seasoning	seasoning
1 egg	1 egg
1½–2 oz. crisp breadcrumbs	40–50 g. crisp breadcrumbs
To fry:	*To fry:*
shallow frying, 2–3 oz. fat or	shallow frying, 50–75 g. fat or
3 tablespoons oil	3 tablespoons oil
OR	OR
deep frying, 1¼–1½ lb. fat	deep frying, generous ½–¾ kg. fat
or 1¼–1½ pints oil	or approximately ¾ litre oil

1. Peel the potatoes, put them into boiling salted water, cook steadily until tender, then drain.
2. Mash, add the margarine, seasoning and a little milk — the mixture should be soft enough to form into finger shapes or rounds. Finger shapes are more suitable for shallow frying.
3. Coat in seasoned flour, then in beaten egg and crumbs.
4. Heat the fat in a frying pan or saucepan.
5. Heat until a cube of bread goes golden brown within 1 minute if using fat, or ½ minute if using oil. If the fat is too hot, the croquettes will break badly.
6. Put the croquettes into the hot fat or oil. If using a frying basket put this into the fat first, then put the croquettes into the fat gently.
7. Fry for a few minutes until crisp and golden brown, in shallow fat they will need turning.
8. Lift out and drain on crumpled tissue or absorbent paper. Serve with meat, poultry or fish.

Cooking time: 35 minutes
Preparation time: 35 minutes
Main cooking utensils: saucepan, frying pan or saucepan and frying basket
Serves: 4–6

Grilled onion and potato slices

Imperial	Metric
2 large onions	2 large onions
4 large potatoes	4 large potatoes
salt	salt
Sauce:	*Sauce:*
1 oz. margarine	25 g. margarine
1 oz. flour	25 g. flour
½ pint milk	250 ml. milk
seasoning	seasoning
2–3 oz. grated Cheddar cheese	50–75 g. grated Cheddar cheese

1. Peel both the onions and potatoes.
2. Slice the onions thinly and potatoes thickly, then cook in boiling salted water until just tender; strain.
3. Meanwhile make the sauce. Heat the margarine in a pan, stir in the flour and cook for several minutes, then gradually stir in the milk, bring to the boil and cook, stirring well, until thickened and smooth; season.
4. Arrange vegetables in a dish with the sauce, top with grated cheese and cook under the grill until crisp and brown. Serve for supper, accompanied by grilled tomatoes.

Variations

Instead of making a sauce put the vegetables into the dish with a very little top of the milk and cheese and grill.
Lyonnaise potatoes: Fry half-cooked sliced potatoes and onions in hot fat.

Cooking time: 30 minutes
Preparation time: 10 minutes
Main cooking utensils: saucepan, ovenproof dish
Serves: 4

Ragoût of tomatoes and peppers

Imperial	Metric
5 green peppers	5 green peppers
seasoning	seasoning
1½–2 lb. ripe tomatoes	¾–1 kg. ripe tomatoes
1 red pepper (capsicum)	1 red pepper (capsicum)
1–2 cloves garlic (optional) and/or 1–2 medium-sized onions	1–2 cloves garlic (optional) and/or 1–2 medium-sized onions
2–3 tablespoons oil	2–3 tablespoons oil
¼ pint white wine	125 ml. white wine
1 teaspoon chopped fresh oregano (wild marjoram) or fresh marjoram or pinch dried marjoram	1 teaspoon chopped fresh oregano (wild marjoram) or fresh marjoram or pinch dried marjoram
1 oz. capers (see note)	25 g. capers (see note)

1. Cut a slice from each green pepper so that the inside core and seeds may be removed.
2. Simmer for about 5 minutes in boiling salted water, drain.
3. Skin the tomatoes if wished, and chop coarsely. Dice the red pepper finely.
4. Crush or chop the garlic and onions, fry in the hot oil with diced red pepper and green peppers, then add the wine, oregano, tomatoes and seasoning.
5. Simmer gently for about 35 minutes.
6. Top with capers and serve with bowls of grated cheese.

Note: Fresh capers are shown in the picture but bottled ones could be used.

Cooking time: 35 minutes
Preparation time: 15 minutes
Main cooking utensil: large saucepan
Serves: 5

Autumn vegetable pie

Imperial	Metric
Rough puff pastry:	*Rough puff pastry:*
8 oz. plain flour	200 g. plain flour
pinch salt	pinch salt
6 oz. lard	150 g. lard
water to mix	water to mix
Filling:	*Filling:*
12 oz. mushrooms	300 g. mushrooms
1 lb. tomatoes	400 g. tomatoes
1 lb. leeks	400 g. leeks
seasoning	seasoning
Glaze:	*Glaze:*
1 egg	1 egg
Garnish:	*Garnish:*
parsley	parsley

1. Sieve the flour and salt, cut in the lard, blend with water. Do not attempt to rub the lard in.
2. Roll out to an oblong shape, fold in three, seal the ends; 'rib', i.e., depress the pastry at regular intervals.
3. Turn at right angles, repeat the procedure to give five foldings and five rollings, put the pastry away between these in a cool place.
4. For the filling, wash and slice the mushrooms, do not peel them as the skin gives flavour.
5. Skin, quarter and remove the seeds from the tomatoes.
6. Wash the leeks well, use the white part only; the green tops can be used in soups and stews.
7. Arrange the vegetables in layers in the pie plate, season well.
8. Roll out the pastry, put a narrow strip round the edge of the plate, cover with a round of pastry, seal the edges and use egg beaten with water for the glaze.
9. Bake for 10–15 minutes, to brown and make the pastry rise, at the higher temperature, then lower the heat for a further 20–25 minutes. Garnish with parsley.

Cooking time: 35 minutes
Preparation time: 30 minutes plus time for pastry to stand
Main cooking utensil: 10-inch (25-cm.) pie plate
Oven temperature: hot to very hot (450–475°F., 230–240°C., Gas Mark 8–9) then moderate (350°F., 180°C., Gas Mark 4)
Oven position: centre
Serves: 6–8

Salads

Salads have become so imaginative today, the following pages give a very few ideas, which I hope you will adapt for yourselves.

Try serving crisp green salads as an accompaniment to hot dishes, they make a change and enable you to use seasonable vegetables, fruit, etc.

To prepare green salads wash lettuce, etc. very gently; if you are too rough you will bruise the fairly fragile leaves. Use cold water, then shake the salad dry in a salad shaker or pat very gently in a dry cloth.

To skin tomatoes, place these in boiling water for about $\frac{1}{2}$ minute, then in cold water and you will be able to remove the skin easily.

To cut tomatoes into a waterlily shape, proceed as follows: Using a small, sharp pointed knife, make zig-zag cuts through to the centre of the tomato and work round. When completed, pull the halves apart gently.

Celery looks most attractive when it forms curls and in the recipe on the right, stages 5–6, directions are given for making these curls.

Radishes can be cut into waterlily shapes as suggested for tomatoes.

Easy salads

Bean salad: Toss cooked green beans in French dressing, page 14, add chopped parsley, chopped chives. It makes an excellent side salad with hot meat dishes.

Celery, beetroot and apple salad: Dice the celery, beetroot and apple. Mix the celery and apple with mayonnaise; toss the beetroot in French dressing (see pages 47 and 14). Shred lettuce and mix with finely chopped spring onions and a little French dressing. Put into salad bowls. Drain the beetroot, mix with the celery and apple just before serving. This salad is good with cold pork, cold duck or ham.

Cheese and carrot salad: Mix cottage or cream cheese with finely chopped gherkin and capers. Form into small balls, roll in finely grated raw carrot. Serve on a bed of shredded lettuce and garnish with rings of tomato and orange. This makes a good light dish or can be served with cold chicken.

Tomato and orange salad: Skin tomatoes, cut away the peel from oranges, removing the white pith at the same time. Lay the tomatoes on a flat dish, top with French dressing (see page 14) and finely chopped chives. Leave for 30 minutes then arrange the orange slices on top. Serve with hot or cold duck or pork.

Slimmers' salad

Imperial	Metric
8 medium-sized tomatoes	8 medium-sized tomatoes
8 oz. cottage cheese	200 g. cottage cheese
4 anchovy fillets	4 anchovy fillets
4 sliced, stuffed olives	4 sliced, stuffed olives
1 carrot	1 carrot
2 sticks celery	2 sticks celery
lettuce leaves	lettuce leaves
2 tablespoons sour cream	2 tablespoons sour cream
few drops tomato ketchup	few drops tomato ketchup
2 teaspoons lemon juice	2 teaspoons lemon juice
pepper	pepper
2 oz. prawns	50 g. prawns
Garnish:	*Garnish:*
paprika pepper	paprika pepper

1. Remove the top from each tomato, scoop out and reserve the seeds and some of the pulp.
2. Stuff the cavity with cottage cheese and chopped anchovy fillets.
3. Top with 2 slices stuffed olives.
4. Place the tomatoes in an hors d'oeuvre dish.
5. Cut the carrot into sticks and slice the celery thinly.
6. Put these into a bowl of iced water to form curls, then arrange on the dish.
7. Arrange the lettuce leaves on a dish for the prawns.
8. Blend together the sour cream, tomato pulp (from stage 1), tomato ketchup, lemon juice and pepper.
9. Blend in the prawns and pile on top of the lettuce just before serving.
10. Sprinkle over a little paprika pepper for garnish. Serve either as an hors d'oeuvre or as a light main course.

Note: Each serving contains approximately 140 calories.

Preparation time: 20 minutes
Main utensil: sharp knife
Serves: 4

Chicken salad

Imperial	Metric
¾–1 lb. cooked chicken	300–400 g. cooked chicken
2 teaspoons oil	2 teaspoons oil
1 clove garlic	1 clove garlic
4 oz. Gruyère cheese	100 g. Gruyère cheese
¼ pint mayonnaise	125 ml. mayonnaise
1 tablespoon lemon juice	1 tablespoon lemon juice
½ teaspoon finely grated lemon rind	½ teaspoon finely grated lemon rind
pinch paprika	pinch paprika
seasoning	seasoning
few sticks celery	few sticks celery
2 hard-boiled eggs	2 hard-boiled eggs
few stuffed olives	few stuffed olives
1 lettuce	1 lettuce
black olives	black olives

1. Cut the chicken into neat pieces, leaving on the skin. Crush the garlic, mix it with the oil and brush this over the chicken pieces.
2. Dice the cheese and mix it with the chicken.
3. Blend the mayonnaise with the lemon juice, rind, paprika and seasoning.
4. Chop the celery, slice the eggs and the stuffed olives.
5. Wash and dry the lettuce thoroughly and arrange it in the salad dishes. Pile the chicken, cheese and celery on top of this and coat with the mayonnaise. Garnish with the sliced eggs and stuffed olives and some black olives. Serve well chilled; this is an ideal dish for a buffet party.

Variation
Mix a small can of tuna with the chicken and omit the cheese. Add strips of green or red pepper instead of the celery.

Preparation time: 20 minutes
Main cooking utensil: mixing bowl, 4 individual salad dishes
Serves: 4

Cauliflower salad

Imperial	Metric
1 medium-sized cauliflower	1 medium-sized cauliflower
1 tablespoon vinegar	1 tablespoon vinegar
2 tablespoons oil	2 tablespoons oil
seasoning	seasoning
2 teaspoons chopped chives	2 teaspoons chopped chives
¼ pint mayonnaise	125 ml. mayonnaise
(see page 47)	(see page 47)
lettuce	lettuce
Garnish:	*Garnish:*
2 hard-boiled eggs	2 hard-boiled eggs
2 tomatoes	2 tomatoes

1. Wash the cauliflower thoroughly and divide it into sprigs. Cook in boiling salted water until just tender. Drain well.
2. Mix the vinegar, oil and seasoning together and toss the cauliflower in this whilst still warm. This helps to keep it moist.
3. Whilst the cauliflower is cooling prepare the mayonnaise.
4. Pile the cauliflower on a bed of lettuce and sprinkle with chives. Garnish with the mayonnaise, quartered hard-boiled eggs and tomato wedges.

Variation
Cook the cauliflower in boiling salted water until just tender, drain well and place on a hot serving dish. Top with crisply fried breadcrumbs and chopped hard-boiled egg and parsley.

Cooking time: 10 minutes
Preparation time: 20 minutes
Main cooking utensil: saucepan
Serves: 4

Coleslaws

Carrot coleslaw

Imperial	Metric
1 small white cabbage	1 small white cabbage
4–6 large carrots	4–6 large carrots
coleslaw dressing (see note)	coleslaw dressing (see note)

1. Remove the outer leaves from the cabbage, then cut it into portions and soak for a short time in cold water. Drain and dry well, shred very finely. Peel and grate the carrots coarsely.
2. Blend the cabbage and carrots together, toss in dressing until thoroughly moistened, allow to stand for 30 minutes.

Apple coleslaw

Imperial	Metric
4–6 sticks celery, finely chopped	4–6 sticks celery, finely chopped
3 dessert apples, peeled and thinly sliced	3 dessert apples, peeled and thinly sliced
4 oz. sultanas	100 g. sultanas
4 oz. chopped walnuts	100 g. chopped walnuts
1 small white cabbage	1 small white cabbage
blue cheese dressing (see note)	blue cheese dressing (see note)

Blend the first four ingredients together, add to the finely shredded cabbage and mix with the dressing, stand for 1 hour.

Note: Alternatively, flavour mayonnaise with a little extra sugar, mixed spice and tarragon or tarragon vinegar. For blue cheese dressing flavour mayonnaise with crumbled blue cheese.

Preparation time: 10 minutes
Main utensil: mixing bowl
Each salad serves: 6–8

Leek salad

Imperial
8 young leeks
Dressing:
4 tablespoons oil
1½ tablespoons vinegar or
   lemon juice
seasoning
Garnish:
2–3 tablespoons chopped parsley
4 oz. coarsely grated cheese,
   Mozzarella or Bel Paese if
   possible

Metric
8 young leeks
Dressing:
4 tablespoons oil
1½ tablespoons vinegar or
   lemon juice
seasoning
Garnish:
2–3 tablespoons chopped parsley
100 g. coarsely grated cheese,
   Mozzarella or Bel Paese if
   possible

1. Wash the leeks and cut them into equal lengths.
2. Cook in boiling salted water until just tender, do not overcook for they must have quite a firm texture.
3. Make the dressing by blending the oil, vinegar and seasoning together.
4. Cool the leeks, then toss in the dressing.
5. Lift out of the dressing and arrange them on a shallow dish.
6. Garnish with bands of chopped parsley and coarsely grated cheese. Serve as a light main dish or an antipasto (hors d'oeuvre).

Variation
Shred a green pepper and a small well-washed fennel root finely. Slice the leeks finely before cooking. Cook till barely tender, drain, mix with the pepper and fennel and toss in the oil and vinegar. Serve piled on a bed of lettuce.

Cooking time: 15–20 minutes
Preparation time: 15 minutes
Main cooking utensil: saucepan
Serves: 4

Celeriac salad with cream cheese dressing

Imperial
2 large celeriac
4 oz. cream cheese and
   2 oz. Cheddar cheese or
   2 oz. Camembert
¼ pint mayonnaise (see page 47)
1 tablespoon lemon juice
2 tablespoons thin cream
Garnish:
black olives
celery leaves or watercress
   (optional)
parsley

Metric
2 large celeriac
100 g. cream cheese and
   50 g. Cheddar cheese or
   50 g. Camembert
125 ml. mayonnaise (see page 47)
1 tablespoon lemon juice
2 tablespoons thin cream
Garnish:
black olives
celery leaves or watercress
   (optional)
parsley

1. Peel the celeriac and grate or cut into matchsticks. Leave it in a bowl of cold water to which a little vinegar has been added whilst preparing the dressing, this prevents discolouration.
2. Put the cream cheese into a bowl. Add the finely grated Cheddar cheese or the Camembert, and beat well.
3. Gradually blend in the mayonnaise, add the lemon juice and cream.
4. Drain the celeriac carefully, mix it well with the dressing and pile it on to a serving dish. Garnish the salad with black olives, chopped parsley and celery leaves or watercress.

Variation
Use all cream cheese instead of a mixture of cream cheese and Cheddar or Camembert. The celeriac can be cut into matchsticks and cooked in boiling salted water until just tender. Drain, chill and serve mixed with a piquant mayonnaise.

Preparation time: 20 minutes
Main utensil: small mixing bowl
Serves: 4

Mushroom and pepper salad

Imperial	Metric
Dressing:	*Dressing:*
4 tablespoons olive oil	4 tablespoons olive oil
juice of 1 lemon	juice of 1 lemon
pinch celery salt	pinch celery salt
shake pepper	shake pepper
good pinch salt	good pinch salt
pinch dry mustard	pinch dry mustard
1 tablespoon chopped parsley	1 tablespoon chopped parsley
Salad:	*Salad:*
1 large green pepper	1 large green pepper
1 large red pepper	1 large red pepper
2 large firm tomatoes	2 large firm tomatoes
8 oz. button mushrooms	200 g. button mushrooms
1 can anchovy fillets	1 can anchovy fillets

1. Blend the ingredients for the dressing together. A screw-topped jar is a good way of doing this; put the ingredients into the jar and shake firmly.
2. Remove the seeds from the red and green peppers. Cut the flesh into narrow strips.
3. Skin the tomatoes; this can be done by putting them into boiling water for 1 minute, then into cold water, or by inserting a fine skewer into the tomato and holding it over heat until the skin breaks.
4. Chop the tomatoes. Wash and slice some of the mushrooms, keeping some whole.
5. Toss the vegetables in the dressing. Arrange in a bowl, and garnish with anchovies.
6. Serve as an hors d'oeuvre or with meat or fish.

Preparation time: 10 minutes
Main utensils: screw-topped jar, salad bowl
Serves: 4–5

Cabbage rose salad

Imperial	Metric
1 large red cabbage	1 large red cabbage
1 small white cabbage	1 small white cabbage
2 grapefruit	2 grapefruit
2 dessert apples	2 dessert apples
4 oz. celeriac or celery	100 g. celeriac or celery
$\frac{1}{4}$ pint mayonnaise (see page 47)	125 ml. mayonnaise (see page 47)
$\frac{1}{4}$ pint sour cream	125 ml. sour cream
2 oz. pecan nuts, walnuts or hazelnuts	50 g. pecan nuts, walnuts or hazelnuts
2 red peppers	2 red peppers

1. Remove the outside leaves from the red cabbage, cut the stalk down to the base of the leaves.
2. Fold back the next two layers of leaves and cut out the centre of the cabbage. This can be cooked as an accompaniment for another meal.
3. Wash the shell in cold water, drain well.
4. Shred the white cabbage finely, wash it well, drain and then dry thoroughly.
5. Cut away the skin and pith from the grapefruit and dice the flesh.
6. Core but do not peel the apples; dice.
7. Peel the celeriac, grate coarsely or shred finely, or chop the celery.
8. Blend the vegetables with the mayonnaise and sour cream, add the nuts and fruit.
9. Discard the core and seeds from the red peppers. Shred the flesh and blend most of it with the salad, save a little for garnish.
10. Pile the salad into the red cabbage shell. Top with a little red pepper.

Preparation time: 15 minutes
Main utensil: mixing bowl
Serves: 8–10

Cheese salad with yoghurt dressing

Imperial
Dressing:
1 5-oz. carton natural
   yoghurt
2 spring onions
1½-inch piece cucumber
seasoning
Salad:
1 small lettuce
½ green pepper
½ red pepper
2 large ripe tomatoes
2 oz. Cheddar cheese
2 oz. Danish blue cheese
few black olives
few green olives

Metric
Dressing:
1 142-ml. carton natural
   yoghurt
2 spring onions
3-cm. piece cucumber
seasoning
Salad:
1 small lettuce
½ green pepper
½ red pepper
2 large ripe tomatoes
50 g. Cheddar cheese
50 g. Danish blue cheese
few black olives
few green olives

1. Blend the yoghurt with the finely chopped spring onions and peeled diced cucumber.
2. Season well and keep in a cool place.
3. Arrange the lettuce on a flat dish.
4. Remove the cores and seeds from the green and red peppers.
5. Slice the peppers, mix with the skinned sliced tomatoes and season.
6. Pile in the centre of the lettuce.
7. Top with the diced cheeses and olives. Serve with the yoghurt dressing.

Variation
Use different cheeses.

Preparation time: 15 minutes
Main utensil: mixing bowl
Serves: 2–4

Fish salad

Imperial
Sharp sauce:
1 tablespoon dry mustard
1 tablespoon sugar
1 tablespoon lemon juice
grated rind of 1 lemon
5 tablespoons wine vinegar
1 small onion
good pinch cayenne pepper
good pinch salt
few drops Tabasco sauce
2 tablespoons chopped dill
Salad:
12 oz. cooked white fish
2 oz. shelled prawns
4 oz. cooked or canned peas
2 hard-boiled eggs, sliced
1 medium-sized cooked beetroot,
   diced
1 lettuce
Garnish:
cucumber slices
few unshelled prawns

Metric
Sharp sauce:
1 tablespoon dry mustard
1 tablespoon sugar
1 tablespoon lemon juice
grated rind of 1 lemon
5 tablespoons wine vinegar
1 small onion
good pinch cayenne pepper
good pinch salt
few drops Tabasco sauce
2 tablespoons chopped dill
Salad:
300 g. cooked white fish
50 g. shelled prawns
100 g. cooked or canned peas
2 hard-boiled eggs, sliced
1 medium-sized cooked beetroot,
   diced
1 lettuce
Garnish:
cucumber slices
few unshelled prawns

1. Make the sauce by blending all the ingredients together in a basin or by shaking them together in a screw-topped jar – the onion should be crushed and the juice only used.
2. Flake the fish and blend with the prawns and the dressing. If wished, a little less of the sharp sauce may be used to give a slightly less moist salad.
3. Add the peas, sliced eggs and diced beetroot.
4. Pile neatly on to a bed of crisp lettuce.
5. Garnish with cucumber slices and prawns. Serve really cold.

Preparation time: 20 minutes
Main utensil: mixing bowl
Serves: 4

Cheese and grapefruit salad

Imperial
2 grapefruit
6 oz. Cheddar cheese
½ small red or green pepper
juice of grapefruit
1 tablespoon olive oil
sugar (optional)
seasoning
Garnish:
lettuce

Metric
2 grapefruit
150 g. Cheddar cheese
½ small red or green pepper
juice of grapefruit
1 tablespoon olive oil
sugar (optional)
seasoning
Garnish:
lettuce

1. Halve the grapefruit on a plate.
2. Remove the segments carefully, put them in a basin, and discard any pips; cut away the skin.
3. Dice the Cheddar cheese and chop the red pepper, discarding the core and seeds; mix with the grapefruit.
4. Pour the juice from the grapefruit into a separate basin and blend with the olive oil, sugar and seasoning.
5. Pour the dressing over the cheese mixture and leave for about 30 minutes for the dressing to flavour the other ingredients.
6. Line the halved grapefruit cases with lettuce and pile the salad in the centre.
   Serve as a light main dish with crisp toast or brown bread and butter.

Variations
Use orange segments and serve in sundae glasses. Top halved peaches with grated cheese or fill centres of pineapple rings with cheese blended with mayonnaise.

Preparation time: 10 minutes plus time to stand
Main utensil: sharp knife
Serves: 4

Chicken salad with cottage cheese sauce

Imperial
8 oz. cooked chicken
4 oz. sliced lean ham
lettuce
watercress or mustard and cress
chicory
pickled onions
Cottage cheese sauce:
1½ level tablespoons redcurrant
  jelly (1½ oz.)
8 oz. cottage cheese
1 level teaspoon horseradish
  cream
¼ pint thin cream
seasoning

Metric
200 g. cooked chicken
100 g. sliced lean ham
lettuce
watercress or mustard and cress
chicory
pickled onions
Cottage cheese sauce:
1½ level tablespoons redcurrant
  jelly (40 g.)
200 g. cottage cheese
1 level teaspoon horseradish
  cream
125 ml. thin cream
seasoning

1. Arrange the sliced meat on a plate with the crisp lettuce leaves, cress, chicory and pickled onions.
2. To make the sauce, melt the redcurrant jelly over a low heat; cool slightly.
3. Blend the ingredients, except the cream and seasoning, together. Fold in the cream and season to taste. Serve the salad with the sauce.

Variations
Use all chicken. A cottage cheese dressing blends with many salads. The jelly may be omitted and a little lemon juice and grated rind used in its place. If cottage cheese is unobtainable use finely grated Cheddar cheese instead.

Cooking time: few minutes
Preparation time: 10 minutes
Main cooking utensil: saucepan
Serves: 4

Maryland chicken salad

Imperial	Metric
1 medium-sized onion	1 medium-sized onion
1 clove garlic (optional) or shake garlic salt	1 clove garlic (optional) or shake garlic salt
8 oz. long-grain rice	200 g. long-grain rice
1 pint chicken stock or water and 1–2 chicken stock cubes	500 ml. chicken stock or water and 1–2 chicken stock cubes
seasoning	seasoning
1 small cooked chicken	1 small cooked chicken
1 small can peas or 4 oz. cooked peas	1 small can peas or 100 g. cooked peas
1 small can cooked green beans or 4–6 oz. cooked beans	1 small can cooked green beans or 100–150 g. cooked beans
1 medium can sweetcorn	1 medium can sweetcorn
1 red pepper	1 red pepper
1 green pepper	1 green pepper

1. Chop the onion, crush the garlic or use garlic salt, put both into the pan with the rice, stock or water and stock cubes.
2. Add seasoning to taste, then bring to the boil, stir briskly with a fork, lower the heat, cover the pan and simmer steadily for 15 minutes or until the rice is tender and has absorbed all the liquid.
3. Add the diced cooked chicken, the well-drained peas, beans and sweetcorn to the hot rice.
4. When cold stir in the diced red and green peppers (discard the cores and seeds).
5. Serve with lettuce, tomatoes and mayonnaise.

Note: This salad makes good use of canned foods, for the chicken could be canned if you are camping and unable to buy ready cooked chicken. Rice salads taste better if most of the ingredients are blended with the hot rice; this gives a good flavour and prevents the rice from becoming dry.

Cooking time: 20–25 minutes
Preparation time: 20 minutes
Main cooking utensils: saucepan
Serves: 6–8

Salami salad

Imperial	Metric
French or vinaigrette dressing (see page 14)	French or vinaigrette dressing (see page 14)
8–12 oz. salami	200–300 g. salami
1–2 hard-boiled eggs	1–2 hard-boiled eggs
2 dessert apples	2 dessert apples
beetroot	beetroot
radishes	radishes
lettuce	lettuce

1. Make the French dressing as directed in the preceding recipe.
2. Slice salami thinly, keep covered until ready to use. Slice hard-boiled eggs. Peel the apple and cut into fingers, dip in dressing to prevent it turning brown.
3. Roll slices of salami round the apple, secure with cocktail sticks.
4. Cut beetroot into slices.
5. Cut the radishes in a vandyke pattern with a sharp knife. Put into cold water and leave for $\frac{3}{4}$–1 hour until they open out like waterlilies.
6. Put the washed lettuce in a serving bowl and arrange the beetroot, radishes, egg and salami and apple rolls on top. Serve with mayonnaise (see page 47) or additional French dressing.

Preparation time: 10 minutes plus time for radish waterlilies
Main utensils: sharp knife, cocktail sticks
Serves: 4

Stuffings and sauces

Stuffings

Many of the meat, fish or other dishes in this book have unusual stuffings, particularly suited to that particular recipe. There are basic stuffings that can be used for many dishes, see below and right.

Parsley and thyme stuffing: This is often known as 'veal stuffing'; there is a recipe for old-fashioned veal stuffing on page 98 (this includes meat).

Make 4 oz. (100 g.) soft crumbs (white bread is usually used, this is very good with wholemeal bread). Mix with 2 oz. (50 g.) shredded suet, melted butter or fat, seasoning, about 2 tablespoons chopped parsley, 1 teaspoon chopped lemon thyme or ¼–½ teaspoon dried herb, little grated lemon rind, seasoning, 1 egg to bind. This makes enough for 4–6 people and is used with chicken, turkey, veal, as well as some fish.

Sage and onion stuffing: Peel 2–3 large onions, chop coarsely to hasten cooking. Simmer in a little well-seasoned water for about 10 minutes, lift out of the stock and chop more finely. Mix with 2 oz. (50 g.) soft breadcrumbs, 1–2 teaspoons freshly chopped sage or ½ teaspoon dried herb. Add 2 oz. (50 g.) shredded suet or melted butter or margarine. Season well, bind with an egg or a little of the onion stock.

This serves 4–6; use with duck, pork, etc.

Chestnut stuffing: Slit the skins of 12 oz. (350 g.) chestnuts and cook steadily for about 10 minutes. Remove the shells and skins while still hot. Place the skinned chestnuts in a pan with ¼ pint (1½ dl.) stock and cook for 15 minutes. Mash with the stock, add 2 oz. (50 g.) butter, 1 teaspoon chopped rosemary, chervil or parsley, 1–2 chopped onions, 4 oz. (100 g.) soft breadcrumbs and seasoning.

Rice stuffings

Cooked rice makes a good stuffing for many foods and a pleasant change from the more familiar crumb mixture. For example, substitute cooked rice for crumbs in both the stuffings on the left-hand side. You will need about 1½ oz. (40 g.) uncooked rice to give you about 4 oz. (100 g.) cooked rice. Other flavourings to add to rice are:

a. Chopped red and green peppers (discard core and seeds), with crushed garlic and lightly fried chopped onions. Use this with pork or veal.

b. Diced celery (use some of the pale green leaves and chop these with parsley or other herbs), finely diced raw chicken or other poultry liver, melted butter or other fat. This blends well with turkey.

c. Well-drained, soaked but not cooked, prunes, grated dessert apple, few sultanas, very little chopped sage and melted butter. Excellent with duck.

Always season rice stuffing well and do not overcook the rice, for it continues cooking in the meat.

To make sauces

A good sauce can turn a pleasant dish into an exceptionally good one, and throughout this book you will find sauces that blend with the various dishes are given under the individual recipes. The following are the two basic sauces, upon which so many other sauce recipes depend.

Brown sauce

Try to use a good flavoured dripping for this, as it makes a great deal of difference to the sauce; failing this use fat. To give the best flavour proceed as follows: heat 2 oz. (50 g.) dripping in a pan, fry finely chopped onion and carrot in this, then blend in 1 oz. (25 g.) flour and cook for several minutes, stirring well. You can allow the flour to turn golden brown, but no darker. Gradually blend in ½ pint (3 dl.) brown stock or water and ½—1 beef stock cube. Bring to the boil, stir until thickened, season and strain. For a quicker sauce you can use just 1 oz. (25 g.) dripping and omit the vegetables, but naturally the flavour is not as good.

To give different flavours to a brown sauce add a little tomato purée; chopped mushrooms, sherry, port wine or Madeira.

White sauce

So many sauces are based upon this recipe, including the sauce mornay below.

Heat 1 oz. (25 g.) butter or margarine in a pan, stir in 1 oz. (25 g.) flour and cook for 2—3 minutes, stir well and do not allow the 'roux', as this is called, to change colour. Gradually blend in ½ pint (3 dl.) milk then bring the sauce to the boil and stir over a low heat until thickened. Season well.

The consistency of the above sauce, and the brown sauce on the left, is known as a 'coating' one, since it should just coat the back of a wooden spoon. If you require a *very thin sauce* then use exactly twice the amount of liquid, i.e. 1 pint (6 dl.). If you require a *very thick sauce* (used for binding ingredients together, and known as a 'panada'), use half the amount of liquid, i.e. ¼ pint (1½ dl.).

To give different flavours to white sauce try a *Béchamel sauce*: in this sauce vegetables are infused with the milk (as stage 1 in the recipe below), before making the sauce as the method above. A *Mornay sauce* is based upon a Béchamel sauce, whereas a cheese sauce is made by adding grated cheese to the cooked white sauce, above. Never overcook the sauce when the cheese is added (see stage 4 below). Anchovy essence, chopped parsley and other flavours can be added to the basic white sauce.

Sauce mornay

Imperial	Metric
½ pint milk	250 ml. milk
small piece onion, celery and carrot	small piece onion, celery and carrot
4–6 peppercorns	4–6 peppercorns
bouquet garni	bouquet garni
1 oz. butter	25 g. butter
1 oz. flour	25 g. flour
seasoning	seasoning
3 oz. Gruyère cheese or 2–3 oz. Gruyère and 1–2 oz. Parmesan cheese	75 g. Gruyère cheese or 50–75 g. Gruyère and 25–50 g. Parmesan cheese

1. Pour the milk into a pan and add the vegetables, peppercorns and bouquet garni. Heat the milk for a few minutes then stand it in a warm place to infuse for about 30 minutes, to bring out the flavour of the vegetables.
2. Heat the butter in another pan, stir in the flour and cook for several minutes.
3. Strain the milk and gradually blend it into the butter and flour, adding a little extra if necessary to give the full ½ pint (250 ml.). Bring to the boil and cook until thickened. Season well.
4. Grate the Gruyère cheese or the mixture of Gruyère and Parmesan cheese which will give the sauce a stronger flavour. Stir the cheese into the sauce and heat gently until the cheese has melted. Do not cook for a long time or the sauce becomes curdled as the protein in the cheese coagulates.
5. Serve as in the picture as an accompaniment to grilled fish. Allow 4 portions of fish and 1–2 oz. (25–50 g.) butter for basting the fish. Grill the fish before adding the cheese, add this at the last minute and pour the sauce over the fish. The sauce also goes very well with cauliflower and hard-boiled eggs.

Cooking time: 10 minutes
Preparation time: 10 minutes plus 30 minutes to infuse the milk
Main cooking utensils: 2 saucepans
Serves: 4 as an accompaniment to a main dish

Egg dishes

Eggs are not only a quickly cooked food, but one that gives a high amount of both protein and iron. In the recipes in this section you will find all the basic methods of cooking eggs, with interesting suggestions for serving these. Remember:

Boiled eggs: Allow only 3½–4 minutes for a soft-boiled egg, up to 10 minutes for hard-boiled eggs; crack the shells of these and plunge into cold water immediately after cooking, this prevents the dark line forming round the yolk (see pages 125 and 126).

Fried eggs: Have the fat sufficiently hot to set the egg, but not *too* hot, otherwise you have a brown skin at the base of the white (see page 126).

Baked eggs: Set fairly quickly, so the egg does not become too hard (see page 127).

Scrambled eggs: Do not cook too quickly or stir too vigorously as the eggs cook (see page 128).

Poached eggs: The recipe on page 129 assumes the eggs are being poached in boiling water; if you prefer an egg poacher make sure the knob of butter or margarine is really hot before adding the eggs..

Omelettes: These vary in their fillings and there are a number of recipes in this section (see pages 130–132). Always make sure the butter or oil is really hot before the eggs are poured into the pan. The technique of making soufflés and pancakes is given on pages 129 and 134 together with interesting flavourings.

Easy guide to egg and cheese dishes
The following gives you help in selecting the right egg and cheese dish for the right occasion.

When you are short of time see pages 36, 108, 125, 126, 127, 128, 130, 131, 132, 135, 137, 138.

When you are short of money see pages 17, 36, 108, 109, 125, 126, 127, 129, 130, 131, 133, 141, 150, 173, 175.

When you want a special dish see pages 51, 108, 109, 127, 128, 130, 131, 132, 134, 189, 191, 220.

For a snack or light meal see pages 120, 121, 124–139, 141.

When you are slimming see pages 115, 119, 120, 127, 129.

Eggs in curry mayonnaise

Imperial	Metric
2 egg yolks	2 egg yolks
2–3 teaspoons curry powder	2–3 teaspoons curry powder
pinch salt	pinch salt
juice of $\frac{1}{2}$ lemon	juice of $\frac{1}{2}$ lemon
pinch black pepper (optional)	pinch black pepper (optional)
pinch cayenne pepper (optional)	pinch cayenne pepper (optional)
up to $\frac{1}{2}$ pint oil	up to 275 ml. oil
about 3 tablespoons chopped chives or green tops of spring onions	about 3 tablespoons chopped chives or green tops of spring onions
6 eggs	6 eggs
Garnish:	Garnish:
few chopped chives (see above)	few chopped chives (see above)
capers	capers
2 large tomatoes	2 large tomatoes
parsley	parsley

1. Beat the egg yolks with the curry powder, salt and lemon juice, add black pepper and a pinch of cayenne pepper if wished.
2. Carefully blend in the oil drop by drop until the mixture thickens.
3. Taste and add a little extra lemon juice if wished.
4. Add chopped chives or onion tops.
5. Divide between four shallow dishes.
6. Hard boil the eggs, halve lengthways, lay them on top of the curry mayonnaise, and top with chopped chives and capers. Garnish with tomato wedges and parsley. Serve as an hors-d'oeuvre or light main dish; if as the latter, serve with salad.

Note: To make sure hard-boiled eggs have no dark line round the yolk, time the cooking carefully – 8–10 minutes is sufficient – crack the shells and plunge into cold water at once.

Cooking time: 10 minutes
Preparation time: 20 minutes
Main cooking utensil: saucepan
Serves: 4

Devilled eggs

Imperial	Metric
Creole rice:	Creole rice:
$\frac{1}{2}$ small onion, peeled	$\frac{1}{2}$ small onion, peeled
$\frac{1}{2}$ stick celery	$\frac{1}{2}$ stick celery
$\frac{1}{2}$ small green pepper	$\frac{1}{2}$ small green pepper
$\frac{1}{2}$ oz. butter	15 g. butter
1 oz. mushrooms	25 g. mushrooms
3 oz. rice	75 g. rice
$\frac{1}{4}$ pint plus 1 tablespoon stock	140 ml. stock
seasoning	seasoning
Eggs and sauce:	Eggs and sauce:
2 eggs	2 eggs
$\frac{1}{2}$ oz. butter	15 g. butter
$\frac{1}{2}$ oz. flour	15 g. flour
$\frac{1}{4}$ pint tomato juice	125 ml. tomato juice
1 teaspoon made mustard	1 teaspoon made mustard
$\frac{1}{2}$ teaspoon Worcestershire sauce	$\frac{1}{2}$ teaspoon Worcestershire sauce
pinch brown sugar	pinch brown sugar

1. To prepare the rice, chop the onion coarsely with the celery and pepper, removing the core and seeds.
2. Fry in the butter for 5 minutes without browning.
3. Add the sliced mushrooms and rice, cook for a further 4 minutes, add the stock.
4. Cover the pan, cook for 20 minutes or until no moisture remains. Season well.
5. Meanwhile hard-boil the eggs and make the sauce.
6. Melt the butter, stir in the flour, cook for 2 minutes, remove from heat.
7. Gradually blend in the tomato juice, boil until thickened, add the remaining ingredients and cook for 5–10 minutes. Season well. Put the rice into a hot dish, top with the halved shelled eggs. Either pour sauce over or serve separately.

Cooking time: 35–40 minutes
Preparation time: 20–25 minutes
Main cooking utensils: three saucepans
Serves: 2

Egg and shrimp curry

Imperial	Metric
⅜ pint boiling water	200 ml. boiling water
1 oz. grated or desiccated coconut	25 g. grated or desiccated coconut
½ onion	½ onion
1 small apple	1 small apple
1 oz. margarine	25 g. margarine
1½ level tablespoons flour	1½ level tablespoons flour
1 teaspoon curry powder	1 teaspoon curry powder
1 tablespoon tomato purée	1 tablespoon tomato purée
juice of ½ lemon	juice of ½ lemon
1 tablespoon black treacle	1 tablespoon black treacle
½ teaspoon salt	½ teaspoon salt
½ pint shrimps	¼ litre shrimps
3–4 hard-boiled eggs	3–4 hard-boiled eggs

1. Pour boiling water over the coconut, leave until cold, then strain. Reserve the liquid.
2. Chop the peeled onion and apple and fry in the fat until golden.
3. Add the flour and curry powder and cook gently for 1 minute.
4. Remove from the heat, gradually blend in the liquid.
5. Cook, stirring, till the sauce comes to the boil and thickens, then add the tomato purée, lemon juice, black treacle and seasoning.
6. Cover the pan, simmer gently for 10–15 minutes.
7. Add the peeled shrimps and halved shelled eggs.
8. Heat for a further 5–10 minutes. Serve with boiled rice and side dishes of yoghurt, fresh cucumber, diced potato, chopped green pepper sprinkled with paprika, sliced tomato with onion rings, peanuts, bananas sprinkled with lemon juice.

Note: This recipe may also be served as an hors d'oeuvre and in this case would serve 4 people.

Cooking time: 30–35 minutes
Preparation time: 30 minutes
Main cooking utensil: saucepan
Serves: 2

Fried egg and vegetable stew

Imperial	Metric
4 good-sized firm tomatoes	4 good-sized firm tomatoes
1 aubergine	1 aubergine
2 green or 1 red and 1 green pepper	2 green or 1 red and 1 green pepper
1 medium-sized marrow or cucumber	1 medium-sized marrow or cucumber
2–3 tablespoons oil	2–3 tablespoons oil
1–2 cloves garlic	1–2 cloves garlic
2 large onions	2 large onions
seasoning	seasoning
chopped parsley	chopped parsley
8–10 eggs	8–10 eggs
fat or oil for frying	fat or oil for frying

1. Skin and chop the tomatoes; dice the aubergine leaving on the skin. Remove the cores and seeds from the peppers and cut the flesh into thin strips.
2. Peel and dice the marrow or cucumber.
3. Heat the oil in a pan. Crush the cloves of garlic and chop the onions finely. Fry until nearly tender in the oil.
4. Add all the vegetables, except the tomatoes, cover the pan tightly and cook slowly until the vegetables are just tender, about 35 minutes.
5. Add the tomatoes 15 minutes before the end of the cooking time, season well.
6. Pile the vegetables on to a hot serving plate, sprinkle with parsley and keep warm.
7. Fry the eggs in some fat or oil allowing one or two per person. Place them on the vegetables.

Cooking time: 35 minutes
Preparation time: 15 minutes
Main cooking utensils: saucepan, frying pan
Serves: 4–5

Eggs à l'ardennaise

Imperial	Metric
8 eggs	8 eggs
good pinch salt	good pinch salt
shake black pepper	shake black pepper
pinch cayenne pepper	pinch cayenne pepper
¼ pint thick cream	125 ml. thick cream
1–2 teaspoons parsley	1–2 teaspoons parsley

1. Separate the egg yolks from the whites.
2. Beat the whites until stiff and whisk in the seasonings.
3. Gradually fold the cream into the fluffy mixture, taking care not to lose the light texture.
4. Spread in a well buttered dish.
5. Make hollows in the cream mixture and put an egg yolk in each.
6. Bake until just set.
7. Top with chopped parsley. Serve with crisp toast, as a light meal with a salad, or as an hors-d'oeuvre.

Variation

Fold 2 oz. (50 g.) finely grated Parmesan cheese into the egg whites. In the picture a little egg white has been left with the yolk.

Cooking time: 15 minutes
Preparation time: 10 minutes
Main cooking utensil: buttered shallow baking dish
Oven temperature: moderately hot (400°F., 200°C., Gas Mark 6)
Oven position: centre
Serves: 4 as a light main dish or 8 as an hors-d'oeuvre

Tomatoes stuffed with eggs

Imperial	Metric
6 very large firm tomatoes	6 very large firm tomatoes
6 eggs	6 eggs
1 tablespoon parsley	1 tablespoon parsley
4 oz. cooked ham (see note)	100 g. cooked ham (see note)
1 oz. butter	25 g. butter
seasoning	seasoning

1. Cut a slice from the top of each of the tomatoes, remove the pulp and chop this finely.
2. Separate the eggs and blend the egg whites with the tomato pulp.
3. Chop the parsley and ham and add them to the tomato mixture.
4. Add half the softened butter and season lightly.
5. Pack into the bottom of the tomato cases.
6. Put the egg yolks on top and season.
7. Butter a dish, stand the tomatoes in it and bake until firm. Serve as soon as they are cooked as a hot hors-d'oeuvre or light supper dish.

Note: Prosciutto or Parma ham may be used instead of ordinary cooked ham but this makes the dish rather expensive.

Variation

Top the egg yolks with a little cream and grated cheese before baking.

Cooking time: 15–20 minutes
Preparation time: 15 minutes
Main cooking utensils: ovenproof dish
Oven temperature: moderately hot (400°F., 200°C., Gas Mark 6)
Oven position: above centre
Serves: 6

Eggs with devilled sauce

Imperial	Metric
8 eggs	8 eggs
seasoning	seasoning
2 oz. butter	50 g. butter
3 small onions or shallots	3 small onions or shallots
scant 1 oz. flour	20 g. flour
½ pint white stock	250 ml. white stock
pinch cayenne pepper	pinch cayenne pepper
2 tablespoons concentrated tomato purée	2 tablespoons concentrated tomato purée
2 teaspoons chopped parsley	2 teaspoons chopped parsley
Garnish:	*Garnish:*
parsley	parsley

1. Beat the eggs lightly with the seasoning.
2. Use ½ oz. (15 g.) butter to brush the insides of the moulds; steam the eggs in a pan of hot water for 10 minutes until firmly set, or use cups in an egg poacher; if these are not deep enough, steam the eggs in 8 cups. Alternatively, fry the un-beaten eggs, turning so they are firm on each side, and cut round the whites to give a neat shape.
3. Chop the onions or shallots very finely and fry in the remaining butter.
4. Stir in the flour, cook for several minutes, then gradually add the stock with the seasoning and a good pinch cayenne pepper.
5. Bring to the boil, cook until thickened, then add the tomato purée and chopped parsley. Pour the sauce over the hot eggs, garnish with parsley and serve with rice, or crisp-bread and butter.

Cooking time: 15 minutes
Preparation time: 15 minutes
Main cooking utensils: 4 individual moulds and steamer or small cups or egg poacher with deep cups, saucepan
Serves: 4

Scrambled eggs with asparagus

Imperial	Metric
5 slices bread	5 slices bread
2 oz. butter	50 g. butter
2 slices ham	2 slices ham
1 small can asparagus tips	1 small can asparagus tips
parsley	parsley
Scrambled eggs:	*Scrambled eggs:*
1–2 oz. butter	25–50 g. butter
8 eggs	8 eggs
seasoning	seasoning
4 tablespoons thin cream or milk	4 tablespoons thin cream or milk
pinch grated nutmeg (optional)	pinch grated nutmeg (optional)

1. Either toast and butter the bread, or fry it on both sides in hot butter. Keep warm.
2. Heat the butter in a pan. Beat the eggs with seasoning, the cream or milk and a pinch of grated nutmeg if wished. Scramble lightly in the hot butter.
3. Pile on to the toast or fried bread.
4. Garnish with asparagus tips, triangles of ham and parsley. Serve immediately as an hors-d'oeuvre or light supper dish.

Variation
Pipérade: Fry 1 finely chopped onion, 2–3 skinned and deseeded chopped tomatoes, and ½–1 red or green pepper in 2–3 oz. (50–75 g.) butter. Beat 6–8 eggs with seasoning but no milk and scramble in the usual way with the vegetables.

Cooking time: 5 minutes
Preparation time: 10 minutes
Main cooking utensils: grill or frying pan, saucepan
Serves: 5

Purée of spinach with poached eggs

Imperial	Metric
1½ lb. fresh spinach	¾ kg. fresh spinach
seasoning	seasoning
3 oz. butter	75 g. butter
3 slices bread, about ⅓ inch thick	3 slices bread, about ½ cm. thick
¼ pint milk	125 ml. milk
½ oz. flour	15 g. flour
1 egg white	1 egg white
1 tablespoon oil	1 tablespoon oil
3 eggs	3 eggs
white pepper	white pepper

1. Wash the spinach well and cook in a pan with seasoning (no water is needed).
2. When cooked, drain well, sieve or chop finely and reheat with 2 oz. (50 g.) of the butter.
3. While the spinach is cooking, soak the bread in the milk in a shallow dish (do not leave too long or it will break up when you take it out).
4. Dip the softened bread in well seasoned flour then into the stiffly beaten egg white.
5. Heat the oil and remaining 1 oz. (25 g.) butter and fry the bread until crisp and brown on both sides.
6. Break each egg into a cup and slide into boiling water. Poach gently until cooked.
7. Put the reheated spinach on a serving dish and arrange the poached eggs on slices of fried bread on top of the spinach. Sprinkle lightly with white pepper and serve as a light lunch or supper dish.

Variation

Sandwich 2 thin slices of bread with slices of Gruyère cheese then coat and fry.

Cooking time: 25 minutes
Preparation time: 20 minutes
Main cooking utensils: 2 saucepans, frying pan
Serves: 3

Potato and tuna soufflé

Imperial	Metric
2 medium-sized old potatoes or 1 small packet instant potato	2 medium-sized old potatoes or 1 small packet instant potato
seasoning	seasoning
1 oz. margarine or butter	25 g. margarine or butter
4 tablespoons milk	4 tablespoons milk
1 medium-sized can tuna fish	1 medium-sized can tuna fish
3 eggs, separated	3 eggs, separated
1 tablespoon chopped parsley	1 tablespoon chopped parsley
½ lemon	½ lemon

1. Peel and cook the potatoes in well salted water, drain, return to the pan and mash until smooth, or prepare instant potato in the pan.
2. Add the seasoning to taste, margarine or butter and milk, then beat until soft and light.
3. Stir in the flaked tuna, together with any liquid in the can, the egg yolks, parsley, grated lemon rind and juice.
4. Finally fold in the stiffly whisked egg whites.
5. Spoon into the greased soufflé dish and bake for 20–25 minutes until just set and brown – do not over-cook. Serve immediately.

Variation

Use 6–8 oz. (150–200 g.) flaked cooked white fish or a medium-sized can salmon.

Cooking time: 40 minutes when using fresh potatoes, or 20–25 minutes when using instant potatoes
Preparation time: 25 or 15 minutes depending on type of potatoes
Main cooking utensils: saucepan, 6-inch (15-cm.) soufflé dish
Oven temperature: moderate (350°F., 180°C., Gas Mark 4)
Oven position: centre
Serves: 4

Mushroom omelette

Imperial	Metric
small can mushrooms or	small can mushrooms or
4 oz. fresh mushrooms	100 g. fresh mushrooms
1 oz. butter	25 g. butter
1–2 teaspoons chopped parsley	1–2 teaspoons chopped parsley
or dried parsley	or dried parsley
seasoning	seasoning
Omelette:	*Omelette:*
8 oz. flour	200 g. flour
seasoning	seasoning
pinch ground coriander	pinch ground coriander
pinch mild paprika	pinch mild paprika
5 eggs	5 eggs
¾ pint milk	375 ml. milk
1–1½ oz. butter	25–40 g. butter

1. Open the can of mushrooms and drain away any surplus liquid, or if using fresh mushrooms wash and dry well.
2. Do not remove the skin of fresh mushrooms unless badly marked, as this will give extra flavour.
3. Toss in the hot butter. Cook fresh mushrooms, but only heat canned ones; add parsley and seasoning.
4. Sieve the flour with the seasoning, coriander and paprika.
5. Gradually beat in the egg yolks and milk. Stand until ready to cook.
6. Just before cooking, fold the stiffly beaten egg whites into the batter.
7. Heat half the butter in the pan; do not use too much for this mixture, otherwise the outside is 'sad' and greasy; there should be just enough to cover the bottom of the pan.
8. Spoon in half the mixture, cook steadily until brown and set, then turn carefully.
9. Repeat with the second omelette.
10. Fill with mushrooms and garnish with tomato and parsley.

Cooking time: 10 minutes
Preparation time: 10 minutes
Main cooking utensils: saucepan or frying pan, 8-inch (20-cm.) omelette pan
Serves: 4

North Sea omelette

Imperial	Metric
3–4 cooked potatoes	3–4 cooked potatoes
2 spring onions	2 spring onions
2 tomatoes, skinned	2 tomatoes, skinned
(see note)	(see note)
1½ oz. butter	40 g. butter
3 eggs	3 eggs
seasoning	seasoning
2 tablespoons chopped parsley	2 tablespoons chopped parsley
3½-oz. can sardines in	99-g. can sardines in
tomato sauce	tomato sauce
Garnish:	*Garnish:*
sprig parsley	sprig parsley

1. Dice the potatoes, chop the spring onions and tomatoes into neat pieces.
2. Put the butter into an omelette pan and heat, then add the potatoes, onions and tomatoes.
3. Turn in the hot butter for about 2 minutes.
4. Beat the eggs with seasoning and half the parsley.
5. Pour over the vegetables and leave for 30 seconds to 1 minute until the eggs have set in a thin film at the bottom of the pan.
6. Tilt the omelette pan and allow the liquid egg to flow from the top of the omelette to the sides of the pan.
7. Cook until the omelette is nearly set, then arrange the sardines on top of the egg mixture in a neat design and put the omelette pan under a hot grill for 2 minutes; top with the remainder of the chopped parsley and a sprig of parsley. Serve immediately.

Note: To skin tomatoes either put them into boiling water for 30 seconds, remove and skin, or spear them with a fork or fine skewer and hold over heat until the skin breaks, then pull it away.

Cooking time: few minutes
Preparation time: 10 minutes
Main cooking utensil: omelette pan
Serves: 2

Spanish omelette with peppers

Imperial	Metric
2 cloves garlic (optional)	2 cloves garlic (optional)
1 large onion	1 large onion
8 large tomatoes	8 large tomatoes
2 large or 4 smaller green peppers	2 large or 4 smaller green peppers
4 tablespoons oil	4 tablespoons oil
seasoning	seasoning
Omelettes:	*Omelettes:*
8 large or 10 medium eggs	8 large or 10 medium eggs
seasoning	seasoning
3 oz. butter or 3 tablespoons oil	75 g. butter or 3 tablespoons oil

1. Crush the cloves of garlic very finely. (Put the skinned clove on a board with a good pinch of salt, crush with the tip of a strong knife.)
2. Chop the onion very finely; skin the tomatoes.
3. Cut the flesh from the green and red peppers into strips, discard the core and seeds.
4. Heat the oil in the pan, fry the vegetables until they are as soft as wished; some people prefer the peppers to be firm, so add these when the onion and tomatoes are nearly soft. If wished, blanch the peppers for a softer texture (see note). Season well.
5. Beat the eggs with seasoning; for a slightly lighter, less rich omelette, add 2–4 tablespoons water.
6. Heat half the butter or oil in an omelette pan, pour in half the egg mixture, allow to set on the bottom, then tilt the pan to allow the liquid egg on top to flow down the sides.
7. When lightly set, tip on to a serving dish; do not fold. Make the second omelette. Serve topped with the very hot vegetable mixture.

Note: Peppers may be simmered for about 5–10 minutes in salted water to give a softened texture.

Cooking time: 15 minutes
Preparation time: 10 minutes
Main cooking utensils: frying pan, omelette pan
Serves: 6–8 as an hors d'oeuvre, 4 people as a main dish

Oven-baked omelette

Imperial	Metric
1 oz. butter	25 g. butter
6 eggs	6 eggs
2 oz. cheese	50 g. cheese
2 skinned tomatoes	2 skinned tomatoes
1 teaspoon chopped parsley or chives	1 teaspoon chopped parsley or chives
seasoning	seasoning

1. Heat the butter for a few minutes.
2. Beat the eggs, then add the grated cheese, thinly sliced tomatoes, parsley and seasoning.
3. Pour into a dish.
4. Cook for 10–15 minutes in the oven until the egg mixture sets.
5. Serve at once, with a salad or potato crisps.

Note: Although this omelette is baked in the oven, care must be taken, as with every other omelette, that it is not over-cooked.

Variations

Add chopped green pepper, removing seeds and core. This may be blanched in boiling salted water for a few minutes before adding to the eggs.
  Add chopped ham or shellfish in place of cheese.

Cooking time: 10–15 minutes
Preparation time: 10 minutes
Main cooking utensil: large shallow ovenproof dish
Oven temperature: hot (425–450°F., 220–230°C., Gas Mark 7–8)
Oven position: centre
Serves: 4

Some omelettes throughout the world

Plain omelette

For each person allow 2 eggs (or use 3 eggs for 2 people). Beat the eggs with seasoning; meanwhile heat a good knob of butter in an omelette pan. Pour in the eggs, allow them to set lightly at the bottom of the pan, then tilt the pan and lift the omelette with a knife so the liquid egg flows underneath. Continue cooking until set to personal taste. Fill if wished, see below, fold or roll, tip on to a hot plate and serve at once.

Bauernomelett (German)

Dice 1 rasher bacon, 1 medium-sized cooked potato and 1 small onion. Fry them in hot butter, then add 4 seasoned eggs and cooked as above; add chopped parsley before serving.

Frittata alla crostina (Italian)

Fry 4 oz. (100 g.) coarse breadcrumbs in 3 oz. (75 g.) butter until very crisp. Beat 4 eggs with seasoning and 2 tablespoons thin cream, pour this over the crumbs and cook as above.

Jewish liver omelette

Fry 1 small, chopped onion in 2 oz. (50 g.) chicken fat, together with 4 oz. (100 g.) finely diced calf's liver. Make an omelette with 4 eggs as above, and add the liver mixture just before folding.

Polish potato pancake

Although called a pancake this has a sufficiently high percentage of eggs to qualify as an omelette. Boil and mash 8 oz. (200 g.) potatoes, sieve if possible to give a smooth purée. Blend with 5 tablespoons milk, 4 egg yolks, seasoning and the stiffly beaten egg whites. Cook in hot butter until golden at the base, then turn and cook on the second side. Sprinkle with grated cheese before serving.

Omelette à la provençale

Imperial	Metric
4 large tomatoes	4 large tomatoes
1 large onion	1 large onion
1–2 cloves garlic	1–2 cloves garlic
1 green pepper	1 green pepper
2 tablespoons oil	2 tablespoons oil
seasoning	seasoning
2–3 tablespoons stock	2–3 tablespoons stock
6 eggs	6 eggs
2 tablespoons thin cream or milk	2 tablespoons thin cream or milk
2–3 teaspoons chopped parsley	2–3 teaspoons chopped parsley
2 oz. butter	50 g. butter
Garnish:	*Garnish:*
chopped parsley	chopped parsley
black olives	black olives

1. Skin and chop the tomatoes and onion.
2. Crush the garlic and chop the flesh from the pepper finely, discarding the core and seeds.
3. Fry steadily in the oil, season well and moisten with stock.
4. Beat the eggs with the cream, season well and add the parsley.
5. Heat the butter in an omelette pan, pour in the egg mixture and allow it to set lightly at the bottom of the pan, then tilt the pan and lift the omelette with a knife so that the liquid egg flows under this. Continue cooking until set.
6. Fill with the hot vegetables, fold up and turn on to a hot plate. Serve at once, garnished with parsley and olives, as a light meal.

Cooking time: 15 minutes
Preparation time: 15 minutes
Main cooking utensils: saucepan, omelette pan
Serves: 4

Savoury egg pie

Imperial

Pastry:
6 oz. plain flour
pinch salt
3 oz. fat
approximately 1½ tablespoons
   water
Filling:
1 onion, chopped
1 oz. fat
¾ pint milk
2 oz. soft white breadcrumbs
3 large eggs
few drops Worcestershire sauce
seasoning
Garnish:
3–4 bacon rashers
watercress

Metric

Pastry:
150 g. plain flour
pinch salt
75 g. fat
approximately 1½ tablespoons
   water
Filling:
1 onion, chopped
25 g. fat
425 ml. milk
50 g. soft white breadcrumbs
3 large eggs
few drops Worcestershire sauce
seasoning
Garnish:
3–4 bacon rashers
watercress

1. Make the pastry as on page 140.
2. Roll out pastry and line the pie plate; flute the edges.
3. Fry the onion in the fat, spread over the pastry.
4. Heat the milk, add the breadcrumbs and the eggs.
5. Blend with the Worcestershire sauce and seasoning.
6. Pour the mixture into the pastry case and bake until the pastry is crisp and the custard set. Halve the bacon rashers, roll them up, and put them on to a skewer; bake on a tin until crisp.
7. Garnish with bacon rolls and watercress. Serve hot or cold with salad.

Cooking time: 45 minutes
Preparation time: 35 minutes
Main cooking utensils: 8- to 9-inch (20- to 23-cm.) pie plate, frying pan, baking tin, skewer
Oven temperature: moderately hot (400°F., 200°C., Gas Mark 6)
Oven position: centre
Serves: 4–6

Onion tart

Imperial

Pastry:
8 oz. plain flour
seasoning
pinch dry mustard
4 oz. butter
1 egg yolk
water to mix
Filling:
1½ lb. onions, peeled weight
4 oz. fat bacon
2 oz. butter
6 eggs
½–1 teaspoon chopped fresh
   sage or ¼–½ teaspoon dried
   sage
½ teaspoon chopped marjoram
   or lemon thyme or ¼ teaspoon
   dried marjoram or thyme

Metric

Pastry:
200 g. plain flour
seasoning
pinch dry mustard
100 g. butter
1 egg yolk
water to mix
Filling:
¾ kg. onions, peeled weight
100 g. fat bacon
50 g. butter
6 eggs
½–1 teaspoon chopped fresh
   sage or ¼–½ teaspoon dried
   sage
½ teaspoon chopped marjoram
   or lemon thyme or ¼ teaspoon
   dried marjoram or thyme

1. Sieve the flour, seasoning and mustard, rub in the butter.
2. Bind with the egg yolk and water.
3. Roll out the pastry and line the flan ring on the baking tray or the sandwich tin.
4. Meanwhile chop the onions very finely, then fry steadily with the chopped bacon in the butter.
5. Beat the eggs with seasoning and herbs, add the onions and bacon and mix thoroughly.
6. For a lightly set pastry, pour the egg and onion mixture into the pastry case and bake for 25 minutes in a hot oven, then lower the heat to moderate and continue baking for a further 20 minutes. For a crisper pastry, bake the pastry blind for approximately 15 minutes (while cooking the onions). Add the egg and onion mixture then return to the oven at a moderate heat for approximately 30 minutes. Serve hot or cold as an hors-d'oeuvre or light main dish.

Cooking time: 45 or 55 minutes (see stage 6)
Preparation time: 25 minutes
Main cooking utensils: 8-inch (20-cm.) deep flan ring and baking tray or sandwich tin, frying pan
Oven temperature: 425°F., 220°C., Gas Mark 7 then 375°F., 190°C., Gas Mark 5
Oven position: centre
Serves: 6–8

Crêpes della nonna

Imperial	Metric
Batter:	*Batter:*
6 oz. flour	150 g. flour
5 eggs	5 eggs
½ pint milk	250 ml. milk
2 tablespoons oil	2 tablespoons oil
seasoning	seasoning
1 teaspoon mustard	1 teaspoon mustard
Filling:	*Filling:*
¾ pint thin white sauce	375 ml. thin white sauce
2 large apples	2 large apples
1 oz. sugar	25 g. sugar
1 egg	1 egg
4 oz. lean ham	100 g. lean ham
4 oz. cheese	100 g. cheese
Topping:	*Topping:*
2 oz. butter	50 g. butter
3 oz. cheese	75 g. cheese
3 oz. ham	75 g. ham
3 large tomatoes	3 large tomatoes

1. Mix together the flour, eggs, milk, oil and seasonings and beat until very light, allow to stand.
2. Make the coating sauce and season well.
3. In a second pan, cook the apples to a soft purée with the sugar and a little water.
4. Blend the egg with the sauce, together with the ham (pounded until smooth) and cheese, cut into cubes.
5. Fry thin layers of batter in very hot butter.
6. Put some sauce filling into each pancake and roll while hot.
7. Cover with the topping made by heating the butter, then adding the finely grated cheese, ham cut into fine ribbons, and the skinned, chopped tomatoes.
8. Garnish with strips of truffle or mushroom. (Mushrooms must, of course, be cooked; the truffle is uncooked.) Put some apple mixture at both ends of the pancakes. Serve hot or cold.

Cooking time: 25 minutes
Preparation time: 30 minutes
Main cooking utensils: omelette or frying pan, 2 saucepans
Serves: 4

Cheese pancakes with mustard pickle

Imperial	Metric
4 oz. plain flour	100 g. plain flour
pinch salt	pinch salt
1 egg	1 egg
½ pint milk or milk and water	250 ml. milk or milk and water
2–3 tablespoons oil or fat	2–3 tablespoons oil or fat
Filling:	*Filling:*
4 tablespoons thick cream	4 tablespoons thick cream
6 oz. Gruyère cheese, grated	150 g. Gruyère cheese, grated
2 oz. Parmesan cheese, grated	50 g. Parmesan cheese, grated
1 oz. butter	25 g. butter
4 oz. celery or grated celeriac	100 g. celery or grated celeriac
seasoning	seasoning
Garnish:	*Garnish:*
mustard pickle	mustard pickle

1. Sieve the flour and salt together.
2. Add the egg and milk and beat well. Strain the batter and leave to stand for a short while.
3. Heat the oil in a pan and fry 8 pancakes until golden (about 1½–2 minutes on each side). Use only enough oil to grease the bottom of the pan for each pancake, make sure this is really hot before pouring in the batter.
4. To make the filling, blend the cream, grated cheese and melted butter in a pan, add the finely chopped celery and season well. Do not cook the mixture or the cheese will become tough.
5. Fill the pancakes with the mixture and roll up firmly. Garnish with generous layers of mustard pickle and serve at once.

Variation

Cream or cottage cheese can be used instead of Gruyère and Parmesan cheese.

Cooking time: 15 minutes
Preparation time: 15 minutes
Main cooking utensil: frying pan
Serves: 4

Scotch pancakes

Imperial
4 oz. flour (with plain flour use
   either 2 teaspoons baking
   powder or ½ small teaspoon
   bicarbonate of soda and
   1 small teaspoon cream of
   tartar)
pinch salt
1 oz. sugar
1 egg
¼ pint milk
1 oz. melted margarine
   (optional)

Metric
100 g. flour (with plain flour use
   either 2 teaspoons baking
   powder or ½ small teaspoon
   bicarbonate of soda and
   1 small teaspoon cream of
   tartar)
pinch salt
25 g. sugar
1 egg
125 ml. milk
25 g. melted margarine
   (optional)

1. Sieve together the dry ingredients.
2. Beat in first the egg, then the milk.
3. Lastly stir in the melted margarine. This is not essential but it does help to keep the scones moist.
4. Grease and warm the griddle, hot plate or frying pan. It is best to use the bottom of the frying pan – the part that usually goes over the heat.
5. To test if the heat is correct, drop a teaspoon of the mixture on the heated surface, and if it goes golden brown within 1 minute, the plate is ready.
6. Drop spoonfuls of the mixture on to the plate.
7. Cook for about 2 minutes, then turn and cook for a further 2 minutes.
8. To test if cooked, press firmly with the back of a knife, and if no batter comes from the sides and the scones feel firm lift out and cool on a wire sieve. Serve with butter, butter and jam or as illustrated, topped with butter and served with a thick apple purée.

Cooking time: 4 minutes each batch
Preparation time: 10 minutes
Main cooking utensil: griddle or thick frying pan
Makes: 8–12 pancakes

Pancakes

Imperial
Pancake batter:
4 oz. flour
pinch salt
2 eggs
just under ½ pint milk
For frying:
little butter or oil
Traditional topping:
sugar
lemon
Fruit filling and topping:
1 lb. peeled cooking apples
3 tablespoons water
2 oz. sugar
3 tablespoons apricot jam
few raisins or sultanas

Metric
Pancake batter:
110 g. flour
pinch salt
2 eggs
275 ml. milk
For frying:
little butter or oil
Traditional topping:
sugar
lemon
Fruit filling and topping:
½ kg. peeled cooking apples
3 tablespoons water
50 g. sugar
3 tablespoons apricot jam
few raisins or sultanas

1. Sieve together the flour and salt.
2. Add the beaten eggs and mix well.
3. Add the milk and beat again.
4. Melt enough butter or oil in a small frying pan just to cover the base.
5. Pour in enough batter to make a thin pancake.
6. Cook on either side until brown.
7. If serving the traditional way, tip on to sugared paper, roll, and serve on a hot dish with wedges of lemon. The pancakes can be kept until ready to serve on an uncovered hot plate over hot water or in the oven.
8. If serving with a fruit topping, simmer the apples with the water and sugar until tender, blend with the apricot jam and raisins. Use half as a filling for the pancakes, roll or fold, then top with the remainder.

Note: Pancakes, traditionally served on a Shrove Tuesday, can be served with various fillings throughout the year.

Cooking time: 10–15 minutes
Preparation time: 10 minutes
Main cooking utensils: frying pan, saucepan
Serves: 4–6

Cheese dishes

Cheese is used in many dishes, not only in this section, but other parts of the book. To find all the cheese and egg dishes, see the Easy Guide on page 124.

When you need to cook with cheese, select the variety carefully. The best cooking cheeses are: Cheddar, Cheshire, Dutch Gouda and Edam, Swiss or French Gruyère and Emmenthal, Italian Parmesan (one of the best cooking cheeses) and Mozzarella, Danish Havarti and Samsoe, together with processed cheeses, cream and cottage cheese; although the latter must not be cooked too quickly, it is ideal as a filling for pancakes, etc. or used in cheese cakes. Do not imagine the above is a complete list of cheeses that can be heated; creamy Camembert can be heated *very slowly* with a little butter and cream to make an interesting sauce or fondue. Danish blue cheese and other veined cheeses can be added to sauces, but particular care must be taken that they do not become too hot.

When cooking cheese in sauces, etc., do not cook for too long a period, or at too high a temperature. If you do the cheese becomes tough and the sauce is inclined to curdle, see recipe page 123. *Cheese is a most valuable protein food*; it also provides essential calcium.

Buy cheese carefully, check it looks pleasantly moist, and store carefully. Soft cheeses, such as Brie, etc., should not be put in the refrigerator.

Freezing egg and cheese dishes

Dishes containing eggs freeze well, the exceptions being any dish that contains whole cooked eggs, such as baked or boiled eggs. The egg, when frozen, becomes tough, 'rubbery' and inedible. This means you cannot freeze sandwiches that contain chopped hard-boiled eggs. Naturally hot soufflés or omelettes would not be frozen, since they must be served as soon as they are cooked. I find it very helpful to freeze small containers of vegetables to use as omelette fillings.

If you have a lot of eggs at one time that cannot be used, then separate the yolks from the whites. Beat the yolks with either a little sugar or with seasoning and put into small containers, mark the number of yolks clearly. The whites should also be packed separately, do not season or sweeten. Use within 8–9 months, thaw out slowly.

Dishes containing cheese freeze well, unless there are other ingredients in the recipe that prevent this. It is not ideal to freeze stocks of cheese, since some flavour is lost, but if you have had a party and there is rather a lot of cheese left over, that could be wasted, then freeze it. Wrap well, and use the cheeses as soon as possible, the harder cheeses tend to lose less flavour than the soft creamy type.

Cheese- and tomato-topped toasts

Imperial
4 thick slices bread
2 oz. butter
4 oz. cheese, Mozzarella,
   Gruyère or Cheddar
4 small tomatoes
little oil or butter
seasoning
½ teaspoon oregano (wild
   marjoram)
small can anchovy fillets
Garnish:
parsley or chervil
tomato wedges

Metric
4 thick slices bread
50 g. butter
100 g. cheese, Mozzarella,
   Gruyère or Cheddar
4 small tomatoes
little oil or butter
seasoning
½ teaspoon oregano (wild
   marjoram)
small can anchovy fillets
Garnish:
parsley or chervil
tomato wedges

1. Toast the bread lightly on both sides.
2. Butter one side of the bread and cover with sliced cheese.
3. Top with the tomatoes, brushed with butter or oil and well seasoned, and a sprinkling of oregano.
4. Cook under the grill until the tomatoes have softened and the cheese has melted.
5. Top with rolls of anchovy fillets and garnish with parsley or chervil and tomato wedges.

Variation
Dip the slices of bread in well-seasoned milk and beaten egg, fry in hot oil or oil and butter until crisp and golden brown. Keep hot. Fry eggs in the hot fat and when nearly set, top with grated Parmesan cheese. Lift out carefully, put on to the hot fried bread and serve with raw tomatoes.

Cooking time: 5 minutes
Preparation time: 10 minutes
Main cooking utensil: grill pan
Serves: 4

Cheese and bacon sandwiches

Imperial
8 thick slices bread
2 oz. butter
8 oz. Cheddar cheese
8 rashers streaky bacon
Garnish:
gherkins
pickled onions
parsley

Metric
8 thick slices bread
50 g. butter
200 g. Cheddar cheese
8 rashers streaky bacon
Garnish:
gherkins
pickled onions
parsley

1. Toast the slices of bread on each side.
2. Spread each slice generously with butter.
3. Slice the Cheddar cheese thinly and arrange the slices on top of the toast.
4. Remove the rind from the bacon, and if the rashers are thick flatten them with a knife and cut them in half. Put these on top of the cheese.
5. Cook under a hot grill until the cheese is melted and the bacon crisp.
6. Lift the second slice of toast with cheese and bacon on top of the first. They should be served immediately with pickled onions and gherkins and garnished with parsley.

Variations
Sliced tomatoes can also be added, or chopped ham used instead of bacon.

Cooking time: 5 minutes
Preparation time: 10 minutes
Main cooking utensil: grill pan
Serves: 4

Frankfurters and cheese

Imperial	Metric
1½ oz. butter	40 g. butter
6 slices bread	6 slices bread
6 slices cooked ham or German garlic sausage	6 slices cooked ham or German garlic sausage
12 small or 6 large frankfurter sausages	12 small or 6 large frankfurter sausages
6 slices Gruyère or Cheddar cheese	6 slices Gruyère or Cheddar cheese
Garnish:	*Garnish:*
parsley	parsley

1. Butter the slices of bread on both sides and heat under the grill or in a hot oven for a few minutes until the butter melts and the bread begins to crisp.
2. Lay the slices of cooked ham on the bread with the whole or halved frankfurter sausages.
3. Top with the sliced cheese, heat under the grill until the topping is very hot and the cheese melted. If preferred, do this in the oven.
4. Top with parsley. Serve as an informal savoury dish.

Variations
Frankfurters in beer: Heat 12 small frankfurters in ½—¾ pint (250—375 ml.) beer instead of water.
Fried frankfurters: Slice frankfurters and fry in 2 oz. (50 g.) butter with 2 sliced, peeled apples, 1—2 oz. (25—50 g.) currants, 4 tablespoons wine and a little cinnamon.

Cooking time: 10 minutes
Preparation time: few minutes
Main cooking utensil: grill pan or ovenproof dish
Oven temperature: hot (425—450°F., 220—230°C., Gas Mark 7—8)
Oven position: hottest part
Serves: 6

Cheese pyramids

Imperial	Metric
1 pint milk	500 ml. milk
4 oz. fine semolina	100 g. fine semolina
4 oz. grated Parmesan cheese	100 g. grated Parmesan cheese
1 level dessertspoon made mustard	1 level dessertspoon made mustard
1 tablespoon Worcestershire sauce	1 tablespoon Worcestershire sauce
dash cayenne pepper	dash cayenne pepper
Coating:	*Coating:*
1 egg	1 egg
approximately 3 oz. breadcrumbs	approximately 75 g. breadcrumbs
fat for frying	fat for frying
Garnish:	*Garnish:*
lettuce	lettuce

1. Grease the sandwich tin and set aside.
2. Heat the milk nearly to boiling point.
3. Stir in the fine semolina, bring to the boil and continue to cook, stirring vigorously, for 3—4 minutes.
4. Remove the pan from the heat, add the remaining ingredients and pour into the prepared sandwich tin.
5. When the mixture is cold, turn on to floured board, divide into eight equal wedges.
6. Brush with beaten egg and coat with breadcrumbs.
7. Heat the fat. Test the heat by putting a piece of bread into it. If this turns golden brown within 1 minute the fat is hot enough.
8. Carefully put the pyramids in and fry on either side until crisp and golden brown.
9. Drain on crumpled tissue or kitchen paper. Stand on end. Top with cutlet frills and serve on a bed of lettuce.

Cooking time: approximately 12 minutes
Preparation time: 10 minutes
Main cooking utensils: 8-inch (20-cm.) sandwich tin, frying pan, cutlet frills
Serves: 4

Potato cheese pie

Imperial	Metric
2 lb. cooked potatoes	1 kg. cooked potatoes
1 oz. butter	25 g. butter
1 egg yolk	1 egg yolk
seasoning	seasoning
milk to mix	milk to mix
8 oz. bacon, made into rolls	200 g. bacon, made into rolls
Cheese sauce:	*Cheese sauce:*
1 oz. margarine	25 g. margarine
1 oz. flour	25 g. flour
½ pint milk	250 ml. milk
seasoning	seasoning
4–5 oz. cheese, grated	100–125 g. cheese, grated
Garnish:	*Garnish:*
apple slices	apple slices
parsley	parsley

1. Sieve or mash the potatoes and beat in the butter, egg yolk and seasoning.
2. Add sufficient milk to make a mixture of a creamy consistency.
3. Line a pie dish or pie plate with two-thirds of the creamed potatoes. Pipe a border with the remainder.
4. Grill until golden brown and crisp.
5. Meanwhile make the sauce. Heat the butter in a pan, stir in the flour and cook for several minutes. Remove from the heat and stir in the milk. Cook until smooth and thickened, season to taste and add the cheese.
6. Pour into the potato pie and keep warm.
7. Grill the bacon rolls and place on the pie. Garnish with apple slices and parsley.

Variation

Omit the bacon and add 2 raw grated carrots to the sauce.

Cooking time: 10–15 minutes
Preparation time: 15–20 minutes
Main cooking utensils: pie dish, piping bag, large pipe, saucepan
Serves: 4

Raisin and cheese pie

Imperial	Metric
Shortcrust pastry:	*Shortcrust pastry:*
12 oz. plain flour	300 g. plain flour
pinch salt	pinch salt
3 oz. margarine	75 g. margarine
3 oz. cooking fat	75 g. cooking fat
approximately 4 tablespoons cold water	approximately 4 tablespoons cold water
Filling:	*Filling:*
12 oz. seedless raisins	300 g. seedless raisins
8–12 oz. cheese, grated	200–300 g. cheese, grated
1 egg	1 egg
2 tablespoons milk	2 tablespoons milk
pinch salt	pinch salt
shake cayenne pepper	shake cayenne pepper
Glaze:	*Glaze:*
little egg white left in the shell	little egg white left in the shell

1. Sieve the flour and salt. Rub in fats until the mixture resembles fine breadcrumbs, then mix to a stiff dough with the cold water.
2. Turn on to a floured board, knead lightly till smooth.
3. Roll out the pastry, use just over half to line the flan ring or tin.
4. Fill with a layer of raisins, then cheese, then a little of the egg beaten with the milk and seasoning.
5. Continue filling the flan like this.
6. Cover with the rest of the pastry.
7. Seal the edges well, decorate the top with pastry leaves, etc.
8. Brush with a little egg white left in the shell.
9. Bake for the time and at the temperature given. Serve hot or cold, instead of a sweet or as a light supper or luncheon dish.

Cooking time: 40 minutes
Preparation time: 30 minutes
Main cooking utensils: 7½- to 8-inch (19- to 20-cm.) deep flan ring and baking tray
Oven temperature: moderately hot (400°F., 200°C., Gas Mark 6)
Oven position: centre
Serves: 4–6

Pastry dishes

Many people believe that pastry-making is an art and that if one is not a born pastry cook the chances of success are rather small.

This is not really true; it is a fact that many people have a natural ability to handle pastry dough, whereas others have to work a little harder to achieve success. The essentials of good pastry are:

1. Weigh the ingredients carefully, so you have a correct balance between fat and flour, etc.
2. Handle the dough carefully; when making short crust pastry, rub the fat into the flour very lightly with the tips of your fingers — do not overhandle.
3. Add liquid gradually to the pastry dough, for if it is too moist the pastry tends to be tough when baked; if it is too dry the pastry crumbles badly.

When a pastry recipe states 8 oz. (200 g.) pastry it means pastry made with that amount of flour, not the completed weight of pastry. Metrication brings certain problems. The accepted equivalent is 1 oz. equals 25 g., whereas the accurate equivalent is 28·35 g. This does not matter on small amounts, but does mean that the equivalent of *8 oz.* is really *226·8 g.*, not *200 g.*, and in turn this will produce a decidedly smaller amount of pastry (although one that is perfectly in proportion) if you follow metric measures rather than the Imperial measures. This may be an advantage if you sometimes have a little pastry dough left over.

To freeze pastry

Pastry of all kinds freezes extremely well so make rather more than you need for one dish, or one meal. Freeze portions of uncooked pastry dough — short, puff, fleur (flan) pastry, etc. Wrap in foil or polythene and label with the amount of flour used, so you know exactly how much pastry is in each package. Uncooked pastry keeps for 2–3 months in the freezer. Defrost slightly before rolling out.

Pies, tarts, etc. can be prepared and frozen without cooking, cover the pie, etc. *after* freezing, so you do not damage the pastry. Thaw out, bake in the usual way or, if you bake from the frozen state, check during baking to see that the pastry does not become too brown before the filling is heated through. Storage time varies with the filling but should not exceed 3 months for meats, etc., 6 months for fruit. You can prepare and bake the dish, cool, then freeze and wrap. Use this method with pies and tarts, but it is particularly suitable for flans such as the Corn quiche, opposite. Reheat gently from the frozen state. Information on freezing, then heating suet crust puddings is on page 56.

Choux pastry see 145 should be baked, cooled, filled, then frozen. *Wrap after* freezing. Use within 5 months if not filled, 2–3 months if filled.

Corn quiche

Imperial
Pastry:
6 oz. plain flour
pinch salt
3 oz. fat
approximately 2 tablespoons
　water, to mix
Filling:
small can sweetcorn
2 eggs
½ pint milk
4–6 oz. grated cheese
seasoning
Garnish:
parsley
tomato

Metric
Pastry:
150 g. plain flour
pinch salt
75 g. fat
approximately 2 tablespoons
　water, to mix
Filling:
small can sweetcorn
2 eggs
275 ml. milk
100–150 g. grated cheese
seasoning
Garnish:
parsley
tomato

1. Sieve the flour and salt, rub into the fat and bind with water.
2. Roll out the pastry and line the flan ring, which should be put on the upturned baking tin for easy removal.
3. Drain the corn and mix with the well beaten eggs; add the milk, cheese and seasoning.
4. Pour into the pastry.
5. Bake for 15 minutes in a hot oven then lower the heat for the remainder of the time.
6. Garnish with parsley and wedges of tomato. Serve hot or cold.

Variation
The classic quiche of France has chopped fried bacon instead of corn. Use chopped mushrooms or shellfish, in place of corn.

Cooking time: 45 minutes
Preparation time: 25 minutes
Main cooking utensils: 7-inch (18-cm.) flan ring and baking sheet
Oven temperature: hot (425–450°F., 220–230°C., Gas Mark 7–8)
　then moderately hot (375°F., 190°C., Gas Mark 5)
Oven position: centre
Serves: 4–6

Steak and kidney pudding

Imperial
Suet crust:
8 oz. flour (with plain flour use
　1 teaspoon baking powder)
4 oz. shredded suet
seasoning
water to mix
Filling:
1 lb. stewing steak
2–3 lamb's kidneys or 4 oz. ox
　kidney
½ oz. flour
seasoning
water or stock

Metric
Suet crust:
200 g. flour (with plain flour use
　1 teaspoon baking powder)
100 g. shredded suet
seasoning
water to mix
Filling:
400 g. stewing steak
2–3 lamb's kidneys or 100 g. ox
　kidney
15 g. flour
seasoning
water or stock

1. To make the suet crust, mix all the dry ingredients together and add enough water to make a firm dough.
2. Line the greased basin with most of the pastry, retaining enough for the cover.
3. Cut the meat into small pieces.
4. Skin, core and chop the kidneys.
5. Mix the meats well together and put into the lined basin, sprinkling each layer with flour and seasoning.
6. Add enough water or stock nearly to fill the basin.
7. Put on the pastry lid, damp the edges and seal well together.
8. Cover with greased greaseproof paper and cloth, or a cloth dipped in boiling water and floured. Leave room for the pastry to swell.
9. Steam for a minimum of 4 hours. Serve with thickened gravy and green vegetables.

Variation
Add finely chopped onions; a few mushrooms; or any vegetable.

Cooking time: minimum of 4 hours
Preparation time: 20 minutes
Main cooking utensils: 2-pint (1-litre) pudding basin, steamer, saucepan, greaseproof paper, cloth
Serves: 4

Onion dumplings

Imperial	Metric
4 large onions	4 large onions
Cheese pastry:	*Cheese pastry:*
6 oz. plain flour	150 g. plain flour
pinch salt, cayenne pepper and dry mustard	pinch salt, cayenne pepper and dry mustard
2½ oz. butter	65 g. butter
4 oz. finely grated Cheddar cheese	100 g. finely grated Cheddar cheese
1½ tablespoons cold water	1½ tablespoons cold water
1 egg	1 egg
1 oz. grated Cheddar cheese	25 g. grated Cheddar cheese
Cheese sauce:	*Cheese sauce:*
1 oz. margarine	25 g. margarine
1 oz. flour	25 g. flour
½ pint milk	250 ml. milk
seasoning	seasoning
3 oz. grated Cheddar cheese	75 g. grated Cheddar cheese

1. Cook onions in boiling salted water for about 1 hour or until tender.
2. Drain and allow to cool slightly.
3. Prepare the cheese pastry.
4. Sieve the flour, salt, cayenne pepper, and mustard.
5. Rub in butter, add cheese and cold water to bind.
6. Knead lightly and roll out to a rectangle 6 inches by 12 inches (15 by 30 cm.).
7. Cut eight strips and brush with beaten egg and sprinkle with grated cheese.
8. Put onions into a dish, cover with cheese strips.
9. Bake until pastry is crisp and brown.
10. To make the cheese sauce, heat the margarine in a pan, stir in the flour, and cook for several minutes.
11. Gradually blend in the milk, bring to the boil, cook until smooth and thickened, add seasoning and grated cheese. Serve the dumplings hot with the sauce.

Cooking time: 1 hour 25 minutes
Preparation time: 25 minutes
Main cooking utensils: saucepan, ovenproof dish
Oven temperature: moderate (375–400°F., 190–200°C., Gas Mark 5–6)
Oven position: above centre
Serves: 4

Sausage meat roll

Imperial	Metric
6 oz. self-raising flour (or plain flour with 1 teaspoon baking powder)	150 g. self-raising flour (or plain flour with 1 teaspoon baking powder)
pinch salt	pinch salt
3 oz. shredded suet	75 g. shredded suet
water to mix	water to mix
Filling:	*Filling:*
12 oz. sausage meat	300 g. sausage meat
2 chopped apples or 2–4 chopped prunes or 3 skinned chopped tomatoes	2 chopped apples or 2–4 chopped prunes or 3 skinned chopped tomatoes
2 chopped onions	2 chopped onions
seasoning	seasoning
1 teaspoon powdered sage	1 teaspoon powdered sage
Garnish:	*Garnish:*
2 tomatoes	2 tomatoes

1. Sieve the flour or flour and baking powder and salt.
2. Add the suet and enough water to make a rolling consistency.
3. Roll into a neat oblong.
4. Mix the sausage meat with the chopped apples or prunes or tomatoes, onions, seasoning and sage.
5. Spread over the suet crust, damp edges and roll like a Swiss roll.
6. Lift on to a baking tin.
7. Bake until crisp and golden brown, lowering heat after 30 minutes if necessary.
8. Garnish with sliced tomatoes. Serve hot, cut in slices.

Variation
Wrap lightly in a floured cloth or greased foil and steam for 1½ hours.

Cooking time: 1 hour
Preparation time: 15 minutes
Main cooking utensil: flat baking sheet or tin
Oven temperature: moderate (375°F., 190°C., Gas Mark 5) then very moderate (350°F., 180°C., Gas Mark 4) if necessary
Oven position: centre
Serves: 4–6

Mushroom pasties

Imperial	Metric
Pastry:	*Pastry:*
8 oz. flour, preferably plain	200 g. flour, preferably plain
pinch salt	pinch salt
2 teaspoons lemon juice	2 teaspoons lemon juice
8 oz. butter	200 g. butter
beaten egg to glaze	beaten egg to glaze
Filling:	*Filling:*
8 oz. mushrooms	200 g. mushrooms
$\frac{1}{2}$ pint stock or milk	250 ml. stock or milk
seasoning	seasoning
1 oz. flour	25 g. flour
2 oz. butter	50 g. butter
grated rind of $\frac{1}{2}$ lemon	grated rind of $\frac{1}{2}$ lemon

1. Sieve the flour and salt, bind with the lemon juice and water, to form an elastic dough.
2. Roll out to a neat oblong, put the butter on the top, and fold pastry over the butter.
3. Turn, seal ends, 'rib' the pastry, roll out.
4. Fold in 3, turn, seal ends, 'rib' again and roll out.
5. Continue until the pastry has had 7 foldings and 7 rollings, put into a cool place between rollings.
6. When ready to make vol-au-vent cases, roll to $\frac{1}{3}$-inch ($\frac{1}{2}$-cm.) thickness, cut into 6–8 squares or oblongs, press a small cutter halfway through the pastry (leave a rim of $\frac{1}{3}$–$\frac{1}{2}$ inch ($\frac{1}{2}$ cm.) round this).
7. Glaze with beaten egg, bake until crisp and golden brown, about 15 minutes. Remove the lids and replace the pastry in a cooler oven to dry out.
8. Slice the mushrooms (unless very small), simmer in half the stock or milk until tender, season well.
9. Blend the flour with the remaining liquid, add to the pan with butter and rind and cook until thickened, stirring.
10. Put the filling in the pastry just before serving.

Cooking time: 30 minutes
Preparation time: 45 minutes plus time for pastry to stand
Main cooking utensils: baking tray, saucepan
Oven temperature: very hot (475°F., 240°C., Gas Mark 9) then moderate (375°F., 190°C., Gas Mark 5)
Oven position: just above centre
Serves: 6–8

Steak and kidney pie

Imperial	Metric
$1\frac{1}{2}$–2 lb. stewing steak	$\frac{3}{4}$–1 kg. stewing steak
4–6 oz. ox kidney	100–150 g. ox kidney
seasoning	seasoning
1 oz. flour	25 g. flour
1 oz. fat	25 g. fat
1 pint stock	550 ml. stock
8-oz. packet frozen puff pastry	226-g. packet frozen puff pastry
little milk to glaze	little milk to glaze

1. Cut the meat into 1-inch (2 cm.) cubes, roll in the seasoned flour.
2. Fry in the hot fat for a few minutes, then gradually blend in the stock and cook until the mixture has thickened slightly.
3. Put a lid on the pan, lower the heat and simmer for approximately $1\frac{1}{2}$ hours.
4. Allow the meat to cool, put a funnel in the pie dish, lift the meat into the dish with a little of the gravy – save the rest to serve with the pie.
5. Roll out the thawed pastry and cover the pie.
6. Form any scraps into leaves, etc., for decoration, brush with a little milk and stick into position.
7. Brush the pie with milk, and make a tiny slit over the funnel to allow the steam to escape.
8. Bake at the higher temperature for 10 minutes, then lower the heat and cook for a further 20–30 minutes. Serve hot with vegetables.

Variation

Add mushrooms; for luxury, add a few oysters.

Cooking time: 2 hours
Preparation time: 35 minutes
Main cooking utensils: saucepan, $1\frac{1}{2}$-pint ($\frac{3}{4}$-litre) pie dish
Oven temperature: hot (450°F., 230°C., Gas Mark 8) reducing to moderately hot (400°F., 200°C., Gas Mark 6)
Oven position: centre
Serves: 5–6

Pastry slices

Imperial	Metric
Flaky pastry:	*Flaky pastry:*
1 lb. plain flour	400 g. plain flour
pinch salt	pinch salt
12 oz. butter or margarine	300 g. butter or margarine
squeeze lemon juice	squeeze lemon juice
cold water to mix	cold water to mix
little water	little water
castor sugar	castor sugar
whipped cream	whipped cream

1. Sieve the flour and salt.
2. Rub in one-third of the fat and mix to a soft, not sticky, dough with lemon juice and cold water.
3. Knead lightly. Roll out to an oblong.
4. Spread half remaining fat in small pieces over two-thirds of the dough.
5. Fold the plain third over the centre and top third down over the centre.
6. Seal edges, turn at right angles.
7. Rib the pastry by pressing the rolling pin down at intervals.
8. Roll out again, repeat stages 4, 5 and 6 with the rest of the fat.
9. Put into a cool place for at least 1 hour.
10. Roll out about $\frac{1}{4}$ inch ($\frac{1}{2}$ cm.) thick to an oblong, 20 by 10 inches (55 by 25 cm.).
11. Trim edges, cut into squares, then triangles or neat slices.
12. Place on baking sheets, brush half or one-third with water and sprinkle with castor sugar for the top layer.
13. Bake for time given.
14. Cool on a wire tray, then sandwich two or three layers with whipped cream. Top with the layer previously sprinkled with sugar.

Cooking time: 15 minutes
Preparation time: 35 minutes, plus time for pastry to stand
Main cooking utensils: baking sheets or trays
Oven temperature: hot (450–475°F., 230–240°C., Gas Mark 7–8)
Oven position: above centre
Serves: 12

French apple flan

Imperial	Metric
Flan or fleur pastry:	*Flan or fleur pastry:*
3 oz. butter or margarine	75 g. butter or margarine
1 oz. sugar	25 g. sugar
6 oz. plain flour	150 g. plain flour
1 egg yolk	1 egg yolk
cold water	cold water
Filling:	*Filling:*
1½ lb. apples, peeled and sliced (see note)	¾ kg. apples, peeled and sliced (see note)
little sugar	little sugar
4 tablespoons apricot jam	4 tablespoons apricot jam

1. Cream the butter and sugar until really soft and light.
2. Add the flour and work together with a palette knife.
3. Stir in the egg yolk and sufficient water to make a rolling consistency.
4. Roll out on a lightly floured board.
5. Fit into the ring or tin, trim edges and bake blind for 10 minutes only. (Place greaseproof paper in the pastry case and fill with baking beans.)
6. Meanwhile, simmer some of the apples with sugar to give thick purée — spread over the half-cooked pastry.
7. Cover with wafer-thin slices of apple and a little sugar, return to the oven until the pastry is brown and apples tender.
8. Cover with melted apricot jam and serve with cream.

Note: To keep apples white, place peeled slices in cold water to which a little lemon juice or salt has been added.

Variation
Use other fruit in place of the apples.

Cooking time: 25 minutes
Preparation time: 25 minutes
Main cooking utensils: 7–8-inch (18–20-cm.) fluted flan ring, baking tray, saucepan
Oven temperature: hot (425°F., 220°C., Gas Mark 7)
Oven position: centre
Serves: 6

Raspberry-filled choux

Imperial	Metric
Pastry:	*Pastry:*
¼ pint water	125 ml. water
1½ oz. butter	40 g. butter
3 oz. flour	75 g. flour
2 medium eggs	2 medium eggs
1 egg yolk	1 egg yolk
Confectioner's custard:	*Confectioner's custard:*
1 level tablespoon cornflour	1 level tablespoon cornflour
½ pint milk	275 ml. milk
2 teaspoons sugar	2 teaspoons sugar
few drops vanilla essence	few drops vanilla essence
or vanilla sugar	or vanilla sugar
2 egg yolks	2 egg yolks
¼ pint thick cream	125 ml. thick cream
Filling:	*Filling:*
1–1¼ lb. raspberries	approximately ½ kg. raspberries

1. To make the pastry, put the water and butter into a saucepan and heat until the butter has dissolved. Remove from the heat and stir in the flour.
2. Cook over a gentle heat, stirring well until the mixture forms into a dry ball.
3. Remove from the heat again and gradually beat in the eggs and egg yolk until the texture becomes smooth and sticky.
4. Pile or pipe into 8 rounds on a greased tray.
5. Cook for about 20 minutes in a hot oven, then lower heat to crisp the pastry.
6. Allow to cool, cut off the tops and remove the sticky inside.
7. Blend the cornflour with the milk, cook until thickened and smooth, add the sugar, vanilla and egg yolks, continue cooking without boiling until very thick.
8. Cool, stirring well, then fold in the whipped cream.
9. Fill the choux with most of the confectioner's custard and fruit. Top with the lids and a spoonful of custard. Serve any remaining fruit round the choux.

Cooking time: 25 minutes
Preparation time: 30 minutes
Main cooking utensils: 2 saucepans, baking trays
Oven temperature: hot (425–450°F., 220–230°C., Gas Mark 7–8)
   then moderate (375°F., 190°C., Gas Mark 5)
Oven position: just above centre
Makes: 8 choux

Californian prune flan

Imperial	Metric
9 oz. plain flour	225 g. plain flour
4½ oz. unsalted butter	115 g. unsalted butter
1½ oz. sugar	40 g. sugar
grated rind and juice of 1 lemon	grated rind and juice of 1 lemon
2 egg yolks	2 egg yolks
few drops vanilla essence	few drops vanilla essence
water to mix	water to mix
Filling:	*Filling:*
6 oz. well-drained cooked	150 g. well-drained cooked
stoned prunes	stoned prunes
8 cooked or drained canned	8 cooked or drained canned
apricots	apricots
1 tablespoon sugar	1 tablespoon sugar
2 teaspoons lemon juice	2 teaspoons lemon juice

1. Sieve the flour and rub in the butter until mixture resembles fine breadcrumbs.
2. Add the sugar and lemon rind, then bind with the lemon juice, egg yolks, vanilla essence and enough water to make a soft dough.
3. Knead lightly on a floured board (the dough will be much stickier to handle than pastry) and press into the greased sandwich tin. If the dough is rather soft to handle leave it in a cool place for about 30 minutes before kneading.
4. Chill the dough in the tin for 30 minutes.
5. Fill the flan with the prunes and apricots, sprinkle with sugar and lemon juice and bake in a hot oven for 15 minutes.
6. Lower heat to moderate and bake for a further 15 minutes or until firm and golden. Serve hot or cold.

Note: The prunes shown in the picture are the stoned type which are tenderised and therefore do not need soaking before cooking.

Cooking time: 30 minutes
Preparation time: 30 minutes plus time for dough to chill
Main cooking utensils: 8- to 9-inch (20- to 23-cm.) sandwich tin
Oven temperature: hot (425–450°F., 220–230°C., Gas Mark 7–8)
   then moderate (375°F., 190°C., Gas Mark 5)
Serves: 5–6

Pasta and rice dishes

Pasta and rice are two versatile and inexpensive foods; they blend with most proteins. This chapter gives a selection of recipes based upon different kinds of pasta and ways of using rice.

It is very important that rice and pasta are cooked correctly, for overcooking spoils both texture and flavour. Follow the directions given in the recipe for timing the cooking and the amount of water to use.

The dishes in this section are not only ideal for family occasions, but would be very suitable for an informal buffet, both rice or pasta dishes are generally favourites with the younger generation. The traditional macaroni cheese is given a 'new look' in the recipe on page 150. This is an excellent meatless main dish, it can be varied in many ways, i.e. add chopped ham or fried bacon to the sauce, use a generous amount of tomatoes, as in the recipe.

Rice is an excellent basis for salads (see page 147) or stuffings. These are described on page 122.

If you have pasta or rice left over, do not waste this. Keep it well covered in the refrigerator. Either put into boiling water for 1 minute to warm or put into cold water and bring this to the boil as quickly as possible, then drain and use.

Easy guide to rice and pasta dishes

The following gives you help in selecting the right rice and pasta dish for the right occasion.

When you are short of time see page 148.

When you are short of money see pages 147, 148, 149, 150, 151.

When you want a special dish see pages 148, 149, 151.

For a snack or light meal see pages 147, 148, 149, 151.

When you are slimming
None particularly slimming — eat sparingly.

Curried rice salad

Imperial	Metric
4 oz. long-grain rice	100 g. long-grain rice
seasoning	seasoning
2 pints water	1 litre water
½ medium-sized cooked chicken	½ medium-sized cooked chicken
2–3 tomatoes	2–3 tomatoes
1 green pepper	1 green pepper
1 red pepper	1 red pepper
Mayonnaise:	*Mayonnaise:*
1 egg yolk	1 egg yolk
pinch salt	pinch salt
pinch sugar	pinch sugar
½–1 teaspoon made mustard	½–1 teaspoon made mustard
1 tablespoon lemon juice	1 tablespoon lemon juice
¼ pint olive oil	125 ml. olive oil
pinch onion seasoning or	pinch onion seasoning or
onion or garlic salt	onion or garlic salt
1–2 teaspoons curry seasoning	1–2 teaspoons curry seasoning
or curry powder	or curry powder
Garnish:	*Garnish:*
parsley	parsley

1. Put the rice into boiling, salted water and cook for about 15 minutes until just tender.
2. Strain the rice and rinse with cold water. Allow to dry.
3. Make a mayonnaise from the egg yolk, salt, sugar, mustard, lemon juice and oil, and season well with onion seasoning and curry seasoning. The secret of a smooth mayonnaise is to beat the salt, sugar, mustard and lemon juice into the egg yolk, then add the oil gradually; if the oil is added too quickly, the mayonnaise will curdle.
4. Remove the skin and bones from the chicken and cut into neat pieces. Blend the rice and chicken with the mayonnaise.
5. Remove the seeds from the tomatoes and peppers and cut into thin strips. Arrange on a dish with the rice mixture and garnish with parsley.

Cooking time: 20 minutes
Preparation time: 20 minutes
Main cooking utensil: saucepan
Serves: 4–6

Fish risotto

Imperial	Metric
2 pints large prawns	generous litre large prawns
1 pint shrimps	generous ½ litre shrimps
4 large tomatoes	4 large tomatoes
3 medium-sized onions	3 medium-sized onions
3 tablespoons oil or 1½ oz.	3 tablespoons oil or 40 g.
butter and 2 tablespoons oil	butter and 2 tablespoons oil
8 oz. Italian or long-grain	200 g. Italian or long-grain
rice	rice
seasoning	seasoning
good pinch powdered oregano	good pinch powdered oregano
or marjoram	or marjoram
good pinch lemon thyme	good pinch lemon thyme
good pinch saffron powder	good pinch saffron powder
4 oz. mushrooms	100 g. mushrooms
Garnish:	*Garnish:*
few unshelled prawns	few unshelled prawns
parsley	parsley

1. Shell the prawns and shrimps, skin the tomatoes.
2. Put the shells and the tomato skins into a pan with 2 pints (generous litre) water or well strained stock, simmer for 20 minutes, then strain.
3. Meanwhile fry the finely chopped onions and chopped tomatoes in oil or butter and oil.
4. Add the rice, turn it in the onion and tomato mixture and add the stock.
5. Bring to the boil, add the seasoning, herbs and a pinch of saffron (if using saffron strands infuse in a little water for 1 hour, strain and add the water).
6. Cook steadily for 15 minutes (with the lid off the pan), add the sliced mushrooms and prawns and continue heating steadily for a further 15 minutes. Garnish with prawns and parsley. Serve with salad.

Cooking time: 50 minutes
Preparation time: 30 minutes
Main cooking utensils: 2 saucepans
Serves: 4–5

Indonesian fried rice

Imperial	Metric
8 oz. Patna (long-grain) rice	200 g. Patna (long-grain) rice
3–4 pints water	1½-2 litres water
2 teaspoons salt	2 teaspoons salt
8 oz. onions	200 g. onions
12 oz. shoulder of pork	300 g. shoulder of pork
4 oz. butter	100 g. butter
12 oz. mixed cooked vegetables	300 g. mixed cooked vegetables
2 tablespoons soy sauce	2 tablespoons soy sauce
1 teaspoon curry powder	1 teaspoon curry powder
seasoning	seasoning
Garnish:	Garnish:
1 egg	1 egg
½–1 oz. butter	15–25 g. butter
2 tomatoes	2 tomatoes

1. Cook the rice in boiling salted water for approximately 12 minutes. Turn into a sieve and separate the grains by holding under running cold water until all the surplus starch is removed; drain.
2. Slice the onions, cut the pork in cubes and fry both in 2 oz. (50 g.) of the butter for 20 minutes, browning slowly.
3. Add the remainder of the butter, the rice, mixed vegetables, soy sauce, curry powder and seasoning. Blend well over the heat until piping hot.
4. Turn into a frying pan or ovenproof dish and garnish with strips of omelette made by cooking the sesoned egg in butter; arrange small wedges of tomato round the edge. Flash under a hot grill for a few moments. Serve immediately, with peanuts, shrimp crisps (see note) and a green salad.

Note: Shrimp-flavoured crisps (or prawn crackers) can be bought dry in packets in this country. They should be fried in deep fat, when they swell to three times their size.

Cooking time: 45 minutes
Preparation time: 20 minutes
Main cooking utensils: saucepan, sieve, omelette pan, frying pan or ovenproof dish
Serves: 4

Curried rice

Imperial	Metric
2 oz. ghee (clarified butter) or unsalted butter	50 g. ghee (clarified butter) or unsalted butter
1 medium-sized onion, chopped	1 medium-sized onion, chopped
1 clove garlic, crushed (optional)	1 clove garlic, crushed (optional)
8 oz. long-grain rice	200 g. long-grain rice
1 tablespoon curry powder	1 tablespoon curry powder
1 pint water	500 ml. water
seasoning	seasoning
4–6 hard-boiled eggs	4–6 hard-boiled eggs
Garnish:	Garnish:
chutney	chutney
Bombay duck	Bombay duck

1. Melt the ghee in a saucepan and fry the chopped onion and crushed garlic.
2. Add the rice and toss in the butter until well coated. Add the curry powder, mix well and fry for a few minutes.
3. Add the water, bring to the boil, season, then lower the heat, cover the pan and simmer for 15–20 minutes, until the liquid is absorbed and the rice is tender.
4. Pile the rice on to a hot dish and place the shelled hard-boiled eggs on top. Garnish with chutney and Bombay duck.

Chinese omelette
Cut 4 oz. (100 g.) chicken breast into small pieces and slice 1 red pepper, 1 bamboo shoot, 2–3 water chestnuts, 2 sticks celery, and 1 medium-sized onion into narrow strips. Toss in 1 tablespoon oil until tender. Blend 1 tablespoon flour, 3 tablespoons water, ½–1 tablespoon soy sauce, 2 teaspoons sherry and seasoning. Put over the chicken and vegetables and cook until slightly thickened. Beat 4 eggs with 2 tablespoons chicken stock and cook in 2 tablespoons oil in a large frying pan until just set. Turn and set second side; serve the chicken and vegetables with the omelette over the top.

Cooking time: 20 minutes
Preparation time: 10 minutes
Main cooking utensil: saucepan
Serves: 4

Danish-style ratatouille

Imperial	Metric
1 aubergine (eggplant)	1 aubergine (eggplant)
seasoning	seasoning
2 onions	2 onions
3 oz. butter	75 g. butter
8 oz. back or streaky bacon rashers	200 g. back or streaky bacon rashers
4 large tomatoes	4 large tomatoes
4 oz. mushrooms	100 g. mushrooms
1 green pepper	1 green pepper
6–8 oz. long-grain rice	150–200 g. long-grain rice

1. Slice the aubergine thinly, do not peel, sprinkle lightly with seasoning and leave to stand while preparing the other ingredients.
2. Peel the onions, cut into rings and toss in the hot butter for 5 minutes.
3. Remove the rinds from the bacon, cut the rashers into pieces.
4. Put it into the pan with the onions, add the rinds to give flavour and fat.
5. Cook for 2–3 minutes, add the skinned, seeded tomatoes, aubergine, sliced mushrooms and strips of green pepper.
6. Season well, cover the pan tightly and simmer until tender, shake the pan from time to time. Remove the bacon rinds.
7. Meanwhile cook the rice until tender. Top the hot rice with the bacon and vegetable mixture.

Cooking time: 45 minutes
Preparation time: 20 minutes
Main cooking utensils: 2 saucepans
Serves: 4–6

Spaghetti alla napoletana

Imperial	Metric
Sauce:	*Sauce:*
1 lb. tomatoes	½ kg. tomatoes
1 onion	1 onion
1 clove garlic (optional)	1 clove garlic (optional)
seasoning	seasoning
2–3 sticks celery	2–3 sticks celery
pinch sugar	pinch sugar
little chopped oregano (wild marjoram)	little chopped oregano (wild marjoram)
little chopped basil	little chopped basil
¼ pint water or stock	125 ml. water or stock
10 oz. spaghetti	250 g. spaghetti
1½–2 teaspoons salt	1½–2 teaspoons salt
2 oz. butter	50 g. butter

1. Skin and chop the tomatoes.
2. Skin and chop the onion finely; crush the garlic on a board with a little salt.
3. Chop the celery.
4. Put the onion, garlic and celery into a pan with the seasoning, sugar and herbs and the stock or water.
5. Bring to the boil and simmer till soft but not a purée.
6. Meanwhile bring 5 pints (2½ litres) water to the boil in a pan, add the salt and cook the spaghetti in this until just tender.
7. Drain well and toss in butter. Arrange the spaghetti on a hot serving dish and spoon the sauce into the centre.

Variation

For a richer tomato sauce simmer 2 oz. (50 g.) diced ham or bacon in the sauce and when the sauce is cooked pass it through a sieve. Reheat the sauce adding 2 oz. (50 g.) butter and a little red wine.

Cooking time: 20 minutes
Preparation time: dependent on sauce, approximately 20 minutes
Main cooking utensils: 2 saucepans
Serves: 4

Fish noodle dish

Imperial	Metric
6–8 oz. bought or home-made ribbon noodles	150–200 g. bought or home-made ribbon noodles
4 fillets whiting	4 fillets whiting
1–1½ oz. butter	25–40 g. butter
seasoning	seasoning
4 oz. cream cheese	100 g. cream cheese
lemon juice	lemon juice
4 oz. mushrooms	100 g. mushrooms
4 oz. cooked peas	100 g. cooked peas
2 oz. prawns	50 g. prawns

1. Put the noodles on to boil in salted water.
2. Lay the whiting fillets on the buttered grid of the grill pan or on foil.
3. Spread the cream cheese over the seasoned fish and sprinkle with lemon juice.
4. Grill steadily for approximately 8 minutes under a moderate heat.
5. Meanwhile cook the mushrooms in a little seasoned water and lemon juice.
6. Drain and add to the drained noodles, with the cooked peas and prawns. Toss in the rest of the butter then arrange in a hot serving dish.
7. Top with the cooked fish. Serve hot with a green salad or vegetables.

Variation

Use thicker fillets of haddock or cod, but these must be brushed with melted butter, grilled on the underside, turned, then topped with the cheese, etc., on the top side.

Cooking time: 20–25 minutes
Preparation time: 20 minutes
Main cooking utensils: ovenproof dish, saucepan, grill pan
Serves: 4

Tomato macaroni cheese

Imperial	Metric
8 oz. macaroni	200 g. macaroni
seasoning	seasoning
½ oz. butter	15 g. butter
½ oz. flour	15 g. flour
¼ pint milk	125 ml. milk
14-oz can Italian peeled plum tomatoes	396-g. can Italian peeled plum tomatoes
8 oz. Cheddar, Gruyère or Mozzarella cheese	200 g. Cheddar, Gruyère or Mozzarella cheese
1 teaspoon made mustard	1 teaspoon made mustard
Garnish:	*Garnish:*
1–2 sliced tomatoes	1–2 sliced tomatoes

1. Cook the macaroni in 4 pints (2 litres) boiling salted water until just tender.
2. Strain and blend with the sauce.
3. To make the sauce, heat the butter in a pan, stir in the flour, cook for 2–3 minutes, then add the milk.
4. Bring to the boil and cook until thickened.
5. Take the pan off the heat so the sauce is no longer boiling.
6. Strain the liquid from the can of tomatoes and add enough water to make up to ¼ pint (125 ml.).
7. Stir into the sauce and heat carefully without boiling so there is no possibility of the sauce curdling. Stir in half the grated cheese, seasoning and mustard.
8. Put half the seasoned tomatoes at the bottom of a dish.
9. Cover with half the macaroni mixture, the remaining seasoned tomatoes and a final layer of macaroni.
10. Sprinkle with the remaining cheese. Garnish with the tomato slices.
11. Brown either in the oven or under the grill. Serve hot with salad or vegetables.

Cooking time: 40 minutes if baking, 20 minutes if grilling
Preparation time: 15 minutes
Main cooking utensils: 2 saucepans, ovenproof dish
Oven temperature: moderately hot (400°F., 200°C., Gas Mark 6)
Oven position: above centre
Serves: 4–6

Pasta mould

Imperial	Metric
8 oz. round or shell pasta	200 g. round or shell pasta
seasoning	seasoning
4 oz. butter	100 g. butter
2 onions	2 onions
1–2 cloves garlic	1–2 cloves garlic
1 tablespoon oil	1 tablespoon oil
1 lb. minced beef	400 g. minced beef
4 oz. mushrooms	100 g. mushrooms
3 large tomatoes	3 large tomatoes
1 pint stock	500 ml. stock
1½ lb. spinach	generous ½ kg. spinach

1. Cook the pasta in 4 pints (2 litres) boiling, salted water until tender, drain and toss in 2 oz. (50 g.) of the hot butter.
2. Pack round the bottom and sides of an ovenproof basin.
3. Fry the chopped onions and crushed garlic in the remaining and oil.
4. Add the meat, the chopped mushrooms, the skinned, chopped tomatoes and the stock. Season well.
5. Simmer steadily for 30 minutes.
6. Meanwhile cook the spinach until tender, seasoning lightly; drain very well.
7. Pack alternate layers of spinach and well-drained meat mixture into the pasta-lined basin. Cover with buttered paper or foil.
8. Bake in the oven for 45 minutes.
9. Simmer the rest of the meat mixture until it is well reduced and thick; keep hot.
10. To serve, turn the mould on to a hot dish and top with the meat mixture.

Cooking time: 1¼ hours
Preparation time: 30 minutes
Main cooking utensils: 3 saucepans, 2-pint (1-litre) ovenproof basin
Oven temperature: moderate (375°F., 190°C., Gas Mark 5)
Oven position: centre
Serves: 6

Green lasagne roll

Imperial	Metric
8 oz. green lasagne	200 g. green lasagne
seasoning	seasoning
1 medium-sized onion	1 medium-sized onion
2 oz. butter	50 g. butter
12 oz. minced beef	300 g. minced beef
4 chicken livers or more	4 chicken livers or more
minced beef	minced beef
2 teaspoons chopped parsley	2 teaspoons chopped parsley
½ pint stock	250 ml. stock
Sauce:	*Sauce:*
2 medium-sized onions	2 medium-sized onions
3 medium-sized tomatoes	3 medium-sized tomatoes
¼ pint stock and ¼ pint white	125 ml. stock and 125 ml. white
wine or ½ pint stock	wine or 250 ml. stock
Garnish:	*Garnish:*
cooked tomato	cooked tomato
cooked peas	cooked peas

1. Cook the lasagne in boiling, salted water until tender, drain and drape over a colander to dry.
2. Chop the onions, fry one in butter, add minced beef, minced or chopped chicken livers, parsley, seasoning and stock.
3. Simmer steadily until a thick purée is formed, about 30 minutes, stirring well as the liquid evaporates to prevent the mixture sticking to the pan.
4. Put a layer of lasagne on a board, spread with the meat mixture. Cover with lasagne, more meat, lasagne, meat and a final layer of lasagne.
5. Form into a neat roll.
6. Put the remaining chopped onions, skinned, chopped tomatoes, stock, wine and seasoning into a casserole with the lasagne roll, cover and cook for 45 minutes.
7. Garnish with baked tomato and peas.

Cooking time: 1½ hours
Preparation time: 35 minutes if buying lasagne
Main cooking utensils: 2 saucepans, casserole
Oven temperature: moderate (350–375°F., 180–190°C., Gas Mark 4–5)
Oven position: centre
Serves: 4

Puddings and desserts

The first recipes in this section deal with baked puddings. It is important to place these in the recommended position in the oven so they do not brown on top before the pudding is thoroughly cooked. These particular recipes vary from a light sponge-type pudding, opposite, to the quickly made crumble topping and old-fashioned cobbler on page 154.

Egg custard puddings are not only easily digested, they are interesting in flavour too. The recipes stress the careful cooking necessary to prevent the egg mixture curdling, i.e. separating, during cooking.

The steamed puddings, that are so famous in this country, should always be light in texture. Apart from the importance of using the recommended proportions of fat and flour, always allow the water to boil rapidly for the first part of the cooking time, for it is during this period that the mixture rises well. Fill up the pan with boiling water when necessary, so you keep a consistent heat under the mixture.

Milk puddings are an excellent way to make sure the family has adequate amounts of this important food. You can give an everyday milk pudding or egg custard a very festive appearance by topping it with caramel or meringue (see pages 156 and 162) or you can give variety of flavour by adding chocolate or coffee powder.

To make a meringue
A meringue as a topping on a flan can turn this into a party dessert without spending too much money. Smaller meringues, which can be filled with fruit or ice cream or cream (see page 167), are one of the most useful 'standbys' for they keep for weeks in an airtight tin.

The secret of making a perfect meringue is:

a. To make sure the whites are really stiff.
b. To add the sugar correctly (see page 167); overhandling of the mixture at this stage could produce a sticky mixture.
c. The correct method of baking, this varies from very slow cooking (see page 167) to speedy browning of the meringue coating in the Baked Alaska (see page 196).

Desserts made with gelatine
A light jellied mould or soufflé is not difficult to make, but check that the gelatine is completely dissolved. You can sprinkle this on to the hot liquid, but I think you will find it easier to dissolve if you soften it in a small quantity of cold liquid, *then* add it to the hot liquid and stir well; or stand the softened gelatine over a pan of hot water and stir until dissolved.

To freeze puddings and desserts

Ice cream or sorbets naturally freeze well, you can freeze in either the freezing compartment of a refrigerator or a home freezer. If using an older-type refrigerator with no star markings, set to the coldest position at least 30 minutes before freezing, return to normal setting when firm. Do not alter the setting on a refrigerator with star markings or home freezer. Quick freezing plus a sufficiently high percentage of cream or full cream evaporated milk, plus not too much sugar, prevent ice cream from having splinters of ice. Use ice cream and sorbets frozen in a refrigerator within a week, but store ice cream up to 3 months, sorbets up to 4 months, in a freezer or where you have 3-star markings in a refrigerator.

Fruit puddings such as crumble can be stored for 6 months, freeze then wrap. Heat gently. *Sponge puddings* can either be frozen before cooking, keep for 1 month, defrost then cook in the usual way; or they can be cooked, then frozen, in which case they can be kept for up to 3 months.

Egg custards only freeze well if made with half cream and half milk or if you freeze the uncooked custard. Use within 2 months in either case.

Easy guide to puddings and desserts

The following gives you help in selecting the right pudding or dessert for the right occasion.

When you are short of time see pages 160, 162, 164, 165, 205.

When you are short of money see pages 154, 155, 156, 157, 158, 159, 164, 165, 219.

When you want a special dish see pages 144, 145, 153, 157, 158, 161, 162, 163, 167, 168, 169, 195, 196, 197, 199, 219.

For a snack or light meal see pages 158, 159, 161, 166.

When you are slimming see pages 165, 167, 195.

Golden apricot pudding

Imperial	Metric
1 lb. fresh apricots	400 g. fresh apricots
¼ pint water	125 ml. water
4 oz. soft brown sugar	100 g. soft brown sugar
Topping:	*Topping:*
3 oz. butter	75 g. butter
3 oz. sugar	75 g. sugar
4 oz. self-raising flour or plain flour and 1 level teaspoon baking powder	100 g. self-raising flour or plain flour and 1 level teaspoon baking powder
4 tablespoons milk	4 tablespoons milk
3 egg whites	3 egg whites
½ oz. flaked or chopped nuts	15 g. flaked or chopped nuts
Golden sauce:	*Golden sauce:*
3 egg yolks	3 egg yolks
1 oz. castor sugar	25 g. castor sugar
3 tablespoons apricot juice	3 tablespoons apricot juice
1 teaspoon lemon juice	1 teaspoon lemon juice

1. Halve and stone the apricots, cook in water with sugar until just tender.
2. Drain fruit, reserving the syrup.
3. Put fruit into the well greased dish.
4. Prepare topping by creaming butter and sugar together until light and fluffy.
5. Fold in the sieved flour and the milk.
6. Whisk egg whites and gently fold into the creamed mixture.
7. Spread over fruit, sprinkle with flaked nuts and bake until firm to touch.
8. 10 minutes before serving, blend egg yolks and sugar together and slowly stir in apricot juice and lemon juice in a basin over simmering water.
9. Whisk until light and foamy. Serve hot with cream or sauce.

Variation

Use any other fruit — plums or rhubarb are particularly suitable.

Cooking time: 1 hour
Preparation time: 20 minutes
Main cooking utensils: saucepan, 2-pint (1-litre) ovenproof dish
Oven temperature: moderate (350–375°F., 180–190°C., Gas Mark 4–5)
Oven position: centre
Serves: 4–6

Fruit cobbler

Imperial
1 can pie filling or fresh fruit
Cobbler:
4 oz. self-raising flour or plain
   flour with 2 level teaspoons
   baking powder
1 oz. margarine
1 oz. sugar
milk to mix

Metric
1 can pie filling or fresh fruit
Cobbler:
100 g. self-raising flour or plain
   flour with 2 level teaspoons
   baking powder
25 g. margarine
25 g. sugar
milk to mix

1. Tip the pie filling into the pie dish and heat for approximately 10 minutes in the oven.
2. Sieve the flour into a basin, rub in margarine until it is the consistency of breadcrumbs, add the sugar and enough milk to make a soft rolling consistency.
3. Roll out to about $\frac{1}{4}$-inch ($\frac{1}{2}$-cm.) thickness.
4. Cut into small rounds and arrange round the edge of the hot pie filling.
5. Bake for nearly 15 minutes towards the top of the oven until golden brown.

Note: When the cobbler (scone mixture) is brown the oven may be reduced to very low in order to keep the pudding hot without burning it.

Variation
Any fruit may be used in this way which makes a very pleasant change from pastry.

Cooking time: 25 minutes
Preparation time: 10 minutes
Main cooking utensils: wide shallow ovenproof dish or pie dish
Oven temperature: hot (425–450°F., 220–230°C., Gas Mark 7–8)
Oven position: coolest part then towards top
Serves: 4

Fruit crumble

Imperial
1 lb. prepared fruit
sugar to taste
little water with firm fruit
Crumble:
2 oz. margarine or butter
4 oz. flour, plain or self-raising
3–4 oz. sugar

Metric
$\frac{1}{2}$ kg. prepared fruit
sugar to taste
little water with firm fruit
Crumble:
50 g. margarine or butter
100 g. flour, plain or self-raising
75–100 g. sugar

1. Prepare the fruit, slicing apples, dicing rhubarb, halving and stoning plums and washing soft fruits.
2. With firm fruits, simmer until nearly tender with sugar to taste and a little water. The mixture must be fairly firm. With soft fruits, there is no need to pre-cook or soften.
3. Put the fruit into the dish.
4. Rub the margarine or butter into the flour, add the sugar and sprinkle over the top of the fruit; press down firmly.
5. Bake until crisp and golden brown. Serve hot, with cream or custard.

Variation
Mix dried fruits with the fresh fruit; add a little spice to the flour or use 1 oz. (25 g.) coconut instead of 1 oz. (25 g.) flour.

Cooking time: 30–40 minutes plus time to cook fruit
Preparation time: few minutes plus time to prepare fruit
Main cooking utensils: saucepan for firmer fruit, pie or ovenproof dish
Oven temperature: moderate (350–375°F., 180–190°C., Gas Mark 4–5)
Oven position: centre or just above centre
Serves: 4

Blackberry roly poly

Imperial	Metric
8 oz. self-raising flour	200 g. self-raising flour
pinch salt	pinch salt
3 oz. butter	75 g. butter
1 oz. castor sugar	25 g. castor sugar
2 level teaspoons finely grated lemon rind	2 level teaspoons finely grated lemon rind
about 4 tablespoons milk to mix	about 4 tablespoons milk to mix
Filling:	*Filling:*
12 oz. fresh blackberries	300 g. fresh blackberries
little water	little water
2–3 oz. castor sugar	50–75 g. castor sugar
3 tablespoons water	3 tablespoons water
Topping:	*Topping:*
1 egg or milk	1 egg or milk
2 level teaspoons castor sugar	2 level teaspoons castor sugar
1 oz. butter	25 g. butter

1. Sieve the flour and salt together.
2. Rub in the butter and add sugar and lemon rind.
3. Mix to a soft dough with the milk, roll out into a rectangle approximately 12 inches by 10 inches (30 cm. by 25 cm.).
4. Cover with 10 oz. (250 g.) of the fruit, to within 1 inch (2½ cm.) of the edge.
5. Moisten the edges of the dough with water, sprinkle the fruit with sugar, then roll up like a Swiss roll.
6. Press joins carefully together to seal then lift into the dish.
7. Make three slits on the top of the roll, brush with beaten egg or milk, sprinkle with castor sugar and dot with butter.
8. Pour 3 tablespoons water into the dish.
9. Bake in a hot oven for 15 minutes then add the rest of the blackberries on top of the slits and reduce heat to moderate for the rest of the time. Serve with cream or custard.

Variation
Use 2 oz. (50 g.) butter only and a little extra milk.

Cooking time: 40–45 minutes
Preparation time: 20 minutes
Main cooking utensil: ovenproof dish
Oven temperature: hot (425–450°F., 220–230°C., Gas Mark 7–8), then moderate (375°F., 190°C., Gas Mark 5)
Oven position: centre
Serves: 4–6

Gingerbread plum pudding

Imperial	Metric
Gingerbread:	*Gingerbread:*
2 oz. margarine	50 g. margarine
3 oz. black treacle	75 g. black treacle
1 oz. golden syrup	25 g. golden syrup
5 tablespoons milk	5 tablespoons milk
1 egg	1 egg
4 oz. plain flour	100 g. plain flour
1 level teaspoon mixed spice	1 level teaspoon mixed spice
1 level teaspoon ground ginger	1 level teaspoon ground ginger
½ level teaspoon bicarbonate of soda	½ level teaspoon bicarbonate of soda
1–2 oz. sugar, preferably brown	25–50 g. sugar, preferably brown
Filling:	*Filling:*
1–1½ lb. plums	½–¾ kg. plums
sugar to taste	sugar to taste

1. To make the gingerbread, heat the margarine, treacle and syrup in a saucepan.
2. Add the milk, allow to cool.
3. Add the egg and beat well.
4. Pour on to the flour, sieved with the dry ingredients.
5. Add the sugar and beat thoroughly.
6. Put the plums at the bottom of the dish with sugar but no liquid.
7. Spread the gingerbread over the top.
8. Bake until firm to the touch.
9. Serve either in the dish or turn upside down on to a hot dish. Serve with cream or custard.

Variation
Other fruit may be used – greengages, pears or apricots blend well with the gingerbread flavour.

Cooking time: 1¼ hours
Preparation time: 15 minutes
Main cooking utensils: 2-pint (1-litre) saucepan, ovenproof dish
Oven temperature: moderate (325–350°F., 170–180°C., Gas Mark 3–4)
Oven position: centre
Serves: 4–6

Bread and butter pudding

Imperial	Metric
3 slices bread and butter	3 slices bread and butter
2–3 oz. dried fruit	50–75 g. dried fruit
2 eggs	2 eggs
1–1½ oz. sugar	25–40 g. sugar
¾ pint milk	425 ml. milk

1. Cut the bread and butter into triangles.
2. Put into the pie dish and add dried fruit.
3. Beat the eggs with the sugar, pour on the warmed milk, then strain over the bread and butter.
4. Bake until just firm and set. Move the pudding towards the top of the oven before serving to encourage the bread and butter to brown and crisp slightly. If baking in a fairly deep dish it will take longer. Serve hot.

Note: This pudding improves if allowed to stand for a short time before it is cooked.

Variation

Make a richer pudding by adding 2 oz. (50 g.) crystallised peel and 4 oz. (100 g.) dried fruit. Top with grated nutmeg before cooking.

Cooking time: 45 minutes
Preparation time: 15 minutes
Main cooking utensil: 2-pint (1-litre) pie dish
Oven temperature: very moderate (325–350°F., 170–180°C., Gas Mark 3–4)
Oven position: centre
Serves: 4

Semolina caramel

Imperial	Metric
Caramel:	*Caramel:*
1 oz. butter	25 g. butter
3 oz. moist brown or granulated sugar	75 g. moist brown or granulated sugar
6 tablespoons water	6 tablespoons water
Pudding:	*Pudding:*
½ pint evaporated milk	250 ml. evaporated milk
½ pint water	250 ml. water
2 oz. semolina	50 g. semolina
1 tablespoon golden syrup or sugar	1 tablespoon golden syrup or sugar
Decoration:	*Decoration:*
soft brown sugar	soft brown sugar

1. Melt the butter, add the sugar and 3 tablespoons water.
2. Stir over a low heat until the sugar is dissolved then boil steadily until a golden brown caramel is formed.
3. Add the rest of the water, boil until the caramel is dissolved in this, then cool slightly.
4. Add the milk and water — heat gently to prevent the mixture curdling.
5. Whisk in the semolina, syrup or sugar and cook, stirring frequently, for 5 minutes.
6. Put into an ovenproof dish — stand this in another tin or dish of water.
7. Cook in the oven until just set — approximately 45 minutes. Serve hot, sprinkled with soft brown sugar, with cream.

Variation

If the pudding is to be served cold, use only 1½ oz. (40 g.) semolina. Rice, sago or tapioca may be used in place of semolina — these will need slightly longer cooking.

Cooking time: approximately 1 hour
Preparation time: 10 minutes
Main cooking utensils: strong saucepan, ovenproof dish, tin or dish for cold water
Oven temperature: moderate (350°F., 180°C., Gas Mark 4)
Oven position: centre
Serves: 4

Rice pudding

Imperial

For a soft rice pudding:
2 oz. round-grain (Carolina)
  rice
1 oz. sugar
1 pint milk
small knob butter or suet
For a firm rice pudding:
3 oz. rice
1 oz. sugar
1 pint milk
small knob butter or suet

Metric

For a soft rice pudding:
50 g. round-grain (Carolina)
  rice
25 g. sugar
500 ml. milk
small knob butter or suet
For a firm rice pudding:
75 g. rice
25 g. sugar
500 ml. milk
small knob butter or suet

1. Wash the rice and put into a pie dish with the sugar, milk and butter or suet.
2. To bake, put the dish in the oven and cook for about 30 minutes; stir, then continue to cook until tender.
3. To steam, cook the pudding covered with greased paper or foil, over boiling water until soft, then brown for a few minutes under the grill.
4. To boil, put the ingredients into the top of a double saucepan or basin over hot water; cover with a lid or foil and cook until soft.
5. Serve hot with fruit or golden syrup; it can be eaten cold.

Variation
Use tapioca, sago, semolina or macaroni instead of rice. All these cereals are better if cooked for a time in a saucepan before being baked. A richer milk pudding is made if a beaten egg is added, this is particularly necessary for a macaroni pudding.

Cooking time: 1¼–2 hours
Preparation time: few minutes
Main cooking utensils: to bake, pie or ovenproof dish; to steam or boil, basin or soufflé dish and double saucepan
Oven temperature: cool (300°F., 150°C., Gas Mark 2)
Oven position: coolest part
Serves: 4

Crème brûlée

Imperial

4 oz. sugar
3 tablespoons water
½ pint thick cream and ¼ pint
  milk or 1 pint thin cream
4 eggs or egg yolks
2 oz. blanched almonds
2 tablespoons icing or brown
  sugar

Metric

100 g. sugar
3 tablespoons water
275 ml. thick cream and 275 ml.
  milk or 550 ml. thin cream
4 eggs or egg yolks
50 g. blanched almonds
2 tablespoons icing or brown
  sugar

1. Make a caramel from 3 oz. (75 g.) of the sugar and 3 tablespoons water.
2. Add to this ¾ pint (425 ml.) of the liquid.
3. Heat gently without boiling until the caramel is absorbed.
4. Pour on to the eggs or egg yolks.
5. Add the remaining 1 oz. (25 g.) sugar and ¼ pint (125 ml.) cream.
6. Cover the top of the basin with buttered paper and cook very slowly in a steamer for about 2 hours or stand the dish in another containing cold water and bake in a slow oven for about 2 hours.
7. Remove the paper.
8. Cover the top with nuts or make a line down the centre as shown in the picture.
9. Sprinkle over the sieved icing or brown sugar and brown under a hot grill. Serve cold, with cream.

Variation
It may be served hot, although the flavour is better when cold.

Cooking time: 2 hours 10 minutes
Preparation time: 15 minutes
Main cooking utensils: saucepan, ovenproof dish or pie dish, steamer (optional)
Oven temperature: very cool (275–300°F., 140–150°C., Gas Mark 1–2)
Oven position: centre
Serves: 4

Grape tart

Imperial	Metric
12 oz. grapes (preferably black)	300 g. grapes (preferably black)
3 oz. sugar	75 g. sugar
¼ pint white wine or water	125 ml. white wine or water
Batter:	*Batter:*
2 oz. butter	50 g. butter
4 oz. sugar	100 g. sugar
2 large eggs	2 large eggs
6 oz. flour (plain or self-raising)	150 g. flour (plain or self-raising)
12 tablespoons milk	12 tablespoons milk
To serve:	*To serve:*
sugar or vanilla sugar (see note)	sugar or vanilla sugar (see note)

1. Remove the seeds from the grapes, but keep grapes whole and do not skin them.
2. Make a syrup with the sugar and liquid, bring this to the boil.
3. Put in the grapes, simmer gently for a few minutes, then lift out.
4. To make the batter, cream the butter well, add the sugar and beat again, then add the beaten eggs.
5. Stir in the flour and milk to give a smooth, thick batter.
6. Blend the well-drained grapes with this.
7. Put into a well-greased baking dish and cook until just firm.
8. Towards the end of cooking time, it may be necessary to cover the top to prevent the fruit drying. Serve cold, topped with plenty of sugar; equally good as a dessert or for tea.

Note: Vanilla sugar is made by putting half a vanilla pod into a jar of sugar. The sugar gradually absorbs the flavour.

Variation

Use other fruit, and use less batter – i.e., 1½ lb. (¾ kg.) fruit and half the ingredients for the batter – this makes it more suitable for a hot dessert.

Cooking time: 45 minutes
Preparation time: 15 minutes
Main cooking utensils: large shallow saucepan, ovenproof dish
Oven temperature: moderate (350–375°F., 180–190°C., Gas Mark 4–5)
Oven position: centre
Serves: 4–6

Treacle tart

Imperial	Metric
Shortcrust pastry:	*Shortcrust pastry:*
8 oz. flour, self-raising or plain	200 g. flour, self-raising or plain
pinch salt	pinch salt
2 oz. margarine	50 g. margarine
2 oz. lard	50 g. lard
about 2 tablespoons cold water	about 2 tablespoons cold water
Filling:	*Filling:*
4 tablespoons soft fine breadcrumbs	4 tablespoons soft fine breadcrumbs
4 tablespoons warmed golden syrup	4 tablespoons warmed golden syrup
juice of 1 lemon	juice of 1 lemon

1. Sieve the flour and salt, rub in the fat until it resembles fine breadcrumbs.
2. Add enough water to make a firm dough.
3. Roll out on a floured board, line the plate, trim and decorate the edges, see below.
4. Prick base with fork.
5. Mix breadcrumbs, syrup and lemon juice. Spread over pastry.
6. Re-roll pastry trimmings, cut narrow strips. Twist them over filling, damping ends so they stick in position.
7. Bake for time and at temperature given; lower heat after 20 minutes if necessary. Serve hot or cold with custard or cream.

Note: To ensure a crisp base to tarts, etc., stand pie plate on baking sheet, heated in oven, or bake pastry blind in a hot oven (425–450°F., 220–230°C., Gas Mark 7–8) for 10 minutes, remove paper and baking beans, add warm filling and complete cooking for 20 minutes in a moderate oven (375°F., 190°C., Gas Mark 4–5). To decorate pastry, either flute by pinching edges with finger and thumb, or press the edges with the prongs of a fork.

Cooking time: 25–30 minutes
Preparation time: 20 minutes
Main cooking utensil: 9-inch (23-cm.) ovenproof plate
Oven temperature: moderately hot to hot (400–425°F., 200–220°C., Gas Mark 6–7)
Oven position: centre
Serves: 4–6

Jam suet pudding

Imperial	Metric
4 oz. flour (with plain flour use 1 teaspoon baking powder)	100 g. flour (with plain flour use 1 teaspoon baking powder)
pinch salt	pinch salt
2 oz. sugar	50 g. sugar
2 oz. shredded suet	50 g. shredded suet
about 2 tablespoons milk	about 2 tablespoons milk
2 tablespoons jam	2 tablespoons jam

1. Sieve the flour or flour and baking powder with the salt; add the sugar and the shredded suet.
2. Gradually stir in the milk, binding the mixture together. This should be a stiff consistency but as flour varies, you may need a little extra milk.
3. Put the jam at the bottom of the greased basin and put the mixture on top.
4. Cover with greased foil or greased greaseproof paper.
5. Steam over boiling water.
6. When cooked, turn out on to a hot dish. Heat more jam as a sauce.

Variation
Use 2 oz. (50 g.) flour and 2 oz. (50 g.) breadcrumbs.

Orange pudding: Add the grated rind of an orange to the mixture. Mix with orange juice instead of milk. Put marmalade at the bottom of the basin.

Cooking time: 1½ hours
Preparation time: 15 minutes
Main cooking utensils: 1½-pint (¾-litre) pudding basin, steamer, saucepan, foil or greaseproof paper.
Serves: 4

Fruit suet pudding

Imperial	Metric
Suet crust pastry:	*Suet crust pastry:*
8 oz. self-raising flour or plain flour and 2 level teaspoons baking powder	200 g. self-raising flour or plain flour and 2 level teaspoons powder
pinch salt	pinch salt
4 oz. shredded suet	100 g. shredded suet
cold water to mix	cold water to mix
Filling:	*Filling:*
1 lb. prepared fruit	½ kg. prepared fruit
2–3 tablespoons sugar	2–3 tablespoons sugar
little water	little water

1. Sieve the flour and salt, add the suet and bind with water.
2. Roll out and use two-thirds to line the pudding basin.
3. Put the prepared fruit into the lined basin with sugar and water if necessary.
4. Cover the remainder of the pastry, seal edges firmly.
5. Cover with greased foil and steam over boiling water for 2 hours.
6. Turn out carefully and serve with hot custard sauce.

Variation
Use different types of fruit. If using hard fruit you need 2–3 tablespoons water; 1 tablespoon water with fruit that softens and makes a little juice (like blackcurrants); no water with fruit like rhubarb that makes a lot of juice. A mixture of fruits can also be used, as in the picture.

Cooking time: 2 hours
Preparation time: 15 minutes
Main cooking utensils: pudding basin, steamer, saucepan, greaseproof paper or foil
Serves: 4

Aeblekage

Imperial	Metric
1½ lb. apples	¾ kg. apples
4 oz. butter	100 g. butter
2–3 oz. sugar	50–75 g. sugar
2 oz. dried brown breadcrumbs	50 g. dried brown breadcrumbs
Decoration:	*Decoration:*
whipped cream (see note)	whipped cream (see note)

1. Peel the apples and slice thinly.
2. Cook gently in half the butter until soft, adding sugar to taste.
3. Mix the sugar and breadcrumbs and brown in the remaining butter. Use a frying pan so the crumbs brown evenly.
4. Allow to cool in the frying pan.
5. Put a layer of the crisp breadcrumbs at the bottom of a bowl, then the apples, then a topping of crumbs.
6. Decorate with whipped cream.

Note: For cream that is very white and light in texture, whip thick cream lightly, then gradually whisk in a little top of the milk.

Variation
Use more crumbs and put a layer of crumbs in the centre. Add lemon juice and a little lemon rind to the apples.
Use rye breadcrumbs for a darker pudding.

Cooking time: 15 minutes
Preparation time: 15 minutes
Main cooking utensils: frying pan, saucepan
Serves: 4

Pear and strawberry shortcake

Imperial	Metric
3 oz. butter	75 g. butter
2 oz. sugar	50 g. sugar
3 oz. plain flour	75 g. plain flour
1 oz. cornflour	25 g. cornflour
pinch salt	pinch salt
Decoration:	*Decoration:*
2 ripe dessert pears	2 ripe dessert pears
juice of 1 lemon	juice of 1 lemon
2–3 tablespoons apricot jam	2–3 tablespoons apricot jam
strawberries	strawberries

1. Cream the butter with half the sugar. Add the flour, sieved with the cornflour and salt.
2. Work to a soft dough and add the remaining sugar.
3. Roll out to ¼ inch (½ cm.) thick and cut into 2½- to 3-inch (6- to 7-cm.) squares.
4. Place on a baking tray and bake until lightly golden, approximately 20 minutes.
5. Cool on a wire rack.
6. Peel, core and slice the pears, sprinkle with lemon juice.
7. Arrange the slices on the shortbread squares, melt and sieve the jam.
8. Brush the pear slices with the cooled apricot jam. Top with unhulled strawberries.

Note: The shortcakes keep well in an airtight tin before topping.

Variation
Use other fruit in season; add 1 oz. (25 g.) chopped nuts to the biscuit mixture.

Cooking time: 25 minutes
Preparation time: 20 minutes
Main cooking utensils: baking tray, saucepan, wire rack
Oven temperature: very moderate to moderate (350–375°F., 180–190°C., Gas Mark 4–5)
Oven position: centre
Makes: 6–7 shortcakes

Raspberry almond shortcake

Imperial	Metric
6 oz. plain flour	150 g. plain flour
4 oz. margarine	100 g. margarine
3 oz. ground almonds	75 g. ground almonds
3 oz. castor sugar	75 g. castor sugar
1 egg yolk to bind	1 egg yolk to bind
Decoration:	*Decoration:*
¼ pint double cream	125 ml. double cream
sugar to taste	sugar to taste
icing sugar	icing sugar
1 medium punnet raspberries	1 medium punnet raspberries

1. Sieve the flour into the mixing bowl.
2. Rub in the margarine until the mixture resembles fine breadcrumbs.
3. Stir in the ground almonds and sugar.
4. Add the yolk of egg, mix together lightly but firmly.
5. Turn on to a lightly floured board and roll out fairly thinly.
6. Cut in three 6-inch (15-cm.) rounds and place on a well greased baking sheet.
7. Bake for time given.
8. Cool on a wire tray.
9. Whisk the cream until stiff. Sweeten.
10. Sandwich the layers with most of the cream. Sprinkle the top with icing sugar and decorate with remaining cream and the raspberries.

Note: The shortcake can be kept for 2–3 days in an airtight tin before decorating.

Cooking time: 20–30 minutes
Preparation time: 20 minutes
Main cooking utensil: greased baking sheet or tin
Oven temperature: moderate (325–350°F., 170–180°C., Gas Mark 3–4)
Oven position: centre
Serves: 6

Honey almond cheesecakes

Imperial	Metric
Pastry:	*Pastry:*
8 oz. plain flour	200 g. plain flour
pinch salt	pinch salt
5 oz. butter or margarine	125 g. butter or margarine
1 oz. sugar	25 g. sugar
1 egg yolk	1 egg yolk
milk to bind	milk to bind
Filling:	*Filling:*
8 oz. cream cheese	200 g. cream cheese
2 level tablespoons honey	2 level tablespoons honey
2 eggs	2 eggs
½ teaspoon powdered cinnamon	½ teaspoon powdered cinnamon
2 oz. blanched almonds	50 g. blanched almonds
Topping:	*Topping:*
2 oz. flaked almonds	50 g. flaked almonds
1 egg white	1 egg white
little honey	little honey

1. Sift the flour and salt and rub in the butter or margarine; add the sugar.
2. Bind with the egg yolk and a little milk.
3. Roll out thinly and line the tins.
4. Prick and bake blind in a hot oven for 10 minutes.
5. Blend the cream cheese, honey, eggs, cinnamon and finely chopped almonds.
6. Put the filling into the pastry cases, top with flaked almonds and brush with egg white.
7. Return to a moderate oven and bake for a further 20 minutes; allow to cool.
8. Brush tops with a little honey before serving cold as a dessert or for tea.

Variation

Flavour the filling with finely grated lemon rind instead of the cinnamon.

Cooking time: 30 minutes
Preparation time: 25 minutes
Main cooking utensils: 12–14 boat-shaped tins, baking sheet
Oven temperature: hot (425°F., 220°C., Gas Mark 7) then moderate (350°F., 180°C., Gas Mark 4)
Oven position: above centre
Makes: 12–14 cheesecakes

Pineapple cream fluff

Imperial
1 medium-sized pineapple
1 egg white
6-oz. can or generous ¼ pint
   thick cream
few drops almond essence
1–2 tablespoons castor sugar

Metric
1 medium-sized pineapple
1 egg white
170-g. can or 150 ml. thick
   cream
few drops almond essence
1–2 tablespoons castor sugar

1. Cut the pineapple into 4 thick slices.
2. Remove the centres with an apple corer.
3. Cut away the skin with kitchen scissors or a sharp knife.
4. Put the pineapple slices into the dish.
5. Whisk the egg white until stiff and whip the cream lightly in a separate basin.
6. Fold the egg white into the cream together with the almond essence.
7. Meanwhile preheat the grill so the topping browns in 1–2 minutes.
8. Spread the cream mixture over the pineapple.
9. Sprinkle with the sugar and brown under the grill. Do not leave too long otherwise the mixture burns. Serve hot or cold.

Note: When whipping egg whites, make sure the bowl is dry and the egg white at room temperature. Whisk sharply.
   Canned cream should be mixed lightly and fresh cream whipped until it just holds its shape.

Variation
Sprinkle the pineapple with Kirsch and/or castor sugar if wished. Use sugar substitute on the topping if you wish for a less fattening recipe.
Pineapple brûlée: Sprinkle the cream with a thick layer of brown sugar and blanched flaked almonds.

Cooking time: 1–2 minutes but grill must be preheated
Preparation time: 10–15 minutes
Main cooking utensil: flameproof shallow dish
Serves: 4

Snow eggs

Imperial
2 eggs
3 oz. castor sugar
¾ pint milk
½ teaspoon vanilla essence
   or vanilla pod (see note)

Metric
2 eggs
75 g. castor sugar
400 ml. milk
½ teaspoon vanilla essence
   or vanilla pod (see note)

1. Separate the egg yolks from the whites and whisk the whites until very stiff.
2. Gradually whisk in 1 oz. (25 g.) sugar, fold in another 1 oz. (25 g.) sugar.
3. Put the milk, the remaining sugar and the vanilla into the saucepan or frying pan. If using a vanilla pod, break it in half and put the two halves into the milk.
4. Allow the milk to become hot, but not boiling.
5. Drop spoonfuls of meringue mixture on to the milk, poach for 2 minutes, then turn the fluffy balls and poach for a further 2 minutes.
6. Lift the balls of meringue out of the milk and drain on a wire rack.
7. Strain the milk over the beaten egg yolks and cook very gently in the top of a double saucepan until the custard thickens sufficiently to coat the back of a wooden spoon.
8. Pour the custard sauce into a shallow bowl or individual glasses and allow to cool; top with the meringues when cold.

Note: The vanilla pod should be rinsed in cold water after use, dried on kitchen paper and either put back in a jar, or into a jar of sugar so that this absorbs the flavour.

Variation
Add a little cinnamon to the custard.

Cooking time: 45 minutes
Preparation time: 15 minutes
Main cooking utensils: large shallow saucepan or frying pan, double saucepan or basin over hot water
Serves: 4

Pots au chocolat

Imperial
4 oz. chocolate, preferably
  plain
1 oz. butter
2 eggs
4 oz. marshmallows
1 tablespoon hot water
Decoration:
grated chocolate

Metric
100 g. chocolate, preferably
  plain
25 g. butter
2 eggs
100 g. marshmallows
1 tablespoon hot water
Decoration:
grated chocolate

1. Put the chocolate, broken into small pieces into the top of the double saucepan or basin, and melt over hot water.
2. Add the butter, egg yolks and the marshmallows and cook, stirring well, until the marshmallows have melted and mixture is smooth and shiny.
3. Add the water, stir well, then allow the mixture to cool, but not set.
4. Whisk the egg whites until very stiff, fold into the chocolate mixture, then put into 4 or 6 individual dishes.
5. When quite cold decorate with grated chocolate.
6. Serve with plain biscuits or fingers of sponge.

Variation
Use coffee essence or strong black coffee in place of the water.

Cooking time: few minutes
Preparation time: 10 minutes
Main cooking utensil: double saucepan or basin over hot water
Serves: 4–6

Tangerine creams

Imperial
2 tangerines
1 oz. loaf sugar
1 level tablespoon custard
  powder or cornflour
⅜ pint milk
¼ pint thick cream or half
  thick and half thin cream
  (see note)

Metric
2 tangerines
25 g. loaf sugar
1 level tablespoon custard
  powder or cornflour
200 ml. milk
125 ml. thick cream or half
  thick and half thin cream
  (see note)

1. Put the tangerines in hot water for a minute, this makes it easier to rub off the 'zest'.
2. Dry the fruit and rub the loaf sugar over the skins while still warm.
3. Take off as much of the yellow skin as possible by rubbing the sugar very hard over the fruit.
4. Blend the custard powder or cornflour with a little cold milk.
5. Bring the remainder of the milk to the boil, pour over the custard powder or cornflour, then return to the pan.
6. Add the sugar and stir over a low heat until thickened.
7. Allow to cool, stirring from time to time, then fold in half the lightly whipped cream.
8. Remove the skin from the tangerines, take out the fruit pulp, discarding the pith and pips only (if any).
9. Blend most of the fruit with the cream mixture, spoon into glasses.
10. Top with the rest of the cream and fruit. Serve as cold as possible.

Note: If using a mixture of cream whip the thick cream first until it holds a shape then gradually whip in the thin cream.

Variation
Use 1 large orange in place of tangerines.

Cooking time: 10 minutes
Preparation time: 15 minutes
Main cooking utensil: saucepan
Serves: 2

Fruit condé

Imperial	Metric
3 oz. round-grain rice	75 g. round-grain rice
¾ pint milk	345 ml. milk
2 oz. sugar	50 g. sugar
¼ pint cream or evaporated milk flavouring (see variation)	125 ml. cream or evaporated milk flavouring (see variation)
Topping:	*Topping:*
8 oz. fresh or canned or cooked fruit	200 g. fresh or canned or cooked fruit
3 tablespoons sieved jam or jelly	3 tablespoons sieved jam or jelly
2 tablespoons water with a little sugar or syrup from canned or cooked fruit	2 tablespoons water with a little sugar or syrup from canned or cooked fruit

1. Put the rice with the milk and sugar into a saucepan or the top of a double saucepan and cook until soft and creamy.
2. Allow to cool, then fold in the lightly whipped cream or milk, together with the flavouring.
3. Put into glasses or a shallow dish.
4. Arrange fresh or well drained canned or cooked fruit on top.
5. Put the jam, water and sugar or syrup into a small saucepan and cook for a few minutes, stirring well until clear.
6. Cool, then brush over the fruit. Serve as cold as possible, with cream.

To whip evaporated milk: Boil the can for 15 minutes open, cool the milk, whisk hard; for a stiffer consistency, dissolve 1 level teaspoon powder gelatine in the hot milk.

Variation
The rice may be given various flavourings, e.g., add a little lemon or orange juice, add a little dried fruit and chopped nuts; stir in 1–2 oz. (25–50 g.) chocolate powder or stir in 1–2 tablespoons coffee essence.

Cooking time: 45 minutes
Preparation time: 15 minutes
Main cooking utensils: saucepans or a double saucepan and an ordinary one
Serves: 4

Rhubarb fool

Imperial	Metric
8 oz. rhubarb	200 g. rhubarb
1 oz. sugar	25 g. sugar
½ oz. custard powder	15 g. custard powder
¼ pint milk	125 ml. milk
½–1 oz. sugar	15–25 g. sugar
Decoration:	*Decoration:*
whipped cream	whipped cream

1. As the rhubarb has to be a firm pulp it is best to cook it without any water.
2. Put the fruit and sugar into a saucepan, over a very low heat, and leave until soft; or cook in the top of a double saucepan over boiling water.
3. Mash or sieve until very smooth, then allow to cool.
4. Blend the custard powder with some of the milk, bring the rest of the milk to the boil, pour over the custard, then return to the saucepan with the sugar and cook until thickened, stirring well, since the mixture is very stiff.
5. Whisk the cool fruit purée and cool custard together until well blended and smooth, adding a few drops of colouring if necessary.
6. Put into glasses and chill, then top with whipped cream. Serve as cold as possible, with plain biscuits or wafers.

Variation
Other fruit may be used instead — try some of the firmer fruits — gooseberries need water.

Cooking time: 15 minutes
Preparation time: 15 minutes
Main cooking utensils: 2 saucepans
Serves: 2

Banana almond fool

Imperial	Metric
½ lemon	½ lemon
½ orange	½ orange
2 ripe bananas	2 ripe bananas
½ oz. ground almonds	15 g. ground almonds
½ oz. blanched almonds	15 g. blanched almonds
¼ pint thick cream	125 ml. thick cream
½ oz. castor sugar	15 g. castor sugar
Decoration:	*Decoration:*
½ oz. blanched almonds	15 g. blanched almonds
(see note)	(see note)
1 tablespoon demerara sugar	1 tablespoon demerara sugar

1. Grate the rind very finely from the lemon and orange, only taking the top 'zest'.
2. Squeeze out the lemon and orange juice.
3. Mash one banana, adding most of the fruit juce.
4. Blend with the ground almonds.
5. Chop the blanched almonds; whip the cream until it just holds its shape.
6. Blend with the banana mixture and castor sugar.
7. Put into individual heat resistant serving dishes and chill well.
8. Slice the remaining banana, dip in the remaining fruit juice, spoon over the fool.
9. Halve the almonds, sprinkle over the bananas and add the brown sugar.
10. Brown under the grill then chill again. Serve as cold as possible.

Note: To blanch almonds, put into boiling water for 1–2 minutes, remove, cool, then take off the skins.

Cooking time: 3–4 minutes
Preparation time: 10 minutes
Main cooking utensils: 2 small heatproof dishes
Serves: 2

Raspberry jewels

Imperial	Metric
1 raspberry-flavoured jelly	1 raspberry-flavoured jelly
1 pint boiling water	550 ml. boiling water
1 pint unflavoured yoghurt	550 ml. unflavoured yoghurt
(4 cartons)	(4 cartons)
Decoration:	*Decoration:*
few raspberries	few raspberries

1. Dissolve the jelly in the boiling water, allow to cool slightly.
2. Divide the mixture between the 4 glasses and as the jelly begins to stiffen, tilt the glasses so the jelly sets at an angle as shown in the picture.
3. When the jelly has set, fill up with the yoghurt.
4. Top with fresh raspberries. Serve as cold as possible.

Variation
Use different flavoured jellies.

Cooking time: few minutes to melt jelly
Preparation time: few minutes
Main utensils: 4 glasses
Serves: 4–5

Iced desserts

In these days, when most of us own a refrigerator and many possess home freezers too, it is comparatively easy to make ice cream or sorbets.

For successful ice cream:

a. Freeze quickly, this is explained on page 153.
b. Use a well-balanced recipe, i.e. one that contains a good proportion of cream or evaporated milk; or use one of the ice-cream powders and follow the directions on the packet. Another economical alternative is to buy cream topping mix, used as an alternative to cream in many recipes; make this up as directions, then add flavouring and freeze.
c. Do not add too much sugar, for this can hinder freezing and if you *really* use an 'overdose', you prevent the mixture freezing at all.
d. Make sure the mixture is light in texture, i.e. do not overbeat cream and make it too solid; often recipes contain a certain amount of egg white which lightens the consistency.

Custard ice cream: Make a sweetened egg custard or fairly thick custard with powder. Cool, then fold in an equal amount of whipped cream or evaporated milk and freeze.

Ways to serve ice cream

Ice cream can form the basis of many simple desserts.

Poires Hélène: The classic name for the dessert on page 205. Serve the chocolate sauce (hot or cold) by itself over ice cream; it is particularly good with a coffee ice cream, then topped with chopped nuts.

Fruit Melba: Put 8 oz. ($\frac{1}{4}$ kg.) raspberries (or equivalent in well-drained frozen or canned fruit), 2–3 tablespoons redcurrant jelly, 1 teaspoon arrowroot or cornflour, blended with $\frac{1}{4}$ pint ($1\frac{1}{2}$ dl.) water or syrup from the canned or frozen fruit into a pan. Sweeten to taste, stir over a low heat until a smooth and thickened sauce. Sieve or emulsify in the liquidiser to give a purée free from pips. Cool. Put ice cream and halved peaches, pears, strawberries or other fruit in glasses; top with a little sauce. Store the rest of the sauce in the refrigerator or make larger amounts and freeze. Use within 1 year.

Coupe Jacques: Coat ice cream and fruit salad with the Melba sauce (above).

Banana split: Put bananas and ice cream into long dishes, then top with either chocolate sauce as page 205 or with Melba sauce above.

Peanut fudge sundae

Imperial	Metric
4 portions vanilla ice cream	4 portions vanilla ice cream
4 oz. seedless raisins	100 g. seedless raisins
Peanut sauce:	*Peanut sauce:*
4 level tablespoons peanut butter	4 level tablespoons peanut butter
6 level tablespoons golden syrup	6 level tablespoons golden syrup
1 tablespoon water	1 tablespoon water

1. To make the sauce, put the peanut butter into a mixing bowl.
2. Gradually add the syrup and water, stir until well blended.
3. Put a spoonful of sauce into each sundae glass, then a layer of ice cream and raisins.
4. Add a further layer of sauce, top with ice cream and more raisins. Serve in tall glasses.

Variations

Use different flavoured ice cream.

Use honey instead of golden syrup. Serve sauce hot instead of cold.

When fresh strawberries or raspberries are in season, these make a delicious contrast in flavour. Arrange layers between the ice cream and raisins.

Preparation time: 5 minutes
Main utensil: mixing bowl
Serves: 4

Sorbets

Imperial	Metric
Orange sorbet:	*Orange sorbet:*
5–6 large oranges	5–6 large oranges
1 lemon	1 lemon
½ pint water	275 ml. water
3–4 oz. sugar	75–100 g. sugar
2 egg whites	2 egg whites
Lemon sorbet:	*Lemon sorbet:*
4 large lemons	4 large lemons
½ pint water	275 ml. water
4–5 oz. sugar	100–125 g. sugar
2 egg whites	2 egg whites

1. Squeeze out the juice from the fruit.
2. Remove any pith from the skins and put the skins with the water into a pan and simmer steadily.
3. Strain carefully to give a clear liquid, add the sugar while hot, stir to dissolve, then add the syrup to the fruit juice.
4. Taste and, if necessary, add more sugar to give a sweeter flavour — remember freezing reduces sweetness slightly; never over-sweeten.
5. Put into the freezing tray, freeze for approximately 30 minutes in the freezing compartment.
6. Whisk the egg whites until stiff, add the partially frozen mixture and fold together.
7. Return to the refrigerator and leave until firm — 45 minutes to 1 hour. In a home freezer the time will be shorter.
8. Serve with whipped cream if liked.

Cooking time: 10 minutes
Preparation time: 15 minutes
Main cooking utensils: saucepan, strainer, freezing tray
Serves: 4–6

Meringues Chantilly

Imperial	Metric
2 egg whites	2 egg whites
4 oz. castor sugar or 2 oz. castor sugar and 2 oz. sieved icing sugar	100 g. castor sugar or 50 g. castor sugar and 50 g. sieved icing sugar
oil or butter to grease tray	oil or butter to grease tray
Crème Chantilly:	*Crème Chantilly:*
¼ pint thick cream	125 ml. thick cream
few drops vanilla essence	few drops vanilla essence
1 oz. sugar	25 g. sugar

1. Whisk the egg whites in a dry bowl until very stiff, then gradually beat in half the sugar and fold in the remainder.
2. For a slightly sticky texture, add a few drops of vinegar to the egg whites when stiff; for a firm texture on the outside, add 1 teaspoon cornflour to the sugar.
3. Put into a piping bag with ½- to 1-inch (1- to 2-cm.) rose pipe and pipe into the desired shape on a well-oiled or buttered tray.
4. For the slightly shiny appearance in the picture, shake a little extra sugar over the meringues before baking.
5. Dry out in the oven until firm, lift off the tray with a warm palette knife and leave to cool.
6. To make the crème Chantilly, whip the cream until it holds a shape, then gradually whip in the vanilla and sugar.
7. Sandwich the meringues together with the cream. This amount of cream gives a fairly thin coating; for a thicker layer plus piping round the edge, use nearly double the amount.

Variation

Meringues glacées: Sandwich together with ice cream and decorate with a little crème Chantilly. Serve at once.

Cooking time: 3–4 hours
Preparation time: 15 minutes
Main cooking utensils: baking tray or sheet, ½- to 1-inch (1- to 2-cm.) pipe and bag
Oven temperature: very cool (225–250°F., 110–130°C., Gas Mark ¼–½)
Oven position: centre or coolest part
Makes: 12 rounds

Orange bombes

Imperial
4 oranges
1 banana, peeled and sliced
2 apples, peeled, cored and chopped
a few canned or fresh cherries
1 pear, peeled, cored and diced
sugar to taste
2 small egg whites
3 oz. castor sugar

Metric
4 oranges
1 banana, peeled and sliced
2 apples, peeled, cored and chopped
1 few canned or fresh cherries
1 pear, peeled, cored and diced
sugar to taste
2 small egg whites
75 g. castor sugar

1. Cut off the tops of the oranges and scoop out the flesh.
2. Remove the pith and skin, add the chopped flesh to the other fruit.
3. Mix together, sweeten if wished.
4. Fill the orange cups with the fruit.
5. Whisk the egg whites very stiffly and fold in the castor sugar.
6. Pipe or pile the meringue on top of the oranges, covering the opening completely.
7. Place under the preheated grill and cook until golden, or put in the oven. Serve immediately with cream.

Variation

Grapefruit may be used in exactly the same way. If you wish to serve the pudding cold, add 4 oz. (100 g.) sugar to the egg whites and cook in a very slow oven (225–250°F., 110–130°C., Gas Mark ¼) for 1 hour.

Cooking time: 4–5 minutes under grill or 12–15 minutes in oven
Preparation time: 10 minutes
Main cooking utensil: pie dish
Oven temperature: moderately hot (375°F., 190°C., Gas Mark 5)
Oven position: centre
Serves: 4

Crème d'ananas

Imperial
3 egg yolks
2 oz. castor sugar
½ pint milk
½ oz. powdered gelatine
1 small can pineapple rings
½ pint thick cream
2 egg whites
Decoration:
little extra cream
angelica

Metric
3 egg yolks
50 g. castor sugar
275 ml. milk
15 g. powdered gelatine
1 small can pineapple rings
275 ml. thick cream
2 egg whites
Decoration:
little extra cream
angelica

1. Beat the egg yolks with 1 oz. (25 g.) sugar, add the warmed milk, pour into the top of the double saucepan and cook (stirring well) over hot but not boiling water until the custard gives a thick coating over the back of a wooden spoon.
2. Meanwhile put the gelatine into a basin.
3. Measure ¼ pint (125 ml.) syrup from the pineapple and add 2–3 tablespoons of this syrup to the gelatine.
4. Heat the remaining syrup in the pan, add the softened gelatine and stir until dissolved.
5. Whisk the hot gelatine mixture into the hot custard, allow to cool and begin to stiffen slightly.
6. Drain and chop all the remaining pineapple finely except for 2 rings.
7. Fold the pineapple and whipped cream into the gelatine mixture.
8. Whisk the egg whites until stiff, beat in the remaining sugar then fold into the pineapple mixture.
9. Spoon into a mould (rinsed in cold water), allow to set. Turn out and decorate with whipped cream, pineapple pieces and angelica.

Cooking time: 15 minutes
Preparation time: 20 minutes, plus time to set
Main cooking utensils: double saucepan, saucepan, 2-pint (1-litre) mould
Serves: 4–6

Coffee party mousse

Imperial	Metric
½ oz. powdered gelatine (1 level tablespoon)	15 g. powdered gelatine (1 level tablespoon)
¼ pint hot water	125 ml. hot water
3 tablespoons coffee essence	3 tablespoons coffee essence
3 egg yolks	3 egg yolks
2 oz. castor sugar	50 g. castor sugar
¼ pint double cream	125 ml. double cream
3 egg whites	3 egg whites
Decoration:	*Decoration:*
8 oz. sponge finger biscuits	200 g. sponge finger biscuits
2–3 tablespoons double cream	2–3 tablespoons double cream
8 hazelnuts or walnut halves	8 hazelnuts or walnut halves

1. Dissolve the gelatine in the water, blend with the coffee essence.
2. Beat the egg yolks and sugar in a basin over a pan of simmering water until thick and creamy.
3. Remove and gradually beat in the coffee and gelatine mixture.
4. When cold (but not set) fold in the lightly whipped cream.
5. Beat egg whites until stiff, fold into the coffee mixture.
6. Pour into a cake tin or mould and chill until firm.
7. To turn out dip the cake tin in hot water for 4–5 seconds and invert on to a flat dish.
8. Trim the sponge fingers to the height of the mousse and set them all the way round it.
9. Decorate the top with the blobs or piped whirls of cream and place the nuts on top. Serve with cream or ice cream.

Cooking time: few minutes to heat water
Preparation time: 20 minutes
Main utensil: 6–7-inch (15–18-cm.) cake tin or mould
Serves: 6–8

Coffee soufflé

Imperial	Metric
3 eggs	3 eggs
2 oz. castor sugar	50 g. castor sugar
2 tablespoons coffee essence or very strong black coffee	2 tablespoons coffee essence or very strong black coffee
¼ oz. powdered gelatine	10 g. powdered gelatine
3 tablespoons water	3 tablespoons water
¼ pint cream	125 ml. cream
Decoration:	*Decoration:*
2 oz. chocolate vermicelli or chopped nuts	50 g. chocolate vermicelli or chopped nuts
whipped cream	whipped cream

1. Separate the egg yolks from the whites, put the yolks into a basin with the sugar and coffee essence.
2. Beat until thick and creamy, this could be done over hot water if wished.
3. Soften the powdered gelatine in water, then dissolve over a very low heat, add to the egg mixture, beating it in thoroughly.
4. Allow the mixture to cool and stiffen slightly, then fold in the lightly whipped cream and finally the stiffly beaten egg whites.
5. Prepare the soufflé dish by tying a band of greaseproof paper around it, to come at least 2 inches (5 cm.) higher than the edge of the dish. Pour the mixture into the dish and leave to set.
6. Remove the paper, then decorate the edge of the soufflé with the chocolate vermicelli and top with cream. Serve chilled.

Variations

Use 1–2 oz. (25–50 g.) melted chocolate powder as well as the coffee to make a mocha soufflé, or omit the coffee for a chocolate soufflé. For a fruit soufflé use ¼ pint (125 ml.) thick fruit purée in place of the coffee.

Cooking time: few minutes to soften gelatine
Preparation time: 25 minutes
Main cooking utensils: saucepan, 5-inch (13-cm.) soufflé dish, greaseproof paper
Serves: 4

Baking

Although the technique of baking varies somewhat with the type of mixture, i.e. does it contain yeast — does it need gentle or vigorous handling, etc., there are certain basic rules to follow:

a. Check carefully on oven temperatures and oven positions.

Although every recipe carries a suggested oven temperature, cookers vary to a certain degree, it is therefore wise to check with your manufacturer's instructions and follow those.

The position in which the food is placed is important. Large cakes etc. should always be placed in the centre of the oven (unless using a fan-heated cooker when every position has the same heat). The purpose of this is to prevent the top of the cake becoming over-browned, before the centre is set.

Small cakes, scones, etc., which need a short baking period, can be baked towards the top of the oven.

b. Follow the method of handling the ingredients, these are mentioned on page 7, but further details are on the right of this page.

c. Test the cake or bread, etc. carefully before bringing this out of the oven; methods of testing are also given on the opposite page. It oftens saves a disappointing result if you are careful about checking this point.

Mixing bread and cakes

Bread made with yeast is mixed by a kneading action, this means pulling the dough with the base of the palm of your hand (often called the heel of your hand); pull and stretch gently, but firmly. You can tell if the dough is sufficiently kneaded by testing with a lightly floured finger. If the impression made comes out, then cease handling the dough, for over-kneading is a bad fault in yeast cookery.

Fairly plain cakes and many biscuits are made by rubbing fat into flour, do this lightly with your fingertips; some of these recipes are on pages 180 and 181. Most of these mixtures can be handled fairly briskly.

Richer and lighter cakes are made by beating the fat and sugar until light, then adding the eggs, etc., this is explained on page 182. Another method of incorporating ingredients is to whisk the eggs and sugar until thick, see the recipe for a sponge on page 184. In these cakes it is *essential* that the flour is incorporated very gently by folding.

Gingerbreads and rather moist-textured cakes are produced by melting some of the ingredients. In this type of cake you can beat the mixture very briskly.

White bread – tin loaf

Imperial	Metric
Yeast liquid:	*Yeast liquid:*
1 teaspoon sugar	1 teaspoon sugar
½ pint warm water	250 ml. warm water
½ oz. fresh yeast or 1 level dessertspoon dried yeast	15 g. fresh yeast or 1 level dessertspoon dried yeast
Dry ingredients:	*Dry ingredients:*
½ oz. lard or margarine	15 g. lard or margarine
1 lb. strong flour	400 g. strong flour
1–2 level teaspoons salt	1–2 level teaspoons salt

1. Dissolve the sugar in the warm water. With fresh yeast add liquid and use immediately, or see next recipe. With dried yeast sprinkle on top of liquid – leave for 10 minutes or until mixture becomes frothy – known as 'letting the sponge break through' or 'sponging'.
2. Rub the lard into flour and salt, sieved into a warm bowl. (All yeast utensils need to be warm.)
3. Add yeast liquid, knead well.
4. Cover bowl with a cloth or put dough into a greased, large polythene bag.
5. Allow to rise until double its size, this takes about 45–60 minutes in a warm place – 2 hours in a cool room. This is known as 'proving'.
6. Re-knead dough (called 'knocking back'); continue kneading until dough springs back when pressed with a floured finger.
7. To shape loaf press to oblong, fold in three and put in a greased warm tin.
8. Prove again until risen to the top of the tin.
9. Bake for time and at temperature given; reduce heat if over-browning.

To test: Knock bottom of loaf – it should sound hollow.

Cooking time: 30–40 minutes
Preparation time: 20 minutes plus time for dough to prove
Main cooking utensil: 1-lb. (½-kg.) loaf tin
Oven temperature: very hot (450–475°F., 230–240°C., Gas Mark 8–9)
Oven position: centre
Makes: 1 small loaf

To freeze bread and cakes

Bread can be frozen in several ways:

a. Bake, cool, wrap and freeze. It is a good idea to slice a loaf, so individual slices can be removed to toast from the frozen state. Use within 6 weeks. Either thaw out at room temperature or wrap in foil and heat in a moderate to moderately hot oven for about 30 minutes for a loaf or 10 minutes for rolls.

b. Prepare the dough to the end of stage 3 or the end of stage 5 as in the recipe above. Put into a well-greased strong polythene bag and freeze. Use within 2 months for plain bread. Remove from the bag, leave at room temperature for 4–5 hours or 12 hours in the refrigerator, then proceed from next stage in the recipe. *Use 50 per cent more* yeast if you plan to freeze uncooked dough.

Cakes can be baked then frozen, use within 2–3 months. If decorated it is advisable to freeze then wrap and to unwrap before defrosting.

To test bread and cakes

Bread is tested as in the recipe above.

Cakes are tested by pressing to see if an impression is left, this is particularly important with light cakes. Page 180, Family fruit cake, stage 7 and page 186 also give other ways of testing cakes.

Easy guide to bread and cakes

The following gives you help in selecting the right bread or cake for a particular occasion.

When you are short of time see pages 175, 176, 177, 178, 180, 181, 182, 183, 184.

When you are short of money see pages 171, 172, 173, 174, 180, 181, 184.

Children will enjoy helping you make cakes, especially those on pages 178, 181, 182, 184, 197.

When you want a special dish see pages 178, 182, 183, 184, 185, 186, 187.

These cakes also make a good dessert see pages 184, 187, 195.

Cob loaf

Cooking time: 30—40 minutes
Preparation time: 20 minutes plus time for dough to prove
Main cooking utensil: flat baking sheet
Oven temperature: very hot (450—475°F., 230—240°C., Gas Mark 8—9)
Oven position: centre
Makes: 1 small loaf

Imperial	Metric
Yeast liquid:	*Yeast liquid:*
1 teaspoon sugar	1 teaspoon sugar
½ pint warm water	250 ml. warm water
½ oz. fresh yeast or 1 level dessertspoon dried yeast	15 g. fresh yeast or 1 level dessertspoon dried yeast
Dry ingredients:	*Dry ingredients:*
½ oz. lard or margarine	15 g. lard or margarine
1 lb. flour	400 g. flour
1—2 level teaspoons salt	1—2 level teaspoons salt
Coating:	*Coating:*
little extra flour	little extra flour

1. Prepare the yeast liquid as in preceding recipe or cream the yeast and sugar, add the warm liquid, sprinkle the top with flour and leave in a warm place until the sponge breaks through.
2. Continue as page 171, stages 2 to 6.
3. To shape the cob loaf, mould dough into a round ball, flatten slightly and cut top of loaf with a sharp knife.
4. Dredge with a little extra flour, put on to a lightly floured tray to prove. Cover with greased polythene if wished and leave till double in size.
5. Bake for time and at temperature given.
6. Test as on page 171. Store in an airtight tin or bread bin.

Note: The liquid in yeast cooking should not exceed 100°F. (38°C.). It is best to use strong flour in bread making.

Variations

Brown bread: Use half white and half wholemeal flour, plus a little extra liquid.
Wholemeal bread: Use all stone-ground flour plus extra liquid to give a soft dough. This takes longer to prove and bake.

Lardy cake

Cooking time: approximately 45 minutes
Preparation time: 25 minutes plus 15 minutes at stage 1, 1—1½ hours first proving, 30—40 minutes second proving
Main cooking utensil: 12- by 7-inch (30- by 18-cm.) tin
Oven temperature: hot (400—425°F., 200—220°C., Gas Mark 6—7), reducing after 20 minutes if necessary
Makes: 14 slices

Imperial	Metric
Bread dough:	*Bread dough:*
½ oz. fresh yeast or 2 level teaspoons dried yeast	15 g. fresh yeast or 2 level teaspoons dried yeast
1 teaspoon sugar	1 teaspoon sugar
about ½ pint tepid water	about 250 ml. tepid water
1 lb. plain flour	400 g. plain flour
½ teaspoon salt	½ teaspoon salt
Filling:	*Filling:*
4 oz. lard	100 g. lard
4 oz. sugar	100 g. sugar
4 oz. currants	100 g. currants
a little spice	a little spice
Glaze:	*Glaze:*
2 tablespoons sugar mixed with 2 tablespoons water	2 tablespoons sugar mixed with 2 tablespoons water

1. Cream yeast with sugar, add the tepid water and a little flour; or blend dried yeast with sugar and a little liquid, stand until softened, cream, add rest of liquid and a sprinkling of flour.
2. Put in a warm place until covered with bubbles, add to the sieved flour and salt.
3. Knead thoroughly, cover with a tea-towel or polythene and allow to prove, i.e., rise until double original size.
4. Knead again, roll out on a floured board to a neat oblong.
5. Put half the lard in small pieces over two thirds of the dough.
6. Sprinkle with half the sugar, fruit and spice, then fold in three, bringing the uncovered piece of dough over first.
7. Give a half turn, repeat 5 and 6.
8. Turn again, roll to a neat oblong, fold, turn and re-roll.
9. Fold once more then roll out to fit warmed tin; score the top.
10. Cover and allow to prove until well risen. Bake in the centre of the oven until golden brown, then remove from tin and test. Knock base, cake should sound hollow. Glaze at once.

Chelsea buns

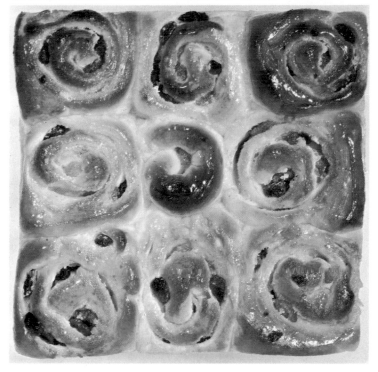

Imperial
Bun dough:
1 oz. sugar
¼ pint warm milk
½ oz. fresh yeast or 2
   teaspoons dried yeast
8 oz. plain flour
pinch salt
Filling:
1 oz. butter or margarine
1 oz. sugar
2 oz. dried fruit
Glaze:
1 tablespoon hot water
1 tablespoon sugar

Metric
Bun dough:
25 g. sugar
125 ml. warm milk
15 g. fresh yeast or 2
   teaspoons dried yeast
200 g. plain flour
pinch salt
Filling:
25 g. butter or margarine
25 g. sugar
50 g. dried fruit
Glaze:
1 tablespoon hot water
1 tablespoon sugar

1. Dissolve 1 teaspoon of the sugar in the warm milk. Stir in the yeast, use at once with fresh yeast or wait 10 minutes with dried yeast until mixture starts to bubble, i.e., the sponge breaks through.
2. Sieve the flour and salt, add rest of sugar and the yeast liquid.
3. Cover with a cloth or put into a polythene bag and allow the mixture to rise, i.e., prove until double its original size (about 50 minutes at room temperature).
4. Knead until smooth, roll out to a neat oblong, spread with softened butter, sprinkle on sugar and dried fruit.
5. Roll up like a Swiss roll, cut into portions and put on to warm tray or in the tin (this gives better shaped buns).
6. Prove for 20 minutes, then bake for time and temperature given until golden brown.
7. Blend water and sugar and brush over the buns. The buns may be reheated to freshen them.

Cooking time: 10–15 minutes
Preparation time: 30 minutes plus time for proving
Main cooking utensil: baking tray or 8- to 9-inch (20- to 23-cm.) square shallow tin
Oven temperature: hot (425–450°F., 220–230°C., Gas Mark 7–8)
Oven position: towards centre
Makes: 9 buns

Cheese roll

Imperial
Yeast pastry:
½ oz. fresh yeast or
   ½ tablespoon dried yeast
2 oz. sugar
at least ¼ pint tepid water
12 oz. plain flour
pinch salt
3 oz. butter
Filling:
12 oz. cream or cottage cheese
grated rind and juice of 1 lemon
   or orange
4–6 oz. sultanas
4 oz. glacé cherries

Metric
Yeast pastry:
15 g. fresh yeast or
   ½ tablespoon dried yeast
50 g. sugar
at least 125 ml. tepid water
300 g. plain flour
pinch salt
75 g. butter
Filling:
300 g. cream or cottage cheese
grated rind and juice of 1 lemon
   or orange
100–150 g. sultanas
100 g. glacé cherries

1. Cream the fresh yeast with 1 teaspoon of the sugar. Add the tepid water and a sprinkling of flour. If using dried yeast, sprinkle the yeast on the tepid water, add 1 teaspoon sugar and a sprinkling of flour.
2. Leave for about 10 minutes until the surface is covered with bubbles.
3. Meanwhile mix the sugar, flour and salt. Add the yeast mixture and, if necessary, more tepid water to give a soft rolling consistency.
4. Knead; roll out to a thin oblong. Put the butter over two-thirds, as in flaky pastry, fold, turn, seal the edges and roll out again, then give a final fold. Leave in a warm place.
5. Knead, roll out to an oblong. Spread with the cheese blended with the lemon or orange juice and rind, the sultanas and half the cherries.
6. Roll up and form into a ring in the greased ring tin (or make into a ring on a baking tray). Leave to prove for 30 minutes, then bake at the given temperature. Decorate with the rest of the cherries.

Cooking time: 40 minutes
Preparation time: 25 minutes plus time for dough to prove
Main cooking utensil: 9-inch (23-cm.) ring tin
Oven temperature: hot (425–450°F., 220–230°C., Gas Mark 7–8)
Oven position: centre
Serves: 8–10

Wholemeal nut bread

Imperial
1 lb. wholemeal flour
2 level teaspoons baking powder
½ teaspoon salt
2 eggs
½ pint milk
2 oz. melted butter
4 oz. chopped walnuts

Metric
400 g. wholemeal flour
2 level teaspoons baking powder
½ teaspoon salt
2 eggs
250 ml. milk
50 g. melted butter
100 g. chopped walnuts

1. Mix together the flour, baking powder and salt.
2. Lightly beat the eggs and add to the dry ingredients with the milk and melted butter.
3. Mix to a smooth soft dough.
4. Add the chopped walnuts.
5. Turn into a well-greased loaf tin.
6. Bake for the time and at temperature given until firm to the touch. Serve with butter, cheese, and tomatoes.

Note: If making wholemeal bread for the first time, be prepared for it to take longer in cooking than white bread since it absorbs more moisture. It is therefore advisable to use a slightly lower oven temperature. Wholemeal bread takes longer to toast, therefore if using an automatic toaster remember it should be re-set when toasting wholemeal bread after white bread.

Variations
Divide dough in two and bake in two 1-lb. (½-kg.) loaf tins for 1 hour. For extra flavour, celery salt may be used in place of ordinary salt.

Cooking time: 1¼–1½ hours
Preparation time: 15 minutes
Main cooking utensil: 2-lb. (1-kg.) loaf tin
Oven temperature: moderate (375°F., 190°C., Gas Mark 5)
Oven position: centre
Serves: 10–12

Raisin bread

Imperial
6 oz. seedless raisins
8 oz. plain flour
2 level teaspoons baking powder
½ level teaspoon bicarbonate of soda
½ level teaspoon salt
3 oz. rolled oats
2 oz. butter
2 oz. sugar
1 egg
½ pint sour milk (or 1 level teaspoon cream of tartar with fresh milk)

Metric
150 g. seedless raisins
200 g. plain flour
2 level teaspoons baking powder
½ level teaspoon bicarbonate of soda
½ level teaspoon salt
75 g. rolled oats
50 g. butter
50 g. sugar
1 egg
250 ml. sour milk (or 1 level teaspoon cream of tartar with fresh milk)

1. Plump the raisins by covering with cold water, bringing to the boil and standing for five minutes. Drain very well.
2. Sieve the dry ingredients, add the rolled oats and raisins.
3. Cream the butter and sugar until light and fluffy, beat in the egg gradually.
4. Add dry ingredients alternately with the sour milk to make a soft dough.
5. Place in the greased and floured loaf tin and bake until firm. Serve sliced fairly thickly and spread with butter.

Note: When baking always check oven temperature with that recommended in your cooker instruction card or book. If using raisins with seeds, remove the seeds by breaking the raisins with your fingers or halving with a knife. Take out the seeds with damp fingers. If the fruit becomes wet, use slightly less milk.

Variation
Add the grated rind of an orange and the juice in place of some of the sour milk.

Cooking time: 50–60 minutes
Preparation time: 20 minutes
Main cooking utensil: 2-lb. (1-kg.) loaf tin
Oven temperature: moderate (350–375°F., 180–190°C., Gas Mark 4–5)
Oven position: centre
Makes: 20 slices

Soda bread

Imperial
1 oz. margarine, optional
8 oz. plain flour
pinch salt
1 level teaspoon bicarbonate of
   soda
¼ pint sour milk or fresh milk
   with 1 teaspoon cream of
   tartar
Glaze:
little milk

Metric
25 g. margarine, optional
200 g. plain flour
pinch salt
1 level teaspoon bicarbonate of
   soda
125 ml. sour milk or fresh milk
   with 1 teaspoon cream of
   tartar
Glaze:
little milk

1. Rub the margarine into the flour (this is not essential, but helps to keep the bread moist).
2. Add the salt, dissolve the bicarbonate of soda in the sour milk, add to the flour.
3. Knead lightly and form into a round loaf.
4. Brush with a little milk.
5. Bake for 15 minutes in a very hot oven then lower the heat to moderately hot for a further 10–15 minutes until the bread is firm to the touch. Serve when fresh with butter.

Note: You can use self-raising flour and fresh milk instead of plain flour and sour milk.

Variation
Raisin soda bread: Add 4 oz. (100 g.) seedless raisins to the flour, add ½–1 teaspoon caraway seeds if wished. Form into a round. Brush top of the bread with melted butter, sprinkle with castor sugar and mark into four portions before cooking.

Cooking time: 25–30 minutes
Preparation time: 10 minutes
Main cooking utensil: flat baking tray or sheet
Oven temperature: very hot (475°F., 240°C., Gas Mark 9), then moderately hot (400°F., 200°C., Gas Mark 6)
Oven position: centre
Serves: 4

Cheese scone round

Imperial
8 oz. plain flour
4 level teaspoons baking powder
½ level teaspoon salt
pinch dry mustard
2 oz. butter
4 oz. grated Cheddar cheese
about ¼ pint milk
Glaze:
1 egg
Topping:
1 oz. grated Cheddar cheese

Metric
200 g. plain flour
4 level teaspoons baking powder
½ level teaspoon salt
pinch dry mustard
50 g. butter
100 g. grated Cheddar cheese
about 125 ml. milk
Glaze:
1 egg
Topping:
25 g. grated Cheddar cheese

1. Sieve the flour, baking powder, salt and mustard together and rub in the butter.
2. Add the grated cheese and sufficient milk to make a soft dough.
3. Knead lightly and roll out to 1-inch (2-cm.) thickness.
4. Cut out rounds with the pastry cutter.
5. Arrange the scones in a ring of eight, on a lightly floured baking sheet.
6. Brush with egg on top and where they touch one another.
7. Sprinkle grated cheese on top.
8. Bake for time and temperature given until well risen and golden brown. Serve them hot or cold at any meal. They make a pleasant change from bread rolls with soup or the main course.

Variation
Use ¼ pint (125 ml.) tomato juice in place of milk or add a little Marmite (yeast extract) to the milk to flavour.

Cooking time: 10–15 minutes
Preparation time: 15 minutes
Main cooking utensil: baking tray or sheet, 2-inch (5-cm.) pastry cutter
Oven temperature: hot (425–450°F., 220–230°C., Gas Mark 7–8)
Oven position: above centre
Serves: 8

Oaties

Cooking time: 20 minutes
Preparation time: 15 minutes
Main cooking utensils: saucepan, 7-inch (18-cm.) sandwich tin
Oven temperature: moderate (350–375°F., 180–190°C., Gas
  Mark 4–5)
Oven position: just above centre
Makes: 8 oaties

Imperial	Metric
4 oz. plain flour	100 g. plain flour
2 level teaspoons baking powder	2 level teaspoons baking powder
½ level teaspoon salt	½ level teaspoon salt
4 oz. rolled oats	100 g. rolled oats
2 oz. castor sugar	50 g. castor sugar
3 oz. black treacle	75 g. black treacle
4 oz. butter or margarine	100 g. butter or margarine
Decoration:	*Decoration:*
little coarse oatmeal or almond nibs	little coarse oatmeal or almond nibs

1. Sieve the flour, baking powder and salt together. Add the rolled oats.
2. Put the sugar, black treacle and butter or margarine into a saucepan and heat until just melted.
3. Mix this into the flour and stir until all the ingredients are thoroughly combined.
4. Press into the greased sandwich tin.
5. Sprinkle the surface of the oaties with coarse oatmeal.
6. Bake for time and at temperature given until firm to the touch.
7. Cut into wedges before the mixture cools. These are excellent for breakfast or for tea, and are delicious split and toasted and spread with butter.

Note: Any basic scone recipe may be used with 50% flour, 50% fine or medium oatmeal — better in this case than rolled oats.

Variation
Use syrup or honey in place of treacle.

American ring doughnuts

Cooking time: about 3 minutes each batch
Preparation time: 15 minutes
Main cooking utensils: 2-inch (5-cm.) cutter, 1-inch (2½-cm.) cutter,
  pan for fat (with frying basket if possible)
Makes: 12–15 doughnuts

Imperial	Metric
12 oz. self-raising flour or 12 oz. plain flour with 2 level teaspoons cream of tartar and 1 level teaspoon bicarbonate of soda	300 g. self-raising flour or 300 g. plain flour with 2 level teaspoons cream of tartar and 1 level teaspoon bicarbonate of soda
½ teaspoon cinnamon	½ teaspoon cinnamon
½ teaspoon mixed spice	½ teaspoon mixed spice
4 oz. margarine	100 g. margarine
3 oz. castor sugar	75 g. castor sugar
1 egg	1 egg
6 tablespoons milk	6 tablespoons milk
1½ lb. fat for frying (should give 3-inch depth in pan)	675 g. fat for frying (should give 7-cm. depth in pan)
Coating:	*Coating:*
castor sugar	castor sugar

1. Sieve together the flour with the dry ingredients.
2. Rub in the margarine until the mixture looks like fine breadcrumbs, add sugar.
3. Stir in the beaten egg and enough milk to give a soft but not sticky, dough.
4. Turn out on to a lightly floured board, knead lightly, then roll out to ¾-inch (1½-cm.) thickness.
5. Cut into 2-inch (5-cm.) rounds, then with the smaller cutter remove the centres.
6. Gather up the parts removed, knead quickly, roll out and continue like this with each batch.
7. Heat the fat to 360°F. (182°C.) or until a cube of bread a day old turns golden in 1 minute.
8. Put in one batch of doughnut rings, fry steadily until golden brown.
9. Lift out, drain on absorbent paper. Roll in castor sugar. Continue like this with each batch. Serve with hot coffee or chocolate.

To make scones

Scones are one of the quickest dishes to prepare and bake; they can be very good, but sadly are often disappointing, due to incorrect handling or baking. Make a scone dough slightly softer than pastry, it should give the kind of mixture that can only just be rolled out. Handle the dough quickly and lightly. Bake the scones quickly. Use when fresh, although they can be stored in a tin for 2–3 days and heated for a short time to freshen them. Scones freeze well, use within 6 weeks. Heat from the frozen state for a short time in a moderately hot oven.

To make a plain scone dough sieve 8 oz. (200 g.) flour with a pinch salt, etc. With plain flour you also need 3–4 *level* teaspoons baking powder or ½ teaspoon bicarbonate of soda and 1 teaspoon cream of tartar. If using self-raising flour it is not essential to add extra raising agent; but if you want very light scones use *just under half* the above quantities. Rub in 1–2 oz. (25–50 g.) butter or other fat, then add seasoning or 1–2 oz. (25–50 g.) sugar, bind with milk or as suggestions on the right. Roll out to about ½–¾ inch (1–2 cm.) in thickness and cut into rounds or triangles. Put on to an ungreased baking sheet, bake towards the top of a hot oven, as Cheese scone round page 175.

New flavours for scones

Use the basic quantities as recipe on the left; do not grease baking sheets for plain scones, but it is better to grease them for the following:

Cheese scones: Follow recipe on page 175, vary by adding little dried fruit or chopped nuts.

Fruit scones: Add 2–3 oz. (50–75 g.) dried fruit to basic recipe; try mixing with grated lemon or orange rind, some juice and some milk.

Oatmeal scones: Use equal amounts of oatmeal and plain flour, with raising agent as plain flour; flavour with fruit, cheese, etc.

Potato scones: Use equal amounts of mashed potato and plain flour, with raising agent as plain flour; particularly good as a sweet fruit scone.

Rich scones: Use 2 oz. (50 g.) butter, then bind with an egg and a little soured cream. Bake slightly more slowly than scones on page 175.

Treacle scones: Omit sugar from recipe on left, add 1–2 tablespoons black treacle and mix with milk; you can use marmalade or honey instead.

Chocolate and walnut cookies

Imperial	Metric
6 oz. self-raising flour or 6 oz. plain flour and 1½ teaspoons baking powder	150 g. self-raising flour or 150 g. plain flour and 1½ teaspoons baking powder
3 oz. butter	75 g. butter
3 oz. brown sugar	75 g. brown sugar
3 oz. granulated sugar	75 g. granulated sugar
½ teaspoon vanilla essence	½ teaspoon vanilla essence
½ teaspoon water	½ teaspoon water
1 egg	1 egg
2 oz. chopped walnuts	50 g. chopped walnuts
4 oz. (1 packet) Chocolate Polka Dots (chocolate chips)	100 g. Chocolate Polka Dots (chocolate chips)

1. Sieve the self-raising flour or plain flour and 1½ teaspoons baking powder.
2. Cream butter, both lots of sugar, vanilla and water until soft and light.
3. Gradually beat in the egg and then flour.
4. Add nuts and Chocolate Polka Dots; the mixture should be quite soft.
5. Drop teaspoons of the mixture on to greased trays, allowing room to spread.
6. Bake for time and at temperature given until crisp and golden brown. Serve with tea, coffee or with a plain sweet.

Note: As this makes a lot of small biscuits you may have to hold back some trays as they must not be baked in the hotter parts of the oven.

Variation
Omit nuts and put in sultanas.

Cooking time: 10–12 minutes
Preparation time: 20 minutes
Main cooking utensils: baking trays or sheets
Oven temperature: moderate (375°F., 190°C., Gas Mark 5)
Oven position: centre
Makes: 40–50

Ginger prune crunch

Imperial	Metric
8 oz. ginger biscuits	200 g. ginger biscuits
4 oz. stoned uncooked prunes	100 g. stoned uncooked prunes
1 oz. walnuts	25 g. walnuts
2 oz. butter	50 g. butter
2 tablespoons golden syrup	2 tablespoons golden syrup
Decoration:	*Decoration:*
castor sugar	castor sugar

1. Crush the ginger biscuits until they are crumbs and small pieces. Do not make too even in texture.
2. Chop the prunes, remove the stones, add chopped walnuts.
3. Melt the butter with the syrup.
4. Pour on to the dry ingredients.
5. Stir together to form a firm mixture and press out in the tin.
6. Leave to become quite cold and firm. Chill if preferred, but do not allow to become too cold.
7. Cut into fingers. Serve sprinkled with castor sugar. Could be served with cooked fruit for a sweet.

Note: You can sometimes buy stoned prunes, which would be good for this recipe.

Variation
Use half chopped figs and half chopped prunes, or all figs, or all dried apricots.

Preparation time: 15 minutes
Utensil for setting: 7-inch (18-cm.) square cake tin or sandwich tin
Serves: 8

Brandy snaps

Imperial	Metric
2 oz. butter	50 g. butter
2 oz. castor sugar	50 g. castor sugar
2 oz. black treacle	50 g. black treacle
1 teaspoon lemon juice	1 teaspoon lemon juice
scant 2 oz. plain flour	scant 50 g. plain flour
½–1 level teaspoon ground ginger	½–1 level teaspoon ground ginger

1. Melt butter, sugar, black treacle and lemon juice together over gentle heat.
2. Add sieved flour and ginger, blend together.
3. Put teaspoonfuls of the mixture on well-greased trays, 5 inches (13 cm.) apart.
4. Bake for approximately 5 minutes until a rich brown and well spread out. Only put one tray in the oven at a time so you can roll without difficulty.
5. Remove from oven, leave to cool for 1 minute until they are easily lifted.
6. While still warm wrap each one round a wooden handle, working quickly. Allow to become firm before lifting on to a wire tray. To serve, fill with fresh whipped cream.

Note: Store brandy snaps in an airtight tin.

Variation
Use golden syrup instead of treacle.

Cooking time: 5–6 minutes
Preparation time: 15 minutes
Main cooking utensils: saucepan, well-greased baking trays or sheets
Oven temperature: moderate (375°F., 190°C., Gas Mark 5)
Oven position: just above centre
Makes: 18 snaps

Sticky gingerbread

Imperial	Metric
4 oz. margarine or lard	100 g. margarine or lard
6 oz. black treacle and 2 oz. golden syrup or use all black treacle	150 g. black treacle and 50 g. golden syrup or use all black treacle
¼ pint milk	125 ml. milk
8 oz. plain flour	200 g. plain flour
2 oz. brown sugar	50 g. brown sugar
1 level teaspoon mixed spice	1 level teaspoon mixed spice
1 level teaspoon bicarbonate of soda	1 level teaspoon bicarbonate of soda
1–2 level teaspoons ground ginger	1–2 level teaspoons ground ginger
2 eggs	2 eggs

1. Warm the margarine or lard, black treacle and syrup.
2. Add the milk and allow to cool.
3. Sieve the dry ingredients into a bowl, add the treacle mixture and the eggs; beat well.
4. Pour into a lined tin.
5. Bake for time and at temperature given until firm to touch.

Note: Try to make gingerbread several days before cutting. The parkin (see below) can be eaten fresh.

Variation

Yorkshire parkin: Use 3 oz. (75 g.) lard instead of 4 oz. (100 g.), use 4 oz. (100 g.) plain flour and 4 oz. (100 g.) medium oatmeal or rolled oats and ¼ level teaspoon salt in place of 8 oz. (200 g.) flour. Make stiffer with 1 egg and 5 tablespoons milk only.

Cooking time: 1¼–1½ hours
Preparation time: 10 minutes
Main cooking utensils: large saucepan, 7-inch (18-cm.) square tin, greaseproof paper
Oven temperature: slow (300 325°F., 150–170°C., Gas Mark 2–3)
Oven position: centre
Makes: 12 pieces

Spiced honey cake

Imperial	Metric
2 oz. butter	50 g. butter
5 oz. honey	125 g. honey
5 oz. Demerara sugar	125 g. Demerara sugar
10 oz. plain flour	250 g. plain flour
pinch salt	pinch salt
1 teaspoon baking powder	1 teaspoon baking powder
1 level teaspoon bicarbonate of soda	1 level teaspoon bicarbonate of soda
1 teaspoon mixed spice	1 teaspoon mixed spice
1 teaspoon powdered ginger	1 teaspoon powdered ginger
1 teaspoon cinnamon	1 teaspoon cinnamon
2–4 oz. chopped peel	50–100 g. chopped peel
1 egg	1 egg
¼ pint milk	125 ml. milk
Decoration:	*Decoration:*
flaked almonds	flaked almonds

1. Heat the butter in the pan, then stir in the honey and sugar, allow to cool.
2. Sieve the flour, salt and baking powder and bicarbonate of soda.
3. Add the rest of the ingredients and beat very well until quite smooth.
4. Put into the prepared tin and top with almonds.
5. Bake until firm to the touch — look at the loaf after about ¾ hour and if browning too quickly lower the heat slightly.
6. Turn out carefully, and allow to cool. Serve sliced and buttered. This loaf keeps well.

Note: To measure honey, dip the spoon in very hot water, shake dry then dip into the jar — 1 level tablespoon equals 1 oz. (25 g.); to weigh honey, flour the scale pans — the honey comes away easily then.

If using self-raising flour you do not need baking powder or bicarbonate of soda.

Cooking time: 1¼ hours
Preparation time: 20 minutes
Main cooking utensils: pan, 2-lb. (1-kg.) loaf tin lined with greased paper
Oven temperature: very moderate to moderate (350°F., 180°C., Gas Mark 4)
Oven position: centre
Makes: 1 loaf

American apple cake

Imperial	Metric
10 oz. self-raising flour	250 g. self-raising flour
1 level teaspoon baking powder	1 level teaspoon baking powder
1 oz. castor sugar	25 g. castor sugar
¾ teaspoon salt	¾ teaspoon salt
4 oz. butter or margarine	100 g. butter or margarine
2 oz. grated cheese	50 g. grated cheese
about ¼ pint milk	about 125 ml. milk
4 eating apples	4 eating apples
2–3 oz. brown sugar	50–75 g. brown sugar
½ teaspoon cinnamon	½ teaspoon cinnamon
1 tablespoon melted butter	1 tablespoon melted butter

1. Sift flour, baking powder, castor sugar and salt together.
2. Rub in butter or margarine and then mix in cheese.
3. Add sufficient milk to make a soft but not sticky dough.
4. Turn on to a floured board and knead dough lightly.
5. Pat out dough in ungreased Swiss roll tin.
6. Pare and core apples, slice thinly.
7. Arrange in rows across dough.
8. Sprinkle with brown sugar and cinnamon mixed together.
9. Brush over with melted butter.
10. Bake for time and at temperature given. Serve sliced with coffee.

Note: When baking always check oven temperatures with that recommended in your cooker instruction card or book.

Variation
Use fresh apricots.

Cooking time: 25 minutes
Preparation time: 15 minutes
Main cooking utensil: Swiss roll tin, approximately 7 by 10 inches (18 by 25 cm.)
Oven temperature: moderately hot to hot (425°F., 220°C., Gas Mark 7)
Oven position: just above centre
Serves: 12

Family fruit cake

Imperial	Metric
8 oz. self-raising flour (or plain flour and 2 level teaspoons baking powder)	200 g. self-raising flour (or plain flour and 2 level teaspoons baking powder)
1 level teaspoon mixed spice	1 level teaspoon mixed spice
½ level teaspoon cinnamon	½ level teaspoon cinnamon
3–4 oz. butter or margarine	75–100 g. butter or margarine
3–4 oz. sugar	75–100 g. sugar
4 oz. currants	100 g. currants
4 oz. sultanas	100 g. sultanas
1 oz. mixed peel	25 g. mixed peel
1 egg	1 egg
about ¼ pint milk	about 125 ml. milk

1. Sieve the flour or flour and baking powder with the spice and cinnamon.
2. Rub in the butter or margarine until the mixture looks like fine breadcrumbs.
3. Add the sugar, dried fruit and peel.
4. Mix with egg and milk to form a soft consistency, i.e., so the mixture drops easily from a knife.
5. Put into the greased and floured loaf tin, making the mixture quite level on top.
6. Bake for the time and at temperature given.
7. Test the cake before removing from the tin. Ensure the cake has shrunk away from the sides of the tin, and when a fine skewer is inserted into the cake it should come out quite clean. Slice and serve. If any mixture is left and becomes cold spread with a little butter and use as bread.

Variation
Use 4–6 oz. (100–150 g.) chopped dates instead of currants and sultanas. Mix with cold tea instead of milk (this gives a very moist cake).

Cooking time: 1–1¼ hours
Preparation time: 10 minutes
Main cooking utensil: 2-lb. (1-kg.) loaf tin
Oven temperature: moderate (350–375°F., 180–190°C., Gas Mark 4–5)
Oven position: centre
Serves: 8–10

Honey, date and walnut cake and Honey loaf

Honey, date and walnut cake

Imperial	Metric
8 oz. plain flour	200 g. plain flour
3 teaspoons baking powder	3 teaspoons baking powder
4 oz. butter or margarine	100 g. butter or margarine
4 oz. castor sugar	100 g. castor sugar
4 oz. sliced stoned dates	100 g. sliced stoned dates
1 oz. chopped walnuts	25 g. chopped walnuts
2 eggs	2 eggs
4 tablespoons milk	4 tablespoons milk
2 tablespoons clear honey	2 tablespoons clear honey

1. Sieve dry ingredients, rub in butter.
2. Add the rest of the ingredients.
3. Pour into a greased tin.
4. Bake for time and at temperature given until firm.

Honey loaf

Imperial	Metric
8 oz. plain flour	200 g. plain flour
1 teaspoon baking powder	1 teaspoon baking powder
1 teaspoon cinnamon	1 teaspoon cinnamon
$\frac{1}{2}$ teaspoon salt	$\frac{1}{2}$ teaspoon salt
4 oz. brown sugar	100 g. brown sugar
$\frac{1}{2}$ pint milk	250 ml. milk
$\frac{1}{2}$ oz. butter	15 g. butter
8 oz. honey	200 g. honey

1. Sieve together the dry ingredients and add the sugar.
2. Warm the milk, butter and honey.
3. Stir on to the dry ingredients and beat well.
4. Put into a floured tin and bake for time and at temperature given until firm to the touch.
5. Serve sliced and spread with butter.

Cooking time: 1–1$\frac{1}{4}$ hours
Preparation time: 15 minutes
Main cooking utensils: 7-inch (18-cm.) square tin; saucepan, 2-lb. (1-kg.) loaf tin or shallow tin
Oven temperature: moderate (350–375°F., 180–190°C., Gas Mark 4–5)
Serves: 10–14

Rock buns

Imperial	Metric
8 oz. self-raising flour (with plain flour 2 level teaspoons baking powder)	200 g. self-raising flour (with plain flour 2 level teaspoons baking powder)
4 oz. lard	100 g. lard
4 oz. sugar	100 g. sugar
4 oz. dried fruit	100 g. dried fruit
1 egg	1 egg
milk to mix	milk to mix
little castor sugar	little castor sugar
Decoration:	*Decoration:*
little castor sugar	little castor sugar

1. Sieve the flour or flour and baking powder.
2. Rub in the lard until it resembles fine breadcrumbs, add the sugar and fruit.
3. Stir in the beaten egg and enough milk to make a sticky consistency.
4. Drop the mixture in small heaps on the greased trays, allowing room for cakes to spread during cooking; sprinkle with sugar lightly before baking.
5. Cook for time and at temperature given until crisp and golden brown.
6. Lift carefully on to a wire cooling tray for cakes are fragile when hot. Sprinkle with more sugar; eat with tea or coffee.

Note: A sticky mixture stands up in peaks when handled with a knife. A slow dropping consistency needs a shake to remove from spoon.

Variation
Add chopped peel, grated rind of fresh orange or lemon.

Cooking time: 12–15 minutes
Preparation time: 10 minutes
Main cooking utensils: 2 baking trays or sheets
Oven temperature: hot (425–450°F., 220–230°C., Gas Mark 7–8)
Oven position: above centre
Makes: 10–12 buns

Victoria sandwich

Imperial
4 oz. margarine or butter
4 oz. castor sugar
2 large eggs
4 oz. self-raising flour (or plain flour and 1 level teaspoon baking powder)
Filling:
3 tablespoons jam
Decoration:
castor or sieved icing sugar

Metric
125 g. margarine or butter
125 g. castor sugar
2 large eggs
125 g. self-raising flour (or plain flour and 1 level teaspoon baking powder)
Filling:
3 tablespoons jam
Decoration:
castor or sieved icing sugar

1. Cream the margarine or butter and sugar until soft and light.
2. Whisk eggs, beat gradually into the butter mixture, if the mixture shows signs of curdling add a little sieved flour.
3. Fold in the sieved flour with a metal spoon, taking care not to overhandle.
4. Put into greased and floured or lined tins.
5. Bake for time and at temperature given.
6. Test cakes before removing from oven. Press gently with finger, if no impression remains the cake is cooked.
7. Cool on a wire cooling tray, sandwich with jam, decorate with castor or icing sugar. In an airtight tin, this cake keeps well for several days.

Note: When baking always check oven temperatures with that recommended in your cooker instruction card or book.

Variations

Coffee sponge: Use 2 small eggs mixed with 1 tablespoon coffee essence.
Chocolate sponge: Use $3\frac{1}{2}$ oz. (110 g.) flour and $\frac{1}{2}$ oz. (15 g.) cocoa.

Cooking time: 20 minutes
Preparation time: 15 minutes
Main cooking utensils: 2 6-inch (15-cm.) sponge sandwich tins
Oven temperature: moderate (375°F., 190°C., Gas Mark 5)
Oven position: about 2 rungs from top of oven
Serves: 6

Surprise cake

Imperial
5 oz. butter
5 oz. castor sugar
3 eggs
8 oz. self-raising flour
4 oz. (1 packet) Chocolate Polka Dots (chocolate chips)
1 tablespoon milk
Icing:
4 oz. butter
$\frac{1}{2}$ teaspoon vanilla essence
3 tablespoons evaporated milk
4 oz. (1 packet) Chocolate Polka Dots (chocolate chips)
1 lb. sieved icing sugar

Metric
125 g. butter
125 g. castor sugar
3 eggs
200 g. self-raising flour
100 g. Chocolate Polka Dots (chocolate chips)
1 tablespoon milk
Icing:
100 g. butter
$\frac{1}{2}$ teaspoon vanilla essence
3 tablespoons evaporated milk
100 g. Chocolate Polka Dots (chocolate chips)
400 g. sieved icing sugar

1. Cream the butter and sugar until soft and light.
2. Gradually add the beaten eggs, stir in a little sieved flour if the mixture shows signs of curdling.
3. Fold in the sieved flour and the Chocolate Polka Dots, lightly dusted with flour, plus 1 tablespoon milk.
4. Put into the greased and floured cake tin, bake for time and at temperature given until the cake is firm to touch.
5. To make the icing, put all the ingredients except icing sugar into a basin or the top of a double saucepan over very hot water, heat until the chocolate is melted, allow to cool, then beat in the icing sugar.
6. Spread over the top and sides of the cake, then swirl with a small flat-bladed knife.

Note: When baking always check oven temperatures with that recommended in your cooker instruction card or book.

Cooking time: $1\frac{1}{4}$ hours
Preparation time: 30 minutes
Main cooking utensil: 7-inch (18-cm.) cake tin
Oven temperature: moderate (325–350°F., 170–180°C., Gas Mark 3–4)
Oven position: centre
Serves: 8–10

Speedy orange cake

Imperial
5 oz. sieved self-raising flour
4 oz. castor sugar
3 oz. shortening (lightened
   cooking fat)
2 eggs
1 tablespoon orange juice
grated rind of 1 orange

Metric
125 g. sieved self-raising flour
100 g. castor sugar
75 g. shortening (lightened
   cooking fat)
2 eggs
1 tablespoon orange juice
grated rind of 1 orange

1. Put all ingredients into a large mixing bowl and stir gently until softened then cream briskly for about 2 minutes until soft and light.
2. Put the mixture into a greased and floured cake tin and flatten the top.
3. Bake for time and at temperature given.
4. Test cake before removing from the oven. It is cooked when shrunk away from the tin and when no impression is left when it is pressed gently but firmly on top with the finger.
5. Turn out and cool on a wire tray. Serve cut in slices.

Note: This method of mixing is only suitable for modern shortening or quick creaming margarine. The same proportion of ingredients can be used with butter or ordinary margarine but it is then important to cream the butter and sugar in the usual way.

Variation
Use lemon rind and juice in place of orange.

Cooking time: 55 minutes
Preparation time: 10 minutes
Main cooking utensil: 6-inch (15-cm.) square or 7-inch (18-cm.) round cake tin
Oven temperature: moderate (350–375°F., 180–190°C., Gas Mark 4–5)
Oven position: centre
Serves: 8

Cherry cake

Imperial
4 oz. butter or margarine
4 oz. castor sugar
2 eggs
few drops vanilla essence
6 oz. plain flour
1 level teaspoon baking powder
3–4 oz. glacé cherries
1½ tablespoons milk

Metric
100 g. butter or margarine
100 g. castor sugar
2 eggs
few drops vanilla essence
150 g. plain flour
1 level teaspoon baking powder
75–100 g. glacé cherries
1½ tablespoons milk

1. Cream the butter and sugar until soft and light.
2. Whisk eggs and gradually beat them into the butter mixture, if the mixture shows signs of curdling add a little sieved flour.
3. Add vanilla essence, fold in sieved flour and baking powder gently with metal spoon.
4. Add the cherries. These should be halved or quartered and coated in flour. If very sticky they should be rinsed in cold water then dried to prevent them from sinking. Then add milk.
5. Put into the greased and floured or lined tin. Level the top.
6. Bake for time and at temperature given.
7. Test cake before removing from the tin. Ensure the cake has shrunk away from the sides of the tin and feels firm to the touch.

Variation
For a richer cake, use 5 oz. (125 g.) butter and 5 oz. (125 g.) sugar, 4 oz. (100 g.) glacé cherries, 2 oz. (50 g.) ground almonds and 6 oz. (150 g.) plain flour, and 3 eggs and no milk.

Cooking time: 1¼–1½ hours
Preparation time: 15 minutes
Main cooking utensil: 6- or 7-inch (15- or 18-cm.) cake tin
Oven temperature: very moderate (325–350°F., 170–180°C., Gas Mark 3–4)
Oven position: centre
Serves: 8–10

Sponge cake

Imperial
2 large eggs
2–3 oz. castor sugar
2 oz. flour (plain can be used
with no baking powder or
with ½ level teaspoon, or use
self-raising flour)
1 dessertspoon hot water
Coating:
little butter
shaking of flour or flour and
castor sugar

Metric
2 large eggs
50–75 g. castor sugar
50 g. flour (plain can be used
with no baking powder or
with ½ level teaspoon, or use
self-raising flour)
1 dessertspoon hot water
Coating:
little butter
shaking of flour or flour and
castor sugar

1. Put the eggs and sugar into a large mixing bowl, and whisk until the mixture is thick and creamy (you see the trail of the whisk). If done over hot water continue beating until the mixture cools again.
2. Sieve the flour at least once.
3. Fold gently into the egg mixture with a metal spoon. Lastly fold in the water.
4. Grease the tin lightly, then coat with flour or an equal mixture of flour and castor sugar.
5. Spoon the mixture carefully into the tin.
6. Bake for time and at temperature given.
7. Test cake before removing from the oven – press with finger, if no impression remains the cake is cooked.
8. Turn the cake out carefully, allowing it 1 minute to cool in the tin. Split and fill with jam or cream.

Variation
Bake in 2 6-inch (15-cm.) sandwich tins towards top of moderately hot oven (400°F., 200°C., Gas Mark 6) for approximately 8–9 minutes.

Cooking time: 20 minutes
Preparation time: 10–15 minutes
Main cooking utensil: 6- to 7-inch (15- to 18-cm.) cake tin
Oven temperature: moderate (375°F., 190°C., Gas Mark 5)
Oven position: centre
Serves: 5–6

Dreamy Swiss roll

Imperial
3 large eggs
3–4 oz. castor sugar
3 oz. flour (plain or self-raising)
1 tablespoon hot water
Filling:
4–6 tablespoons warm
strawberry jam or defrosted
or well drained canned
strawberries
Coating:
1 packet dream topping
6–7 tablespoons milk
To decorate:
1–2 tablespoons jam or few
well drained strawberries

Metric
3 large eggs
75–100 g. castor sugar
75 g. flour (plain or self-raising)
1 tablespoon hot water
Filling:
4–6 tablespoons warm
strawberry jam or defrosted
or well drained canned
strawberries
Coating:
1 packet dream topping
6–7 tablespoons milk
To decorate:
1–2 tablespoons jam or few
well drained strawberries

1. Put the eggs and sugar into a large mixing bowl, and whisk until the mixture is thick and creamy (you see the trail of the whisk); if done over hot water, continue beating until the mixture cools again.
2. Sieve the flour at least once.
3. Fold gently into the egg mixture with a metal spoon. Lastly, fold in the water.
4. Pour into the lined, greased tin.
5. Bake for time and temperature given.
6. Test before removing from oven – press with finger, if no impression remains, the cake is cooked.
7. Turn on to sugared paper, spread with jam or strawberries, roll firmly.
8. For the coating, whisk the dream topping into cold milk until fluffy and thick, spread over the cold Swiss roll.
9. Decorate with jam or strawberries.

Cooking time: 7–10 minutes
Preparation time: 15 minutes
Main cooking utensil: lined Swiss roll tin
Oven temperature: moderately hot to hot (400–425°F., 200–220°C., Gas Mark 6–7)
Oven position: near top
Serves: 8

Baking for all occasions

In this chapter you will find cakes that are suitable for most occasions.

For example a plain Victoria sandwich can become a very special Mother's day cake, see recipe below. This same mixture would be ideal for a children's party cake, for it can be baked 1–2 days ahead and iced, so there is no last-minute rush. For small babies the even lighter sponge cake, opposite, would be ideal. Cover with a soft glacé icing, made by blending icing sugar with water or fruit juice to moisten. Pour this over the cake and decorate in a suitable way.

For very special occasions, i.e. Christmas, adult's birthday cakes or even wedding cakes, you will find the rich fruit cake on page 186 is ideal. There are suggestions for decorating it on the same page. A rich cake like this keeps for some weeks, indeed it improves with keeping, so you can prepare this well ahead of the special occasion.

A rich gâteau is not only served for tea, but it is excellent for a dessert and there are several in this book (see pages 187 and 195). Remember cakes freeze well, so if you have a home freezer prepare the cake, decorate and use within 6 weeks. Handle carefully so you do not harm the decoration. Do not freeze rich fruit cakes.

Some designs for cakes

Turn a simple cake into an interesting celebration one. If you have made a round cake it could become:

A glamorous hat: Coat the cake with pretty coloured icing. Make a frill of ruffled paper or ribbon for the brim. Add piped flowers and a ribbon decoration.

A circus ring: Coat the cake with icing. Make a round of coloured cardboard for the roof of the 'Big Top', secure to the centre of the cake by sticking it to a barley sugar stick. Have a parade of toy clowns and animals round the edge of the top of the cake.

A drum: Build up a narrow rim round the top of the cake with marzipan, coat whole cake with icing. Pipe bands of gay colours round the sides of cake, put two drumsticks of marzipan or barley sugar on top.

A ballet ring: Decorate the iced cake with piped flowers to make it look very pretty and feminine, then add small ballet figures.

A parcel: Coat a square or oblong cake in icing, then pipe the 'string' in another colour. Pipe the address and greetings on top.

A book: Shape the short ends of an oblong cake to look like an opened book. Coat with icing, pipe on greetings then complete with a ribbon book-mark.

Mother's day cake

Imperial	Metric
4 oz. margarine	125 g. margarine
4 oz. castor sugar	125 g. castor sugar
grated rind of 1 lemon	grated rind of 1 lemon
2 eggs	2 eggs
4 oz. self-raising flour	125 g. self-raising flour
Lemon icing:	*Lemon icing:*
4 oz. margarine	125 g. margarine
12 oz. sieved icing sugar	350 g. sieved icing sugar
good 2 tablespoons lemon juice	good 2 tablespoons lemon juice
Decoration:	*Decoration:*
yellow colouring	yellow colouring
cake board	cake board
1 rose spray	1 rose spray
band ribbon	band ribbon

1. Cream the margarine and sugar until soft and light, with the lemon rind.
2. Gradually beat in the eggs, adding a little sieved flour if the mixture shows signs of curdling.
3. Fold in the rest of the flour; if the eggs are small add 1 dessertspoon water (lemon juice could be used).
4. Put into the greased and floured tins and bake for time and at temperature given, until firm to the touch.
5. Turn out and allow to cool.
6. To make the icing, cream the margarine and half the sugar until soft, add the remaining icing sugar with the lemon juice, beat again. Save some for piping.
7. Use a little icing to sandwich the cakes together, put the remainder into a basin over a pan of hot water, beat until smooth, glossy and soft.
8. Pour over the cake and allow to set.
9. Tint the small amount of icing left a deeper colour and pipe the word MOTHER. Lift on to a cake board, put rose and ribbon in position.

Cooking time: 20 minutes
Preparation time: 40 minutes
Main cooking utensils: 2 7-inch (18-cm.) sandwich tins, basin,
    No. 1 or 2 writing pipe, icing syringe or greaseproof paper bag
Oven temperature: moderate (375°F., 190°C., Gas Mark 5)
Oven position: second rung from top
Serves: 8–10

Making a rich fruit cake

The cake recipe below is suitable for keeping for some weeks before icing. To give a very moist texture, prick the cooked cake at 10-day intervals and soak with a little sherry, brandy or rum.

First prepare the cake tin

Take a 9-inch (23-cm.) square or a 10-inch (26-cm.) round cake tin. Cut a round of brown paper and two rounds of greaseproof paper to fit the base. Cut a double round of greaseproof paper to fit round the inside. Snip the base of this band at regular intervals, so it fits flat at the bottom. Press the band into the cake tin, then add the brown paper and then the greaseproof paper rounds. Grease lightly. Tie a deep band of brown paper round the outside of the cake tin.

You will notice I have given the more accurate metric measures rather than working on the accepted 25 g. as being equivalent to 1 oz. This is to give you the same sized cake, whether you use Imperial or metric measures.

Do not overbeat this particular cake mixture, for it is not a light cake, like a sponge. Plain flour with no raising agent can be used in the cake.

To make and bake a rich cake

Cream 10 oz. (280 g.) butter, 10 oz. (280 g.) moist brown sugar, the finely grated rind of 1 lemon and 1 orange, and 1 tablespoon black treacle.

Beat 6 eggs with 2 tablespoons sherry or brandy and gradually blend into the creamed mixture.

Sieve 12 oz. (340 g.) plain flour, 1 teaspoon mixed spice, $\frac{1}{2}$ teaspoon ground cinnamon and 1 oz. (25 g.) ground almonds; stir into the butter and egg mixture.

Add 3 lb. (scant $1\frac{1}{2}$ kg.) mixed dried fruit, 6 oz. (170 g.) chopped glacé cherries, 6 oz. (170 g.) chopped blanched almonds and 6 oz. (170 g.) chopped candied peel. Stir into the cake mixture gently and carefully.

Spoon the mixture into the prepared cake tin, see above. Smooth the mixture on top and press gently with damp, but not too wet, knuckles. This helps to keep the cake flat on top and also prevents it becoming hardened with baking.

Bake for approximately $4\frac{1}{4}$–$4\frac{1}{2}$ hours in the centre of the oven. Allow 1 hour at a very moderate heat (325 °F., 160 °C., Gas Mark 3). Lower the heat to slow, (275–300 °F., 140–150 °C., Gas Mark 1–2) and continue the cooking. Check carefully and lower the heat if the cake is becoming too brown. Test as page 180 (under Family fruit cake), then follow another test. Listen carefully, an uncooked rich cake makes a distinct 'hum'. Cool in the tin; turn out when cold.

To marzipan a rich fruit cake

The usual coating for a rich fruit cake is a layer of marzipan and two layers of royal icing.

If preferred you can use a lighter fondant-type icing and details of this are given below.

First brush away any surplus crumbs from the cake, make sure it is quite level on top. It often is a good idea to turn the cake upside-down and use the base as the top, since this is 100 per cent flat.

Coat the cake with sieved apricot jam or egg white before putting on the marzipan.

To make enough marzipan to coat the top and sides of the 9–10 inch (23–26-cm.) cake:

Mix together 1 lb. (scant $\frac{1}{2}$ kg.) ground almonds, 8 oz. (220 g.) sieved icing and 8 oz. (220 g.) castor sugar, a few drops almond essence and the yolks of 4 large eggs. Roll out on a lightly sugared board, then make into a round or square large enough to coat the cake, or cut a round or square for the top and a band to go round the sides of the cake. If using the latter method with a round cake, roll the cake on the band of marzipan so it adheres to this, then press on the top round.

Neaten the marzipan coating by rolling lightly and quickly with a rolling-pin or use a jam jar to neaten the sides of the cake.

To ice a rich fruit cake

Before icing the cake, decide whether you want to leave the marzipan for 48 hours to dry out. I dislike this method, for the marzipan is nicer if moist, but if it has been handled a lot the oil from the ground almonds will soak through the icing. I prefer to paint the marzipan with egg white and ice at once.

To coat the top and sides of the cake with two coats and to allow some icing for piping you should:
Whisk 7 egg whites lightly; add 2–3 tablespoons lemon juice, then gradually beat in $3\frac{1}{2}$ lb. ($1\frac{3}{4}$ kg.) sieved icing sugar. Beat until smooth, white and shiny, do *not* overbeat. For a softer icing add $\frac{1}{2}$–1 tablespoon glycerine. Take out a third of the mixture, cover the rest with a damp cloth, so it does not harden. Spread the icing over the top and sides of the cake, then neaten with long sweeping movements, using a warm palette knife. Allow to dry, then repeat with some of the remaining icing. When this is quite dry, you can pipe round the sides and any design you require on the top of the cake.

For a Christmas snow effect sweep up the icing in peaks with the tip of a knife.

For a softer fondant icing use 1 egg white to 1 lb. ($\frac{1}{2}$ kg.) icing sugar, plus the glycerine and lemon juice. This is not suitable for piping or wedding cakes, but stands up in peaks for a snow effect.

Festive cream gâteau

Imperial	Metric
6 oz. butter or margarine	150 g. butter or margarine
6 oz. castor sugar	150 g. castor sugar
2–3 drops vanilla essence	2–3 drops vanilla essence
3 eggs	3 eggs
6 oz. self-raising flour	150 g. self-raising flour
2 tablespoons hot water	2 tablespoons hot water
Filling and topping:	*Filling and topping:*
½ pint double cream	250 ml. double cream
4 tablespoons rose hip syrup	4 tablespoons rose hip syrup
Decoration:	*Decoration:*
5–6 tablespoons lightly toasted desiccated coconut	5–6 tablespoons lightly toasted desiccated coconut
few segments mandarin orange	few segments mandarin orange
a few halved walnuts	a few halved walnuts

1. Cream the butter or margarine and sugar until soft and light, adding the essence.
2. Gradually beat in the eggs, adding a little sieved flour if the mixture shows signs of curdling.
3. Fold in the flour and hot water.
4. Line the tin with greaseproof paper, make sure this stands above the top of the tin to support the cake.
5. Bake for time and at temperature given until firm to the touch.
6. Cool, cut into 3 strips.
7. Whip the cream lightly, then gradually add the rose hip syrup, taking care not to overbeat.
8. Sandwich the layers together with some of the rose hip cream.
9. Coat sides of the cake with the cream and roll in the coconut.
10. Top with cream, mandarin orange segments and walnuts and pipe rosettes of cream on top if wished. Serve as a special cake for tea or instead of a sweet.

Cooking time: 30 minutes
Preparation time: 35 minutes
Main cooking utensils: 12- by 8-inch (30- by 20-cm.) Swiss roll tin, greaseproof paper
Oven temperature: moderate (375°F., 190°C., Gas Mark 5)
Oven position: just above centre
Serves: 10–12

Midsummer gâteau

Imperial	Metric
3 eggs	3 eggs
4 oz. castor sugar	100 g. castor sugar
2½ oz. self-raising flour (or plain flour with ½ teaspoon baking powder)	65 g. self-raising flour (or plain flour with ½ teaspoon baking powder)
½ oz. cocoa	15 g. cocoa
Filling:	*Filling:*
½ pint thick cream	250 ml. thick cream
12 oz.–1 lb. strawberries	350–450 g. strawberries
little sugar	little sugar

1. Whisk the eggs and sugar until thick. Fold in the sieved dry ingredients.
2. Pour into the well greased and floured or lined sandwich tins.
3. Bake for time given – the 7-inch (18-cm.) cakes take a few minutes less than the deeper 6-inch (15-cm.) cakes.
4. Test to see if cooked – when cooked they should be firm to the touch.
5. Turn out carefully and cool.
6. Split each cake through the centre.
7. Whip the cream until it holds its shape, but is not too stiff.
8. Spread between the cakes with the sliced or halved fruit and sugar to taste.
9. Top with the cream and whole strawberries and serve as a dessert or for tea.

Variation

Use 3 oz. (75 g.) flour and omit the cocoa. Fill with other fresh or well drained canned or frozen fruits as available.

Cooking time: 15–20 minutes
Preparation time: 25–30 minutes
Main cooking utensils: two 6-inch (15-cm.) sandwich tins (rather deep ones) or two 7-inch (18-cm.) shallow tins
Oven temperature: moderately hot (375–400°F., 190–200°C., Gas Mark 5–6)
Oven position: above centre

Catering for parties

The following pages give recipes for all kinds of parties, from dinner parties to barbecues.

Christmas catering

One of the most important family celebrations is at Christmas time, and as poultry is the favourite at this time you should consult pages 90 to 101 and page 198. A home-made Christmas pudding recipe is on page 199 and the rich fruit cake, together with directions for icing this, on page 186. Make both cake and pudding well before the Christmas party so they mature in flavour.

Freezing food for parties

If you have a freezer use this wisely, so you can prepare much of the food beforehand, and avoid the last-minute panic so often associated with entertaining. At the beginning of each major section you will find information on freezing. If you consult these pages they will help you to select the dishes to make ahead.

Do not imagine you must spend an undue amount of money or excessive time in preparing party food. The Easy Guide to entertaining will help you choose the right dishes for the time and money available on that particular occasion.

Easy guide to entertaining

The dishes below are specially suitable for entertaining and have been divided into savoury and sweet recipes. (These are additional to those in this chapter.)

If you are short of time

choose the savoury dishes on these pages: 9, 10, 11, 13, 14, 15, 40, 189, 190, 191, 192.
choose the sweet dishes on these pages: 160, 162, 164, 165, 205.

If you are short of money

choose the savoury dishes on these pages: 12, 14, 16, 17, 37, 40, 41, 62, 63.
choose the sweet dishes on these pages: 157, 158, 160, 161.

If you and your guests are slimming

choose the savoury dishes on these pages: 9, 10, 15, 40, 58, 59, 191.
choose the sweet dishes on these pages: 185, 187.

In addition to the dishes in this special section,

look at special savoury dishes on pages 11, 12, 15, 16, 17, 28, 29, 30, 31, 39, 40, 41, 42, 43, 44, 45, 49, 50, 51, 53, 58–61, 67–69, 71–73, 76, 80, 81, 82, 89, 92–101, 105, 108–112, 115, 117, 118, 148, 149.
Look at special sweet dishes on pages 144, 145, 153, 157, 158, 161, 162, 163, 167, 168, 169, 178, 182, 183, 184, 185, 186, 187.

Cheese straws

Imperial	Metric
8 oz. plain flour	200 g. plain flour
good pinch salt	good pinch salt
shake pepper	shake pepper
pinch dry mustard	pinch dry mustard
shake celery salt	shake celery salt
5 oz. butter	125 g. butter
4 oz. firm Cheddar cheese, very finely grated	100 g. firm Cheddar cheese, very finely grated
2 egg yolks	2 egg yolks
To glaze:	*To glaze:*
2 egg whites	2 egg whites

1. Sieve the flour and seasonings.
2. Rub in the butter until the mixture resembles fine breadcrumbs; add the cheese.
3. Bind with egg yolks, knead lightly.
4. Roll out firmly, but gently on a lightly floured board until about a ¼ inch (½ cm.) in thickness.
5. Cut into very narrow fingers.
6. Re-roll any pastry left and make into rings and extra fingers.
7. Put on to lightly greased baking trays and brush with the lightly beaten egg white.
8. Bake until crisp and golden brown.
9. As these are very fragile allow to cool on the baking tray for a few minutes, then transfer to a wire tray to finish cooling.
10. Serve the straws through the rings or place in tall glasses. These are ideal to serve at a cocktail party.

Note: Store in an airtight tin.

Variations

Cut the straws a little thicker, then twist before baking. Or, when cooled dip each end in mayonnaise, or one end in paprika pepper and the other in finely chopped parsley.

Cooking time: 8–10 minutes
Preparation time: 15 minutes
Main cooking utensils: baking trays
Oven temperature: hot (425–450°F., 220–230°C., Gas Mark 7–8)
Oven position: near top
Makes: approximately 48

Interesting dips

A savoury dip makes an excellent celebration dish. It can be served with a variety of foods, e.g., potato crisps, small biscuits, tiny carrots, pieces of celery, raw cauliflower. Quantities below make a good-sized bowlful which will serve about 8.

Commercial flavourings for dips: It is possible to buy excellent dehydrated flavourings for dips, e.g., green onion, etc., and these can be blended with a cottage cheese dip, as below, to give a different flavour. Following the directions on the packet, add the dip flavouring to the recipes below.

Cottage cheese dip
Blend 12 oz. (300 g.) cottage cheese with ¼ pint (125 ml.) dairy soured cream, 3–4 tablespoons mayonnaise and the dip flavouring. If you find the mixture a little too thick, blend in a little extra cream or mayonnaise; add a little brandy or sherry to taste.

Cheddar cheese dip
Grate 1 lb. (½ kg.) Cheddar cheese, blend with ¼ pint (150 ml.) thick and ¼ pint (150 ml.) thin cream, seasoning, 3 tablespoons diced gherkins and 3 tablespoons chopped olives. Dip flavourings may be added if wished. A little port gives an excellent flavour.

Avocado and cheese dip
Use either of the previous recipes and add the pulp from 1 large ripe avocado pear. Do not cut the pear until ready to use as the flesh discolours easily. The dip flavourings may also be added if wished.

Canapés and open sandwiches

Cocktail snacks
Spear the following with cocktail sticks:
1. Emmenthal in fancy shapes (cut with a pastry cutter), dipped in paprika, topped with a slice of gherkin and a pearl onion.
2. Sliver of red pepper wrapped around the top of a piece of Gruyère and then a pearl onion.
3. Gruyère with a stuffed olive.
4. Layers of Sbrinz (see note), each spread with herb butter (see note) or herby cottage cheese, and topped with a rosette of herb butter.
5. Gruyère with a piece of pineapple dipped in curry powder.
6. Gruyère with a black olive.
7. Slices of Gruyère with slices of pimento topped with a gherkin slice.
8. Emmenthal with a slice of candied lime or orange peel.
9. Slices of Gruyère with slices of gherkin, topped with a rolled anchovy.
10. Gruyère with a slice of preserved apricot.
11. Gruyère with a slice of mushroom.
12. Gruyère with a preserved or maraschino cherry.

Open cheese sandwiches
Spread butter on thinly sliced bread and add a thin layer of mustard or mayonnaise. Cover with slices of Emmenthal or Gruyère cheese, cut to the shape of the bread. Garnish with tomatoes, slices of hard-boiled egg, gherkins and olives.

Cheese-butter canapés
Blend equal quantities of butter and grated Swiss cheese (see note), season and spread, or pipe on $\frac{1}{4}$-inch ($\frac{1}{2}$-cm.) thick slices of bread.

Note: You can put cheese spread into three bowls and vary the basic flavour with chopped herbs, tomato purée or caraway seeds. Sbrinz is a hard cheese, if unobtainable, use Parmesan. For herb butter, blend chopped herbs with butter.

Mixed hors d'oeuvre

A simple selection of ingredients, as in the picture, make a delicious hors d'oeuvre.

All foods should have dressing with them, so no extra oil or vinegar or mayonnaise need be served.

Russian salad
Mix cooked diced fresh vegetables or canned vegetables or frozen vegetables with mayonnaise. To make a more unusual salad, chopped hard-boiled eggs and chopped ham may be blended with the vegetables.

Salami
A selection of salami should be sliced neatly; rings of raw onion and watercress sprigs are a colourful garnish.

Potato salad
Dice cooked potatoes while hot, mix with mayonnaise and grated raw onion or chopped spring onion or chives. Chopped parsley, diced gherkin, capers may also be included and a garnish of paprika pepper and chopped parsley give colour.

Gherkins, sliced cucumber tossed in French dressing, sliced or whole stuffed, green or black olives are generally included.

Rollmop or Bismarck herrings, bought in jars if wished, should be topped with rings of raw onion.

Egg mayonnaise
Coat whole or halved hard-boiled eggs with mayonnaise, top with chopped parsley and paprika pepper; or fill the whites of hard-boiled eggs with shrimps, prawns, crab meat, etc., blended with mayonnaise and topped with sieved egg yolk.

Cheese puffs

Imperial	Metric
8 oz. frozen puff pastry	200 g. frozen puff pastry
2 oz. grated Parmesan cheese	50 g. grated Parmesan cheese
1 egg white	1 egg white

1. Roll out the pastry until paper thin.
2. Sprinkle with most of the cheese, fold in three, roll out again until $\frac{1}{8}$ inch ($\frac{1}{4}$ cm.) thick.
3. Cut into $\frac{1}{2}$-inch (1-cm.) strips about 3 inches ($7\frac{1}{2}$ cm.) in length, brush with egg white, top with the rest of the cheese.
4. Bake for about 12 minutes above the centre of the hot oven.

Cheese rolls

Imperial	Metric
9 large wafer-thin slices bread	9 large wafer-thin slices bread
3 oz. cream cheese	75 g. cream cheese
1 oz. grated Parmesan cheese	25 g. grated Parmesan cheese
seasoning	seasoning
1 tablespoon chopped chives	1 tablespoon chopped chives
little butter	little butter

1. Halve the slices of bread, remove the crusts.
2. Mix the cream and grated cheeses, add the seasoning and chives, spread over the bread. Roll, secure with cocktail sticks.
3. Brush with melted butter, bake for 2—3 minutes in the centre of the hot oven.

Mushroom croûtes

Fry 18 small rounds of bread in $1\frac{1}{2}$ oz. (40 g.) butter. Drain well and put in an ovenproof dish. Fry 18 mushroom caps and stalks in another $1\frac{1}{2}$ oz. (40 g.) butter. Put the caps on the bread, fill with 4 oz. (100 g.) cream cheese and put the stalks in the centre. Heat for a few minutes in the oven.

Cooking time: see method
Preparation time: for 3 recipes 50 minutes
Main cooking utensils: 2 baking trays, frying pan, ovenproof dish
Oven temperature: hot (450—475°F., 230—240°C., Gas Mark 8–9)
Oven position: see methods
Makes: about $3\frac{1}{2}$ dozen savouries

Imperial	Metric
2 large or 4 medium-sized crabs	2 large or 4 medium-sized crabs
$\frac{1}{4}$ cucumber	$\frac{1}{4}$ cucumber
2 apples	2 apples
$\frac{1}{4}$ pint mayonnaise	125 ml. mayonnaise
grated rind and juice of 1 lemon	grated rind and juice of 1 lemon
black pepper	black pepper
Garnish:	*Garnish:*
sliced cucumber	sliced cucumber

1. Pull the claws from the crabs, crack them and remove the meat. Open the body shell, remove the inedible stomach bag and the grey fingers where the smaller claws join the body.
2. Peel and dice the cucumber and mix with the crab meat.
3. Core and dice the apples; if they are a good colour do not peel them. Blend the apples with the cucumber and crab meat and mix in the mayonnaise, lemon rind and juice and a sprinkling of black pepper.
4. Serve in a shallow dish, topped with sliced cucumber, with a green or mixed salad. This dish is ideal for a buffet party.

Crab ramekins

Prepare 1 large or 2 medium-sized crabs as above. Heat 2 oz. (50 g.) butter, fry a small chopped onion and 4 oz. (100 g.) sliced mushrooms. Blend in 1 oz. (25 g.) flour, cook for several minutes, add $\frac{1}{2}$ pint (250 ml.) milk, bring to the boil and cook until thickened. Season well, add 4 medium-sized, cooked, diced potatoes and flaked crab meat. Put into 4 individual dishes, top with 2 oz. (50 g.) breadcrumbs mixed with 2 oz. (50 g.) melted butter. Bake for about 15 minutes in a moderately hot oven (400°F., 200°C., Gas Mark 6) until crisp and golden.

Preparation time: 15 minutes
Serves: 6—8

Paella

Imperial	Metric
2 tablespoons oil	2 tablespoons oil
1 chopped onion	1 chopped onion
3 skinned tomatoes	3 skinned tomatoes
3–4 oz. long-grain rice	75–100 g. long-grain rice
pinch saffron powder	pinch saffron powder
1 pint chicken stock	550 ml. chicken stock
seasoning	seasoning
1 small green pepper	1 small green pepper
¾–1 lb. white fish, preferably skate or other firm-textured fish	300–400 g. white fish, preferably skate or other firm-textured fish
4–5 oz. prawns	100–125 g. prawns
Garnish:	*Garnish:*
few prawns in their shells	few prawns in their shells
chopped parsley	chopped parsley

1. Heat the oil in a large frying pan; fry the finely chopped onion and large pieces of tomato for a few minutes.
2. Add the rice, turn in the oil, then add the saffron blended with the chicken stock. Season well.
3. Simmer gently for 5–10 minutes.
4. Add the chopped green pepper, removing seeds and core, and the pieces of fish.
5. Cook until both fish and rice are soft.
6. Add the prawns, heat for a few minutes only.
7. Garnish with prawns and parsley. Serve with salad.

Variation

A more authentic paella is made by adding 1–2 crushed cloves of garlic, tiny pieces of uncooked chicken in place of white fish, and mussels and lobster as well as prawns.

Cooking time: 25–30 minutes
Preparation time: 15 minutes
Main cooking utensil: frying pan
Serves: 4

Stuffed pork pâté

Imperial	Metric
2 lb. raw pork	1 kg. raw pork
1 onion	1 onion
2 cloves garlic	2 cloves garlic
2–3 tablespoons fresh parsley	2–3 tablespoons fresh parsley
salt	salt
black pepper	black pepper
4 small eggs	4 small eggs
Stuffing:	*Stuffing:*
4 oz. stoned prunes	100 g. stoned prunes
4 oz. cooked ham	100 g. cooked ham
4 oz. Gouda cheese	100 g. Gouda cheese
Topping:	*Topping:*
6 oz. Gouda cheese	150 g. Gouda cheese
watercress	watercress

1. Put the pork, onion and garlic through a mincer, mince or chop the parsley.
2. Mix the meat, onion, garlic and parsley well together.
3. Season generously with salt and freshly ground black pepper.
4. Beat the eggs and stir them into the mixture.
5. Line the tin with half the mixture.
6. Fill the centre with the stuffing of chopped prunes, ham and diced cheese. Cover with the remaining meat.
7. Lay greased foil on top and bake for the time and temperature given, standing the tin of pâté in a dish of cold water.
8. Turn out on to a hot ovenproof dish, top with sliced cheese and place under the grill, or in a very hot oven, till the cheese melts and colours. Garnish with watercress and serve hot with green salad and hot toast.

Variation

Omit the cheese from the filling and topping and serve the pâté cold.

Cooking time: 2 hours
Preparation time: 20 minutes
Main cooking utensil: 2-lb. (1-kg.) loaf tin
Oven temperature: very moderate (325–350°F., 170–180°C., Gas Mark 3–4)
Oven position: centre
Serves: 10–12

Boeuf en croûte

Imperial

Pastry:
12 oz. plain flour
pinch salt
4 oz. butter or fat
¼ pint water
Forcemeat:
1 tablespoon olive oil
1 clove garlic
1 large onion or 2 shallots
good pinch finely chopped
    fresh tarragon or pinch
    dried tarragon
8 oz. pork sausage meat
Filling:
1½–2 lb. fillet or rump steak
    in one piece
Glaze:
1 egg
Garnish:
watercress

Metric

Pastry:
300 g. plain flour
pinch salt
100 g. butter or fat
125 ml. water
Forcemeat:
1 tablespoon olive oil
1 clove garlic
1 large onion or 2 shallots
good pinch finely chopped
    fresh tarragon or pinch
    dried tarragon
200 g. pork sausage meat
Filling:
¾–1 kg. fillet or rump steak
    in one piece
Glaze:
1 egg
Garnish:
watercress

1 Sieve the flour and salt into a bowl. Melt the butter or fat with the water, pour this over the flour, knead together and keep warm until ready to roll out.

2. Heat the oil, fry the finely chopped or crushed garlic and chopped onion in this, add the herbs and sausage meat.

3. Roll out the pastry, spread with the forcemeat, then lay the steak on top and wrap the pastry round it; seal the ends.

4. Decorate with pastry leaves, made from the trimmings. Brush with beaten egg.

5. Lift on to a lightly greased baking tray, bake for 25 minutes in a hot oven, then lower the heat. For rare steak, allow an extra 25 minutes, for well done steak, either cook the steak for 25 minutes before putting it on the pastry or allow a further 40–45 minutes. Garnish with watercress when cold.

Cooking time: see stage 5
Preparation time: 25 minutes
Main cooking utensils: saucepan, baking tray
Oven temperature: hot (425–450°F., 220–230°C., Gas Mark 7–8)
    then moderate (375°F., 190°C., Gas Mark 5)
Oven position: centre
Serves: 6–8

Kulibyaka

Imperial

Flaky pastry:
12 oz. plain flour
pinch salt
4 oz. lard
4–5 oz. margarine
cold water to mix
Filling:
8 oz. sole or other white fish
3 oz. cooked rice
1 chopped hard-boiled egg
1 onion
2 oz. sliced mushrooms
3 oz. melted butter
seasoning

Metric

Flaky pastry:
300 g. plain flour
pinch salt
100 g. lard
100–125 g. margarine
cold water to mix
Filling:
200 g. sole or other white fish
75 g. cooked rice
1 chopped hard-boiled egg
1 onion
50 g. sliced mushrooms
75 g. melted butter
seasoning

1. Sieve the flour and salt, divide the fats into three.

2. Rub in one third, bind with water to give a soft elastic dough.

3. Roll out to an oblong.

4. Put half the fat in small dabs over two thirds of the dough, bring up the plain part and bring down the top, making a closed 'envelope'. Turn at right angles, seal the ends and roll out; repeat with the remaining fat and fold, seal and roll once more. Roll into an oblong 16 by 8 inches (40 by 20 cm.).

5. Cook and flake the fish, spread it over half the pastry and cover with the rice, egg and seasoning.

6. Fry the finely chopped onion and mushrooms in 1 oz. (25 g.) butter, add to the filling, season well. Fold over the pastry to make a square, seal the edges and make slashes on top.

7. Bake for 25 minutes then lower the heat for the final 15 minutes if the pastry is becoming too brown.

8. Lift on to a serving dish, brush with melted butter and pour any excess butter through one of the slits on top. Serve hot.

Cooking time: 40 minutes
Preparation time: 35 minutes
Main cooking utensil: baking tray or sheet
Oven temperature: hot (425–450°F., 220–230°C., Gas Mark 7–8)
    then moderate (375°F., 190°C., Gas Mark 5)
Oven position: centre
Serves 4–6

Moussaka

Imperial	Metric
3 oz. butter	75 g. butter
8 oz. onions	200 g. onions
2 large aubergines	2 large aubergines
1–1½ lb. potatoes	½–¾ kg. potatoes
Sauce:	*Sauce:*
1 oz. butter	25 g. butter
1 oz. flour	25 g. flour
½ pint milk	250 ml. milk
seasoning	seasoning
2–3 oz. cheese	50–75 g. cheese
1 egg	1 egg
1 lb. minced meat	½ kg. minced meat
2–4 tomatoes	2–4 tomatoes
Garnish:	*Garnish:*
parsley	parsley

1. Heat the butter and fry the sliced onions until tender but not broken.
2. Remove the onions from the butter, then fry sliced aubergines and thinly sliced potatoes turning until well coated.
3. Make the sauce, heat the butter, then add the flour and cook for several minutes, remove from the heat, then gradually add the milk, stirring.
4. Bring to the boil and cook, stirring, until thickened and smooth; add seasoning and the grated cheese and beaten egg – do not cook again.
5. Arrange a layer of the aubergine mixture in the dish, top with the well-seasoned meat, onion, and sliced tomato.
6. Put a small amount of sauce on each layer and continue filling the dish ending with a layer of sauce.
7. Cover with lid and cook for 1½ hours. (Remove the lid for the last 30 minutes, to allow the top to brown.)
8. Serve garnished with parsley.

Cooking time: 2–2½ hours
Preparation time: 35 minutes
Main cooking utensils: large frying pan, covered casserole
Oven temperature: very moderate (325–350°F., 170–180°C., Gas Mark 3–4)
Oven position: centre
Serves: 4–6

Beef stroganoff

Imperial	Metric
1¼–1½ lb. fillet of beef	about ¾ kg. fillet of beef
seasoning	seasoning
2 small onions	2 small onions
3 oz. butter	75 g. butter
3–4 oz. mushrooms	75–100 g. mushrooms
¼ pint smetana (soured cream, see note)	125 ml. smetana (soured cream, see note)
1 dessertspoon flour	1 dessertspoon flour
pinch mustard	pinch mustard
little extra smetana	little extra smetana
Garnish:	*Garnish:*
parsley	parsley

1. Cut the meat into thin strips 2 inches (5 cm.) long and season.
2. Fry the chopped onion in hot butter until golden coloured.
3. Add the sliced mushrooms to the onions and add the meat and fry for 5 minutes.
4. Blend the smetana with the flour and mustard and pour into the pan.
5. Stir well, cover the pan, simmer gently for 10 minutes until the meat is tender.
6. Add more smetana before serving with rice or creamed potatoes and a green salad. Garnish with parsley.

Note: If smetana is not available use fresh cream soured with 1 tablespoon lemon juice.

Variations
2 tablespoons brandy can be added to the sauce at stage 6.
1 tablespoon tomato purée can be added at stage 4.

Cooking time: 25 minutes
Preparation time: 15 minutes
Main cooking utensil: large covered saucepan
Serves: 4–5

Pineapple fruit salad

Imperial
1 large pineapple
about 1 lb. mixed fruits, grapes,
  fresh or frozen raspberries
  or strawberries, blackberries,
  segments of orange, diced
  ripe pears
Syrup:
approximately ¼ pint white
  wine
1 tablespoon honey
2 tablespoons Kirsch

Metric
1 large pineapple
about ½ kg. mixed fruits, grapes,
  fresh or frozen raspberries
  or strawberries, blackberries,
  segments of orange, diced
  ripe pears
Syrup:
approximately 125 ml. white
  wine
1 tablespoon honey
2 tablespoons Kirsch

1. Cut the stalk end from the pineapple.
2. Remove all the pulp and dice this neatly.
3. Slit the grapes and take out the pips, skin if liked.
4. If using frozen fruit allow this to defrost, but do not let it become too soft, otherwise it loses both flavour and texture.
5. Cut the skin away from the orange so the outer pith is also removed, and cut the segments to discard skin and pips; prepare pears last to keep them a good colour.
6. Mix all the fruit with the pineapple and cover with syrup.
7. To make this heat the ingredients slowly in a saucepan.
8. Pile back into the pineapple case.
9. Serve chilled with cream or ice cream.

Variation

Canned fruit salad can be used in place of the mixed fresh fruits. The canned syrup can be used instead of the one above.

Cooking time: few minutes
Preparation time: 15 minutes
Main cooking utensil: saucepan
Serves: 6

Chocolate nut gâteau

Imperial
12 oz. plain flour
10 oz. unsalted butter
6 oz. ground almonds
8 oz. sieved icing sugar
Filling:
½ pint thick cream
3 oz. icing sugar
3 oz. chopped blanched
  almonds or ground almonds
4 oz. chopped walnuts
Icing and decoration:
12 oz. plain chocolate
1 oz. butter
2 oz. sieved icing sugar
3 tablespoons water
½ pint thick cream
halved walnuts

Metric
300 g. plain flour
250 g. unsalted butter
150 g. ground almonds
200 g. sieved icing sugar
Filling:
250 ml. thick cream
75 g. icing sugar
75 g. chopped blanched
  almonds or ground almonds
100 g. chopped walnuts
Icing and decoration:
300 g. plain chocolate
25 g. butter
50 g. sieved icing sugar
3 tablespoons water
250 ml. thick cream
halved walnuts

1. Sieve the flour into a large bowl, add the butter.
2. Rub in with the tips of the fingers. Do not over-handle as the percentage of butter is very high.
3. Add the ground almonds and icing sugar; knead very well.
4. Divide the mixture into three equal rounds to fit the tins.
5. Line the bottom of the tins with greaseproof paper and brush these and the sides lightly with melted butter.
6. Put in the rounds of mixture and bake until firm. Allow to cool.
7. Whip the cream until it just holds its shape. Gradually whip in the sugar and nuts.
8. Sandwich the cakes together with this mixture.
9. Coat with the chocolate icing made by melting the chocolate with the butter, sugar and water.
10. Allow this to set, then decorate with piped cream and halved walnuts.

Cooking time: 40 minutes
Preparation time: 45 minutes
Main cooking utensils: 3 8- to 9-inch (20- to 23-cm.) cake or
  sandwich tins, greaseproof paper, double saucepan
Oven temperature: (300–325°F., 150–170°C. Gas Mark 2–3)
Oven position: near centre
Serves: 12–14

Baked Alaska

Imperial
1 square or round of sponge
  or cooked pastry
fruit
1–2 blocks ice cream
5 egg whites
5–10 oz. castor sugar (see
  stage 5)
Decoration:
few glacé cherries
angelica

Metric
1 square or round of sponge
  or cooked pastry
fruit
1–2 blocks ice cream
5 egg whites
125–250 g. castor sugar (see
  stage 5)
Decoration:
few glacé cherries
angelica

1. Put the sponge or pastry into the dish or on to the board.
2. Top with the fruit; although some juice may be allowed to soak through a sponge, keep the fruit well-drained if using pastry.
3. The dessert is nicer if fresh fruit is mashed with sugar to give a more moist texture.
4. Put the ice cream on top of the fruit and sponge or pastry.
5. Whisk the egg whites until very stiff, gradually beat in half the sugar, then fold in the remainder. (The quantity of sugar may be varied according to personal taste — the sweet is just as successful with the smaller amount.)
6. Pile or pipe over the ice cream and sponge; it is essential to cover the sweet completely. Decorate.
7. Put into the oven until tipped with brown.

Note: This is much better served hot, although it can stand for up to 20 minutes without the ice cream melting.

Cooking time: 3–5 minutes
Preparation time: 10 minutes, plus time to prepare the sponge or pastry
Main cooking utensil: ovenproof dish or board covered with foil
Oven temperature: very hot (475–500°F., 240–250°C., Gas Mark 9–10)
Oven position: just above centre
Serves: 6–8

Scottish trifle

Imperial
4 sponge cakes
2–3 tablespoons raspberry jam
2 large macaroon biscuits
3 tablespoons water
3–4 oz. castor sugar
4–5 tablespoons light sherry
2 oz. seedless raisins
1–2 oz. blanched almonds
2 eggs
2 egg yolks
1¼ pints milk
piece lemon rind
few drops vanilla essence
Decoration:
¼–½ pint thick cream
few ratafias
few blanched almonds
glacé cherries

Metric
4 sponge cakes
2–3 tablespoons raspberry jam
2 large macaroon biscuits
3 tablespoons water
75–100 g. castor sugar
4–5 tablespoons light sherry
50 g. seedless raisins
25–50 g. blanched almonds
2 eggs
2 egg yolks
700 ml. milk
piece lemon rind
few drops vanilla essence
Decoration:
150–250 ml. thick cream
few ratafias
few blanched almonds
glacé cherries

1. Split the sponge cakes and sandwich them with the jam.
2. Put them into the serving dish and add the macaroon biscuits, broken into pieces.
3. Heat the water and 2 oz. (50 g.) of the sugar over a low heat until the sugar has dissolved; add the sherry.
4. Spoon over the sponge cakes; sprinkle the raisins and coarsely chopped blanched almonds on top.
5. Meanwhile beat eggs and egg yolks with remaining sugar.
6. Add the warm milk, lemon rind and essence, pour into the top of the double saucepan over hot water and cook gently, stirring, until custard coats the back of the wooden spoon.
7. Cool slightly, remove the lemon rind then pour over the sponge cakes.
8. Allow to cool and decorate with the whipped cream, ratafias, almonds and glacé cherries. Serve chilled.

Cooking time: 15 minutes
Preparation time: 20 minutes
Main cooking utensils: saucepan, double saucepan
Serves: 6–8

Imperial	Metric
4 oz. butter	100 g. butter
4 oz. castor sugar	100 g. castor sugar
4 oz. chopped blanched almonds	100 g. chopped blanched almonds
1 oz. chopped glacé cherries	25 g. chopped glacé cherries
1 oz. chopped walnuts	25 g. chopped walnuts
1 oz. sultanas	25 g. sultanas
2 oz. chopped candied peel	50 g. chopped candied peel
1 egg	1 egg
1 oz. shredded blanched almonds	25 g. shredded blanched almonds
Coating:	*Coating:*
3–4 oz. plain chocolate (chocolat couverture)	75–100 g. plain chocolate (chocolat couverture)

1. Put the butter and sugar into a saucepan and heat gently until melted.

2. Stir in the chopped almonds and other ingredients, except the shredded almonds, adding the well-beaten egg last.

3. Put small teaspoons of the mixture on well-greased baking trays, allowing plenty of space for the biscuits to spread out.

4. Bake until golden brown.

5. After the biscuits have been in the oven for about 5 minutes, remove the trays and sprinkle shredded almonds over the top. If the edges of the biscuits seem to be spreading out, draw them together with a palette knife, then return the trays to the oven. Lower the heat after 10 minutes if they are becoming too brown.

6. When cooked, allow the biscuits to cool for a few minutes, then remove from the trays and cool on the rack.

7. Heat the chocolate in a basin over hot water until softened, coat the bottom surface only of the biscuits with the chocolate.

Cooking time: 20 minutes
Preparation time: 15 minutes
Main cooking utensils: saucepan, baking trays, wire rack, double saucepan or basin over saucepan of hot water
Oven temperature: (360–375°F., 180–190°C., Gas Mark 4–5)
Oven position: just above centre
Makes: 12–14 biscuits

Dutch celebration meal dishes

Cheese and chicory hors d'oeuvre
Wash 2 heads of chicory and pull away 8 of the outer leaves. Chop the remainder of the leaves and put them into a bowl with 1 small onion (cut into rings), 1–2 tomatoes (cut into wedges) and 2 oz. (50 g.) diced Edam cheese. Blend with salad dressing, pile into individual bowls and garnish with the chicory leaves.

Pork and cheese crumble
Remove the bones and excess fat from 4 pork chops. Heat 1 oz. (25 g.) butter in a frying pan, fry the chops in this until golden brown. Peel and slice 2 medium-sized onions thinly; put them into an ovenproof dish and cover with a large can of tomatoes. Season and add 1 teaspoon sugar. Place the chops on top of the tomatoes. Blend 5 oz. (125 g.) soft white breadcrumbs with 4 oz. (100 g.) grated Gouda cheese. Sprinkle over the chops and bake for 1 hour in the centre of a moderate oven (325°F., 170°C., Gas Mark 3). Lift the lid and continue cooking for another 30 minutes. Serve topped with raw or fried onion rings.

Lemon chiffon flan
Cream 3 oz. (75 g.) butter with 1 level tablespoon golden syrup. Crush 6 oz. (150 g.) digestive biscuits, and work these into the butter mixture with 1 teaspoon ground cinnamon. Line an 8-inch (20-cm.) flan dish or flan ring on a serving plate with this. Put it into the refrigerator for several hours to chill. Meanwhile dissolve a lemon-flavoured jelly in ½ pint (275 ml.) water, add the grated rind and juice of 1 lemon, cool and stiffen slightly. Whisk hard with a small can evaporated milk. Spoon into the flan case and when firm decorate with whipped cream and crystallised lemon slices.

Serves: 4

American Thanksgiving menu

Prawn and citrus fruit cocktail
Remove the pulp from 2 large oranges and 1 grapefruit. Blend with a 5-oz. (142-ml.) carton soured cream. Add 2 tablespoons mayonnaise, 1 teaspoon tomato ketchup and 4–6 oz. (100–150 g.) shelled prawns. Put into glasses, top with prawns and a little tomato ketchup.

Roast turkey with celery and herb stuffing
Mix 8 oz. (200 g.) soft crumbs from a brown or wholemeal loaf with 8 stalks finely chopped celery, 3 tablespoons chopped parsley, 1 teaspoon chopped lemon thyme, the grated rind and juice of 1 lemon, 1 finely chopped onion, 4 oz. (100 g.) shredded suet or melted margarine and 2 eggs or 3 egg yolks. Put into an 8- to 10-lb. (4- to 4¾-kg.) turkey; either cook in a very moderate oven allowing 30 minutes per lb. (½ kg.) and 30 minutes over or in a hot oven allowing 15 minutes per lb. (½ kg.) and 15 minutes over. Baste well with melted fat or butter. Serve with roast potatoes, corn and beans and cranberry and apple sauce.

Cranberry and apple sauce
Simmer 1 lb. (½ kg.) peeled apples and 8 oz. (200 g.) cranberries with ¼ pint (150 ml.) water and 3–4 oz. (75–100 g.) sugar until tender.

Coffee chiffon
Make 1 pint (500 ml.) strong coffee. Soften ¾ oz. (20 g.) gelatine in a little cold coffee, stir into the hot coffee and heat until dissolved. Allow to cool and stiffen slightly then fold in ½ pint (250 ml.) lightly whipped cream, 2–3 oz. (50–75 g.) finely chopped pecans or walnuts. Whisk 3 egg whites (left from the stuffing) very stiffly, gradually whisk in 2–3 oz. (50–75 g.) castor sugar and fold into the coffee nut mixture. Pile into a dish, serve with sweet biscuits.

Serves: 6–8

Celebration dinner menu

Turkey and cranberry soup
Melt 3 oz. (75 g.) butter, and fry 2 chopped onions, 2 chopped carrots and 2 chopped celery stalks until tender. Stir in 1½ oz. (40 g.) flour, cook 3 minutes. Blend in 2 pints (1 litre) turkey stock, 2 tablespoons chopped parsley and 4 tablespoons cranberry jelly. Cover pan, simmer 35 minutes, season.

Pork with lemon and apple stuffing
Score the skin on the leg of pork, brush with oil and season very lightly. Weigh the joint and allow 25 minutes cooking time per lb. (½ kg.) plus 25 minutes over. Start in a hot oven (425°F., 220°C., Gas Mark 7) and reduce to 400°F., 200°C., Gas Mark 6 after 40 minutes. Cut the tops off 6–8 small dessert apples, scoop out centres and chop flesh with 5 oz (125 g.) breadcrumbs, grated rind and juice of 1 lemon, 1 large onion, finely chopped, 2 oz. (50 g.) melted butter and seasoning. Cook for about 30 minutes. Serve the pork with stuffing.

Chocolate pear tipsy cake
Sieve together 6 oz. (150 g.) self-raising flour (or plain flour and 1½ teaspoons baking powder) and 2 tablespoons cocoa, add 5 oz. (125 g.) soft brown sugar, 5 tablespoons corn oil, 5 tablespoons milk, 2 egg yolks and 1 teaspoon rum. Lastly fold in 2 whisked egg whites. Pour into a lined and greased 7-inch (18-cm.) cake tin and bake at 325°F., 170°C., Gas Mark 3 for about 50 minutes until firm. Turn out and cool, then split and sandwich with whipped cream and sliced dessert pears (dipped in lemon juice). Top with cream and chocolate curls.

Apple and mincemeat sundaes
Cook 2½ lb. (1¼ kg.) sliced apples with a little water, lemon juice and sugar. Beat to a purée and tint green. When cold, fold in 3 whisked egg whites. Spoon layers of apple and mincemeat into glasses. Top with cream and glacé cherries.

Serves: 6–8

Frosted fruit

Imperial
approximately 8 oz. fruit (see note)
1 egg white
approximately 3 tablespoons castor sugar

Metric
approximately 200 g. fruit (see note)
1 egg white
approximately 3 tablespoons castor sugar

1. Prepare the fruit, remove the stalks, but leave grapes in tiny neat bunches, wash and dry thoroughly.
2. Remove the pith and pips from orange segments without spoiling the shape.
3. Leave redcurrants and blackcurrants in bunches where possible.
4. Rinse away surplus syrup from glacé cherries, leave fresh cherries on stalks.
5. Beat the egg white very lightly with a fork, do not attempt to make it white and frothy. Brush the fruit with this.
6. Either dust the fruit with castor sugar from a fine sifter or dip in sugar.
7. Leave to dry in a warm place for several hours, then serve.

Note: Use white and black grapes; soft fruit such as red, black or white currants; glacé cherries or fresh cherries.

Preparation time: 10 minutes
Main utensil: fine pastry brush
Serves: 4–6

Christmas pudding

Imperial
4 oz. flour
2 oz. breadcrumbs
1 teaspoon mixed spice
1 level teaspoon cinnamon
1 level teaspoon nutmeg
4 oz. shredded suet
4 oz. brown sugar
4 oz. grated apple
1 small carrot, grated
4 oz. mixed crystallised peel
4 oz. currants
8 oz. raisins
4 oz. sultanas
2 oz. prunes or dried apricots, chopped
4 oz. almonds, chopped
grated rind of ½ lemon
juice of ½ lemon
grated rind of ½ orange
1 tablespoon golden syrup
¼ pint ale, beer or milk
2 eggs
Brandy butter:
4 oz. butter
6 oz. icing sugar
2 tablespoons brandy

Metric
100 g. flour
50 g. breadcrumbs
1 teaspoon mixed spice
1 level teaspoon cinnamon
1 level teaspoon nutmeg
100 g. shredded suet
100 g. brown sugar
100 g. grated apple
1 small carrot, grated
100 g. mixed crystallised peel
100 g. currants
200 g. raisins
100 g. sultanas
50 g. prunes or dried apricots, chopped
100 g. almonds, chopped
grated rind of ½ lemon
juice of ½ lemon
grated rind of ½ orange
1 tablespoon golden syrup
125 ml. ale, beer or milk
2 eggs
Brandy butter:
100 g. butter
150 g. icing sugar
2 tablespoons brandy

1. Mix the ingredients and leave overnight, then stir again.
2. Put into the greased basin or basins, cover with foil, greaseproof paper or a cloth. Grease both the inside and outside of the paper to keep the pudding dry on top.
3. Steam or boil for time given, allowing longer time for one pudding. Remove the covers when cooked, then put on dry covers and re-steam for 2–3 hours when needed.
4. Cream the butter and icing sugar together for the brandy butter. Beat in the brandy. Serve with the pudding.

Cooking time: 6–8 hours
Preparation time: 45 minutes
Main cooking utensils: 1 or 2 basins, foil or greaseproof paper or cloth.
Serves: 12–16

Easy New Year's party

Complete menu serves: 6—8

Les crudités
Set a tray with crisp salad ingredients — raw cauliflower sprigs, strips of carrots or coarsely grated carrot, rings of raw onion, sticks of celery, radishes, chicory, etc. Serve with nuts, dried fruit and French dressing (see page 14).

Hot canapés
Stuffed prunes: Stone large lightly cooked prunes and fill the centres with a little cottage cheese. Wrap each prune in half a rasher of bacon and secure it with a cocktail stick. Bake or grill until the bacon is crisp.
Cheese filled canapés: Wrap strips of kipper fillet round cheese cubes. Heat for 1 minute until cheese softens.
Wrapped mushrooms: Wrap strips of kipper fillet or half rashers of bacon round button mushrooms, grill or bake until the mushrooms are cooked.

Mushroom quiche lorraine
Line an 8-inch (20-cm.) flan ring with 8 oz. (200 g.) short-crust pastry and bake blind for about 15 minutes in a hot oven. Beat 3 eggs and 1 egg yolk with seasoning, $\frac{1}{2}$ pint (250 ml.) thin cream and $\frac{1}{4}$ pint (125 ml.) milk then mix in 6 oz. (150 g.) fried chopped bacon, 4 oz. (100 g.) fried sliced mushrooms and 6 oz. (150 g.) grated cheese. Spoon into the pastry case and bake for about 45 minutes (325°F., 170°C., Gas Mark 3) until set. Serve hot or cold with salads.

Orange cream baskets
Cut tops from 8 large oranges. Scoop out pulp, cut flesh into small pieces. Soften 1 oz. (25 g.) gelatine in $\frac{1}{4}$ pint (125 ml.) cold water then stand over hot water to dissolve. Mix with orange segments and $\frac{1}{2}$ pint (250 ml.) soured cream. When nearly stiff, fold in 4 whisked egg whites, mixed with 2 oz. (50 g.) castor sugar. Pile into orange cases and leave to set. Decorate with angelica.

Cider sherry cup

Imperial
1 flagon (2 pints) dry or sweet cider
$\frac{1}{4}$ pint lemon squash (undiluted)
$\frac{1}{4}$ pint orange squash (undiluted)
$\frac{1}{4}$ pint sherry (if using dry cider, a sweet sherry is a good idea)
$\frac{1}{2}$ pint cold water or soda water
Decoration:
1 dessert apple
1 orange
$\frac{1}{4}$ medium-sized cucumber
sprigs mint

Metric
1 flagon (generous litre) dry or sweet cider
125 ml. lemon squash (undiluted)
125 ml. orange squash (undiluted)
125 ml. sherry (if using dry cider, a sweet sherry is a good idea)
250 ml. cold water or soda water
Decoration:
1 dessert apple
1 orange
$\frac{1}{4}$ medium-sized cucumber
sprigs mint

1. Put the cider, squashes and sherry into a bowl. Add the water but if using soda water do not add this yet. Mix well.
2. Slice the apple, orange and cucumber thinly and add to the cup with the mint.
3. Leave in a cold place for 2—3 hours.
4. If using soda water add this just before serving.
5. Spoon the cup from a large bowl into small glasses or wine glasses. The rims can be frosted by brushing them with a little egg white and dipping them in castor sugar.

Preparation time: 10 minutes
Main utensil: large bowl
Makes: 8—10 glasses

Punch marquise

Imperial	Metric
1 lemon	1 lemon
1 bottle sweet or medium-sweet white wine (Sauternes, Entre-deux-Mers, Graves)	1 bottle sweet or medium-sweet white wine (Sauternes, Entre-deux-Mers, Graves)
4 oz. sugar (depending on wine used)	100 g. sugar (depending on wine used)
1–2 cloves	1–2 cloves
small piece cinnamon stick	small piece cinnamon stick
¼–½ pint brandy, depending upon personal taste	150–250 ml. brandy, depending upon personal taste
Decoration:	*Decoration:*
1 seedless lemon	1 seedless lemon

1. Pare the rind from the lemon, discarding the white pith, which could make the drink bitter.
2. Put the wine, sugar, lemon rind and spices into a saucepan and heat until boiling point is reached — do not allow to continue boiling.
3. Strain into a hot bowl.
4. Add the brandy, heated in the pan for 1–2 minutes, then ignite the drink.
5. Leave for 1–2 minutes, when the flame will doubtless have burnt itself out. Top with slices of lemon.

Variation
Add ¼ pint (125 ml.) moderately strong, very well-strained tea to the wine.

Preparation time: 10 minutes
Main cooking utensil: saucepan
Serves: 8

Mulled wine with oranges

Imperial	Metric
2 medium-sized oranges	2 medium-sized oranges
½ pint water	250 ml. water
2–4 oz. sugar (see stage 4)	50–100 g. sugar (see stage 4)
1 bottle Bordeaux or Burgundy (see note)	1 bottle Bordeaux or Burgundy (see note)
Decoration:	*Decoration:*
1 seedless orange	1 seedless orange
nutmeg	nutmeg

1. Remove the peel thinly from the oranges with a sharp knife and put it into the saucepan.
2. Add the water and some of the sugar.
3. Simmer for about 5–6 minutes, strain and return the liquid to the pan.
4. Add the wine, heat until just at boiling point, taste and if desired add a little well-strained orange juice and more sugar. The amount of sugar varies according to personal taste and the sweetness or dryness of the wine. If adding orange juice, reheat for a minute as this needs to be very hot.
5. Spoon into hot glasses or pour into a hot bowl or jug, decorate with halved thin slices of orange (keep the peel on for colour) and grated nutmeg.

Note: Choose Médoc or Bordeaux rouge (claret) or Mâcon or Bourgogne rouge (Burgundy).

Variation
Mulled port: Use the same recipe and method as above, but substitute 2 medium-sized lemons and 1 bottle port for the oranges and red wine and decorate with lemon and powdered cinnamon. In both recipes, the drink may be sweetened with honey in place of the sugar.

Heating time: 10 minutes
Preparation time: 10 minutes
Main cooking utensil: saucepan
Makes: 8–10 glasses

Children's parties

Ideas for younger children

Even the smallest child enjoys a special celebration for a birthday or other occasion. Do not make too many unfamiliar or elaborate dishes, for tiny children often are conservative in their tastes. Prepare simple food that looks colourful and interesting. I find it a good idea to have all the food very small (about the size of a 10p piece).

Sandwiches can be cut out into rounds, hearts, etc. with biscuit cutters and filled with grated cheese, yeast extract, scrambled egg, honey, mashed banana, etc., or make small versions of some of the open sandwiches on page 203.

Most children love *sausages*, so cut larger sausages into slices and put on to cocktail sticks or make midget sausage rolls and serve them with crisps.

Small *scones* can be topped with honey or jam. The recipe for *doughnuts* on page 176 can be adapted to make very small rounds and these will be very popular, so will little biscuits and baby meringues. Follow the recipe for *meringues* on page 169, but reduce the cooking time to about half. Bake the *Victoria sandwich or sponge* (see pages 182 and 184) in a flat tin, cut into fancy shapes and ice.

Serve milk or milk shakes, tea, squash, plus ice cream and jelly but avoid creamy desserts or too much chocolate.

Ideas for older children

Many older children will enjoy helping to plan and cook for their own parties. I have given dishes suitable for informal parties in this section, but there are many other dishes throughout the book that children could cook for their friends.

The dishes on these pages are particularly easy for children to make: 9, 11, 83, 164, 165, 166, 168, 175, 177, 178, 199, 209.

When you or the children are short of time see pages 130, 131, 137, 138, 164, 165, 176.

Although suitable for special occasions, these are economical dishes see pages 165, 166, 168, 196.

For a snack or light meal see pages 124–138, 147–151.

Consult the various chapters for slimming dishes.

Savoury fish cakes

Imperial	Metric
1¼ lb. white fish (weight without bone and skin)	good ½ kg. white fish (weight without bone and skin)
seasoning	seasoning
2 medium-sized onions	2 medium-sized onions
2 medium-sized tomatoes	2 medium-sized tomatoes
2 oz. margarine	50 g. margarine
2 oz. bread (weight without crusts)	50 g. bread (weight without crusts)
4 tablespoons milk	4 tablespoons milk
Coating:	*Coating:*
little flour	little flour
seasoning	seasoning
1 egg	1 egg
2 oz. crisp breadcrumbs	50 g. crisp breadcrumbs
To fry:	*To fry:*
2–3 oz. fat	50–75 g. fat

1. Cook the fish in a little well salted water until just tender, drain well and flake.
2. Meanwhile peel and chop the onions and tomatoes.
3. Fry steadily in the hot margarine until soft.
4. Soak the bread in the milk while the onions, tomatoes and fish are cooking.
5. Mash the bread with a fork, add the onion mixture, fish and seasoning.
6. Mix very well and chill for a time.
7. Form into 8 flat cakes, coat in seasoned flour, then egg and crumbs.
8. Fry until crisp and golden brown.
9. Drain on absorbent paper and serve on a bed of cooked spinach or creamed potatoes or spaghetti.

Variation
Add chopped anchovy fillets to the fish mixture.

Cooking time: 25 minutes
Preparation time: 20 minutes, plus time to stand
Main cooking utensils: saucepan, frying pan
Serves: 4

Danish open sandwiches

These delightful sandwiches can be made small enough for party savouries or substantial enough for a main meal. Cut the bread thinly and spread each slice lavishly with butter; lettuce is usually put under the topping. The following sandwiches are all shown in the picture beginning at the top and working from left to right.

1. Sliced hard-boiled eggs and sliced tomatoes.
2. Luncheon meat, with horseradish cream, prune and an orange twist.
3. A rissole, topped with diced beetroot, gherkin and cucumber.
4. Smoked pork loin, cheese, tomato and parsley.
5. Frankfurters and potato salad with mustard mayonnaise, bacon, onion rings and parsley.
6. Chicken with gherkin and tomato.
7. Sliced gammon, mayonnaise and mixed vegetables.
8. Tongue and liver pâté, with aspic, onion and tomato.
9. Diced chicken and mushrooms in mayonnaise with cucumber, tomato and paprika.
10. Ham with a dessert apple ring, mayonnaise and a cherry.
11. Cooked sausages, red cabbage and onion rings.
12. Pork with crisp crackling, red cabbage, prune, gherkins and an orange twist.
13. Diced beetroot and peas in mayonnaise with hard-boiled egg, pineapple and cucumber.
14. Liver pâté with crisp bacon and fried mushroom slices.
15. Ham slices filled with diced vegetables in mayonnaise with pineapple and a cherry.
16. Canned pork and ham with mixed vegetables in mayonnaise, tomato and cucumber.

Sausage rolls

Imperial	Metric
8 oz. sausage meat	200 g. sausage meat
Rough puff pastry:	*Rough puff pastry:*
8 oz. plain flour	200 g. plain flour
pinch salt	pinch salt
4–6 oz. fat (lard or a mixture of margarine and lard)	100–150 g. fat (lard or a mixture of margarine and lard)
1 dessertspoon lemon juice (optional)	1 dessertspoon lemon juice (optional)
water to mix	water to mix
Glaze:	*Glaze:*
little egg and water or milk	little egg and water or milk

1. To make the pastry, sieve the flour and salt; cut the fat into pieces.
2. Add the fat to the flour, but do not rub it in; mix with the lemon juice and enough water to form a stiff dough.
3. Roll into a long strip and fold in three.
4. Seal the ends, give the pastry a half turn.
5. Repeat stages 3 and 4 twice more.
6. Roll the pastry into a long strip and roll the sausage meat into a strip the same size as the pastry.
7. Place the sausage meat on the pastry, brush the edges with water, fold over and seal. Flake the edges, flute if wished.
8. Cut the roll into 12 medium or 16 small pieces, place on an ungreased baking sheet.
9. Make slits on each piece and glaze with egg and water or milk.
10. Bake for 10 minutes in a hot oven then reduce the heat for the remainder of the time. Serve hot or cold.

Variation

Make the rolls cocktail size and cook for 12–15 minutes only.

Cooking time: 15–20 minutes
Preparation time: 25 minutes
Main cooking utensil: baking sheet
Oven temperature: hot (450°F., 230°C., Gas Mark 8) then moderately hot (375–400°F., 190–200°C., Gas Mark 5–6)
Oven position: just above centre
Makes: 12–16 rolls

Stuffed sausages with grilled cheese

Imperial	Metric
8 canned frankfurter sausages	8 canned frankfurter sausages
4–6 oz. Gruyère cheese	100–150 g. Gruyère cheese
4 large or 8 small rashers bacon (streaky or back is ideal)	4 large or 8 small rashers bacon (streaky or back is ideal)

1. Poach the sausages in the brine from the can for 5 minutes.
2. Lift out, drain well and pat dry on absorbent paper.
3. Slit down the centre and insert a finger of cheese into each.
4. Remove the rind from the bacon and cut any long rashers in half.
5. Roll these round the stuffed frankfurters and secure with wooden cocktail sticks.
6. Cook under a hot grill or over a barbecue fire, turning once or twice until the bacon is crisp and the cheese melted. Serve as a light snack. These are ideal for a barbecue.

Variation

Spread mustard or chutney in the sausages before filling them with the cheese.

Cooking time: 10 minutes
Preparation time: 5 minutes
Main cooking utensils: saucepan, grill or barbecue
Serves: 4

Stuffed baked potatoes

Imperial
4 large old potatoes
little melted fat or oil
  or little seasoned flour
Filling:
1 oz. margarine or butter
seasoning
4 oz. finely chopped
  cooked ham or boiled
  bacon or cooked meat
  or corned beef

Metric
4 large old potatoes
little melted fat or oil
  or little seasoned flour
Filling:
25 g. margarine or butter
seasoning
100 g. finely chopped
  cooked ham or boiled
  bacon or cooked meat
  or corned beef

1. Scrub and dry then prick the potatoes, to prevent the skin bursting.
2. To crisp the skin rub the outside with melted fat or a little oil – or roll in a very little seasoned flour.
3. Put on the baking tray or sheet.
4. Bake in a moderately hot oven until soft.
5. Slit the skin at once for a plain baked potato to give a 'floury' texture as the steam escapes, but when stuffing, cut a slice from the top and scoop out most of the inside.
6. Mash this with the margarine and seasoning, add the ham and pile back into the cases.
7. Re-heat if wished for a further 10 minutes. Serve for a light supper or lunch dish, topped with more butter.

Variation
Use grated cheese, or fried tomatoes and bacon rashers. Cook the potatoes in a moderate oven (325–350°F., 170–180°C., Gas Mark 3–4) for 1½–2 hours.

Cooking time: 1–1¼ hours
Preparation time: few minutes
Main cooking utensil: baking tray or sheet
Oven temperature: moderately hot (400°F., 200°C., Gas Mark 6)
Oven position: centre
Serves: 4

Pears and ice cream with chocolate sauce

Imperial
4 medium-sized ripe pears
lemon juice
block vanilla ice cream
Sauce:
6 oz. plain chocolate
few drops vanilla essence
1 oz. butter
2 tablespoons water
1 oz. castor sugar
2 teaspoons golden syrup
Decoration:
chocolate curls

Metric
4 medium-sized ripe pears
lemon juice
block vanilla ice cream
Sauce:
150 g. plain chocolate
few drops vanilla essence
25 g. butter
2 tablespoons water
25 g. castor sugar
2 teaspoons golden syrup
Decoration:
chocolate curls

1. To make the sauce, chop the chocolate into small pieces and put it into a basin or the top of a double saucepan with the other ingredients; if serving the sauce cold use double the amount of water as the sauce thickens as it cools.
2. Melt over hot, but not boiling water; if the water is too hot the sauce loses its shine and becomes hard, rather than melting.
3. Peel, halve and core the pears.
4. Sprinkle with lemon juice and cover, if allowing to stand, to keep the colour.
5. Spoon the ice cream into glasses with the pears then top with the hot or cold chocolate sauce.
6. Decorate with curls of chocolate. To make these scrape along a block of chocolate with a sharp knife and the thin wafers of chocolate will curl. For large curls, melt the chocolate, pour on to a tin and leave to set, then proceed as above. Serve with wafers.

Variation
Moka sauce: Use strong coffee instead of water for the sauce.

Cooking time: few minutes
Preparation time: 10 minutes
Main cooking utensil: basin and saucepan or double saucepan
Serves: 4

Barbecues and picnics

Planning a picnic

There is no longer any need to consider sandwiches the only kind of picnic food. Nowadays when so many of us travel by car you can plan quite elaborate and varied dishes as well.

There are occasions though when your picnic menu needs to be simple or easily transported; the special needs for these occasions are covered on pages 212 and 213.

If you enjoy regular picnics it is worth considering the purchase of special picnic equipment, i.e. a picnic hamper, so you have crockery, cutlery, etc. always available; an insulated carrying bag, which means that cold food really does stay cold for a long time. Vacuum flasks, not only for hot or cold drinks but the wide-necked variety which enables you to transport fruit salads, ice cream, stews, etc. These are also ideal for baby food.

In addition to the special dishes in this section of the book see the column on the right, this lists some of the dishes in other chapters which could be adapted for picnic food.

If you have a freezer you can freeze so many dishes, see various chapters (including sandwiches – except with hard-boiled egg filling), ready for a picnic when the sun chooses to shine.

Planning a barbecue

Barbecues have become very popular and they give you an opportunity to entertain your friends with the minimum of fuss and effort. There are many barbecues that can be purchased if you do not feel you could build your own, and many are not particularly expensive.

Barbecue food is simple food but the method of cooking gives it a special flavour. There are a number of suggestions in the pages that follow, but many other dishes in this book would also be suitable for barbecues or picnics. All of these are quickly prepared. Always make sure the barbecue fire is really hot before you start to cook, for slow cooking will make the food dry and unappetising.

If you are short of money see pages 17, inexpensive soups – 19, 21, 22, 23–65, 69, 71, 82, 83, 87, 92, 93, 98, 139, 141, 208, 211, 212

When you want a special barbecue or picnic dish see pages 92, 93, 98, 209, 210, 211, 212.

When you are slimming choose these barbecue or picnic dishes: see pages 210, 213 (part), 115–121.

Barbecued sandwiches

Imperial	Metric
4 long French loaves	4 long French loaves
4–5 oz. butter or margarine	100–125 g. butter or margarine
1–2 cloves garlic	1–2 cloves garlic
Filling 1:	*Filling 1:*
4 oz. Cheddar or Gruyère cheese	100 g. Cheddar or Gruyère cheese
medium can baked beans	medium can baked beans
Filling 2:	*Filling 2:*
4–5 large cooked sausages	4–5 large cooked sausages
2 tablespoons tomato ketchup	2 tablespoons tomato ketchup
½ tablespoon made mustard	½ tablespoon made mustard
Filling 3:	*Filling 3:*
medium can salmon	medium can salmon
2 tablespoons mayonnaise	2 tablespoons mayonnaise
2 tablespoons chopped gherkins	2 tablespoons chopped gherkins
Filling 4:	*Filling 4:*
4 oz. Cheddar or Gruyère cheese	100 g. Cheddar or Gruyère cheese
2 tomatoes	2 tomatoes
seasoning	seasoning
4 oz. cooked ham or salami	100 g. cooked ham or salami

1. Slit the loaves lengthways and spread with the creamed butter or margarine blended with the crushed garlic.
2. Mix the grated cheese and baked beans (do not use all the liquid from the can) and spread this over half the first loaf.
3. Slice the sausages thinly, mix with the ketchup and mustard, spread this over half the second loaf.
4. Blend the drained flaked salmon, mayonnaise and gherkins together and spread this over half the third loaf.
5. Spread half the fourth loaf with the diced or grated cheese blended with the chopped or sliced tomatoes, the seasoning and chopped ham or salami.
6. Put the plain halves over the fillings, wrap in foil and heat. Serve cut in fingers, with salad.

Cooking time: 15 minutes
Preparation time: 10 minutes
Main cooking utensils: foil, barbecue
Serves: 8–12

Devilled pork chops

Imperial	Metric
4 rosy dessert apples	4 rosy dessert apples
little oil	little oil
4 thick pork loin chops	4 thick pork loin chops
6 tablespoons crisp breadcrumbs	6 tablespoons crisp breadcrumbs
2 teaspoons dry mustard	2 teaspoons dry mustard
1 teaspoon curry powder	1 teaspoon curry powder
Sauce:	*Sauce:*
2 tablespoons oil	2 tablespoons oil
2 medium-sized onions	2 medium-sized onions
1 tablespoon cornflour	1 tablespoon cornflour
½–1 tablespoon mustard,	½–1 tablespoon mustard,
1 teaspoon curry powder	1 teaspoon curry powder
½ pint brown stock or water and 1 stock cube	250 ml. brown stock or water and 1 stock cube
1 tablespoon Worcestershire sauce	1 tablespoon Worcestershire sauce
seasoning	seasoning

1. Core the apples, slit round the skins, then brush with oil.
2. Put on to the foil and cook for 30–35 minutes.
3. Put the pork chops on the bars (allowing a total of 20 minutes cooking time).
4. Cook for 10 minutes only then remove the chops and press both sides into the crumbs mixed with the mustard and curry powder.
5. Return them to the barbecue and complete the cooking.
6. Meanwhile put the oil for the sauce into the saucepan.
7. Add the chopped onions and cook for several minutes.
8. Stir in the cornflour, mustard and curry powder.
9. Blend in the stock or water and stock cube and the sauce and season.
10. Cook until thickened. Serve the chops with jacket potatoes and the hot sauce. Do not spoon the sauce over the meat too soon for it will spoil the crisp outside.

Cooking time: 30–35 minutes
Preparation time: 15 minutes
Main cooking utensils: barbecue, foil, saucepan
Serves: 4

A new look for kebabs

If planning a barbecue there is nothing more attractive than colourful and appetising kebabs. You need long metal skewers — never try to eat the food directly from the skewers for they become extremely hot, but pull the food from the skewers with a fork on to a plate.

Always baste the food well while cooking over the barbecue, using either melted butter or fat or oil. Season this, add a little lemon juice or make a spiced sauce as the recipe on page 207.

Sausage and fruit kebabs

Since the sausages need longer cooking than the fruit it is a good idea to cook them partially first, cool, then put on to the skewers with the fresh fruit.

Put thick chunks of dessert apple, pieces of banana and wedges of orange on the skewers as well as the sausages. Cook until the fruit is very hot and the sausages thoroughly cooked.

Fish and vegetable kebabs

Dice firm fleshed fish — discard any skin or bones. Put on to skewers with tiny mushrooms, small partially cooked onions, tiny firm tomatoes and squares of red and green pepper flesh. Baste well during cooking. Serve with lemon or the sauce on page 207 (made more suitable for fish by using fish stock and the grated rind and juice of a lemon, in place of brown stock).

Cheese and bacon kebabs

Halve rashers of streaky bacon and wrap round cubes of Cheddar or Gruyère cheese. Thread on to skewers with button mushrooms and small firm tomatoes. Baste the vegetables, but not the bacon, and cook until the bacon is crisp; do not overcook.

Mustard steaks

Imperial	Metric
6–8 large steaks, rump, fillet or sirloin	6–8 large steaks, rump, fillet or sirloin
oil for grilling	oil for grilling
Sauce:	*Sauce:*
2 tablespoons French mustard	2 tablespoons French mustard
1 tablespoon made English mustard	1 tablespoon made English mustard
4 tablespoons frying oil	4 tablespoons frying oil
good shake pepper	good shake pepper
pinch salt	pinch salt
$\frac{1}{4}$ pint brown stock	125 ml. brown stock

1. Mix all the ingredients for the sauce together and keep this warm over the barbecue fire.
2. Brush the bars with oil, put the steaks on the grid and brush with the sauce.
3. Cook for 2–3 minutes, turn with tongs or a long-handled fork if the fire is fierce. Brush again with sauce.
4. Continue cooking to personal taste. Serve with rolls heated over the barbecue and with salad.

Note: Whatever kind of barbecue you use allow time for the charcoal to heat through (this varies a great deal but a minimum of 35 minutes is usual). The barbecue is ready to use when the charcoal glows red. Brush the bars of the grid well with melted fat or oil so the food does not stick and keep the meat, etc., well basted during cooking. Use either butter, oil or fat. The simplest food to barbecue is a steak or chops and the recipe gives a new flavour to steak. If the steak is very thin then do not start cooking it too early. Turn the steaks halfway through the cooking period.

Cooking time: 5–10 minutes according to taste
Preparation time: 5 minutes
Main cooking utensils: barbecue
Serves: 6–8

Barbecued desserts

The easiest and most pleasant desserts are made with fresh fruits. Here are some suggestions:

Ginger apples
Core 4 medium to large cooking apples, slit the skins round the centre. Stand the apples on a double thickness of foil. Blend 2 heaped tablespoons golden syrup with 6 tablespoons crushed gingernut crumbs and 4 tablespoons raisins. Press into the middle of the apples and gather the foil round the fruit. Cook over the barbecue for about 45 minutes. Serve with hot golden syrup mixed with chopped preserved or crystallised ginger.

Jamaican oranges
Cut away the peel from 4 large oranges, stand them on a double thickness of foil. Sprinkle them with rum and brown sugar and gather the foil round the oranges. Cook over the barbecue for 12–15 minutes. Bananas can be cooked in the same way, but allow 10 minutes only.

Coconut peaches
Halve large firm peaches and remove the stones. For 4 peaches allow 2 oz. (50 g.) butter or margarine, 2 oz. (50 g.) brown sugar and 3 oz. (75 g.) desiccated coconut. Sandwich the halves together with the coconut mixture. Sprinkle with lemon or orange juice and wrap in a double thickness of foil. Cook for about 15 minutes over the barbecue.

Luxury picnic

The picture shows a most luxurious looking picnic menu but this is very simple to prepare. It does need last minute arranging and transport to carry dishes, etc. The main course is a substantial salad.

Fried chicken
Joint 2 small chickens or buy about 6–8 chicken legs. These keep more moist than the breast, so are better for a picnic. Fry steadily in fat or oil for about 15 minutes. Drain very well on absorbent paper, then wrap carefully in foil.

Gammon cornets
Ham could be used instead. Cut the gammon or ham into thin slices and wrap in foil or polythene. Prepare the filling and put this into a screw-topped jar. To make this, mix some finely chopped celery, red pepper, chopped nuts and mayonnaise together. Spread a little on each slice of cooked gammon or ham and roll into a cornet.

Beetroot
Dice, toss it in oil, vinegar and seasoning and carry in a screw-topped jar.

Oranges
Cut away the peel and pith, slice, toss in oil, vinegar, seasoning and chopped chives and carry in a screw-topped jar.

Potato and vegetable salads
The easiest way to have these is to buy cans, and take these unopened. Remember the can opener.

Serve this with a green salad, tomatoes, cucumber, red pepper — all of which can be prepared just before serving. Bread or rolls, butter, fresh fruit and wine complete the menu.

Savoury meat loaf

Imperial	Metric
1 oz. butter	25 g. butter
1 large onion	1 large onion
1 canned or fresh red pepper	1 canned or fresh red pepper
1 cooking apple	1 cooking apple
1 lb. sausage meat	½ kg. sausage meat
8 oz. fresh breadcrumbs	200 g. fresh breadcrumbs
2 tablespoons chopped parsley	2 tablespoons chopped parsley
grated rind of ½ lemon	grated rind of ½ lemon
seasoning	seasoning
1 egg	1 egg
Garnish:	*Garnish:*
watercress	watercress
red pepper	red pepper

1. Melt the butter and fry the finely chopped onion until soft.
2. Cut four strips of red pepper and chop the rest. Peel and grate the apple and mix the apple and pepper well with all the other ingredients.
3. Press the mixture into a greased loaf tin.
4. Smooth the top and cover with greaseproof paper. For a moist instead of crisp outside, stand the tin in a dish of cold water.
5. Bake until firm to the touch.
6. Turn out and serve cold with toast and butter, strips of red pepper and sprigs of watercress.

Note: This loaf will keep for 1–2 days in a cool place. It can be left in the tin and covered with a layer of melted butter to keep the top moist.

Variation

Use finely minced pork instead of sausage meat, add ½–1 teaspoon chopped sage, thyme.

Cooking time: 1½ hours
Preparation time: 20 minutes
Main cooking utensil: loaf tin
Oven temperature: moderate (375°F., 190°C., Gas Mark 5)
Oven position: centre
Serves: 4

Pork pie

Imperial	Metric
Hot water crust pastry:	*Hot water crust pastry:*
12 oz. flour	300 g. flour
pinch salt	pinch salt
5 oz. lard	125 g. lard
¼ pint water	125 ml. water
Filling:	*Filling:*
4 oz. streaky bacon	100 g. streaky bacon
1½ lb. pork fillet	¾ kg. pork fillet
seasoning	seasoning
pinch powdered ginger	pinch powdered ginger
1 tablespoon water	1 tablespoon water
1 beaten egg to glaze	1 beaten egg to glaze
Jelly:	*Jelly:*
1 pig's trotter	1 pig's trotter
1 pint water	550 ml. water
bay leaf	bay leaf
1 onion	1 onion

1. Sieve the flour and salt into a mixing bowl.
2. Heat the lard and water, cool slightly, pour over the flour and knead well until smooth.
3. Roll out two thirds for lining the tin or mould this into the pie shape with your hands, keep the rest warm.
4. Fill the pie-crust with the diced bacon rashers, diced pork, seasoning, ginger and water.
5. Roll out the rest of the pastry, make a lid, seal the edges firmly, make a centre slit and a rose decoration.
6. Brush with egg. Bake for about 2 hours until golden brown, standing the tin on a baking sheet.
7. Boil the pig's trotter in the water with a bay leaf and the onion for about 1 hour, then remove the onion, bay leaf and pig's trotter and boil rapidly until reduced to about 5 tablespoons strong liquid.
8. Remove the pie from the tin, cool, allow the stock to cool, then pour it through the centre hole with a funnel. Serve cold.

Cooking time: 2 hours
Preparation time: 30 minutes
Main cooking utensils: cake tin (with loose base) or proper raised pie tin that unlocks, saucepan
Oven temperature: moderate (350–375°F., 180–190°C., Gas Mark 4–5)
Oven position: centre
Serves: 4–6

Imperial	Metric
Dough:	*Dough:*
½ oz. yeast	15 g. yeast
1 teaspoon sugar	1 teaspoon sugar
¼ pint tepid water	125 ml. tepid water
10 oz. plain flour	250 g. plain flour
pinch salt	pinch salt
1 tablespoon oil	1 tablespoon oil
Topping:	*Topping:*
2 onions	2 onions
1 tablespoon oil	1 tablespoon oil
1 oz. butter	25 g. butter
1 lb. tomatoes	½ kg. tomatoes
2 tablespoons tomato purée	2 tablespoons tomato purée
seasoning	seasoning
2–4 oz. mushrooms	50–100 g. mushrooms
½ teaspoon chopped oregano or marjoram or pinch dried herbs	½ teaspoon chopped oregano or marjoram or pinch dried herbs
2 teaspoons chopped parsley	2 teaspoons chopped parsley
2 oz. grated Parmesan cheese	50 g. grated Parmesan cheese

1. Cream the yeast with the sugar, add the tepid liquid and a light sprinkling of flour and leave in a warm place until the surface is covered with bubbles.
2. Sieve the flour and salt, add the oil and yeast liquid. Knead well, allow to prove (rise) in a large greased polythene bag or covered bowl until double its original size, about 1 hour.
3. Meanwhile toss the very finely chopped onions in hot oil and butter, add the skinned, deseeded tomatoes, tomato purée, seasoning, half the mushrooms, the finely chopped herbs and 1 teaspoon of parsley. Cook to a thick purée and cool.
4. Roll out the dough to 10-inch (25-cm.) round, put on a baking tray, cover with purée, top with the sliced mushrooms, grated cheese and remaining parsley.
5. Leave to prove again for 20–25 minutes. Bake for 20 minutes in a hot oven, then for a further 15 minutes at moderate.

Cooking time: 45–50 minutes
Preparation time: 30 minutes plus time for dough to prove
Main cooking utensils: saucepan, baking tray
Oven temperature: hot (425–450°F., 220–230°C., Gas Mark 7–8) then moderate (375°F., 190°C., Gas Mark 5)
Oven position: centre
Serves: 5–6

Garden luncheon menu

Vol-au-vent

Roll out 1 8-oz. (226-g.) packet frozen puff pastry ½ inch (1 cm.) thick and cut into rounds. Make a circle in each with a smaller cutter. Bake in a very hot oven (450°F., 230°C., Gas Mark 8) for 10–15 minutes until brown. Lift out the centre circles and dry out the cases for a few minutes in a cool oven. Cool the cases. Make the filling by mixing 8 oz. (200 g.) flaked cooked fish or chopped cooked chicken, ham or mushroom with 4–5 tablespoons mayonnaise. Fill the vol-au-vent cases with filling and replace the lids. Serve with salad and mayonnaise.

Orange and lemon mousse

Dissolve ½ lemon jelly in ½ pint (275 ml.) boiling water. Allow to set in the bottom of a 2-pint (1-litre) mould. Whisk 2 egg yolks with 2 oz. (50 g.) sugar until thick. Dissolve 1 oz. (25 g.) gelatine in 1 20-oz. (567-ml.) can orange juice, heated. Pour on the egg yolks, allow to cool and begin to stiffen, then fold in ¼ pint (125 ml.) lightly whipped cream and 2 stiffly beaten egg whites. Spoon over the lemon jelly and set. Turn out to serve.

Serves: 4

Garden picnic

When the weather is fine take food into the garden. The pie combines meat and vegetables and is easy to serve. The jellied sweet is most refreshing.

Corned beef pie au gratin

Cook and mash about 12 oz. (300 g.) potatoes. Heat 1 tablespoon oil in a pan, add 1 chopped onion and cook for several minutes. Mix with about 14 oz (300 g.) diced corned beef, 3—4 skinned sliced tomatoes, 1 green pepper (cut into narrow strips, with the core and seeds discarded). Put this mixture into an ovenproof dish. Blend 5—6 tablespoons evaporated milk with enough water to give ½ pint (250 ml.). Heat 1 oz. (25 g.) butter in a pan, stir in 1 oz. (25 g.) flour, then the liquid. Bring to the boil, cook until thickened, add 3 oz. (75 g.) grated Cheddar cheese and seasoning. Pour over the corned beef mixture. Sprinkle with another 1 oz. (25 g.) cheese. Spread or pipe the mashed potatoes round the edge of the dish and heat for 25 minutes in the centre of a moderately hot oven (400°F., 200°C., Gas Mark 6).

Orange jelly creams

Open a can of mandarin oranges. Drain off the syrup and add enough water to make ¾ pint (400 ml.). Dissolve a packet of lemon or orange jelly in this and allow to cool and begin to stiffen. Whisk in ¼ pint (125 ml.) evaporated milk and most of the orange segments. Put into sundae glasses and top with the rest of the orange segments and a slice of banana if liked.

Note: These dishes are ideal if cooking in a caravan for they are based mainly on canned foods.

Serves: 4

Seaside picnic

Dutch apple soup

Peel 1 lb. (½ kg.) cooking apples, put into a pan with 1 pint (½ litre) water, the grated rind and juice of 1 lemon, 1 diced red pepper (discard core and seeds) and 3 oz. (75 g.) seedless raisins Bring to the boil, cook to a soft pulp. Beat well to make the mixture smooth. Blend ½ tablespoon cornflour with ¼ pint (125 ml.) water, stir into the soup with 2 oz. (50 g.) sugar, cook until thickened slightly; chill. Add 4 tablespoons thick cream and a little chopped parsley. Carry in a vacuum flask.

Tuna and pear scallops

Make shortcrust pastry with 8 oz. (200 g.) flour, etc. (see page 140), roll out and line eight small scallop shells. Prick the pastry, bake for 15 minutes in a hot oven (425°F., 220°C., Gas Mark 7). Heat 1½ oz. (40 g.) butter in a pan, stir in 1½ oz. (40 g.) flour, gradually blend in ½ pint (125 ml.) milk. Bring to the boil, cook until thickened and smooth. Add 1 tablespoon tomato ketchup, 1 finely grated onion, 1 finely chopped green pepper (discard core and seeds), 1 teaspoon capers, 1 teaspoon lemon juice, a medium can flaked tuna fish and 1 peeled diced pear. Season well. Spoon into half the pastry shells and top with the other shells.

Lemon chiffon

Blend 2 teaspoons cornflour with the grated rind of 2 lemons (use top zest only) and 1 pint (generous ½ litre) milk. Bring to the boil, cook until thickened slightly, pour over 3 egg yolks, beaten with 2—3 oz. (50—75 g.) sugar. Return to the saucepan and cook gently, without boiling, until thick. Soften, then dissolve ½ oz. (15 g.) gelatine in 2 tablespoons lemon juice. Whisk into the cold custard. When nearly set fold in 3 stiffly whisked egg whites. Leave to set in paper cups. Decorate with lemon rind and apple pieces, dipped in lemon juice.

Serves: 4

This menu is refreshing for a hot weather picnic. Take iced tea, French bread and butter plus extra fruit, lettuce and tomatoes.

Rollmop salad
Drain a medium jar of rollmop herrings at home and put back in the jar. Dice cooked beetroot and dessert apples, toss in lemon juice and carry in polythene bags. Arrange the salad as shown in the picture and top with parsley (also carried in polythene).

Savoury quiches
Make shortcrust pastry with 8 oz. (200 g.) flour, etc. (see page 140) and line four individual deep foil dishes or patty tins. Bake blind for 10 minutes in a hot oven (425°F., 220°C., Gas Mark 7). Meanwhile beat 2 eggs with seasoning, 4 oz. (100 g.) diced cooked ham, 2 oz. (50 g.) diced cooked tongue, $\frac{1}{4}$ pint (125 ml.) milk, 3 tablespoons thick cream and 4 oz. (100 g.) grated Cheddar cheese. Spoon into the pastry cases and bake for 40 minutes in a very moderate oven (325°F., 170°C., Gas Mark 3). Top with parsley. As a variation, omit tongue and add a diced apple to the filling.

Orange rice baskets
Cut a slice from 4 large oranges, scoop out the flesh from the fruit, discard pips, pith, etc. Put the pulp into a basin and mix with 1 small can rice pudding and 2 ripe peeled diced pears (tossed in a little lemon juice). Carry this mixture in a screw-topped jar or wide-necked vacuum flask. Spoon into the orange cases, top with a little cream (carried in a separate container) and make the slice removed into wings. If more convenient serve in picnic cups.

Serves: 4

This menu would be too cumbersome to carry if travelling other than by car. Take red wine or beer, and coffee.

Les crudités
Prepare most of the food at home, carry in polythene bags. Divide a small cauliflower into bite-sized pieces, peel and cut young carrots into strips, wash spring onions. Arrange on plates with sliced salami, halved tomatoes, apple slices (dipped in lemon juice). Top with French dressing made by blending salt, pepper, little made mustard, 1 tablespoon chopped parsley, 6 tablespoons salad oil and 2 tablespoons lemon juice (carry this in a screw-topped jar).

Sausagemeat patties
Make raised pie pastry by heating 5 oz. (125 g.) lard or fat with $\frac{1}{2}$ pint (250 ml.) water and a pinch of salt. Pour over $1\frac{1}{4}$ lb. ($\frac{1}{2}$ kg.) plain flour, knead well and roll out while hot. Line 12 deep patty tins with two thirds of the pastry. Blend $1\frac{1}{4}$ lb. ($\frac{1}{2}$ kg.) sausagemeat, 2 rashers chopped bacon, 1 egg, 1 chopped onion, good pinch sage, seasoning and 2 tablespoons chopped parsley. Divide this between the patty tins, brush rims with a little beaten egg, put on lids of the pastry. Glaze with egg and bake for 15 minutes in a very hot oven (450°F., 230°C., Gas Mark 8) then reduce the heat to very moderate (325°F., 170°C., Gas Mark 3) for 1 hour.

Pear and chocolate whirls
Make $1\frac{1}{2}$ pints ($\frac{3}{4}$ litre) thick sweet custard. Dice 3 firm pears, toss in lemon juice, then stir into the almost cool custard. Spoon into picnic cups, top with chocolate drops, which soften slightly and make whirls. Chill. Take whipped cream in a screw-topped container, put on desserts before serving.

Serves: 6

Catering for invalids

A well-balanced and interesting diet is important when catering for someone who is ill, or recovering from an illness. Naturally this must be planned to follow medical advice and special dietary needs. Cook all foods in the most easily digested way. Try to encourage the invalid to have an adequate amount of protein foods, milk, fish, poultry, etc. together with fruit and fresh vegetables too. On the other hand, do not fuss unduly if your patient does not appear to be interested in food for a time.

Home-made soups are a good choice when the invalid does not feel like making an effort to eat solid food. See pages 18–31 and right.

Fish is one of the most easily digested foods; in the fish section, starting page 32, are a number of ideas. Remove skin and bones from fish before cooking or serving to someone who is ill and who might find it an effort to do it themselves.

To steam fish: Put on to a plate, add seasoning, a little butter and milk if allowed, cover with foil or a plate. Stand this over boiling water.

Milk is generally considered one of the essential foods in a general invalid light diet and milky puddings a good way of using this valuable protein (see pages 156, 157, and 162).

Make the food and tray look interesting and your invalid will soon be enjoying your cooking again.

Refreshing drinks for invalids

Make certain there is a jug of a refreshing drink for an invalid, especially if he or she has a fairly high temperature. Keep the jug covered.

Drinks containing fresh orange, lemon or grapefruit juice are thirst-quenching and contain valuable Vitamin C, which is important at all times, but especially when one is not well.

Speedy lemonade: Halve lemons, squeeze out all the juice, put the cut halves into a heatproof jug. Add boiling water and sugar, honey or glucose to sweeten. Press the lemon halves once or twice. Leave until cold, then add the lemon juice. Serve with ice or soda water.

Speedy orangeade: Make this in the same way as the lemonade above. I like to add just a little lemon flavouring (juice only or juice plus 1 lemon) to the oranges, for this makes the drink sharper and more refreshing.

Appleade: Add diced apples to the lemons in the recipe above, or flavour apple juice with fresh lemon.

Pineapple cocktail: Mix grapefruit juice and pineapple juice or other citrus fruits with the pineapple.

Vichyssoise soup

Imperial
4 medium-sized leeks
2 oz. butter or margarine
3 small potatoes
¼ pint water
1 pint chicken stock, or water
and chicken stock cube

1 level teaspoon salt
pinch pepper
¼ pint thick cream
Garnish:
chopped chives or spring onion
   tops

Metric
4 medium-sized leeks
50 g. butter or margarine
3 small potatoes
125 ml. water
generous ½ litre chicken stock,
or water and chicken stock
cube
1 level teaspoon salt
pinch pepper
125 ml. thick cream
Garnish:
chopped chives or spring onion
   tops

1. Use the white part of the leeks only, wash well and chop.
2. Melt the butter in a pan and cook the leeks slowly for 10–15 minutes, without letting them brown.
3. Peel the potatoes and cut in cubes.
4. Add to the leeks with the water and stock.
5. Season, cover pan and simmer for 25 minutes until the potatoes are soft.
6. Rub the mixture through a sieve, return to the pan, add the cream and heat, but do not boil.
7. Serve either hot or chilled and sprinkled with chopped chives or finely cut spring onion tops.

Note: Store in the refrigerator. If reheating, do so gently.

Variation
Add 1 small onion, chopped. If serving cold, use ¼ pint (125 ml.) white wine in place of water.

Cooking time: 45 minutes
Preparation time: 15 minutes
Main cooking utensils: large saucepan, sieve, ovenproof dish
Serves: 4–6

Grilled plaice and orange butter

Imperial
4 good-sized plaice fillets
2 oranges
1 oz. butter
seasoning

Metric
4 good-sized plaice fillets
2 oranges
25 g. butter
seasoning

1. Wash and dry the fish well.
2. Grate the rind from one orange and squeeze out the juice.
3. Blend the rind with most of the butter and a little seasoning. Chill in the refrigerator until required.
4. Rub the rest of the butter over the grid of the grill pan so that the fish does not stick.
5. Heat the grill, then put the fish under it and cook until tender. Add the orange juice to flavour it as it cooks.
6. Divide the orange butter into four portions and place one on top of each fillet.
7. Garnish with segments of the second orange and serve with a green vegetable or green salad.

Variation
Use lemon rind and juice. Cut down the butter slightly and put the fish on foil so that it keeps in its juices and flavour.

Cooking time: 7 minutes
Preparation time: few minutes
Main cooking utensil: grill
Serves: 4 small or 2 large portions

Jamaican plaice

Imperial	Metric
2–3 oz. butter	50–75 g. butter
4 large plaice fillets	4 large plaice fillets
seasoning	seasoning
2 bananas, sliced	2 bananas, sliced
2 oz. blanched almonds	50 g. blanched almonds
juice of 1 lemon	juice of 1 lemon

1. Melt the butter carefully.
2. Use a little to grease the dish, arrange the fish in it, season lightly and brush with more butter.
3. Cover with a lid or foil.
4. Cook until the fish is tender and opaque.
5. Fry the sliced banana in the rest of the butter for 2–3 minutes.
6. Arrange the fish on a hot dish.
7. Top with the bananas and the almonds tossed in the remaining butter and lemon juice. Serve with salad or green peas.

Variation
Use sole or whiting.

Cooking time: 15 minutes
Preparation time: 10 minutes
Main cooking utensils: ovenproof dish, saucepan
Oven temperature: moderate (375°F., 190°C., Gas Mark 5)
Oven position: above centre
Serves: 4

Veal à l'orange

Imperial	Metric
8 oz. veal fillet	200 g. veal fillet
1 small onion	1 small onion
½ pint white stock	250 ml. white stock
seasoning	seasoning
1 small orange	1 small orange
2 small young carrots	2 small young carrots
4 oz. long-grain rice	100 g. long-grain rice
1 oz. butter	25 g. butter
¾ oz. flour	20 g. flour
pinch saffron powder	pinch saffron powder
2 tablespoons thick cream	2 tablespoons thick cream

1. Dice the veal; peel the onion and keep it whole. Put the veal, onion, stock and seasoning into a pan.
2. Bring the stock to the boil.
3. Lower the heat, simmer for 40 minutes or until the meat is tender; remove the onion.
4. Cut away the peel from the orange, remove the bitter white pith then cut the orange rind into narrow strips. Soak in 4 tablespoons water for 30 minutes.
5. Peel the carrots, cut into neat matchsticks and put with the orange rind. Add a little seasoning and simmer in a covered pan for 20 minutes.
6. Cook the rice in ½ pint (250 ml.) boiling salted water.
7. Heat the butter in a pan, stir in the flour and cook for several minutes. Add the strained veal stock and bring to the boil.
8. Cook until thickened, tip in the orange rind, carrots and any liquid left, together with the pinch of saffron powder and the cream.
9. Stir over a low heat until smooth. Add the cooked veal and blend.
10. Arrange a border of rice round the serving dish and garnish with an orange cut into slices. Spoon veal mixture in the centre of the dish, top with chopped parsley.

Cooking time: 1 hour
Preparation time: 25 minutes
Main cooking utensils: 3 saucepans
Serves: 2

Baked eggs en cocotte

Imperial
1 oz. lard
4 oz. mushrooms
4 eggs
seasoning

Metric
25 g. lard
100 g. mushrooms
4 eggs
seasoning

1. Divide the lard between the dishes placed on the baking tray.
2. Place in the oven for about 5 minutes to melt the lard.
3. Wash and slice mushrooms (there is no need to peel them if they are the button kind) and add to the melted lard.
4. Return to oven and cook for about 10 minutes.
5. Break 1 egg into each dish on top of the mushrooms. Season.
6. Return to the oven and cook for another 10 minutes until the eggs are set. Serve on small plates, with hot toast.

Variations

Use asparagus tips instead of mushrooms or add grated cheese and cream over top of eggs before baking. Tiny pieces of crisp bacon can also be added to the eggs.

Cooking time: 25 minutes
Preparation time: 10 minutes
Main cooking utensils: 4 small ovenproof dishes, baking tray or sheet
Oven temperature: moderate (375°F., 190°C., Gas Mark 5)
Oven position: centre
Serves: 4

Surprise soufflé

Imperial
3 tablespoons oil
2 onions, chopped
1½ lb. minced meat
4 oz. mushrooms, sliced
seasoning
3 eggs
1 small packet instant potato
1 oz. butter
2 tablespoons milk
2 teaspoons finely chopped
   parsley
good pinch ground nutmeg

Metric
3 tablespoons oil
2 onions, chopped
¾ kg. minced meat
100 g. mushrooms, sliced
seasoning
3 eggs
1 small packet instant potato
25 g. butter
2 tablespoons milk
2 teaspoons finely chopped
   parsley
good pinch ground nutmeg

1. Heat the oil in a pan.
2. Lightly fry the onion, meat and mushrooms in the oil until brown.
3. Add seasoning to taste, continue cooking for 15 minutes, stir well.
4. Spoon into the soufflé dish.
5. Separate the egg yolks from the whites.
6. Make up the instant potato as directed on the packet.
7. Beat in the butter, milk, egg yolks, parsley, nutmeg and seasoning.
8. Whisk the egg whites stiffly and fold into the potato mixture, then pour on to the minced meat mixture.
9. Bake for 45 minutes, until cooked and golden brown. Serve immediately.

Cooking time: just over 1 hour
Preparation time: 20 minutes
Main cooking utensils: saucepan, 3-pint (1½-litre) soufflé dish
Oven temperature: moderately hot (375°F., 190°C., Gas Mark 5)
Oven position: centre
Serves: 4–6

Chicken supreme

Imperial	Metric
4 oz. rice	100 g. rice
water	water
salt	salt
1 oz. butter	25 g. butter
1 oz. flour	25 g. flour
½ pint chicken stock	250 ml. chicken stock
¼ pint milk	125 ml. milk
2 egg yolks	2 egg yolks
2 tablespoons cream	2 tablespoons cream
cooked breasts of 2 young chickens or 1 large fowl divided into 4 joints	cooked breasts of 2 young chickens or 1 large fowl divided into 4 joints
squeeze lemon juice	squeeze lemon juice
4–6 oz. mushrooms	100–150 g. mushrooms
1–2 oz. butter	25–50 g. butter
Garnish:	*Garnish:*
1 hard-boiled egg	1 hard-boiled egg

1. Cook the rice. Method 1: Put the rice with a generous ¼ pint (150 ml.) water into a pan with ½ teaspoon salt, bring to the boil, stir, cover tightly, lower heat and leave for 15 minutes. No straining is necessary. Method 2: Put the rice into 2 pints (1 litre) boiling water, with a good teaspoon salt, cook for 18–20 minutes, strain, rinse in cold water and reheat, or rinse in boiling water.
2. Make a sauce with the flour, butter, chicken stock and milk, then add the egg yolks beaten with the cream.
3. Put in the chicken breasts, heat for about 10 minutes without boiling, then add a squeeze of lemon juice.
4. Fry the mushrooms in the butter.
5. Arrange the well-drained rice on a hot dish, put the chicken breasts and sauce on top and garnish with chopped hard-boiled egg. Arrange the mushrooms round the dish.

Cooking time: 30 minutes
Preparation time: 20 minutes
Main cooking utensils: 3 saucepans
Serves: 4

Milk chicken

Imperial	Metric
2 small roasting chickens approximately 2½ lb. (when trussed)	2 small roasting chickens approximately 1¼ kg. (when trussed)
2 sticks celery	2 sticks celery
1 pint water	500 ml. water
seasoning	seasoning
½ oz. flour	15 g. flour
½ pint milk	250 ml. milk
1 oz. butter	25 g. butter
1 egg yolk	1 egg yolk
Garnish:	*Garnish:*
1–2 hard-boiled eggs	1–2 hard-boiled eggs
1–2 bananas	1–2 bananas
cooked peas	cooked peas

1. Put the whole chickens (or joint these if the pan is not sufficiently large) into a pan, add the diced celery, water and seasoning.
2. Bring to the boil, remove any scum from the top of the liquid, cover the pan, lower the heat, simmer gently – allow 45 minutes for jointed chicken, 1 hour for whole birds – until tender but unbroken; lift on to hot dish.
3. Blend the flour with half the milk, stir into the stock, cook until thickened.
4. Add the butter and the egg blended with remainder of the milk, and cook gently without boiling for several minutes.
5. Strain some of the sauce over the birds, then garnish with the sliced hard-boiled egg, bananas and peas. Serve with the rest of the sauce and creamed potatoes.

Variation

Serve with cooked macaroni instead of potatoes; add a little cream and sherry to the sauce at stage 4.

Cooking time: 1–1¼ hours
Preparation time: 15 minutes
Main cooking utensil: large saucepan
Serves: 6–8

Wine jelly

Imperial
1 bottle red or white wine
¾ oz. (1½ level tablespoons) powdered gelatine
5 tablespoons hot water
3 oz. sugar
Decoration:
grapes or other fresh fruit
Cream sauce:
2 egg yolks
1½ oz. icing sugar
few drops vanilla essence
¼ pint cream

Metric
1 bottle red or white wine
20 g. (1½ level tablespoons) powdered gelatine
5 tablespoons hot water
75 g. sugar
Decoration:
grapes or other fresh fruit
Cream sauce:
2 egg yolks
40 g. icing sugar
few drops vanilla essence
125 ml. cream

1. Pour the wine into a basin.
2. Soften the gelatine in the water then stir until dissolved.
3. Add to the wine, together with the sugar.
4. Pour into a mould, rinsed out in cold water, and allow to set.
5. Turn out on to a wetted plate to enable the jelly to be moved into the centre of the plate if it has been turned out to one side.
6. Decorate with grapes.
7. To make the cream sauce, stir the egg yolks and icing sugar until the sugar has dissolved, add the vanilla essence and the whipped cream. Serve as cold as possible with the cream sauce.

Variation
Make a fluffy cream sauce. Whisk the egg yolks and sugar over a pan of hot water until thick and light, then continue to whisk until cool, fold in vanilla and whipped cream. Use fresh fruit juice instead of wine.

Cooking time: few minutes to dissolve gelatine
Preparation time: 15 minutes
Main cooking utensils: saucepan, 9-inch (23-cm.) ring mould
Serves: 8

Chocolate casserole pudding

Imperial
3 oz. margarine
3 oz. sugar
3 eggs
3 oz. flour (with plain flour use 1 level teaspoon baking powder)
1 oz. cocoa
good ½ pint milk
Decoration:
little castor sugar

Metric
75 g. margarine
75 g. sugar
3 eggs
75 g. flour (with plain flour use 1 level teaspoon baking powder)
25 g. cocoa
275 ml. milk
Decoration:
little castor sugar

1. Cream the margarine and sugar until soft and light.
2. Gradually beat in the egg yolks, then fold in the sieved flour, cocoa and the milk. You may find the mixture curdles but this is quite in order.
3. Lastly fold in the stiffly beaten egg whites.
4. Put into the greased casserole and stand in a tin of water.
5. This pudding will separate during cooking and give you a very light fluffy texture on top with a more moist saucelike texture underneath.
6. If you want a slightly crisp topping, do not cover the casserole. If you wish the topping to be soft, put a lid or foil on the casserole.
7. Bake for the time and at temperature given.
8. Sprinkle the top with sugar and serve hot or cold with cream or custard.

Variation
Use coffee in place of milk or omit cocoa and use the grated rind of 2 lemons and juice of 2 lemons and enough milk to give 13 tablespoons.

Cooking time: 45 minutes
Preparation time: 15 minutes
Main cooking utensils: shallow casserole, tin for water
Oven temperature: very moderate to moderate (350–375°F., 180–190°C., Gas Mark 4–5)
Oven position: centre
Serves: 4–5

Cheese aigrettes

Imperial	Metric
3 tablespoons corn oil	3 tablespoons corn oil
¼ pint water	125 ml. water
2½ oz. plain flour	65 g. plain flour
½ oz. cornflour	15 g. cornflour
good pinch salt	good pinch salt
shake pepper	shake pepper
shake cayenne pepper	shake cayenne pepper
2 eggs	2 eggs
2 oz. Cheddar or Parmesan cheese, finely grated	50 g. Cheddar or Parmesan cheese, finely grated
good 1 pint corn oil for frying	generous ½ litre corn oil for frying
Garnish:	*Garnish:*
little grated Cheddar cheese	little grated Cheddar cheese
parsley	parsley

1. Put oil and water into the saucepan and bring to the boil.
2. Remove from the heat and gradually stir in flour and corn-flour, sieved with the seasonings.
3. Beat well and return to a low heat, stirring until the mixture forms a dry ball and leaves the sides of the pan quite clean.
4. Remove from heat once again, cool slightly and beat in the eggs.
5. Lastly stir in the grated cheese.
6. Heat the oil to 375°F. (190°C.), or until a cube of stale bread goes golden brown in just under 30 seconds.
7. Drop spoonfuls of the mixture into the hot oil and fry until crisp and brown.
8. Drain on crumpled tissue or kitchen paper and garnish with cheese and parsley. Serve hot.

Variation
Add 1 oz. (25 g.) finely chopped nuts at stage 5.

Cooking time: few minutes and 4–5 minutes for frying
Preparation time: 15 minutes
Main cooking utensils: saucepan, pan for oil
Makes: about 24 cocktails-size aigrettes

Cheddar mousse

Imperial	Metric
1 oz. butter	25 g. butter
1 oz. flour	25 g. flour
½ pint milk	250 ml. milk
4 oz. grated Cheddar cheese	100 g. grated Cheddar cheese
seasoning	seasoning
2 level teaspoons tomato purée	2 level teaspoons tomato purée
2 level teaspoons made mustard	2 level teaspoons made mustard
little cayenne pepper	little cayenne pepper
2 level teaspoons powdered gelatine	2 level teaspoons powdered gelatine
1 tablespoon cold water	1 tablespoon cold water
2 tablespoons boiling water	2 tablespoons boiling water
2 egg yolks	2 egg yolks
2 egg whites	2 egg whites

1. Prepare the soufflé case by tying a wide band of double greaseproof paper round the outside so that it extends above the rim for 2–3 inches (5–8 cm.).
2. Make a cheese sauce. Melt the butter in a pan and add the flour. Cook for 2–3 minutes, stirring all the time.
3. Remove from the heat and blend in the milk. Return to the heat and bring to the boil. Boil gently for a few moments, then stir in the grated cheese and seasoning.
4. Add the tomato purée, the mustard and cayenne pepper.
5. Soften the gelatine in the cold water and dissolve in the boiling water.
6. Add the egg yolks and dissolved gelatine to the cheese sauce, stirring over gentle heat until it thickens. Do not boil.
7. Cool, stir occasionally and when almost set, fold in the stiffly beaten egg whites.
8. Pour into the prepared soufflé case.
9. Set in a cool place. When set, remove the paper carefully, drawing it back and helping it with the blade of a knife. Garnish with cucumber fans. parsley and serve with a salad.

Cooking time: 10 minutes
Preparation time: 25 minutes
Main cooking utensils: saucepan, 5-inch (13-cm.) soufflé dish
Serves: 4

Questions and answers

This book covers most general aspects of cooking as well as giving recipes, both basic and unusual. There are, however, certain points that crop up very often in the letters I receive and I thought it might be helpful to have some of these points answered.

Freezing

Q. Why is it that certain mixtures curdle after they have been frozen and reheated?

A. It could be that the curdling is nothing to do with the freezing, but simply that the mixture, generally a sauce or a stew containing wine and cream, etc., is reheated too quickly. If you consider that normally these ingredients are added towards the end of the cooking time and are never boiled, it means that reheating after freezing should be done most carefully.

It is a fact, however, that sauces, stews and soups thickened with flour do have this tendency to separate out. Personally I find I get much better results if I thicken with cornflour or potato flour. If using potato flour, use exactly the same amount as you would with ordinary flour. If using cornflour, however, use only half the amount, e.g. if a sauce contains 1 oz. (25 g.) flour, use ½ oz. (15 g.) cornflour.

If it is possible to freeze the mixture without cream and wine, and to add these when the food is hot, you stand a far better chance of a smooth mixture.

I do feel that people get rather over-anxious about this threat of curdling, for the remedy is fairly simple, whisk very sharply or put the mixture into a blender and it is smooth again. If you find that it is rather thinner than you would wish, all you need to do is add the thickening later.

Shellfish

Q. Many people who live by the sea, and who can obtain shellfish fairly reasonably, do cook and freeze them and they sometimes complain about the shellfish being rather tough after freezing them.

A. This may be because they are defrosted too quickly. I like to bring the shellfish out of the freezer and allow it to defrost at room temperature, then use. There is another reason, however, why shellfish can be tough and this is nothing whatsoever to do with freezing. It is because it is overcooked, either in the initial stages or when added to a sauce or other mixture.

If you have live crab, lobster, etc., there are two ways of dealing with them; either put the fish in cold water, bring slowly to boiling point, lower the heat and simmer for a few minutes until the fish turns bright red or plunge into boiling water and simmer very gently until the fish changes colour. Lobsters and crab take approximately 7 minutes per lb. (½ kg.) by the second method, prawns and shrimps take 2–3 minutes only.

Cakes

Q. Many people worry about the fact that one is told to freeze a decorated cake without wrapping.

A. The reason for this is fairly obvious, if you cover the decorations while they are soft you would harm them. The short time in the freezer, without the cover, is not harmful but do remember to cover after freezing.

General cookery questions

Q. If you have no double saucepan what is the best way to deal with creamy mixtures to prevent curdling?

A. Stand a good-sized basin over a pan of hot, but not boiling, water. Make sure it is safely balanced and whisk briskly.

Q. Is there any way to prevent a skin forming on custard sauce as it cools?

A. There are several ways:

a. Put a piece of damp greaseproof paper over the sauce.
b. If the recipe uses ½ pint (3 dl.) liquid, make the sauce with about three-quarters of this amount. Pour the remainder of the cold liquid over the sauce. This makes a barrier between the sauce and the air and no skin will form. Before reheating or serving, whisk the mixture briskly to incorporate the cold liquid.
c. Make the sauce without any particular precautions, then just before serving put into your liquidiser and emulsify. This gives a very smooth sauce but one that tends to be a little thinner than usual so you may want to simmer for a few minutes.

Casseroles

Q. Sometimes a meat and vegetable casserole appears to have a reasonably thick sauce but as it cooks the sauce becomes rather thinner.

A. This is because of the amount of water present in most vegetables, as the vegetables cook the water is extracted. All you have to do is add a little thickening before serving. If you are thickening at this stage, there is no question that cornflour is better than flour.

Cakes

Q. How do you prevent the butter or margarine and sugar mixture curdling?

A. By not adding the eggs or liquid too quickly. If you have a slight sign of curdling, fold in a little of the flour. It is important to prevent the mixture separating in this way since it does tend to spoil the texture of a cake.

Some people prefer to add a little of the beaten egg, then fold in a little sieved flour, more egg and more flour; there is no reason not to do it this way.

Index